The Philosophic Process
in Physical Education

WILLIAM A. HARPER, Ph.D.
Associate Professor of Physical Education
Emporia Kansas State College

DONNA MAE MILLER, Ph.D.
Professor of Physical Education
University of Arizona

ROBERTA J. PARK, Ph.D.
Supervisor of Physical Education
Coordinator, Hearst Gymnasium
University of California, Berkeley

ELWOOD CRAIG DAVIS, Ph.D.
Emeritus Professor of Physical Education
University of Southern California
Lecturer, California State University, Northridge

THIRD EDITION

LEA & FEBIGER   *Philadelphia 1977*

RUTH ABERNATHY, Ph.D.

Editorial Adviser
Professor Emeritus, School of Physical and Health Education
University of Washington, Seattle 98105

Library of Congress Cataloging in Publication Data

Main entry under title:
The Philosophic process in physical education.

(Health education, physical education, and recreation series)
First–2d ed. entered under E. C. Davis.
Includes index.

1. Physical education and training—Philosophy. I. Harper, William Arthur, 1944– II. Davis, Elwood Craig, 1896– The philosophic process in physical education.

GV342.D3   1976   796′.01   76–10373

ISBN 0–8121–0565–6

First Edition, 1961
Second Edition, 1967
Third Edition, 1977

Printed in the United States of America

Print number: 4   3   2   1

To Kathleen and Carol Ann

Foreword

This new edition of *The Philosophic Process in Physical Education* takes the reader on a voyage from which the authors hope he will return with a deepened insight in the meaning of philosophic inquiry and an enriched perspective on physical education. Elwood Craig Davis, who originally charted the course, and Donna Mae Miller, who co-authored the first revised version, are joined by Roberta J. Park and William A. Harper. Together, the four authors have explored new territory and given added dimensions to the original work. Through it all they have remained true to Davis's main belief that philosophy is action and that the novice philosopher first learns by doing. This belief sets the tone of the journey and, in my opinion, it is the main guarantee for a rewarding experience to the readers of *The Philosophic Process.*

In the literature of physical education, books touching on philosophy are far outnumbered by books dealing with scientific aspects of physical activity. I have the distinct impression that in physical education, as elsewhere, there is a benign toleration of philosophers "as slightly annoying but harmless curiosities" in a modern world. There is little necessity, on the other hand, for pointing to the tremendous impact the sciences have had on the theoretical underpinnings of physical education. Yet, I hope that especially the scientifically oriented students of physical education will venture in *The Philosophic Process,* if only because the first steps on the road toward philosophizing are as relevant for the scientist as they are for the philosopher in physical education.

The deterrents to straight thinking that sidetrack the novice philosopher in the journey to real insight are equally applicable to scientific thought. In my statistics classes, for example, probability statements have a tendency to take on a life of their own. A statistically significant difference merely represents the inference that two populations in all probability are different with respect to a particular variable. It makes no statement whatsoever about the biological, physiological, or psychological significance of that difference. Yet statistical significance often is confused with practical significance and the journals of our profession are cluttered with significant results that attest to the wicked magic of words.

Much deeper rooted than occasional lapses in scientific inference is the view that the sciences provide us with the ultimate insight into reality. When the success of the sciences in reshaping our world, not to mention our own bodies, is considered, such a conception is not surprising. It certainly has left its mark on the theory of physical education. It becomes, therefore, so much more important to recognize that this view, far from being a scientific inference, is in fact a philosophic position. Philosophers often refer to this position as *scientism* and carefully distinguish it from science itself. Scientism asserts that "real" knowledge can only be gained through the scientific method. As such, it is an uncompromising philosophic position with a closed view of reality. It is one thing to say that sciences such as anatomy and physiology have made valuable contributions to the study of human movement; it is something else to claim that human movement can *only* be understood in terms of scientific knowledge. In the first instance, one merely affirms the usefulness of science and the scientific approach; in the second, one disregards the limitations of science and lapses into scientism.

It would be absurd to blame scientists, who of necessity work within the confines of the scientific method, for the philosophic position of scientism. At the same time, this rigid philosophic stance may help the novice philosopher discover the importance of investigating the presuppositions that underlie scientific knowledge or, for that matter, any kind of knowledge. One of the essays in *The Philosophic Process* deals with presuppositions, but an example here may be helpful. Suppose a physical educator makes a mechanical analysis of the long jump. As a result of this analysis, he gains certain knowledge of the jump. To answer the question of what kind of knowledge he obtained, we must understand the presuppositions of a mechanical analysis. The most crucial presupposition, I think, is that the jumper is reduced to physical mass, that his body is considered as an object in space. Does this invalidate mechanical knowledge of long-jumping? Certainly not. But it does put restrictions upon such knowledge. "Given that the human body is nothing but physical mass," one could say, "the following observations about the long jump are valid." It would be presumptuous to claim that mechanical or other scientific knowledge we have of the long jump represents the only valid knowledge of this human activity. The situation is somewhat analogous to the famous experimental qualifier: "All things being equal. . . ." Unfortunately for scientists dealing with human behavior, things hardly ever are equal.

Scientism is but one of many isms that crowd the field of philosophy. An entire section of *The Philosophic Process* is devoted to a discussion of these philosophic systems. The authors extend a strong invitation to the reader to discover the rich heritage of philosophy. In doing so, they do not want to browbeat novice philosophers into systematic submission. To the contrary, the authors challenge the reader to approach the wisdom of the past with an open mind, ready to ask critical questions. I find this approach refreshingly different from texts that offer a philosophy of physical education by mere extrapolations from time-honored philosophic positions. It has always struck me as ironic that idealistic or realistic philosophies of physical education often have been inferred from the writings of philosophers who never bothered to shine their light on the subject of physical activity. The wisdom of the past should be approached as any edifice of knowledge: with a reverence that does not obscure the critical faculties.

In one of the early chapters in *The Philosophic Process*, the novice philosopher is admonished to take distance, to stand back, to become a disinterested spectator. Perhaps a word of caution is in order. Indeed, the person who gets totally involved in a movement or committed to a cause may suffer myopia. The football coach on the sideline can analyze certain situations better than the linemen on the field. The television crew in a blimp has a great perspective on the lines of battle. Someone who watches football exclusively from a blimp, however, may soon develop *blimpism*; he gains a sharp eye for the great lines but he becomes oblivious to the clash of helmets, the power of controlled violence, and the feelings of utter exhaustion experienced by the mortals below. The view from the top is derived perspective, valid only insofar as it helps one to gain insight into the essence of football. That point is well made in Chapter 16, in which one of the authors discusses the phenomenological method. The modern philosopher understands the need to take distance, but he also recognizes that he has to be where the action is: back "to the things themselves!" *The Philosophic Process* is a modern book in that it rejects the "philosophy of the ivory tower" and opts for the primacy of the act—the act of doing and the act of thinking.

Finally, the reader who ventures on the journey toward better understanding needs to develop a vocabulary. Sometimes it may seem to the novice philosopher as though he has arrived in a thoroughly foreign country. From my experience I can say that the authors have developed valuable aids for communication: the language is clear, the jargon minimal. That is essential for a pleasant journey. I am reminded of a logical positivist who strayed into a meeting of phenomenological philosophers. The man became exceedingly excited at the "unscientific" descriptions of the phenomenologists and interrupted the last speaker repeatedly by asking: "What do you mean by that?" The exasperated phenomenologist finally silenced him by countering with "What do you mean by 'what do you mean'?"

Eugene, Oregon   JAN BROEKHOFF

Preface

In spite of extensive revisions in this edition, we are more strongly than ever committed to the two convictions that triggered both the original and second editions. They are:

> . . . that reading, talking and reporting *about* a something—in short—that knowledge *about* is not enough to bring the mature student to *understanding* the something, or its place in the world. That height is reached by climbing, by *action,* and by extending one's involvement, and that physical education acutely needs to apply its resources to the task of utilizing the philosophic process.

Physical educators are reaching the point in increased numbers where the action suggested in the foregoing statement is accepted as both a challenge and an obligation. The need for and utilization of the philosophic process are beginning to be demonstrated and openly acknowledged in almost every phase of physical education—research, administration, teaching, curriculum planning, professional writing, and the like—as never before.

Increased numbers of professional persons elect to study philosophy, either through formal course work or by means of disciplined self-teaching. This popular, stepped-up interest, however, loses much of its benefit to physical education if it does not result in the individual pushing beyond "knowledge about." There also needs to be improvement in that human ability and proclivity to engage in commonplace philosophizing.

Performing the philosophic process awarely and trying to improve one's ability in this process are directly related to "know thyself." Some branches of philosophy have features that motivate the reader to turn his thoughts inward. But otherwise, no aspect of philosophy is so effective at helping the individual person come to know so many things about himself as purposely and awarely philosophizing and then trying to improve his skill in it.

Improved philosophizing has been described as thinking straight, toward a purpose with cogency and awareness. At its best, the philosophic process is something like journeying—mental journeying. It arises from an inner need, a target, a selected direction and is adventurous pursuit— a "going after."

The third edition "goes after" the philosophic process in particular. Accordingly, the thrust of this widely rewritten and pointedly reorganized book is to help the professional learn more about how to think, not what to think. For this reason it is necessary to understand that the frequent use of the phrase *physical education* is meant to include physical education *in the large*. The temptation to trumpet in any particular disciplinary focus has been largely avoided.

After the reader has been personally invited to engage in the act of philosophizing, Part I, *Philosophy as Action*, aims to help the student to develop and refine his ability to philosophize, to direct reasoned beliefs toward a goal, to see that reasoned beliefs derive from thinking, to avoid error and dangers in philosophizing, and to view clearly the essence of this process. The suggestions in these five chapters emerge from the process employed by thinkers throughout history as they sought the wisdom by which man lives.

Chapters 7 to 12 comprise Part II, *Philosophy as Heritage*. The reader is led to see that philosophic activity produced the subject matter or *substance* of philosophy. The origins, definitions, branches, positions, systems, and modes of thought are presented as the philosophic wisdom of the present and the past. Throughout, examples are taken from physical education.

Part III, *Philosophy as Quest*, and Part IV, *Philosophy as Discovery*, present original essays speaking to different themes. They are brief examples of philosophizing in physical education. They endeavor to exemplify the spirit of desiring to know (questing), or claiming (however tentatively) to know (discovering). Each essay is followed by a short critique for the purpose of inviting further thought on the theme.

Following the four parts of "going after" the philosophic process are the Appendix and Glossary. Appendix A suggests 34 different activities for practicing one's philosophizing skill, both for the individual student and for classes of students studying philosophy. Appendix B summarizes in chronological perspective some of the better known philosophers of the Western world. The Glossary assists the student philosopher in becoming more comfortable with some of the more technical vocabulary found in philosophic literature.

The reader may be interested to know that this edition was written so that each author responded to the chapters written by the other authors, and in turn, considered all suggestions regarding his chapters that came from the other authors.

We are thankful to Minnie Lynn. Not only was she motivationally helpful in initiating the writing of the original edition, but her professional thought and practice reflect her dedicated belief in the philosophic process and its spirit of awe, doubt, curiosity, and continuous inquiry.

It is not possible to acknowledge all those persons who have had some connection with this or the earlier editions. Suffice it to say that such a book involves the goodwill and cooperation of many without whose insights the book may not have been undertaken or revised. It is with great pleasure that we offer this revisiting of the philosophic process to physical educators. Should this book help students of philosophy (which is to say, students of life) see the advantages and enjoyment of joining in this never-ending quest, then it will have served its intended purpose.

Emporia, Kansas WILLIAM HARPER
Tucson, Arizona DONNA MAE MILLER
Berkeley, California ROBERTA J. PARK
Northridge, California ELWOOD CRAIG DAVIS

Contents

Contents

IV. Philosophy as Discovery

A NEW TASK BEGINS, THEN. LITTLE BOAT, TO SEA ONCE MORE!

—Ortega

1

Introduction: The Quest Begins

HUMAN NATURE LOSES ITS MOST PRECIOUS QUALITY WHEN
IT IS ROBBED OF ITS SENSE OF THINGS BEYOND, UNEXPLORED
AND YET INSISTENT.

—A. N. Whitehead

PHILOSOPHIZING: A HUMAN COMMONPLACE

Persons of good reason who can communicate can and do philosophize.
"My philosophy of _____ is _____." Such a statement is commonly
heard. Ideas of philosophy are expressed extensively or briefly, depend-
on the occasion, topic, speaker, background, and culture.

Novice philosophers talk and write about such things as *values* (preferences, importance), *purposes* (goals, aims), *ethics and morals* (standards of human conduct), *aesthetics* (beauty), *justice, truth,* and their
opposites. Every day we hear, see, or read bits and pieces of ancient and
modern personal philosophizings in conversations, classrooms, television
programs, documents, books, movies, the press, periodicals, public ad-
dresses, laboratories, radio, and the marketplace. Typically heard snatches
serve as examples. "I am responsible to no one but myself." "Ends never
justify the means." "The universe was not created." "You can't be ethical
in a practical world." "The most important thing in this experiment is
_____." "Let's feed the world's starving people before we drown in
our own affluence."

Less profound fragments of an overall philosophy of life are reflected
in a philosophy of a profession. "The master value of physical education
is _____." "The most important task of the teacher is _____." "My
philosophy of coaching is _____." "My view of competition in athletics
for the performer is _____."

There is nothing new or strange about contemporary adult persons
"doing" philosophy. Philosophizing began after mankind fashioned and
invented words that permitted and encouraged the process. The first

1

hard evidence discovered so far to support this statement was found in Egypt in the Pyramid Texts of over 5,000 years ago.[2] Today's philosophizing among Americans differs from nineteenth century American philosophizing in several ways. For example, we modern persons have lost much of our predecessors' apprehension of the word "philosophy." Most of us wish to avoid being identified with the abstract or with the posture of the self-styled intellectual. More philosophic books and periodicals at every reading level are available than ever before. A wider variety of alternatives than in former times is available to those who wish to enrich or revise their philosophies in each ingredient of philosophy—values, purposes, relationships, ethics, and the like.

Not the least of the forces encouraging the individual to philosophize is the array of eminent philosophers who favor the philosophizing of *people*. Ortega, A. N. Whitehead, Mortimer Adler, and E. A. Burtt are examples. Ortega tells his audiences that they can become philosophers if they make the effort. Adler challenges his readers with the six conditions that prevail if philosophy is to be philosophy (rather than the effort to make it a science or some adjacent discipline). Three of the six conditions are that it should be made a *public* enterprise, it should be connected with life, and it should be related to the universe.[1]

The hesitant reader might gain courage to try purposely to philosophize by recalling that the early Grecian thinkers were not aware of what it was they were doing. There were no words to identify what they were doing. Other persons began to refer to the Greek philosophers as "friends of looking," "inquirers," and "investigators." Eventually, Pythagoras hit on the term "philosophos," that is, "philosopher." It is significant that he named the *doer*. *What* he did, that is, the product, was named later. Today, those who philosophize (even when aware of it) may not know what it is they are doing. As they talk, write, and think about *certain* things, they may be philosophizing even though it is about the ordinary experiences and events of day-to-day living. The word "may" in the last sentence suggests that the *way* one thinks also is involved in the process. The quality of philosophizing can be improved, as will be apparent in the discussion that follows. Improvement begins to seem important, for philosophizing can assist in a better understanding of self; some of life's most disturbing and persistent personal problems with which other disciplines are not concerned can be treated; more meaning is found in everyday living; perspective is gained and the individual begins to be better organized and to see life and see it whole; problems of society begin to be better understood, as is the nature of human existence.

Ability to Philosophize is Challenged. A skeptical reader expresses doubt that he should bother to improve his skill in philosophizing. He asks, "If almost everybody philosophizes at the beginner's level, why bother to improve? We all understand we are novices, so we understand each other, and that's good enough for me. Frankly, I'm not interested in becoming a *philosopher!*"

Skepticism and doubt are prime ways philosophy began. They still are catalysts or source-springs of philosophizing, if the skepticism is genuine and the doubt authentic. They help to launch the search for truth or the nearest thing to truth we know. One purpose of this book is to attempt to assist in this quest. Included in this purpose is to help the mature novice philosopher feel the need of gaining the advantages improvement brings.

Philosophizing is Like a Sport. One does not have to be a top-notch athlete to feel the need or desire to improve one's skill, strategy, and knowledge of the sport. One sensible, professional philosopher has compared learning to philosophize with learning to play a sport, be it tennis, golf, football, or any other. Both the novice in sport and the beginner in philosophizing are well aware of top-grade performers in each endeavor. These neophytes also are aware that there are many others in the novitiate class. For example, the gap is wide between the novice tennis player and the champion. Yet, it must be admitted that both are playing tennis. The boundary lines, balls, nets, racquets, scoring plan, rules, and purpose (hit the ball over the net within the boundary lines) are the same. There is no question of the awkwardness and the like of the beginner. However, one of the forces that help to motivate him, which may be overlooked, is the vast number of tennis players of varying abilities between him and the expert. He sees the possibility of moving up. All he has to do is to work on his game—practice. This *continuum* of proficiency from beginner to superstar forms a series of steps from bottom to top. Adler thinks this analogy should be significant to the novices in philosophizing, and refers to Will James's belief that man cannot help but philosophize once he sees what life is all about and what it means to human beings.[1]

Life's Intangibles Persist. As vital as it is to pursue happiness and enjoy life, man does not grow and mature by dodging life's problems and questions. This particularly seems to be the case when life's intangibles shoulder onto the scene.

Let us attempt a quasi-experiment in the area of intangibles. Listed below are some conditions that face most of the persons of this country. They have been presented by an eminent historio-philosopher. On a scale of 0 to 5 (high), what is your rating of the importance of each item? If an item should be of absolutely no concern to you, rate it 0 (zero). Compare your rating of each item with that of a well-known friend.

Seekers after power have spawned dangerous shifts from freedom to license

Technology has become exalted

Art has been abased
Moral and ethical codes have been flawed or discarded
Marriage and the family have lost their moorings
Useless luxuries have twisted asceticisms
Human behavior is typified by irresponsibility
Only novel ways are sought, with consequences ignored
Shallow experimentation has replaced the tried and true
Western values are threatened without a fair trial
Man has become disenchanted
Probable results of war have become alarming
Women have been freed
Religious beliefs and faith have been replaced by material concerns
Human effort is lured by uncertainties at the cost of reliability in government, social responsibility and social will

Does the list present a picture so familiar that you are indifferent to a malaise which some believe infests this nation? Is even this abbreviated list too serious to be considered in the early pages of a book? Does this list leave you disinterested to the weal and woe it presents? Is this picture inaccurate or exaggerated? You may be interested to learn that it reflects conditions listed by Will Durant in 1928.[3]

The fact that such conditions have persisted for at least a half-century in this country may catch some reader more interested in the intangibles facing his profession's future rather than his own future. Shall we join him as members of a department of physical education? Assume that we can openly discuss with other faculty members of this department matters that challenge us as we look at our mutual profession, which, let us pretend, embraces interinstitutional athletic sports and physical fitness. The following list includes some of the conditions facing this profession at this time, which also existed at the time Will Durant published his delightful *Mansions of Philosophy* in 1929. Add other items that exist today and existed at the close of the 1920s. If you wish, rate these items and compare them as previously suggested.

Professionalism in college athletics
Imbalance between theory and practice in program planning
Failure of parents to appreciate the contributions of physical education to American culture
Little agreement among professional members as to chief purposes and major values of this discipline
Need of ethics in the conduct of college athletics
Lack of adequate instruments for evaluating students in physical education classes
Degree of pedantry in classes in physical education activities
Efficacy of the principle of equality for faculty personnel

Few readers would find it difficult to extend this brief list, particularly if the limitation of the time (1928–1929) is removed. One reason for the persistence of intangible problems is that they are not amenable to solution by scientific methods. Many of them are philosophic. Although an individual might be extremely competent in the performance of the duties connected with his position as a physical educator, and he may be rather facile in philosophizing as a novice (without knowing it), he may have done nothing to improve himself in *philosophizing*. This lack of improvement explains in large part why *many of the problems of physical education, evident a half-century ago, persist*. Another reason for this situation is that man's ability to solve intangible problems of several kinds—social, political, religious, psychologic—has always been frustratingly slow. Part of man's humanness is his difficulty to understand himself and others and the universe.

Some related factors involved in this complex situation are that (1) most of the time and effort of many men and women in physical education are spent teaching students whose prime interest is *in physical education;* (2) many of the most able members of this profession devote all possible opportunities to writing and/or directing and engaging in research; (3) few members have become interested in philosophy as it could be applied to this profession. Some of these, not knowledgeable *in* physical education, have become esoteric. The positive impact of the others is starting to be visible in the thoughts about and practice of physical education; and (4) except for those included in the previous sentence, the three factors operate as forces against the efforts of members of this profession to tackle the intangibles that limit, obstruct, and plague physical education. In the meantime, additional problems and questions arise, many of which are intangibles within philosophy's province.

Is All Theorizing Philosophizing? Through the centuries there have been many attempts to identify the questions that fall within the province of philosophy. Mortimer Adler, for four decades, worked on the knotty question of what are the first-order questions with which philosophy alone is concerned, and what are second-order questions shared with some other disciplines such as psychology or religion. The partial list that follows clarifies the puzzle that faces the novice philosopher: when you theorize are you philosophizing? Some second-order questions are interspersed with the first-order ones in this list.[1]

Right and wrong
Human virtues, values, and vices
Justice
Man's duties and responsibilities
Characteristics of a good society
Man's rights and those of society

Human aspirations
Kinds of causes
Freedom and indeterminism
The nature of man's soul
The nature of man
The nature of consequences
The nature of causation
Powers of the mind
Freedom of the will
The nature of change
Human happiness
Speculative questions of being and nonbeing
Major goals of life
Purpose(s) of life
Relationships with other persons and with society

Even this shortened list indicates the sorts of questions the philosophizer thinks about—that which humans should do, be, possess, and strive for; the nature and meaning of life in the universe; and the consequences of whatever happens to people in this world. The improving philosophizer is also concerned with the *how* of thinking and knowing, the *what* of human thought and action, and that which *is* (existence).

The beginning philosopher who improves in this process triggers the effort to make positive steps rather than negative ones, even when conditions are adverse. In the meantime, he becomes knowledgeable of the product of the professional philosopher, and is more apt to be challenged to make the effort to improve. Thus, in the face of negative conditions that confront and weigh on mankind, some conditions are beyond understanding, such as the great senseless forces—hurricanes, earthquakes and other natural catastrophes. As man better understands and assesses the source of unhappiness and trouble, the more ways are apt to open for the resolution of them. The understanding of philosophy as *action* is essential to find the ways to a better world.

PHILOSOPHIZING LEADS TO SUBSTANCE

Early in this book the novice philosopher will be encouraged to go directly to work to ferret out his beliefs about certain broad categories, namely, life, education, and physical education. This strategy is much like the method of having the beginning tennis player play the game *before* he has received theoretical introduction to even the rudiments of the sport. The point is to let the beginner experience the whole before the analyses of the parts of the sport are revealed. It is only *after* the student philosopher tries the philosophy "game" that he or she is gradually introduced to the particulars of how to improve his or her philosophizing ability and the substance of the philosophizing of experts.

Later in this book, well after the novice has learned some of the "inside secrets" of better philosophizing, the pros, the philosophic superstars, are put on stage. It is in the *substance* of their philosophizing that the basic heritage of philosophy resides.

Why Do Philosophers Disagree? One of the first things the novice philosopher is likely to note about this philosophic heritage is that philosophers disagree. For some, this fact is reason enough not to begin the quest. For others, these legendary disagreements are the very reasons for questing, for if everything were known clearly there would not be much stimulus to philosophize.

Aristotle opened his *Metaphysics* with the words, "All men by nature desire to know." If this desire is pursued, it is inevitable that the desire is satisfied in many different ways and by many different truths. There is a point at which the philosophizing person takes a stand, even if it be a tentative stand. It is in taking a stand that the *substance* of philosophy arises. The word "substance" actually derives from the Latin *substare*, which means to stand or be under.

Our philosophic heritage reveals that philosophers have stood nearly everywhere. Let that not discourage the novice from getting into the philosophic arena. Fuller reminds us that there is permanent conflict in the basic nature of the philosophic enterprise.[4] Owing to temperamental bias, conflicting moral and religious preferences, special human interests dominating most philosophic systems, and ever-changing accumulation of facts and evidences, skirmishes, battles, and wars are a persistent part of philosophizing:

> The history of philosophy is in large part the chronicle of an unremitting struggle to bring within the same focus the good, the beautiful, and the true, and to contemplate them all as a single, self-consistent, all-explanatory object in which all our aspirations, including our yearning to satisfy our curiosity, find equal and complete fulfillment.

The Novice Reacts to Ideas. Aspiring to improve philosophizing ability the physical educator will react to the *substance* left us by the professional philosophers. The wayfaring student philosopher will actively consider this heritage as he comes to know his own mind. Will he accept everything presented? Will he reject everything, preferring to go his own way? Will he be influenced by the prejudices of his instructor? Will he accept many ideas from *one* philosopher because this expert states his views in such a way that the novice likes them? Will he allow this textbook to influence his choices, if it is found to sponsor certain views? Will he be persuaded to follow a view because it is in fashion, is modern, or is popular?

It is against this philosophic landscape that the novice will be forced to hold on to, modify, or jettison his personal beliefs. The beginner will be *influenced*. In seeking the basis for intelligent decisions, purposes, values, the sincere beginner aspiring to improve his philosophizing skill will study many diverse ideas, some of which are conflicting in themselves. This philosophic galaxy provides a source for the discovery of one's constellation of beliefs.

Philosophers Are Men of Action. Whatever the philosophic school of thought, slant, or persuasion, the foremost philosophers are men of action. Not unlike men and women physical educators, they are active persons, however, in a slightly different way. Although it may be that the typical philosopher is not traditionally active physically (and might well be more so), so the physical educator might well take the initiative in more actively trying to improve his or her thinking skills.

The philosophers of old demonstrated what it means to initiate. They saw the need to improve their skill in dealing with man's problems in a philosophic manner. They actually made a beginning; they set to the business of thinking. They reasoned. They examined basic assumptions. They discovered purposes.

Physical educators can learn from this *kind* of action. It is the necessary preliminary to the more visible action to which physical educators are accustomed. All too often physical educators have dealt with the second sort of action (program development, teaching methods, professional preparation, and the like) without tending to the first. That is, we physical educators have sometimes been inclined to take practical action before thinking about why we are going to do what it is we are about to do, or how we are going to do it once we know what we are about to do. Many of our past problems have their source in this kind of *unreflective* action. To be and do otherwise is to philosophize.

Disciplined Self-distancing. Some persons have said that the good philosopher is one who can maintain a "distance" between himself and the subject matter. In other words, the better the philosopher, the greater the distance between his gazing and that which he is scrutinizing. For example, a football tackle has less visual perspective about his relationship to other players during a game than does the coach on the sideline. The coach in the booth in the grandstand has still more perspective than either of the other two. If there were a coach directly above the playing field in a blimp or a helicopter, he would have still better general perspective of the game, and even more as the aircraft moved. Distancing of oneself from the scene of the action usually means *gaining in perspective.*

The ideas of substance in our philosophic heritage result not only from taking a stand, but also from standing back. Such disinterested viewing enables the reflective person to avoid jumping to conclusions, to describe what he sees, to draw the correct conclusion from the proper premises.

Insofar as physical education is concerned, the novice philosopher stands back, gaining perspective on the profession itself, on the whole of professional preparation, and on the interrelationships between physical education and other disciplines of study. What is more, these three aspects of physical education are further viewed through time, attending to physical education's yesterday, today, and tomorrow.

Disciplined self-distancing allows the philosopher to see that the gradual development of physical education over the years—however discontinuous, periodic, and unpredictable—forms its heritage. This heritage is the source-spring of what this discipline, in all of its facets, is today. The physical educator learns what physical education was successively, from year to year, as programs of all kinds were changed and the results or consequences (immediate and deferred) are viewed. Some of these were distinct gains, such as Thomas D. Wood's so-called natural program; the adoption of the essence of John Dewey's doctrine of interest; and, the establishment of principles (where they are valid) as suggested by W. G. Anderson and first consummated by J. F. Williams. Other outcomes of physical education as it evolved represent mistakes and failures, as occur in all professions. In addition, this profession's heritage, as seen in perspective, includes such inescapable elements as the contributions of professional men and women; the overall culture; the conditions prevailing at the time—political, economic, educational; the beliefs and life styles of the people; the influence of international relationships. Such forces not only paralleled the flow of physical education's heritage, but also formed a sort of womb within which physical education developed.

Having perspective as one views physical education today includes finding and examining these same sorts of elements *as they exist today*. One of the explanations for why physical education today is different from what it was years ago is that the paralleling forces are different. The financial picture in the country or in education may be different, and to mention one other example, the status of physical education in the minds of the public and/or leading educators may be different.

The third temporal factor is the future. The techniques of futurism have focused attention on the possibilities of using them on an increasing number of disciplines. As they are made more valid and reliable in the educational process, physical education may join space exploration and medicine and some aspects of industry and business in benefiting from the techniques of futurism. Then physical education might find them assistive to philosophy's chief way of regarding the future, *specula-*

tion. One reason that philosophic speculation (obvious in the works of many first-rate philosophers) is used sparingly in physical education is that most members of this profession are held responsible for the outcomes of speculation in action.

The three temporal ways of viewing physical education perspectively apply to such foundations of the profession as professional preparation and physical education's other programs, as well as its administration and instructional operations. Many of the fads, movements, and bandwagons appearing in any profession that tolerates and welcomes new ideas and creativeness and encourages or does not object to trying novel ideas and practices from other disciplines are examples of speculation. Not all speculation is philosophic. One mark of philosophic speculation is that the creator begins with some reasonable basic assumptions. This obvious first step is not always candidly admitted or identified. In fact, a few of the great professional philosophers occasionally have speculated at length, utterly unaware that their entire stand on a given matter was based on some assumptions that were suspect or at least not beyond reasonable doubt. One common minor example of this error in physical education is speculation about the desirability of borrowing some method, content, principle, or practice from a related discipline in which it has been eminently successful. The assumption that may escape notice is that there are a sufficient number of similar elements present in physical education to enable successful results to emerge. Gaining skill in seeing perspectively includes avoiding this often overlooked error.

Nevertheless, having perspective in considering the interrelationships with other fields of study and appropriate disciplines includes the finding of and speculation about ways that physical education may contribute to them, as well as vice versa. In this process the *parts* of the disciplines must be sought. Then these parts are considered for their fittingness in the related or other discipline. It is here that care should be exercised in speculating about their fittingness. Overall, this is analysis—synthesis, a dissection–integration process.

If any discipline is to be accepted professionally, improvement in the art of disciplined distancing from the details of one's vocation removes one from the dangers of professional self-preoccupation. It helps physical educators to move beyond the physical, exercise per se, the movement movement, humanistic education, perceptual-motor learning, sport and the like, as isolated concerns. Perspective helps physical educators to become observant of pertinent happenings and trends in other disciplines. Members of other professions know something that seems to remain opaque to too many physical educators. If any discipline is to be accepted by the people in a culture, it must establish the idea and accomplish the fact that it does *contribute to the culture's values.* Better yet, some of the discipline's prime values must parallel similar-level values of the culture. This sort of identification is the responsibility of the discipline and the professionals comprising it. It is not the responsibility of the society. Figuratively, the members of society sit back and say, "Show us!"

The understanding of philosophy as heritage can equip the novice philosopher with guides against which to compare or contrast his own thoughts. The study of professional thinkers and their thoughts provides the physical educator with the opportunity to survey many of the more significant philosophic ideas.

PRACTICE MAKES PERFECT

"Practice makes perfect" is an old saying, but there is truth in it. As the novice philosopher improves his adroitness in philosophizing, he more closely approaches self-knowledge, as well as practical wisdom about life in general, and education and physical education in particular. Yet it is difficult to practice *at the outset* on the best-from-the-past theories as given to us by the professional thinkers. Usually many of these theories have benefited from years of reflection, or at least have withstood years of strong criticism.

The last two parts of this book are provided chiefly for the student philosopher to *practice* his or her skill before stepping into larger and perhaps weightier battles. In these two parts, Philosophy as Quest and Philosophy as Discovery, brief essays on small segments of a philosophic area are presented. The short treatises were written *not* to be the last word on the subject, nor to reveal *the* answer to a question. Rather, each essay is followed by a short critique (sometimes written by the author of the essay itself) to encourage the student to react to the essay, to go into action himself, and to distance himself from the subject of the essay. It is through these philosophic acts that *substance* is discovered.

All in all, the physical educator who chooses to improve his or her ability to philosophize should now begin to sense the adventure in discovering philosophy as *action,* as *heritage,* as *quest,* and as *discovery.* Let us *now* begin the journey!

OF ALL HUMAN AMBITIONS AN OPEN MIND EAGERLY EXPECTANT OF NEW DISCOVERIES AND READY TO REMOLD CONVICTIONS IN THE LIGHT OF ADDED KNOWLEDGE AND DISPELLED IGNORANCES AND MISAPPREHENSIONS, IS THE OLDEST, THE RAREST AND THE MOST DIFFICULT TO ACHIEVE.

—James Harvey Robinson

PERSONS . . . PHILOSOPHIZE BECAUSE THEY WANT TO UNDER-
STAND THE WORLD THEY LIVE IN. I BELIEVE THAT, IN SOME
DEGREE OR OTHER, EVERYONE WANTS THIS. EVERYONE IS A
BUDDING PHILOSOPHER, NOT PERHAPS IN THE SENSE THAT HE
WANTS TO SPOIL A GREAT MANY PAGES WITH VERY LARGE
WORDS, BUT IN THE SENSE THAT HE IS GENUINELY INTER-
ESTED IN THE GREAT METAPHYSICAL PROBLEMS.

—Brand Blanshard

PERHAPS THE MOST VALUABLE RESULT OF ALL EDUCATION IS
THE ABILITY TO MAKE YOURSELF DO THE THING YOU HAVE
TO DO, WHEN IT OUGHT TO BE DONE, WHETHER YOU LIKE IT
OR NOT; IT IS THE FIRST LESSON THAT OUGHT TO BE LEARNED;
AND, HOWEVER EARLY A MAN'S TRAINING BEGINS, IT IS
PROBABLY THE LAST LESSON THAT HE LEARNS THOROUGHLY.

—Thomas Henry Huxley

References

1. Adler, M.: *The Conditions of Philosophy.* New York: Atheneum, 1965, pp. 2–49, 68–70.
2. Breasted, J. H.: *The Dawn of Conscience.* New York: Charles Scribner's Sons, 1947, pp. 32–43.
3. Durant, W.: *Mansions of Philosophy.* Garden City, N.Y: Garden City Publishing Co., Inc., 1929, pp. vii–x.
4. Fuller, B. A.: *A History of Philosophy,* rev. ed. New York: Henry Holt and Company, 1945, pp. 10–15.

Selected Reading

Burtt, E. A.: *In Search of Philosophic Understanding.* New York: The New American Library, Inc., 1965, pp. xiii–23.
Danto, A. C.: *What Philosophy Is: A Guide to the Elements.* New York: Harper & Row, 1968, pp. xi–xiv, 1–16.
Ortega y Gasset, J.: *What is Philosophy?* New York: W. W. Norton and Company, Inc., 1960, pp. 7–28.
Ortega y Gasset, J.: *The Origin of Philosophy.* New York: W. W. Norton and Company, Inc., 1967, pp. 7–46.
Schweitzer, A.: *The Decay and Restoration of Civilization.* London: Adams and Charles Black, 1971, pp. 1–25.
Whitehead, A. N.: *The Aims of Education.* New York: The Macmillan Company, 1929.
Whitehead, A. N.: *Adventures of Ideas.* New York: The Macmillan Company, 1933, pp. 283–305.

I

PHILOSOPHY
AS ACTION

THE PHILOSOPHER . . . EXPLORES THE WORLD OF IDEAS OVER
TRANQUIL PATHS. AND NOW LIKE A BUTTERFLY HE FLUTTERS
OVER THE OCEAN SHORE, DARTING OUT OVER THE WATER; HE
SPIES A SHIP IN WHICH HE WOULD LIKE TO GO ON A VOYAGE
OF DISCOVERY.

—Karl Jaspers

To philosophize is to venture into action. The chapters in this part describe the actions peculiar to the philosophic process. Chapter 2 helps the novice philosopher take stock of his present beliefs before calling them into question. Chapter 3 points the voyaging questioner toward the goal of reasoned beliefs. Chapter 4 discusses the vehicle for discovering reasoned beliefs, namely, thinking. Chapter 5 cautions the adventuring thinker to be on the lookout for certain predictable dangers during the quest. The last chapter considers the "soul" of the philosophic process itself, manifested in analysis and synthesis.

References for Part I begin on page 87.

2

Getting Under Way

WE SHALL NOT CEASE FROM EXPLORATION AND THE END
OF ALL OUR EXPLORING WILL BE TO ARRIVE WHERE WE
STARTED AND TO KNOW THE PLACE FOR THE FIRST TIME.
—*T. S. Eliot*

Persons can live without philosophizing. It is possible and common to live an entire lifetime without using the greater portion of one's mental abilities. Most of the behavior of mankind, although not done altogether without thought, often does not get the attention of careful and sustained thinking. Frequently, one's really vital choices such as life style, wife or husband or neither, vocation and avocation, and religion have a way of happening almost mysteriously. They just happen!

Because people can exist without philosophizing does not mean that they ought to. Frankly, most of us currently reign over a mental region (difficult though it is to admit it) that is sheer clutter! In this disorderly heap we frequently find vague and confused thoughts; few real convictions; many borrowed but undigested opinions; prejudices—lots of prejudices; unexamined assertions, suppositions, and sentiments; beliefs about a great many things, often accepted on sheer faith; and amid our occasional good sense, plenty of nonsense.

Is it any wonder that when one's mind is called on to perform what miracles it can, the tangled content is more often even further bound up, not liberated? It is much easier, when facing a problem, to surrender to the acutely pervasive forces of public opinion, established routine, or tradition. Even when there are intentional efforts to help the student deal with ideas—such as in schools—all too often the powerful tool of thought is confused with some smaller capacity such as memorizing, recalling of trivia, recognition of some remote facts, or recitation of rules, formulas, or sequences. To live in the world without bothering to sustain the resolve to think hard and straight about things is not difficult, if Barzun is right that "a pleasantly retarded mind contributes to everybody's ease."[3]

Persons who do not enjoy the "sleep of reason," such as idea hunters, seem to have in common what the delightful thinker Ortega calls *alertness*.[19] Think for a moment about the coach who compliments one of his or her players by saying, "That kid has eyes in the back of her head." The coach is telling the world that the player is on guard, watchful, circumspect, prepared. She is able to take in the field of play at all times, to know where she is at each moment, to anticipate movements and changes of direction at the instant. In short, this player, like the best of them, is *alert*.

Learning to be alert is one outcome of improving philosophizing skill. One is on the lookout—vigilant, watchful—ready to put one's mental house in order, to make ideas clear, to distinguish between good and bad arguments, to define terms, to speak with authority. As Ortega puts it,

> . . . the only man who truly thinks is the one who, when faced with a problem, instead of looking only straight ahead, toward what habit, tradition, the commonplace, and mental inertia would make one assume, keeps himself alert, ready to accept the fact that the solution might spring from the least foreseeable spot on the great rotundity of the horizon.[19]

HOW TO BECOME ALERT

One way to become alert in one's journey in ideas is through the pinpointing of one's *presently held ideas and beliefs*. Discovering what one has ideas and beliefs about and what one has not thought enough about to have developed beliefs or to have gained ideas is a sensible way to start. Ideas and beliefs come in the form of *words*. Beginning with words is no mean undertaking. Pindar, the great Grecian poet, reminds us, "the word in its power can be the spur to battle."

Today words are so taken for granted that it is easily forgotten that in man's early development one reason he did not think well was that he *did not have the words to think with*. So fundamental is this relationship that words still lead to words that are needed to communicate more accurately. Even then, many ranking philosophers find it necessary to invent words to more accurately say what current language prevents them from saying. We picture our problems with words and figures. A great many of our human relationships depend on words. Words are philosophic tools. In the words of the late J. Bronowski (*The Ascent of Man*): "Indeed, language as we use it has something of the character of a hunting plan. . . ."

You now have the chance to experiment with your beliefs and ideas in three familiar spheres: life, education, and physical education (see diagram, p. 19). The *words* technique will provoke your thoughts as you conduct this exercise. This means that there are clusters of words closely involved with *life,* another cluster for *education,* and still another group of words connected with *physical education.* Each word triggers beliefs and ideas, if we have any, related to that word. Perhaps most of the ideas and beliefs are highly personal. They are yours. Some words will elicit many ideas and beliefs. Other words will elicit but a few. Their number and their quality depend on your experiences, your imagination, your thinking about, as well as the breadth and depth of your experiences, and the versatility and liveliness of your imagination.

In order to gain some familiarity and a little skill in using words in this way, some initial practice may be helpful. Practice in the use of words related to life and to education, in the manner prescribed below, suggests that physical education is inescapably linked with life and with education. This practice also helps the novice philosopher improve on the ability to deal with words in a *philosophic manner.*

LIFE

Begin the exercise by conceiving the three selected areas as concentric circles (see diagram below). The largest circle is, of course, life. Most persons know more about life than about their professions (or even themselves). Certainly life is less technical than one's profession, and more easily discussed than abstractions of education.

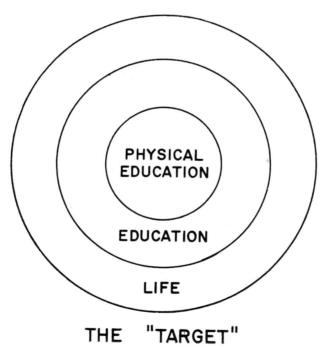

THE "TARGET"

First, what are the main ingredients, the main elements, that make up life and living? As indicated previously, we recognize these elements through *words*. Only 75 words are suggested in the list, and it probably could be multiplied by 100. Should the list include elements that do not seem to apply to your personal experiences, they may be omitted. Many others may be added. Should *all* elements within life be included, many challenges to thinking would be presented as philosophic statements are written or elicited.

Second, a short statement (about 50 words) or "telegram," is written for *each element* or word. The statement should not define the word. It is much better to use a good dictionary in order to find the definition. Rather, the short statement describes some of the essentials of the element; it explains how or why the word is significant or meaningful to the soon-to-be-alert person. The selected word may have significance to the individual because of its disvalue! It may have meaningfulness in and of itself. It may have value because of what it leads to, serves, or makes possible. It could have meaningfulness because of its insignificance! It is important at this beginning stage that the statements be personally held ideas or beliefs. (Why do *you* think this element has value or significance in life? What are these things to *you*?)

The following incomplete list of words represents ideas that crop up again and again in life. (The words are purposely listed in no particular order.) When the statements have been written, the intending philosopher will have made a definite step toward taking stock of some mental ideas in his own unique and largely private collection.

happiness	God	peace	love	culture
ideals	ideas	morals	character	progress
tradition	labor	divorce	children	marriage
values	right	virtue	wealth	reason
capital	war	civilization	knowledge	ethics
science	mind	good	evil	history
reality	religion	life	truth	soul
body	liberty	freedom	temperance	sense(s)
punishment	space	will	principles	custom
democracy	art	courage	duty	honor
citizen	quality	cause	law	quantity
judgment	experience	evolution	opinion	nature
philosophy	memory	pleasure	pain	competition
cooperation	medicine	man	justice	emotion
change	beauty	universal	opposition	friend

Here are four samples not examples taken from the efforts of students.

Life: a rare awakening, a bursting forth of freshness, a bubbling over.

Beauty: Ideals—hidden in hearts—preserved in love—the physical body —the soul of man—sometimes an imposter—or disguised—but *there,* if we care to take the time to look.

Custom: Wending one's thoughts, *custom* arrives from antiquity, demonstrating dependencies of today upon yesterday providing basis for decision.

Freedom: To climb a peak, to plunge in crystal clear waters, to gaze at the heaven, to live with nature—those unrestrained moments waiting; this is *freedom.*

There is a difference between *present* beliefs and *permanence* of beliefs. Not many individuals know what beliefs they *might* hold tomorrow. *The best that anyone can do is to express what are his present beliefs.*

As the reader begins to improve his philosophizing ability through what-I-believe statements, something needs to be added if the importance of being personally organized is to be significant.

In some ways, life's elements or ingredients are like knockdown parts. For each day in the overall span of years, putting the knockdown parts together so that they *make sense* is the inescapable human task. For the intelligent, *organized* person the put-together parts have to do *more* than merely make sense. They should lead to *personal* satisfaction. The parts must be assembled in terms of some vast overall personally selected purpose. It is *this* purpose that provides the basis of organized personal living.

If life is pictured as a sphere, the knockdown parts are within the sphere. During childhood and early adolescence these parts are apt to be helter-skelter in daily living. Many also are incompatible. The individual is unsure of what to believe or even what he believes, not to mention why. New, puzzling experiences are added continually as the individual attends high school and perhaps college, marries, and goes to work, not necessarily in that sequence. Where do the many new, strange-shaped beliefs fit within the sphere? For the disorganized person, the knockdown parts are misfits, incongruent as the predecessor parts. Some persons unnecessarily *go through life perpetually disorganized.* They may be intelligent, charming, sociable, but their lives are in disarray, out of gear. They are not unlike the 12 generals trying to win a war by riding forth at once in 12 different directions.

The possession of a set of personally selected ideas and beliefs is far from being enough. Disconnected fragments must be unified around an overall purpose, the master magnet at the center of life. It draws *all else* to itself, including lower-level purposes. When this happens, almost every part of living *drops into place.* Each new addition is drawn into place. By adulthood, this master purpose is apt to represent a supreme value. Some choose happiness. Others select helping humanity. Still others do the will of God. There are those who select improvement or progress. A few say preservation of our kind. A few select personal survival. For younger people, their personally selected master magnet often does not seem to them large enough in size or scope. To them it often seems trivial, too material, or too immediate, as they compare it with the master purpose of mature persons. But as long as it is *the* most important purpose that the individual can select and identify at the time, it will enable him or her to be organized and to focus personal energies and efforts, for his or her stage of maturity. Time usually brings sufficient growth to achieve a larger personal master purpose.

If one is to avoid an arrested state, there will be a willingness—yes, an eagerness—to seek and accept a better supreme purpose in one's personal life. This view matches the Hindu admonition "Don't Cling!" Someone says, "Don't cling to anything! Not *anything*?" If he but recalls that his present concept of almost everything has changed since he was a five-year-old, he begins to see that it is the clinging that *prevents* improving, maturing, advancing. As long as a person resolutely and blindly clings to all his tightly gripped beliefs, he cannot begin to mature. Seeing life and seeing it whole calls for *change!* The emphasis on changing one's beliefs does not mean changing *all* of one's beliefs, changing many immediately, or even one of them instantly. A fully adequate substitute must be at hand before any change is made. Without a valid alternative, a vacuum results, with the emergence of frustrating confusion. However, seeing life and seeing it whole does indicate the *examination* of beliefs.

We have been considering some of the elements of life, with abbreviated written statements of personal beliefs, as a start both toward a partial sketch of a personal philosophy of life and toward the improvement of one's skill in philosophizing. This bare beginning serves as a temporary backdrop for philosophies of education and of physical education. Such considerations may aid an individual to see how shaky most of his beliefs actually can be. "But they are mine. I have a right to them!" protested a serious student who quite missed the point. He forgot a fundamental guideline—beliefs need to be *examined continually.* If examination is missing, one is prevented from moving from merely being informed toward understanding and wisdom. Even one's master purpose of life may be expected to change a number of times during one's lifetime. Such a *summum bonum* as "reverence for life" evolved for Albert Schweitzer only after many years of numberless experiences at varied locations, creative and humanitarian efforts, profound thought, and several previous master purposes of life sequentially emerged over the years. The novice philosopher should follow the authentic philosopher's example of bringing unity and organization to his or her thoughts on life. If one runs into contradictory beliefs, inconsistency, or, for that matter, any result or condition that seems to require a reconciliation of beliefs, he or she is fortunate. An important clue has been discovered. There is the need to think a bit more carefully, the need to scrutinize these problematic beliefs and ideas. In unity and organization of thinking, one must remain ever alert to the idea of a master purpose. A novice archer does not draw the bow, take aim, and let the arrow fly, if there is no target.

EDUCATION

Within the larger, outer circle which stands for life is the next one, education. We suggest that the reader place some of his ideas about this field before himself, using the words listed below in a systematic manner. As soon as this is done, a somewhat unified picture of one's beliefs about education and its place in life begins to form. In addition, a closer, clearer backdrop for much of physical education takes shape.

Some elements of education are listed below. In order to uncover and fashion a few of one's thoughts on education, we again suggest that concise statements be formulated for each element. As before, definitions of these elements *must* be avoided. Definitions force one to miss the point of ferreting out one's *personal* beliefs. The statements should describe the element (word) in terms of its value, its vital ingredients, its possible consequences, its significance in education, as well as its personal meaningfulness.

We suggest that the novice philosopher (of education) keep in mind that (1) some, perhaps many, of the general beliefs prepared for the philosophy of life may prove useful (they should!); (2) many of the words (listed below), which trigger and identify ideas about education, also inevitably suggest ideas about physical education; (3) when possible, one's statements for education should be worded in *general* terms, so that they refer to education in general.

The following list of 80 words should trigger ideas of education that could start a personal stock-taking to help to delineate one's present position toward this sphere of human activity.

democracy	learning	success	failure	promotion
society	cooperation	group	method(s)	curriculum
teacher	student	activity	tests	whole child
development	maturation	teaching	needs	well-being
community	parent	man	leisure	awards
grading	evaluation	fundamentals	heredity	environment
effort	interest(s)	facts	facilities	school board
praise	punishment	knowledge	opinion	profession
salary	discipline	blame	change	social distance
potential(s)	academic level	standards	talent(s)	taxation
mass media	teacher education	policies	elective	attendance
requirements	independence	shortage(s)	character	federal aid
home	public relations	work	supervision	dependence
administration	liberty	norms	aptitude	personality
essentials	academic freedom	recruitment	selection	welfare
extra pay	overtime	unions	frills	teaching load

Here are a few "telegram" statements written by some students about some of these sample elements of education:

Student: lazy—eager—hope of the world—moving out of the nest, trying wings—cross between oyster, sponge, and some catalyst.

Unions: inner conflict, can I join one and still be a true professional?

Academic freedom: overly sensitive teacher-professor; don't tread on me—imagined encroachment—on the defensive—yet, a must—education, the last stronghold of many kinds of truth.

Failure: some must; consequence of standards; every man fails at something; who decides at what one must not fail; great men, magnificent failures because they dared to try; choose between success and low crossbar, and failure and high crossbar.

The list of 80 ingredients or elements of education is a fraction of a complete list. If some other ingredients seem better suited to your personal experiences and beliefs, there should be no hesitancy to use them. The individual gains some skill in different kinds of philosophic thinking as she or he seeks, finds, and expresses the abbreviated statement of beliefs about education that are of personal value or disvalue, significance or marked insignificance, importance or inconsequence.

As one writes these statements, he or she becomes aware that personal beliefs and ideas about a selected word (e.g., grading) are influenced, in part, by what he or she already has written about some related, previously treated word (e.g., evaluation or tests). This cannot be prevented. It should cause no concern. Beliefs and ideas of the average person are seldom housed in separate, isolated compartments, and certainly there should be free interplay among them.

For this exercise, it might prove fruitful if closely related words are grouped and treated consecutively. For example, those having to do with *administration* or with the *community* would be treated together.

Just as we discovered when reflecting on our beliefs about life, it is crucial to be alert to *unity* and *organization*. One ought to be on the lookout for incompatibilities, inconsistencies, contradictions, discrepancies, and unintelligibilities.

PHYSICAL EDUCATION

As the exercise continues, an initial difficulty arises when this same general process is applied to physical education. If the purpose of learning more about the use and misuse of the philosophic process is to learn more about one's chosen profession, then how can one confidently know *in advance* enough about physical education to have any beliefs about it? Indeed, this is a peculiar problem.

Most persons, especially those who have chosen physical education as a career, have a rough enough idea of their profession. Even though physical education in the large seems to encompass a wide assortment of activities not usually considered to be strictly educational (such as professional sports, fitness institutes, health spas, the sandlot, beauty salons, or the YMCA and YWCA), the trunk of physical education seems rooted in the schools. Furthermore, even for persons (such as camp directors, sports reporters and broadcasters, club pros) in the wide array of vocational pursuits connected with physical education, the essentials usually are learned in school.

Most physical educators work in schools, colleges, and universities, thus it is to be expected that the third circle representing physical education is within the circle representing education. As seen in this perspective, professional efforts in physical education are viewed with education as the immediate backdrop, and life as the eventual and larger backdrop. Thus, many of the ideas and beliefs written for the two larger areas have direct connections with beliefs and ideas of physical education. This, however, is not a reason for avoiding the "telegrams" approach to this discipline. Rather, a more immediately useful step involves guidelines that lead toward being more systematic, thorough, and organized in one's philosophizing about physical education. The next chapters undertake to deal with this key function.

In the meantime, and for the sake of comparison with the centers of belief of life and of education, the following elements suggest some of the ideas about which one would write in his professional philosophy.

sportsmanship	carry-over	skill	rewards	endurance
strength	calisthenics	competition	amateurism	character
physical fitness	intramurals	health	recreation	coeducation
athletics	elementary program	high school program	combatives	dance
organic vigor	sociomoral values	first aid	skill tests	aim
excuses	principles	drill teams	exercise	body dynamics
weight training	motor learning	performance	team play	elementary supervision
socialization	objectives	equipment	supplies	facilities
conditioning	body image	requirement	elective	public use
dualism	coordination	adaptives	rehabilitation	safety
fatigue	fees	kinesiology	biologic bases	posture
development	growth	carriage	play	sports
games	aquatics	self-defense	outdoor activities	drill
fundamental skills	whole-part	transfer	guidance	health examination
research	biological values	ability levels	classification	conduct
demonstration	individual differences	emotional control	publicity	relaxation
sensory aids	achievement scales	physique	practice	gymnastics

Here are four sample "telegrams" written by students about elements of physical education:

Sportsmanship: important, but fading fast; fair play; do unto others.
Competition: what you do in all categories of living; must have competitive spirit; striving against or with others.
Play: ultimate freedom; watch a child—then you will know play; a kind of spirit.
Research: independent learning; checking things out against what is supposed to be true . . . pursuing truth; the pillars of a profession.

The list of 85 words brings an immediate definiteness to thinking through one's professional philosophy, as far as physical education per se is concerned. As will be seen later, additional definiteness is made possible as the *functions* and the *areas* of the philosophy of any discipline are brought into focus. Still more definiteness results when consideration is given to the kind of basic category, such as physical education *programs*, used. Should the main categories be named for the different *phases* of the physical education *program*, such as intramurals, athletics, dance, adapted physical education? Should they be named after the main *tasks* of the physical educator—teaching, evaluation, administration, and so on? Should they be named for the *persons* who may be involved in an overall philosophic statement such as students, faculty, administrators, members of the community?

WHERE ARE WE NOW?

We are under way. Living with, rather than without, improving our philosophizing ability is a choice each of us makes. To elect to become better at philosophizing is to be willing to travel from chaos to order, from the unknown to the known, from echoing others to independent thought. The transformation to the *alert* professional can be hastened along by the use of a technique whereby one uses some loaded *words* as triggers of ideas to the discovery of what one presently believes. Whether one finds the mind empty, full, or more probably somewhere in between, the novice philosopher has recognized the need for getting under way and the inexorable duty to explore personally the nooks and crannies of his mind.

ALMOST ALL REALLY NEW IDEAS HAVE A CERTAIN ASPECT OF FOOLISHNESS WHEN THEY ARE FIRST PRODUCED, AND ALMOST ANY IDEA WHICH JOGS YOU OUT OF YOUR CURRENT ABSTRACTIONS MAY BE BETTER THAN NOTHING.

—Alfred North Whitehead

THERE IS NO ADEQUATE DEFENSE, EXCEPT STUPIDITY, AGAINST THE IMPACT OF A NEW IDEA.

—P. W. Bridgman

MANKIND CAN FLOURISH IN THE LOWER STAGES OF LIFE WITH MERELY BARBARIC FLASHES OF THOUGHT. BUT WHEN CIVILIZATION CULMINATES, THE ABSENCE OF A COORDINATING PHILOSOPHY OF LIFE, SPREAD THROUGHOUT THE COMMUNITY, SPELLS DECADENCE, BOREDOM, AND THE SLACKENING OF EFFORT.

—A. N. Whitehead

3

Searching for Reasoned Beliefs

MOST OF OUR SO-CALLED REASONING CONSISTS IN FINDING
ARGUMENTS FOR GOING ON BELIEVING AS WE ALREADY DO.
—James Harvey Robinson

If we do not know our beliefs, it is usually because we have not looked for them. We may not have hunted down the words by which our beliefs are expressed. Once the search gets under way the alert professional becomes more fully acquainted with his own peculiar constellation of beliefs. However, most of us feel a need to move beyond merely finding our beliefs. We, then, must discover if they are *reasoned beliefs*.

Suppose we were expected to answer the question: "What is physical education?" After thinking over the question for a short while we might search out our beliefs and devise a "telegram" such as the following.

> Physical education is an integral phase of education concerned with the physical, mental, and social growth, development, and adjustment of the individual.

This statement may be regarded as fairly representative of some professionals' verbal or written responses to our question. In truth, just so we keep to the facts, this statement may not be only typically representative, it actually does appear in the literature of physical education.[5] And, as is true with this statement, most responses to the question are quickly followed by a list of various activities through which these things apparently are claimed to occur.

So far then, we can say that some people actually do believe this statement. But merely because it is believed, or because the statement appears in print (or is verbalized in professional meetings), there is no good reason *yet* to accept the belief. What is in order now is to subject this claim to truth (and all others like it) to strict scrutiny. What, we might ask, does the belief in question already suppose to be certain (or guaranteed) in order for it to be true? In other words, we ask not whether it is or is not true, but *what has to be known quite clearly before it can possibly be true.*

To already suppose is to *presuppose.* There are some obvious and other less obvious presuppositions in the example before us. Just exactly what has been taken for granted?

1. That there is something called physical education in the first place, in order to even define it.
2. That what is referred to as physical education can be defined at all (as opposed to other ways of delineating it such as measurement or description).
3. That one knows what education is or ought to be in order for physical education to be an integral phase of it.
4. That, if physical education is *concerned with* certain things as a phase of education, these concerns are unique enough to distinguish the substance of physical education from that of other subject matters.
5. That we even know how to understand this notion of *being concerned with.*
6. That human beings actually consist of certain *aspects,* referred to as social, mental, and physical.
7. That we know what *each* of these aspects is.
8. That it is the proper function of education to contribute to or alter or affect these aspects, if they exist.
9. That physical education can indeed actually *do* something in each of these alleged aspects, and do it intentionally.
10. That there is not only some need or justification for growth and development in each aspect, but also a need to *adjust* human being to these areas (implies some kind of unspecified standard or norm of behavior against which persons are measured or judged). What could it possibly mean to *adjust* the individual socially, physically, and mentally?

It is now clear that one cannot risk stopping the philosophic process after identification of personally held beliefs. Even popular and inoffensive beliefs, like those concerning the profession of physical education, often depend on a vast number of *assumed truths.* Without the vigilant looking of the *alert* professional, one's beliefs may be true. But, unfortunately, genuine and sincere questing usually shows they are not true!

THE ROLE AND POWER OF REASONED BELIEFS

The personal philosophy of physical education that the individual formulates consists of words, as we presented in Chapter 2. Basically, these words are woven into statements. Even when the facts are involved, the individual selects those facts in which he is interested. He *interprets* them as his beliefs indicate or dictate. He *applies* them as he wishes—in accordance with his beliefs. It hardly needs saying that his values, ideals, purposes, the premises he uses, his assumptions, generalizations, hypotheses, and so on, are his beliefs. Some are the kinds of beliefs that constitute his philosophy. No matter how well-intentioned beliefs may be, however, *they are potentially dangerous until searched, identified, and examined.*

There is another reason one's beliefs are of interest and even concern to a professional person. They play a key role in his behavior and conduct. As has been said so often in a variety of ways, a person does not do all that he believes, but whatever he does springs from his system of beliefs.

As the world shrinks in size and as man's proximity to other men increases through faster communication, what the individual believes increasingly touches, intrudes, and becomes the concern of all mankind. It should not take another triumvirate such as Hitler, Stalin, and Mussolini to make humanity see the sense of that. Not to know the limitations of beliefs is not to know what the world teaches.

Despite sincere wishful thinking to the contrary, man has almost no *reasoned* beliefs. They are intimately related to and involved in the individual's experiences, as yet unexamined. Thus, one's beliefs are not only deeply personal, they are also essential. Most of one's beliefs are impregnated with feeling. Most personal beliefs are intermixed or interwoven. It therefore is not surprising that beliefs are among one's most precious possessions. Recall but a few of the many men and women throughout history who quite willingly gave up their lives for personal beliefs. Such acts are found throughout the world.

The role that beliefs play in one's philosophy (and thus in one's life) is again to be seen in those ends or aspirations toward which one strives. The individual's destiny, as far as he or she is concerned, is determined by personal choices. The bases for such choices constitute some of one's profound personal beliefs.

The power of beliefs surreptitiously arises in part from their incognito status. They also work unlabeled and in silence, in the shadows. How seldom they are identified by the individual! Almost never is their force even sensed. If they were recognized for what they are and then examined, it seems reasonable to think that many beliefs would be modified or nullified and jettisoned. But this process of identifying and searching for one's beliefs almost never comes off. It seems to demand too much tenacity, mental agility, and detective work, so tricky is the mind, so thin-skinned is man's self-esteem, and how tempting is expediency!

The severity of the consequences of this common human frailty should be motive enough to drive the person to action. Without the identification and examination of one's beliefs, generalizations may forever remain false. Biases may remain untouched. Conclusions may remain unwarranted. Faulty principles may be accepted readily. It stretches credulity to see how easily beliefs persist *in the face of available, contradictory facts, reason, and experience.* A small pool of half-truths do not form an ocean of, or even one, truth.

There is at least one outstanding reason for the value of the formulation of a personal philosophy of one's professional discipline. It spreads before him those beliefs with the most impact in the determination of personal and professional thought, practice, and destination. For the first time in his life, the individual can scrutinize the significant parts of what he believes.

INFLUENCES TO ACTION

The attempt to search diligently for authentic reasoned beliefs on which to base personal and professional action is, indeed, an individual project. Ultimately, the end result of this effort is one's own, regardless of the beliefs of others, and one should have the courage to express personal beliefs in written philosophic statements.

Nevertheless, there is always the unknown, unsensed, or unrecognized influence of one's associates, one's professors of major subject areas, and one's readings. Such influence may be largely uncontrollable.

There are two schools of thought about wide use of such aids. How does one proceed to search out of one's own thoughts what one believes about one's profession? Followers of one school advocate that the novice philosopher read a great deal so that the advantage of the accumulated wisdom of the profession may be used.

Believers in the second view advocate the avoidance of seeking the ideas of others about physical education, especially when writing a personal philosophy. They place great value on the *individual's* thinking through independently. A thought of John Locke touches on this second school of thought, *"reading furnishes the mind only with material of knowledge; it is thinking that makes what is read ours."* The advocates of the second school of thought claim noticeable strides made in personal and professional growth of individuals who have gone through this more personally demanding process. They put great store on the novice philosopher's presentation and development of personal ideas *regardless of his or her disagreement with the leading authorities.* They sharply question the value of an advanced student being satisfied with quoting or paraphrasing the ideas of the leaders and experts during this attempt to search for his or her own beliefs. They point out that the best education brings the student to the threshold of his best thinking.

The second school of thought also holds the view that *after* students have given their best, as they go through the challenging process of thinking through their philosophies, they almost invariably become avid readers of top writers in a wide variety of the disciplines of knowledge. These developments are not mere accelerations of interest; they represent *leaps* forward! There follows a *new* way of viewing and appraising one's work and one's profession.

Regardless of when outside influences are most effective—and people differ as to the timing of these influences—this is one of the surest ways to improve the profession. To use an example from another field, the well-known sculptor Phillip McCracken succinctly worded it this way: "Influences—meaning new ways of seeing and understanding things through the ideas and actions of men interpreting them—must be SOUGHT for a mind to *grow*." He went on to make the observation that much that transpires before us, day in and day out, goes by unnoticed, without value to us. He added that if we bother to filter out the bits that may be valuable to us, they become a part of us. If permitted and aided, "These bits grow and join together to form larger wholes, and make a fuller picture of things for us."

It is such individuals as the aforementioned who have prompted changing the meaning of a profession from a panoramic window through which one looks out upon the universe, to "a thoroughfare which provides passages for its ideas and services, and, for those of other fields to meet, be exchanged, interact, and inter-serve, grow and advance together."

Today is there a vast, unplanned, mass reaction against the consequences of specialization and overreliance on the expert? Does physical education as a profession need more individual members who want to gain a breadth of view and an appreciation for the purposes, and to become familiar with at least the general content of such disciplines as anthropology, archeology, mathematics, and zoology, to mention but a few? Is there a need to find more ways to serve better, and more ways that others may better serve physical education?

Sometimes it appears that physical education has some valuable ideas and services, without *seeing* and *grasping opportunities* to make them count. Other disciplines also may have dynamic ideas and helpful services for physical education. It may seem paradoxical that, on the heels of building a philosophy of physical education, the reader is urged to turn his attention away from his handiwork. Should the individual not be encouraged to return at once to improve her or his own profession? This lies at the base of encouraging the individual to explore the efforts of others quite outside the profession. Does it not seem incredible that the real and false storms swirling around education's head have some persons content with their ideas, practices, and even yesterday's hopes? Does one lack the desire and ability to have new ideas fundamental and vital enough to bring about changes in areas that indicate need for improvement? Many unexpected kinds and numbers of new ideas come through wide acquaintanceships with other professions.

One never knows where a bit of wisdom may be seized. The search often requires an open mind, ready to grasp whatever has a holding power (remember Ortega's "alert man"). For example, who would expect to run across some wisdom on a golf course? The golf professional Angel De la Torre had just finished giving several months of instruction to a persistent adult player. As this determined, novice golfer walked off the practice tee after the last goodby at the end of the season, the old pro called him back. Quietly, reassuringly, he said, "And now that you have a fairly good golf swing, remember this one thing. No one ever built a golf swing for . . . one is ever a-building it! *Ever* a-building it."

REASONS TO BELIEVE

Genuine philosophic beliefs must be based on some *kinds of reasons* in order to qualify as having been *reasoned*. These reasons can be understood as the sources of and evidences for the belief.

The sources and evidences underlying beliefs in general include such things as hearsay, hunch, guess, fancy, faith, speculation, unverified opinion, anybody's opinion, conviction, authoritative opinion, experts' agreement, facts, hypotheses, theories, principles, laws. Some people like to think of these as arranged in a hierarchy of preferences. Thus, as we gain more knowledge, our beliefs become more reasonable as they become more reasoned.

Of all the sources and evidences at hand, some are preferable to others, especially in terms of reliability and verifiability. If one's views about the profession are admittedly based on hearsay, hunch, or guess, no one could place much confidence in them. However, the individual is not always free or able to base personal beliefs on the preferred kind of ingredients such as verifiable judgment or facts supporting a set of beliefs. For example, one of the areas that a philosophy embraces is *hypothesis*. Yet, a hypothesis often stems from a hunch or a guess. In addition, some of the ingredients that do not appear at the preferred end of the list are of great value in philosophy. Speculation is an example. It is one of philosophy's most typical activities, leading as it does from the known to the unknown.

Certainly laws and principles appear more stalwart than anybody's opinion. Again, by their nature, some beliefs cannot demand or receive strong support in terms of verifiability. Yet the beliefs are necessary. Some of the beliefs of almost any man may be buttressed by strong supports from verification. Nonetheless, at least some beliefs of any man will have weak supports. Again, one way to put away childish things is to select beliefs that are as soundly supported as possible. Another mark of maturity is to find the evidences supporting one's beliefs, and then to examine both the beliefs and the evidences. Although much of what one believes is based on hearsay and guess, what about a fact or two?

One faces a disappointing experience if one happens to be a person who stops examining or analyzing as soon as someone says, "It's a fact." The word not only has a halo borrowed from science, but another halo from the idea that a fact is clear-cut, definite, reliable, and so on. However, a fact must be examined. For one thing, what *kind* of a fact is being discussed? "Water boils at 100° C. at normal atmospheric pressure" is one kind of fact. "Our school program offers 17 different activities" is quite a different kind of fact. "Bill and I waited for you on the corner for 30 minutes" is a third kind of fact. The *first* kind of fact pertains to the environment as viewed by the sciences. The *second* refers to circumstances and situations. The *third* has to do with direct, verifiable personal experiences. It is not enough to think or say that one's beliefs are supported by facts. Obviously, facts are not of the same quality, the same reliability, the same verifiability, or the same significance.

One should be willing to examine *any* facts that support beliefs. If this is done, the fact in question loses some of its prestige. In this fast-moving time, a scientific fact used to support a belief may be discarded tomorrow. Even in the most exact sciences, facts are superseded by later facts. Facts are replaced and remain viable only as a historical marker of the advance of science. Thus, should a personal belief be based on a given fact jettisoned later, does not one's belief need to be reexamined?

One ought to be curious about the judgment of experts regarding the place, interpretation, value, and importance of a fact. Not only may one's judgment of such matters be inexpert, but if the fact is the result of observation, one continually has to be aware that the human senses are noted for the inaccuracy of their reporting. The old saying "a fact's a fact," of course, may not be a fact! So many persons do not get *all* of a fact. They turn to something else as soon as they have a bit of the fact—particularly if the bit agrees with or seems to prove something in which they are interested. The result is that most of the factually supported beliefs of some individuals actually are founded on half- or quarter-facts.

From a consideration of other evidences of beliefs, one encounters four *major* bulwarks. They are hypothesis, theory, principle, and law. A word or two about them may suggest how they may be used to come to grips with the process of independent thinking.

A *hypothesis*, in the philosophic process, is a generalization of low probability. It is a conjecture that embraces at least one fact and attempts to explain that fact or what it may lead to. When one says, "If so and so is a fact, then this and that probably will happen," he sees that hypothesis and hypothetical come from the same root. A hypothesis, in a sense, is stronger than a fact in that it goes beyond the fact that it includes. It may lead to related or even new facts. In research, hypothesis is, of course, a tentative supposition that accounts for known fact(s) and serves as a springboard for further inquiry by which it may or may not be proved.

A *theory* in philosophy is a statement of higher probability than a hypothesis and of less probability than a law. It is less specific and precise than a law. It may include a verified hypothesis, but it always includes at least one unverified hypothesis. Thus, one speaks of the theories of light. Physical education, being chiefly based on some other disciplines, is supported by a number of borrowed theories but few laws. For example, in psychology most of the beliefs are based on propositions that are still in the theory stage. Leading psychologists admit this is one major reason why psychology is not yet a science.

A *principle* in philosophy is somewhat unlike the same term used in physical education. In physical education, principle means, roughly, a belief used as a guide to action. As used in philosophy, principle is regarded as a fundamental truth. When these two meanings are combined (since the interest is in philosophy of physical education), one discovers the meaning as a fundamental truth that serves as a guide to action. There are few, if any, fundamental truths (in the sense of great, ultimate truths) in physical education. There are some scientifically determined facts; there are some common consistent experiences of the race and of the profession; there are the results of man's intuition and insight; and there are the outcomes of the philosophic process—any or all of which may lead to generalizations which lead to some beliefs used as guides to action. (The professional philosopher *might agree* that the relationship between life and activity, and between activity and a basic enjoyment or satisfaction, would constitute a fundamental truth.)

A *law* is a generalization of wide application and high probability. It comes closest of all the philosophic supports to verified experience. It describes perceptible relations among phenomena. It describes constant connections between phenomena, considering certain conditions or circumstances. It says, "This will happen when or if these conditions exist." There are, of course, no laws in physical education. There are laws in the sciences on which this profession rests, such as physics, physiology, and chemistry. Despite such borrowed supports, it is possible, unfortunately, for a person actually to hold *beliefs* that are in contradiction to laws even when he knows the laws. Such "outlaw" beliefs exist because some persons do not carefully search out their beliefs, nor do they examine and reexamine the evidences for their beliefs. They do not select beliefs that are as strongly supported as they could be. They do **not change** beliefs from weakly supported to strongly supported ones when this is possible. In short, they *almost* seem to prefer the path that leads from indifference to consciously selected ignorance.

MISTAKEN IDENTITY OF BELIEFS

It is admitted that despite encouragement, help, and opportunity, it is possible for a person to resist the fascinating experience of discovering the threshold of one's mind. One reason for resistance given by a few persons who have started to synthesize their beliefs, after really examining them, is that they are ashamed of the lack of quality. This condition should discourage no one. Not many individuals feel elated when they display all their beliefs before themselves. This, of course, is one of the reasons the experience of writing a philosophy has proved so productive of leaps toward maturity.

Some other persons resist the chance to find out what it is they believe because they foresee that they may want to change some of their beliefs. Not only do some of these individuals believe that beliefs should not be changed, but they also may have some undesirable yet cherished beliefs they do not wish to change. Although they believe in the worthiness of truth and exert effort pursuing it, they avoid or reject it if some cherished belief is jeopardized by the very truth which was sought and found!

If the philosophizing person is sincere in questing, there are times when various forces—some from within, some from without—indicate a change in a belief or two. Even when care and attention are given to the process of the search for and the discovery of philosophic beliefs, good reasons that require careful reappraisal and even dispossession of an undesirable belief often spring up. These are times when we must admit to a case of "mistaken identity." We are simply mistaken, either about the belief or about the sources of and evidences used to support it. Once again, the *alert* person is *ever* a-watching!

As the wisdom of the ancient Hindu admonition "don't cling!" is faced, what are some aids to help one *change a belief*? What have men who have changed large and small beliefs, even major purposes or basic values, done? Here are a few suggestions.

1. For the less decisive, less determined person, there must be a genuine desire to improve, a dissatisfaction with the old, a decided willingness to let go of the old and try out the new. Such an attitude might well be accompanied by a defiance of the fear to be wrong again, of failure. The possession of an all-covering purpose of life helps a great deal.

2. After deciding on the best substitute for the old belief, the latter is almost physically pushed out as the new belief is pulled in. This process demands not only considerable desire, but also a substantial amount of

perseverance. The individual should avoid remaining in the sea of confusion.

3. If a person sincerely wants to change, the door of acceptance must be kept open long enough to try out the new proposal. The individual should remain teachable, coachable. Personal suggestions from oneself and perhaps others may have to be accepted. Also, one should make sure that one wants to *follow through* to a desirable conclusion.

4. If the person wants to take on a new belief, he should make sure the old belief should be jettisoned. What will be the consequences? An analytic ability is needed, in addition to the ingenuity and clarity of identification, to know *exactly* what belief it is that is being discarded or revised. This definiteness of identification also serves as a basis of judgment in the consideration of the validity of the new, proposed belief.

5. As the person continues to want to change the belief and before the right substitute is found, possible substitutions are gathered and examined one by one. One mentally tries each of them for fit; he or she experiments mentally with each one for validity as a qualified substitute, in addition to anticipating probable consequences.

6. There is no way to estimate how long it will take a person to give the tentatively selected substitute belief a reasonable tryout. Some beliefs, by their nature, are important but put to use only occasionally. Other beliefs may be used several times a day. Certainly final acceptance is postponed until adequate evidence indicates the satisfactoriness and workability of the new belief.

7. The new belief, having proved compatible and perhaps catalytic, is connected to other, presently held, related beliefs. Opportunities are made or awaited to appraise the functioning of this relationship. No longer does intellectual cowardice prevent testing one's belief.

8. One now faces the possibility that other beliefs will be changed or revised, as beliefs continue to be examined and reexamined.

Whether or not a new or revised belief is to be accepted depends on such criteria as:

1. Is this belief compatible with related, presently held beliefs?
2. Is it a desirable *enough* belief to bother to accept it?
3. To what degree is it supported by enough respectable evidence?
4. Is this belief trustworthy in terms of the kind of conduct it will elicit?
5. Is it valid? On examination does it measure up to what it purports to be?
6. Am I capable at the present time of including it in my constellation of beliefs?

7. Do I really understand precisely what this belief is, what it implies and what its consequences are, now and later, to myself and to others?
8. Do I clearly see the presuppositions on which the belief is based? What has to be certain before it can possibly be true?
9. Is the belief practical?
10. How applicable is it? To what degree and how widely applicable is it?

PREMATURE ARREST OF PHILOSOPHIC DEVELOPMENT

Persons may be prematurely arrested in their philosophic development. They go so far, or at least a little way, and then stop. Despite what has been said, some persons are concerned about themselves and others being persuaded too easily to change their beliefs—particularly those that relate to the major values of society or of their life styles. In short, these persons believe that it is better psychologically to retain the old beliefs— and that they will be happier in so doing. They feel that people are not strong enough to change one or more of their basic beliefs through the years. Their advice is, "Cling to what you believe!"

How flexible should a person be in this matter of retaining beliefs? In what respects, in what areas, should he be flexible or inflexible?

One of the attributes looked for particularly in advanced graduate students is mental, social, and emotional flexibility. Perhaps it is more accurate to say mental, social, and emotional inflexibility is apt to be cause for concern. One reason for the purported importance of flexibility is that experience has indicated that the inflexible, advanced graduate student appears to be less teachable. Prejudices are jettisoned with difficulty as are favorite ideas or former professional learnings. This retards the student's receiving and accepting the new. He appears to learn slowly. If old ideas are jettisoned solely to keep up with the class, but are still believed, emotional troubles may emerge. The individual also may feel that to show the degree of flexibility desired by professors of his major subject area drives out the qualities of determination and perseverance which purposely were developed through the years. The individual may feel that he is being asked to change too quickly. As one fine doctoral candidate put it, "Can one conform to this indication to shed inflexibility so much that he loses his integrity? If so, is the degree worth it?"

In assuming the ever-watchful philosophic stance, here are some speculative recommendations about flexibility and inflexibility that may be helpful.

1. Most professional persons are somewhat concerned about the kinds of labels placed on them. They want to avoid unwanted labels. The three ancient and honored professions (medicine, law, and theology) are concerned about labels. They prefer that *they* accept the responsibility for

the standards and conduct of their members rather than courts of law. Publics have come to expect quality of behavior from members of the three professions, and exceptions to this behavior are rare enough to be newsworthy. The point here is not that labels given by an occasional person should be of great concern to an individual. Rather, it is that if a person is labeled inflexible by a number of his or her associates and seniors who know him or her, the need to examine personal behavior might be considered seriously.

One should not confuse perseverance with inflexibility. It might help to look at some of the synonyms for the two words. Synonyms for inflexibility are absolute, fixed, unalterable, uncompromising, rigid, unbending, unchangeable. Those for perseverance are steadfast, constant, enduring, diligent, firm, sustained. Both words are words of degree. One cannot say that a slightly inflexible person is the same as a rather persevering one. The key to the distinction may seem to rest in the words "fixed" and "firm," or "rigid" and "resolute." There probably is something to the suggestion that part of the difference between an inflexible person and a persevering person arises from the way he acts and reacts, together with what seem to be his attitudes.

2. The person who would develop some additional flexibility might try to go all out to participate in several *different kinds* of activities, viewpoints, interests—possibly quite unlike his usual ones.

3. Versatility in participation and involvement should be extended over a period of time. That is, the individual might try to *persevere* in the pursuit of versatility!

4. The watchword for living "nothing in excess" is another aid toward the avoidance of inflexibility. In this life style, one makes sure that *balance* is a dominant force. This ideal of the Greeks did not preclude temporary concentration on the development of talents.

5. It is helpful to *examine* circumspectly, patiently, and honestly one's decisions, goals, assumptions, and personal standards of conduct. During this scrutinizing of these mental actions, it is essential but difficult to *avoid rationalization*.

6. The individual who others think is inflexible should *make certain* that what he does and says is self-determined and that he takes full *responsibility for the consequences*.

7. Some inflexible persons lack *empathy*. They appear to be insensitive to the fact that most people expect others to be flexible in certain well-known relationships and situations.

8. Usually the flexible person is careful of the things on which he places the label *important*. An astonishing number of troublesome involvements spring from *placing this label on unimportant things*. What is urgent is not necessarily important. The ultra-serious individual may find it difficult to reserve this label only for truly important matters. The

person who others feel is inflexible may help to diagnose his problem by looking into the degree to which he regards life and living as only extremely serious concerns. The point is not that life is or is not a serious business; rather, it is a matter of how a person persistently *feels* about it, what attitude is taken toward life, and what life brings to the individual.

The willingness to identify and examine the bases on which one's written philosophy rests does not mean that one will renounce the foundation of one's beliefs. Nor does it mean that major changes in the constellation of personal beliefs suddenly will be effected. Nevertheless, if one is to improve the soundness of the foundation and supports of personal beliefs, and if the beliefs themselves are to be upgraded, they must be examined and known for what they are.

WHERE ARE WE NOW?

The novice philosopher has now encountered the powerful idea of *reasoned beliefs*, that is, having beliefs is not necessarily the same as having reasoned beliefs. Aside from being introduced to the role and power of such reasoned beliefs, the wayfaring apprentice thinker should now understand and appreciate the influence on, the sources of, and the evidences for such beliefs. In remaining ever alert to the widely diverging quality of beliefs, the professional is forever open to change and always will bear at least one solid mark of maturity—reasoned flexibility.

(BELIEFS) HAVE ABOUT THEM A QUALITY OF "ELEMENTAL CERTITUDE," AND WE ESPECIALLY RESENT DOUBT OR CRITICISM CAST UPON THEM . . . THE "REAL" REASONS FOR OUR BELIEFS . . . CAN DO MUCH TO DISSIPATE THIS EMOTIONAL BLOCKADE AND RID US OF OUR PREJUDICES AND PRECONCEPTIONS.

—James Harvey Robinson

THAT HAPPINESS ENDURES WHICH COMES FROM THE GRINDING TOGETHER OF ANGUISH AND ECSTASY AND FROM THE INTENSITY OF THE GRINDING. THAT KNOWLEDGE IS TRUE WHICH COMES FROM SEARCHING INTO DOUBTS AND BELIEFS, AND FROM THE DEPTH OF THE SEARCHING.

—Chao Tze-chiang[25]

I CAN WELL CONCEIVE A MAN WITHOUT HANDS, FEET, HEAD (FOR IT IS ONLY EXPERIENCE WHICH TEACHES US THAT THE HEAD IS MORE NECESSARY THAN FEET). BUT I CANNOT CONCEIVE MAN WITHOUT THOUGHT; HE WOULD BE A STONE OR A BRUTE.

—Pascal

4

Thinking: The Vehicle

WE COME TO KNOW WHAT IT MEANS TO THINK WHEN WE
OURSELVES TRY TO THINK. IF THE ATTEMPT IS TO BE SUC-
CESSFUL, WE MUST BE READY TO LEARN THINKING.

—*Martin Heidegger*

We are now ready for the attempt to learn to think better than we already do. If reasoned beliefs are to be the *end* of the journeying process, we must become acquainted with the *means* by which such ends are to be known, the vehicle for our journeying, *thinking*. Without thinking, reasoned beliefs will be but a fast-fading dream provoking interesting, if wistful, professional chatter, but never actually emerging.

That we have reasoned beliefs means we have already thought, thinking being the vehicle. So important is this statement for the professional physical educator that we should examine it more closely.

If the past and present moments of physical education were testimony to our having understood the proper sequence between thinking and having reasoned beliefs, there would be few occasions for physical educators to improve in this respect. Misunderstanding of the necessary sequence between thought and belief often leads to our having to think, so to speak, *backwards*. That is, we are forced to think after, not before, taking our position. For example, the requirement to engage in physical education in the schools, historically speaking, has produced some of this backtracking to which we refer. Many of the more colorful reasons and explanations for requiring physical education were given to account for an already existing practice. The beliefs underlying this practice surfaced only by *thinking back* to discover what we must have believed in order to have taken the action in the first place.

In sum, thinking leads to *reasoned beliefs;* reasoned beliefs lead to wise and often courageous action. In the words of Hermann Hesse, "Practice ought to be the consequence of thought, not the other way round."[15]

In the discussion that follows we shall include the *types* of thinking, some *requirements* of thinking, and a few *guidelines* for thinking.

TYPES OF THINKING

What are the possible beginnings of thinking? Such conjectures should not reach past the speculative stage. However, it is interesting to join the biologists, psychologists, and anthropologists and note that, from observing animal behavior, thinking appears to be of the trial-and-error method, a probing, groping kind of behavior. In Kohler's famous experiments, manipulation and gross experimentation seem to be used in such ways that it *appears* that the chimps are thinking it over, that they get ideas.

One cannot help but wonder what occurred that first enabled man to think. Was there some *developing* trait(s) or ability(ies) in prethinking man that enabled man to become a thinker? Was it a possession *already* a part of Homo sapiens when he emerged?

Exactly what constitutes thinking? Is it the ability to anticipate action before muscular movements occur, which seems to characterize the behavior of the higher animals? Is it the kind of memory that lower animals appear to demonstrate?

We turn now from this fascinating speculation to a brief consideration of some different kinds of thinking, the various models of our vehicle that may serve the student philosopher.

1. There are times when one *mentally wanders* without any particular purpose or goal for thoughts, lighting momentarily on this item and that item without planning, lighting momentarily on still another topic that might be far removed from the first. So unplanned is this type of thinking that it is not even mental browsing. Yet, on rare occasion an excellent idea or thought is stumbled on in this manner. There are those who would not classify this kind of thinking as real thinking.

2. One of the least understood types of thinking is *intuitive* thinking. This immediate, direct knowing is not classified by some psychologists as thinking. Others regard it as related to nonconscious thinking. Whatever this ability is, some individuals seem to be more intuitive than others and make use of it to discover their hierarchies of beliefs. For the average individual, however, beliefs might be formed from the more tangible, direct kinds of thinking.

3. *Creative thinking* is somewhat more clearly understood than intuitive thinking, but apparently nonconscious thought may be involved in this, too. Poets, inventors, and other creative thinkers of note have attempted to assist in the understanding of what happens when a new idea, a solution, suddenly comes to them.

Most of them seem to believe that the chief steps are (1) the stage of total absorption in the subject; (2) the mental stage in which there is interaction of ideas; (3) the period of incubation of ideas; and (4) the birth or inspiration stage. This categorization is an artificial and imperfect one, for often the periods overlap or do not occur in sequence and, whereas some of the process may be engaged in consciously and deliberately, much of it may be subconscious.

There is not space to discuss the components of these various stages. Perhaps it will suffice to dwell briefly on one, the stage of immersion or absorption. It is during this stage that one becomes saturated in the material for thinking. Brewster Ghiselin reflects this spirit of thoroughness when he suggests that every creative person must attain full understanding and mastery of his medium, and skill, ingenuity, and flexibility in handling it.[13] It is during this stage also that information is gathered. Dewey stated, "We can have facts without thinking but we cannot have thinking without facts." It is acknowledged, however, that the creative thinker learns to respect intuition as well as facts. It also is during this immersion or saturation stage that patterns and relationships are sought. As James Webb Young pointed out, an idea is nothing more or less than a *new combination* of old elements, and the ability to make new combinations is heightened by an ability to see relationships.[29] Whitehead referred to the fact that Newton brought together the thinking of Galileo, Kepler, and others and abstracted their laws.[28]

In the vital stage of saturation there is need to gather raw materials through all sorts of media. The opportunities follow no pattern. Providing periods of quiet and relaxation, turning to another task, setting an expectant attitude or atmosphere are examples. Most persons gifted with this creative mental ability agree that *direct* seeking is often fruitless. However, there are those who advocate quite the opposite. Not only do they gather together several persons to directly think of all possible ideas related to the subject, but they also include those who know nothing about the subject! In fact, they feel that there may be an advantage in not knowing the limitations and the basic assumptions. Is this a gilded futility?

Group thinking has become the center of much interest in recent years and might result in expanded, helpful information for the average person. *Brainstorming*, as popularized by Osborn, involves picking a time and place, and creating a mood for helping groups to speed the discovery of new and imaginative approaches to problems.[20] At the same time it should be noted that in some ways the group process is considered as a possible inhibitor of creative thinking. Once taught the techniques of group ideation, some individuals with active imaginations may profit more from solitary meditation.

The point is that the more areas of experience accessible to thought, the greater the prospects of creative thought. As James Webb Young pointed out, every creative advertising person had the noticeable characteristic of being an extensive browser in all areas: "For it is with the advertising man as with the cow: no browsing, no milk."[29]

It cannot be overemphasized that ideas must be allowed to grow before they are trampled underfoot. Seemingly wild ideas can lead to entirely new approaches. Many ideas deserve to be allowed to live long enough to sink at least one or two roots. If they survive they ought to be granted a chance for further growth. One ought to be curious and patient enough to see what happens if a branch or two erupts from the central stem. Permitting ideas to grow instead of cutting their roots tends to encourage the acquisition of more ideas, or of obtaining them more easily.

There is, of course, a long history of resistance to new ideas. Ideas are always in danger of being rejected because they conflict with accepted ideas, beliefs, and practices, or because the person offering the idea lacks professional standing or seniority. In this connection physical educators should practice what the writers in creativity call the "art of suspending judgment." There is a great need for the experts, and those not yet in that category, to exert intelligent efforts to motivate vast numbers in the profession to be considerate of the other person's ideas. Some of the more experienced persons may feel that "I've tried about everything and I now know what works." The less experienced persons may feel that times are changing. They feel this view calls either for trying out some of the ideas that failed previously, or for trying out new ideas. Part of the dilemma in this situation springs from the less experienced individual's failure to *think through* the various limiting factors and the various possible consequences of his ideas. On the other hand, sometimes the more experienced person rejects abruptly, tersely, and definitely ideas proposed by a junior staff member, without explanation or encouragement for him to try again.

The previous paragraph does not exhaust the difficulties that sometimes confront the relationships of these two groups. Neither does it erase the fact that in some situations persons in these two groups do produce ideas. They have *exerted intelligent efforts to encourage the emergence of ideas.* "The notion that the creative imagination, especially in its highest exercise, has little or nothing to do with facts is one of the pseudodoxia which die hard." (John L. Lowes)

4. *Problem-solving* thinking has been well outlined by Dewey.[10] His well-known five steps are (a) occurrence of a difficulty, (b) identification and definition of the difficulty, (c) suggestion of possible solutions, (d) expansion and development of the suggested idea for solution through the reasoning process, and (e) extension of observations and experiment leading to acceptance or rejection of the idea. Two additional steps have been suggested as necessary for the description of the complete act of problem-solving. Bryson pointed out that Dewey's first step may be the beginning of thinking for the trained mind, but for the untrained

mind there is a prior step.[7] This is a searching of memory for a similar difficulty wherein some part at least was solved, and that part resembles some aspect of the present puzzle. In fact, Bryson goes on to say that there does not have to be a conscious seeking of a similar situation, only to try to remember a feeling of triumph and the events related to it.

The *second* addition to Dewey's five steps comes from Kelley, who suggested that after the finding of a solution that works, there is a "mental looking ahead" as one appraises the new solution in terms of possible future needs.[17]

A possible *third* additional step is the identification of the two or more elements that form any problem. This seems to promise helpful suggestions for possible solutions of the problem. It is problem-solving thinking that usually is referred to as *reflective* thinking. Because one meets many small puzzling situations every day, he has occasion to use this kind of thinking rather frequently. Identification of the elements at the outset may assist in the solution of a problem. For example, a teacher wants a given position. One qualification is a doctoral degree, which this teacher lacks. The problem's elements are (1) the want of the requirement, (2) the requirement, and (3) the lack of the requirement. Cancellation of any one element may solve the problem.

5. Quite in contrast to problem-solving is the type of thinking that might be called "reverie," "musing," or "contemplation," wherein one is lost in thought. When in reverie, it is difficult afterward to explain just what one was doing. About all one can say is, "Oh, I was just thinking about_____." With both reverie and musing, it seems that quietly and slowly things are mentally juggled, possibilities are turned over again and again. Perhaps a little differently, contemplation might be illustrated by the sports-minded person who has saturated himself with a mass of details about the sport in which he is extremely interested. He hunts for every possible kind of information that might be pertinent. He delves into all the nooks and crannies of each kind of information. He mentally views each and all details and pulls them together in new combinations. In a sense, this is a step beyond creative thinking. The subject is contemplated over and over again in every new relationship. The subject is approached from every conceivable angle. Nothing is overlooked. Most persons find themselves contemplating a great deal, especially in the early stages of wondering what it is they believe when they are awakening to the idea of reasoned beliefs.

6. Closely tied to contemplation is *meditation*. In fact, so close are they in meaning that many philosophers use the words interchangeably. For example, Karl Jaspers does not distinguish between these two philosophic acts.[16] Yet, his description of contemplation/meditation/reflection differs from the understanding of contemplation just presented (5).

The differences are substantial enough to warrant the separation of meditation from other acts like it, but which are not it.

In leading the philosophic life, Jaspers speaks of the need to follow the two paths of solitary meditation and communication with men. Solitary meditation is a total immersion in the depths of personal existence. Such meditation is a *thinking back* on one's daily doings. Our conduct—all our actions, thoughts, moments of strength and weakness, feelings, and experiences—is summoned before us. We tally, so to speak, our day. We learn what we can from these particular moments of our existence.

Even further, however, such meditation includes *thinking in the present* about personal tasks or duties, in short, one meditates on what should be done now. From the assessment of the quality of our day, we make judgments about the practical tasks yet before us.

If meditating becomes a force in one's life, it provides

> the dominant tone that carries me through the day in its countless activities. . . . For in these moments when I return home as it were to myself I acquire an underlying harmony . . . (these moments) give my life cohesion and continuity.[16]

7. There are numerous occasions when the individual tries to catch or to *comprehend* some meaning in what is already known (but not understood), or what someone else already knows and may be trying to help one understand. This thinking also is used in the process of discovering truths. The person tries to translate ideas into words that are meaningful to him. He tries to translate what he reads or hears into his own words, yet still have them represent what the other person meant. As simple as it may seem, this type of thinking is difficult enough that a great many individuals never pursue it far, being satisfied with half understanding. This accounts in part for an individual's knowing *what* he believes but not knowing *why* he believes it instead of something else, or in knowing but not really understanding what he believes.

8. One of the familiar kinds of thinking is the reconstruction or *recall* of something forgotten for the present. Also included is the recalling again and again of something related to the emotions. Immediate and simple recall uses the barest minimum of this kind of thinking. It is when one does not remember but continues to try that it is used. One probes one's mind and even talks to it to try to remember. In fact, elaborate expensive schemes have been devised to aid recall. It is the various maneuvers taken that constitute this kind of thinking. Man does not comprehend remembering and its antonym *forgetting*. They are both selective but the way(s) in which they occur is not understood. Not many individuals will be able to formulate a galaxy of beliefs without resorting to recall.

It is well to note that, although the manipulation of memories is the main instrument for thinking, memories are unreliable. They are not free of error and the impact of emotions. Frequently it is the trivial that is remembered and the essential that is forgotten. Nevertheless, memory can be trained. In fact, memory is the basis for almost every type of thinking.

9. When one tastes good food or watches a beautiful cloud formation or watches a good play, there may be a type of thinking which is difficult to describe, because these same things might stimulate some of the other types of thinking. For example, a master director might watch a play and be prompted to try to recall how an actor previously interpreted the part. The particular shade of thinking referred to in this type is probably best symbolized by the word "gratifying," or even "enraptured." That is, there may be in one's thoughts a response to exquisiteness, the delicacy of the taste of the food, a response to the skill of the acting, an enjoyment of the gracefulness of the dancer's movements. Sometimes in reading a book or a poem one stops to let the beauty of the word sing through his mind. Some of the things that the individual holds as beliefs may have this characteristic of appeal or attractiveness. The point is that a person might permit himself to think appreciatively, as he philosophizes, as he tries to express inner feelings and thoughts.

10. Most persons wish to think well of themselves and also wish others to think well of them. They constantly protect their self-esteem. One way this is done is neither admirable nor mature, but it does permit escape. One *rationalizes.* If he figures out ways to get even, crawls out of some embarrassing situation, finds an excuse for poor or tardy work and so on, he is rationalizing. Even when he catches himself in the act of rationalizing, he may find reasons for doing so! In the identification, selection and pulling together of beliefs into a constellation, there are times he should and must ask the philosophic "Why?" This is often the time rationalization begins!

SOME REQUIREMENTS OF THINKING

Five indispensable conditions concerning the vehicle called "thinking" might help the apprentice philosopher to carry out the philosophic process.

1. *Intelligent striving,* making the effort to try, constitutes a good share of thinking. When one's thinking has not produced the desired result, one may have a feeling of failure or frustration. But the matter should be judged differently. When the result is *attained,* thinking along this line tends to stop. Some of the deepest, sharpest, best thinking in the world is done when the direct goal is not attained.

It sometimes helps to recall that man tends not to think, at least reflectively, until forced to do so. When pain or snags appear, when man is *stopped*, he then begins to think, to find a way to relieve the pain or to get around the roadblock.

If we are to think, there must be something to think *with*. There are two ideas here. One is the presence of adequate properly functioning cells and tissues. The other is that there must be something on which to work mentally—ideas, experiences, behavior, and their symbols, words. The individual who has had a broad, rich background of experiences, who has developed such abilities as decision-making, foresight, and self-reliance, and who has made the effort to understand what he has learned *should* be able to think better than the opposite kind of person. He simply has more to think *with*, and part of the implication is that he had found that it pays to use what he has as he thinks!

The need for ideas and experiences, and words that express them meaningfully, suggests that there must be something to think *about*. This in turn suggests that the individual must extend and expand his concepts, his vocabulary, his experiences, his knowledge, and his ways of meeting life. As indicated earlier, the paths to wisdom begin with response to being curious, doubting, and wondering about. That is, the individual responds to questions, problems, challenges, conflicts, confusion, controversy, and the like. The philosopher's mental habit of seeing all sides of an issue and of facing a plethora of life's issues develops that most enviable ability of taking it all in stride. One could almost generalize by saying that a *little* facing of life's issues is a dangerous thing.

2. The failure to recognize an issue that can affect one is quite as fatal as the lack of the ability to rise to meet it successfully. Another way to *avoid* improving one's chances to have stimulating things to think about is to reject a challenge, even when it is pointed out. The recognition of a challenge for what it is is a crucial step forward. It focuses one's ideas, energies, time, abilities, and effort. It also triggers the necessary planning. If these preliminary steps are taken in time and are effective, one takes the next step, which was highlighted by Toynbee: *arising to successfully meet the challenge.* There also is the more fundamental challenge "What do I believe?"

Even young persons not fortunate enough to go to college at times consider the three great philosophic challenges: "Who am I?" "Where am I?" "Why am I here?" All the answers are *beliefs,* beliefs based on some kind of thinking. Thus, this reference to challenges includes the present challenge to philosophize.

3. One of the more obvious requisites of the good thinker is the ability to *discriminate,* as has been discussed. He should be able to appraise the relative worth of the facts, ideas and temporarily held beliefs. He should be able to select the best and discard the worst. He also should know when he has an adequate number of facts in order to justify stating his present beliefs.

4. The good thinker has the ability to *draw reasonable generalizations* and justifiable conclusions. This is of particular interest to the task of philosophizing. "Because of this and that, I believe thus and so." One continually draws conclusions. In the formulation of a philosophy, generalizations may be connected with any or all types of thinking, and may be based on anything from hunch to strongly verified judgment. Sound generalizations are based on the most appropriate kinds of thinking for tasks at hand, on the best available facts or information, and on good reasoning. They *must* be based on sound premises.

All generalizations (including this one) should be *scrutinized* and *analyzed,* beginning with the premises and continuing until the general statement is formulated. Each one should be *compared* with the larger generalizations accepted as reasonable and worthy to be major guides. This means that many conclusions may be held tentatively—long enough for thinking to move ahead.

In fact, in the formulation of a philosophy, one may expect to find the majority of minor beliefs to be of this *tentative* type. To some persons this is a source of impatience. They become frustrated. Some even lose self-confidence. They feel they should be surer of more beliefs; yet this self-criticism is often inappropriate. As a person gains in the ability to see life or his profession in larger wholes, as he gains in becoming an understanding person, he becomes aware of the *fewness* of life's or his profession's certitudes. Even though generalizations are made circumspectly, one is forced to regard most of them as tentative. This, however, does not prevent carrying on work and play like other human beings who have to do the same thing. Man holds some beliefs throughout his life, yet he holds them tentatively. He simply never found better ones. Self-criticism would be in order if one stopped trying, stopped examining beliefs and other generalizations, accepted weakly based and poorly supported generalizations as worthy of permanent acceptance, without efforts to the contrary.

5. One reason we never build a philosophy because we are ever a-building it is related to the admirable trait of *remaining sensitive to what is going on.* Where are the rough spots? At what stage in the formulation of a given belief did some difficulty appear? Should one try a different kind of thinking on a particular matter? What new approach might one try? Is this difficulty caused by lack of knowledge? Is this the only reasonable conclusion possible based on this information? Can the various parts of the supporting information be recombined or realigned? What would happen if basic assumptions were scrutinized?

These examples of possible rough spots encountered in philosophizing should not be viewed as weaknesses so much as opportunities to seek an improved philosophy. To be content with the old way even though it is effective, to accept without examination and reexamination, to view facts or philosophic ingredients in isolation, to expect easy answers to profound questions, to explain away a need to synthesize, to accept expert opinion without an effort to analyze, compare, and understand it, and to accept status quo without scrutiny and surveillance—these should be viewed not only as weaknesses but also as insensitivities.

GUIDELINES FOR THINKING

A few guidelines may prove helpful in learning more about thinking as a means to action.

1. Acknowledge beforehand the possibility that some errors in reasoning and generalization may creep into the philosophic process. This planned alertness aids in the prevention or eradication of such errors.

2. Guard against talking from ignorance. Even in a philosophy of one's profession, the scope of coverage is broad. One should not expect to have exact and current information in *all* details of the profession. One should expect to *become informed* if matters are encountered about which one knows little, yet about which one should have well-founded and soundly supported beliefs.

3. Find out the meanings of terms, select the one that seems to fit best, and permit thinking to move forward at least tentatively. The attempt to find the perfect meaning of some terms is futile in some cases. Sometimes meanings change with situations. Indecision not only prevents but also confuses thinking in such instances. Nevertheless one should keep in mind that he is working with a tentatively accepted meaning. When a change is indicated, again, it should be done with dispatch.

4. Be willing and ready to doubt the right to feel sure of what appears to be true. Then, examine not only the matter at hand but also the doubt itself.

5. Use analogy as the basis of reasoning with caution, and be skeptical of all such reasoning.

6. Recognize, identify, and label what is subjective and what is objective, but fear or subserve neither.

7. Acknowledge that even intelligent, well-educated persons are human enough to tend to see in situations and the behavior of others what they are looking for. Such acknowledgment aids in the prevention of blindness to the fallibility of sense experiences.

8. Reduce intellectual bric-a-brac to a minimum during the thinking act. One guide to follow in this effort is to practice thinking in and with simplified terms, words, and concepts.

9. Develop versatility in viewing personal beliefs from different perspectives. For example, in the use of the philosophic function *examination*, carry it out first from one vantage point and then from another. As beliefs are examined, one of the easiest and most fruitless plans to follow

is to persist in using one set of assumptions as a given belief is scrutinized. Persistence in mental digging in one spot beyond a reasonable point usually produces no new ways of looking at a given belief.

Any one of these and similar suggestions may be greatly elaborated, but one is selected for comment here. Its pertinency will be apparent as it is discussed. A number of excellent causes have appeared to be failures because of the way they were interpreted and used. One of these is the concern about better communication among human beings. Among other aspects of this complicated matter is a familiar philosophic area, the meanings of words and terms. So seriously has this concern about meanings been taken by some persons that in professional meetings, for example, no progress is made toward the goals of the business at hand until there is agreement as to the absolute meaning of all key words. In fact, in some instances the importance of meanings has come to mean that the groups involved may not move ahead with the business at hand until there is *unanimous* agreement as to the precise meaning of key words!

A solution for this self-imposed dilemma has been made by William Templeman, Professor Emeritus of English, University of Southern California. His proposal is that an approximate, sensible description or definition of the word be tentatively agreed on by the *majority* in order that the work of the group may move ahead. Then, as it becomes necessary (if it does) to further refine the original statement, let it again be done just enough to enable work to proceed. This process is continued until the work is accomplished and the meaning of the word has gradually been formulated.

Such a plan not only enables busy people to apply their talents to the tasks of responsibility, but also assures that the meanings of words are forged in the situations in which they are crucial. Too frequently, the other plan of attempting to find agreement on refinements of meanings does not stand up as work proceeds.

This discussion of the place of the meaning of words should not lead one to conclude that in the formulation of a personal philosophy of physical education (or of any other discipline) one may be casual or irresponsible about the use of words. However, no one should conclude that it is possible to reach a precise exactness in the meaning of most words. The English language is notoriously imprecise. Yet, it is of importance in discussing matters of consequence for the majority of those involved to agree on the meaning of key terms.

In the formulation of a personal philosophy of physical education, the novice philosopher should clarify the meaning of pivotal words in order not only that he be understood but also that needless argument be avoided.

The limitations of language as a tool of communication are so well known that all philosophers of note have found it necessary to either invent words or give their own unique meanings to key terms. Such concerns should not influence one to forget that the test of *wisdom* is to be found in the application of knowledge to life. Thus, the significance of Dr. Templeman's comments becomes apparent. In the words of Felix Frankfurter, *"The ultimate accomplishment of a thinker is found not in his books nor in his opinions, but in the minds of men."*

WHERE ARE WE NOW?

In learning more about the vehicle called "thinking," we have been reminded of the various types of thinking and some of the requirements of and guidelines for thinking. Aside from learning more about the thinking processes, the student philosopher should also understand the urgent need to put some of these actions into play. Realization of the necessary and sequential connection between thinking and reasoned beliefs leads the alert professional person to knowledge, and finally to the wise use of what is known. It is this fundamental means of conveyance called *thinking* that gives birth to alternatives, helps the individual see all possibilities, allows one to anticipate consequences, and assists one to judge rightly and act in accord with those judgments.

What is more, thinking is nothing less than an essential element in an intelligent life style. Every person in this discipline should think before, not after, he acts. How else will physical education move beyond the inviting tendencies to imitate other disciplines, to be dazzled by the glitter of what is in fashion, to be mesmerized by the promises of the charlatan, and to surrender when under attack—often before the first shot is fired?

IF WHEN THOUGHT IS NEEDED, NOBODY DOES ANY THINKING, IF EVERYONE ASSUMES THAT SOMEONE ELSE IS THINKING, THEN IT IS CLEAR THAT NO ONE IS THINKING EITHER FOR HIMSELF OR FOR ANYBODY ELSE. INSTEAD OF THOUGHT, THERE IS A VAST, INHUMAN VOID FULL OF WORDS, FORMULAS, SLOGANS, DECLARATIONS—IDEOLOGIES!

—Thomas Merton

THE ORGANIZED POLITICAL, SOCIAL AND RELIGIOUS ASSOCIATIONS OF OUR TIME ARE AT WORK TO INDUCE THE INDIVIDUAL MAN NOT TO ARRIVE AT HIS CONVICTIONS BY HIS OWN THINKING BUT TO MAKE HIS OWN SUCH CONVICTIONS AS THEY KEEP READY-MADE FOR HIM. ANY MAN WHO THINKS FOR HIMSELF AND AT THE SAME TIME IS SPIRITUALLY FREE, IS TO THEM SOMETHING INCONVENIENT AND EVEN UNCANNY.

—Albert Schweitzer

THE THIRD-RATE MIND IS HAPPY WHEN IT IS THINKING WITH THE MAJORITY. THE SECOND-RATE MIND IS HAPPY WHEN IT IS THINKING WITH THE MINORITY. A FIRST-RATE MIND IS ONLY HAPPY WHEN IT IS THINKING.

—A. A. Milne

5

Avoiding Predicament, Peril, and Pitfall

THE ROAD TO WISDOM?—WELL, IT'S PLAIN
AND SIMPLE TO EXPRESS:

ERR

AND ERR

AND ERR AGAIN

BUT LESS

AND LESS

AND LESS.

—*Piet Hein*

Who can forget that most famous journey of all, given to the world by Jules Verne, *Around the World in Eighty Days?* Phileas Fogg's mad race around the world stemmed from a near-irrational wager with members of the Reform Club that he could do it in 80 days:

"You have a strange way, Ralph, of proving that the world has grown smaller. So, because you can go round it in three months."

"In eighty days," interrupted Phileas Fogg. . . .

"Yes, in eighty days!" exclaimed Stuart, who in his excitement made a false deal. "But that doesn't take into account bad weather, contrary winds, shipwrecks, railway accidents, and so on."

"All included," returned Phileas Fogg, continuing to play (cards) despite the discussion. . . .

Stuart, whose turn it was to deal, gathered them up, and went on: "You are right theoretically, Mr. Fogg, but practically—"

"Practically also, Mr. Stuart," (calmly retorted Fogg; adding quietly) "The unforeseen does not exist."[26]

It was not that Fogg was certain that no disasters would befall him. Nor was it that he was cocksure that if disaster occurred he knew exactly what kind of danger it would be. It was only that Fogg's brash claim "the unforeseen does not exist" meant that the possibility of disaster is *foreseeable*.

So it is with the journeying in the philosophic process. The thinking (means) by which we are to discover reasoned beliefs (end) should not be considered free from dangers. Yes, it is extremely important to undertake such thinking, but the undertaking *in no way guarantees* solid results. It is foreseen that the novice philosopher—and for that matter occasionally even the professional philosopher—will get into predicaments, perils, and pitfalls. This chapter submits for the consideration of the beginner in philosophy unforeseen dangers he may thereby come to foresee.

PREDICAMENT

Predicaments are of two sorts. One kind is a state of affairs over which the individual in the predicament has little or no control, such as being a victim of a natural disaster. A second kind of predicament is the situation into which persons *actually get themselves,* a more frequent occurrence than the first. Potentially, persons are quite able to influence or control some threatening forces. Most human relationships fall into the second category. On a person-to-person (or group-to-group) basis, the predicament exists because of the person's behavior.

The philosophic process directly concerns predicaments of the second sort, those the individual gets himself into. Does not the position seem reasonable that, if the novice philosopher attends carefully to thinking before and not after acting, a great number of predicaments can be avoided? One *can* learn to foresee what many may think unforeseeable. The following three quite avoidable situations are examples of common predicaments that often hinder the taking up of the philosophic process itself.

1. *Overconcern for the practical* prevents a number of persons in the practical arts (e.g., physical education) from thinking straight. Paradoxically, by being practical they believe that they are doing down-to-earth thinking. No theories for them! The devotee of this line, if he actually follows it, ceases to grow. He fails to see that imagination, theory, and speculation often lead to a better way. There is disagreement among the practical thinkers as to what the word "practical" means. To some it means what is obviously useful. To others it is geared to anything that does not require use of the intellect. Then, there are those who have the old favorite test; does it work? Still another is can I *see* the results, are they tangible? A respectable percentage of those with ample experience in physical education who go on to advanced graduate study are frank to say that the practical line became a millstone around their professional necks. Not until they began to ask questions (what? why?

why not? of what value?) and attempted to answer these questions did a new excitement in and of physical education begin.

"Self cross-examination" calls into question, at one time or another, the sensibleness of almost every practice that has been taken for granted for years. Results of studies have led researchers to question learning theories, coaching techniques, teaching practices, skill progressions, training schedules and routines, curriculum values, administrative styles, and even design and care of equipment and facilities insofar as such matters assist in excellent performance in athletics.

One way out of this predicament of being preoccupied with the practical to the neglect of other, often better, possibilities is to ask questions. About this active resolve to question Erwin Straus is quite clear:

> Only by questioning do we obtain answers. The question puts into words that something has become questionable to ourselves. Questions disturb and questioners are a nuisance. They disturb the well-being of immediate sensory existence, the comfort of moving along old tracks.[24]

2. *Security hampers philosophizing.* Productiveness in the philosophic quest can be thwarted by the individual's side-stepping the difficult, dodging the new and seeking security. The search for security makes one neither brave nor free. It expands no ideas and challenges no abilities. Yet chasing the attractive shadow security is one of the characteristics of current American life. The fascination and reward of venturing into unknown or uncertain endeavors seem to have been forgotten. Security has become an opiate. It has dulled the proclivity for adventure. As Walter H. Judd put it, "We say we want peace when what most of us really want, I think you will agree, is to be left in peace—undisturbed in our comfort and security."

Teaching, for example, is losing its vigor for those who fail to seek the adventure of the meritorious, and who fail to defy the insecurity of competition. One of the possible subtle consequences of overconcern for material security is a spreading of the security complex into other phases of the individual's life. Some teachers may still have grounds for concern about the financial remuneration afforded them. Educational administrators at all levels are now familiar with vaunting requests for automatic, graduated salary increases, pension plans, sick leaves, insurance, and other fringe benefits. Not that some extra compensation may not be appropriate, but rather that personal security becomes a fetish, almost a way of life. In the past, the great contributions of teachers to humanity would have fallen dramatically short of those actually made if the teachers had permitted concern for personal material goods to hamper their imaginations and dwarf their efforts.

Some individuals permit material security to become a power pattern. Whatever the results of the intrusion of labor unionists' concerns into public education at all levels may be, it has pushed some teachers into using material security as their major concern *as teachers*—as their *summum bonum*. Indeed, it is difficult for the art of teaching to survive when one's ears are tuned to the jingle of money and not to the students' cry for help.

As more persons attempt advanced graduate study, one becomes aware that some of them do not complete the requirements, do not measure up, or do not tackle the difficult because they have become too security conscious. They do not hear the clarion call. They appear to lack adventuresomeness. They seem to prefer to remain at anchor in some snug harbor. This trait is so well described by Wilfred Noyce that a bit of it is presented here.[18] Noyce was a member of the British team that climbed Mt. Everest in 1953. He points to the adventurer's pity for the nonadventurous spirit as expressed by Antoine de Saint-Exupéry in *Wind, Sand and Stars*. In a bus that took him to his airfield, the French flier had listened to the conversation of office clerks.

> I heard them talking to one another in murmurs and whispers. They talked about illness, money, shabby domestic cares. Their talk painted the walls of the dismal prison in which these men had locked themselves up. And suddenly I had a vision of the face of destiny.
>
> Old bureaucrat, my comrade, it is not you who are to blame. No one ever helped you to escape. You, like a termite, built your peace by blocking up with cement every chink and cranny through which the light might pierce. You rolled yourself up into a ball in your genteel security, in routine, in stifling conventions of provincial life, raising a modest rampart against the winds and the tides and the stars. You have chosen not to be perturbed by great problems, having troubles enough to forget your own fate as man. You are not the dweller upon an errant planet and do not ask yourself questions to which there are no answers. You are a petty bourgeois of Toulouse. Nobody grasped you by the shoulder while there was still time. Now the clay of which you were shaped has dried and hardened, and naught in you will ever awaken the sleeping musician, the poet, the astronomer that possibly inhabited you in the beginning.[22]

The quest for personal security might be likened to the forces that restrict or cripple any creative process. Eric Fromm, describing a condition of creativity, refers to the ability to accept conflict and tension resulting from polarity, rather than to avoid these experiences. Wrote Fromm, "Conflicts are the source of wondering. . . . If one avoids conflicts one becomes a smoothly running machine, where every effect is immediately leveled off, where all desires become automatic, where all feelings become flattened out."[2]

Abraham Maslow's selected subjects were different from the average person's in that they did not cling to the familiar nor was their quest for truth a catastrophic need for certainty, safety, definiteness.[2] Similarly, Carl Rogers describes the condition closely associated with a potentially creative act as "openness to experience."[2] Here again the implication is lack of rigidity, inhibition, defensiveness, fearfulness of the new and strange, additional sparks to light the magic flame of creativeness.

William James, describing an "enthusiasm of self-surrender" suggests that if we are set free of our demands for guarantees, securities, and timidities, we will float and sing.

John Gardner pointed out that self-renewal depends on men's capacity to remain versatile, not to be trapped by techniques and routines, not to be imprisoned by comfortable habits.[12] The self-renewing person is always exploring new things and does not mind a failure now and then as long as he is learning and growing. Those who are willing to deny themselves "easy exits," to use Gardner's phrase, keep a sense of wonder, curiosity, zest, and of caring about things.

Other traits of those who are speculative, creative and venturesome that seem worthy of emulation include curiosity, zest for living, turning a failure into a success, making difficulties for themselves, seeking danger, using intelligent fear, living life as a drama.

For the individual to overly desire security is for him to have missed being *alive* and to have chosen the path to the professional doldrums. The philosopher is not fearful of letting his mind s-t-r-e-t-c-h. He projects his ideas into the stream of life. There is no backing-into life and what it brings. One should remind oneself again that the rewards of philosophy are in the *seeking*.

3. *Socialization* is another stifling dogma that infects twentieth century life and is an obstacle to man's searching activities, which are necessary to carry through the philosophic process. Powerful pressures that encourage and reward youth in group adjustment (to belong, to be accepted, to be agreeably subservient, to be contented, to be popular) exist in society.

In 1933, Albert Schweitzer warned that, along with the neglect (even mistrust) of thinking in this age, forces are at work that try to take away from individuals their essential uniqueness.[23] Efforts are made to merge persons into various organizations, the strength of an organization being measured by the degree of unity and exclusiveness attained. Thus, says Schweitzer, for his whole life long,

> the man of today is exposed to influences which are bent on robbing him of all confidence in his own thinking. . . . From every side and in the most varied ways it is dinned into him that the truths and convictions which he needs for life must be taken by him from the associations which have rights over him. The spirit of the age never lets

him come to himself. Over and over again convictions are forced upon him in the same way as, by means of the electric advertisements which flare in the streets of every large town, any company which has sufficient capital to get itself securely established, exercises pressure on him at every step he takes to induce him to buy their boot polish or their soup tablets.[23]

In the early 1960s the danger of conformity had been pointed out by many thoughtful writers and speakers. The conformity of a large segment of the American youth was exposed and discussed in numerous books and magazine articles. For example, a study by the Horace Mann-Lincoln Institute of School Experimentation found that bright students would even hide their abilities for fear of becoming unpopular. Potentially brilliant pupils even in this private school accepted the values of mediocre people around them instead of holding to their own standards. A 1961 Gallup poll of teenagers concluded that they wanted little and were unwilling to risk what they had. *Life* magazine even referred to collegians in the early 1960s as most comfortable in groups, even tending to make dates in fours and sixes. The students showed no strong urge to glorify or to rebel against their surroundings. They were without public heroes or villains. They were reported to be not so wild as their parents, nor so hard-working. They griped less and hoped less. In another generation or two they should be ready for the hive, predicted this view.

The prediction turned out to be wrong, if the later 1960s was any indication. From many, many forces, some kind of awakening occurred, especially on the college and university campuses. Students, scarcely noticed as a subculture in times past, suddenly began questioning—*everything!* The entire system was challenged, in many cases even the existing laws. With legal and sometimes extralegal actions, causes such as college and university governance, civil rights, the military, freedom of speech, big government, industry, even the police were espoused. At first, it was thought that these stirrings were just a few hot spots of typically unorthodox behavior, a striking out of the oversocialized victims to these outcomes. After all, unorthodox behavior has been one of the characteristic marks of most youths since time immemorial. Some youths have not escaped feeling like showing off their displeasure at the society into which they are beginning to take an increasing part. Even as occurred in the later years of the 1960s, a few youths in most free nations down through the years have defied the law of their homelands.

However, the nationwide (even worldwide) disruption was not merely the rebelling without a cause of a few youths. The times were right for what was to be a large-scale and painful reevaluation of the entire politico-religio-socio-educational organization. Reevaluation of this complexity is still going on today. The overt rebellion of many youths, including the excesses on both sides of the battle lines, contributed to what has been called the "age of accountability," as those who accepted the need for change attempted to take constructive steps. Some of this observable activity sprang from idealism, paradoxical though it may appear. Some, consequently, was a sincere desire to demonstrate a reaction against or for some attendant cause. Except for an exceptional individual, most of these young persons did precisely what their counterparts did. They ran to their peer groups for sympathy, solace, pity, support, and solutions to their problems. Overstressed social objectives force the continued use of *the group* as a crutch, a defense, a haven, a device to postpone a facing-up to life on one's own.

"Socialitism"* gave way to momentary individualism, both of which have given way to something in between. The present-day proclivity to make the necessary changes in government, education, law, and the like, *within the system,* is an encouraging sign that a balance is possible. Within one decade, the pendulum of social change has swung from one excess to the other, and now may be moving somewhere near the middle of its swing. This balance may reflect the development of persons who are willing to join the various institutions in order to help. They are becoming stable, mature, *thinking* persons. They have the ability to work and think within the group, but also the courage to think and work independently.

If young persons continue to remain as they have been, we can expect instances when they are preoccupied with individualism and instances when they join the "lonely crowd." Neither end of the pendulum's swing is healthy for either individual or community. No doubt the balance between socialitism and individualism in education will continue to command observation. There is no better place than in halls of learning to determine the proper relationship between the individual and the group, if we *think*.

One enduring truth is that men and women who move mountains and work wonders have not done so because they adjusted well to their peer groups. Ruth St. Dennis, at age 85, described her youthful philosophy in one word, "balance," which she claimed is maintained because the mind is fed with loneliness. "There is creative value in loneliness. Don't be afraid of it. If you learn to handle it, you won't become a sheep."

Thoreau described independence in biting verse: "Great God, I ask thee for no meaner pelf than that I may not disappoint myself. . . . And, next in value, which thy kindness lends, that I may greatly disappoint my friends." Of course, independence can bring unpopularity. Emerson

* For convenience, we have coined the word "socialitism" to refer to the deleterious condition of the oversocialized individual.

must have had this in mind when he observed, "For nonconformity the world whips you with displeasure." Emerson asked, however, "Is it so bad to be misunderstood?" Pythagoras, Socrates, Jesus, Luther, Galileo, Copernicus, Newton, and "every pure and wise spirit that ever took flesh" were misunderstood. To be great is to be misunderstood, although being misunderstood is not a sign of greatness.

If an individual mentally wraps his cloak about himself before venturing forth in life, he will probably do the same when he undertakes to formulate his personal philosophy of physical education, which would be another serious obstacle to the completion of this task. Such an undertaking has enough obstacles without bringing to it a hesitancy to come to grips with the problems. Fortunately, only a few men and women in physical education lack adventuresomeness.

PERIL

Overconcern with the practical, with security and comfort, and with herdlike thinking must be confronted and overcome if philosophizing is to have the mark of independent thought. Not only does the intending philosopher contend with predicaments like these, avoidable though they are, but he watches for inevitable exposure to other dangers.

1. *Overclaiming* is one of the most common perils. Attempting to make small things look great; trying to rest the case on some inconsequential point; using cliches and catch phrases as supports and proofs; using *is* ("so-and-so *is*") instead of "it appears to be" or "in my opinion"; employing *all* or implying *all* when the fact is that only some or almost all fits the case; and, one of the more common, using one or a few examples or one's untested experience as sufficient evidence to draw a conclusion.

2. *Making misleading statements,* usually without an intention to deceive, can be illustrated by the following samples. "Professor Blank says football players seldom get As or Bs in his courses. This certainly shows that he either is against athletics or believes athletes are dumb." "I believe adjustment to the group is a major value because its importance makes it of major concern to man." "Your description of 'good teaching' is interesting but that isn't *really* good teaching. Now really good teaching is . . ." (and then proceeds to set up his own concept). "I believe all disciplinary cases are due to a lack of character, because lack of character arises from those who are undisciplined." "I know the order in which teaching operations like demonstration, motivation, and explanation should occur. I arrange them according to the way they occur in class. They occur this way because this is the way I have planned for and arranged them." "The secret of a good program is to have equal amounts of conditioning activities, aquatics, individual and dual sports, and so on. This is the truly balanced program. Any other kind is warped

and skewed and extreme." "The opponent of physical education is an opponent of the welfare of man." "Those who claim that the essence of good departmental administration is the development of all who come in contact with it are really saying that trained guidance counselors make the best departmental heads."

3. *Playing up to the audience* may occur when an individual prepares a philosophy which he knows some important person may read. It occurs if some of the ideas and beliefs presented are thereby insincere or slanted. Anything of this sort destroys a good deal of the value of independent thinking and seriously compromises the person's integrity.

4. *Posturing* in the journey through ideas applies to fewer individuals than the other obstacles discussed. It may occur as one writes or speaks of those philosophic *operations* in which one is somewhat expert. The philosophic quest is difficult. The individual is not accustomed to identifying beliefs on so many matters, much less examining them or synthesizing them. Thus, when he comes to some part about which he not only knows his own mind but also perhaps knows more than several other persons, he is apt to posture. He tends to become dogmatic, be oversure of his position, be authoritarian, show little patience with hypothetical or real opponents of his view, and even employ words of condemnation.

5. *Mislabeling* is one of the familiar perils. Because a person wants things to come out his way, he chooses words or misinterprets them in order to bolster his way. Some examples are using vague but fine-sounding terms when not sure of one's position; beginning with a statement with which almost anybody would agree, followed later by the doubtful point; substituting an idea that appears to be similar to one's view because the latter is more difficult to justify, then bringing in one's view as if it were synonymous with the substitute. Other examples include attempting to present half-truths as the whole truth; labeling an opposing position as complex and confused (which it may be!); ignoring the "if" in "If so-and-so is true, then we certainly can . . ." then proceeding as though the hypothetical part were actually true. Still other examples are using the word of an authority in one discipline as if he were an authority in the area under discussion (e.g., quoting John Dewey in psychology); referring to the findings of a modest, limited, loosely conducted survey as research; treating an analogy as though it were fully representative of the basic point being made; and presenting a view that one knows may be in error but which, at the moment, helps to support one's belief—turning a fantasy into a fact.

6. *Loose thinking* is a quickly recognized reason why an individual fails to formulate a systematic synthesis of his beliefs. The loose thinker seems unaware of half-truths. He draws unwarranted conclusions. He is not self-critical of the quality, direction, or level of his thinking. He often fails to get all of a fact. He may disregard facts that are counter

to his prejudices, without realizing it. He usually is not orderly in his thinking.

7. *Emotional involvement* has an honored place in the best that man has done, thought, and been. When this characteristic *strongly* asserts itself in a personal interest, it may become an obstacle to good thinking. Personal interest can be so emphasized and insisted on that almost everything else seems unimportant. Perspective is lost. Sound thinking becomes difficult, even impossible. Potential relationships, thus, are not seen. Even ordinary conversations are turned to the point of emotional focus. The individual seems tied to this one concern. He is quite disinterested in anything that does not bear on this cherished subject. He becomes the slave of the idea, rather than the idea being a concept that he controls.

8. *Lack of maturity* is an obstacle referred to previously in connection with being responsible for one's beliefs and opinions. Some symptoms of the immature person that work against sound or straight thinking are fear of negative reactions of others to one's views; talking or acting impulsively, later regretting it, and then insisting it is "not my fault"; talking or acting for effect; not possessing beliefs, convictions, or standards for which one will take a stand; lack of confidence, to the extent and in ways that are related to the individual's losing his individuality; an unwillingness to come to grips with the present; having well-established tendency to worry and fret about what has happened and about which nothing can be done; being satisfied (apparently) with off-top-of-head thinking; overemphasis on adjustment to the group and getting along with everybody; persistent rejection of self-discipline; being quick with an alibi; the seeming inability to foresee unwanted consequences of things said and done; and the seeming inability to anticipate responsibility, face it, and carry it through. Any one of these symptoms appears to influence an individual's quality of thinking. Perhaps a more important consideration is that these and similar characteristics tend to agglutinate (cluster)—and sometimes the clusters are large in size, in number, and in significance.

9. *The closed-door attitude* toward the new or the different operates to the detriment of the kinds of thinking required to formulate a philosophy of life. It is characterized by limited self-questioning, curiosity, or doubt. Blind, unexamined acceptance of and dependence on what the individual believes *now* is typical. When a different view from the currently held one is presented, it is not considered owing to intellectual cowardice. Personal experiences, personal opinions (unverified), and personal ideas often form the limits of vision. The individual is pilloried to the past, to the familiar. He seems unable to think straight because he appears to avoid the requisites of such thinking.

10. *Gullibility* is encountered more frequently than might be apparent because it does not bear the label. There is the individual preparing for

a test of comprehension or a graduate entrance examination who spends precious weeks reading the eight-inch-thick dictionary! There is the student who pursues a graduate degree for the express purpose of adding to his knowledge who never has a moment to synthesize, appraise or apply what he knows. Another kind of gullibility seems to emerge in the person who fails to study or listen circumspectly. Most philosophers are not cynical, but they often have to be skeptical. They permit themselves to be alert enough to know there are vested interests.

11. *The biased mind* is somewhat like the closed-door attitude. One difference is that the biased person will accept the new if it agrees with his bias. The biased mind also differs in that it forces itself to include a part of the past, present, and future. The biased mind and the practical mind usually result in narrow-minded individuals. They remind one of William Palley's gem: *"There is a way of thinking and acting which is a bar to all progress, a proof against all argument, a way to keep the mind in everlasting ignorance—and that is contempt before examination."*

12. *Pedantic verbiage* is one of the sly obstacles seldom recognized by the user. Wherever advanced students gather, it is encouraged. This is a hard-to-identify danger. The user is overconcerned about employing the latest complicated words to describe simple or simplified educational or physical education processes. It is quite possible for an erudite professor to invent and use fancy terms without preventing him from thinking soundly and well. However, imitative students who attempt to do like-wise often end up "saying words"! The meaning of their discourse is soon lost in falseness or vagueness. Those who object to professional verbiage also point out that because the meanings are seldom sharp, more escape from responsibility is possible. Those who defend new words point out that it not only enlivens the vocabulary but also helps to build or create one. Nevertheless, when the goal and concern of the individual become pedantic verbosity instead of clear thinking, as philosophic processes are developed, *thinking* is apt to suffer. Expressing one's self complexly and verbosely is not the way to clarity.

PITFALLS

As if it were not enough for the novice philosopher to have to be on the alert for predicaments and perils, there is yet more danger that can be foreseen. In thinking through toward reasoned beliefs, the philosophizing person will encounter some well-concealed traps. These pitfalls come quite without warning, and vary in size, form, and location. Three of the more common pitfalls are discussed to assist the thinker to expect these and others like them.

Arguing at the Opinion Level. One large trap into which many an unsuspecting philosophic wayfarer falls shows up in verbal expression as well as in the written word. Almost any conversation of 15 minutes or more reveals parts of the speaker's informal philosophy. Almost any six pages or more of written material similarly reveals some basic belief. The pitfall referred to is that professional persons appear to spend more time and space *arguing at the opinion level than discussing at the reflective level.* These two ways of expressing one's self are not as black to white but they are distinguishable.

We will digress for a few sentences in order to gain perspective for some of the comments that follow. Philosophy, as is known, begins with unrest. It is the unrest of curiosity, doubt, and wonder. It is the unrest of controversy, challenge, failure and troublesome issues. The resulting disequilibrium compels the person to seek equilibrium, which often means searching for the best information possible for a solution or a resolution of issues. The information in turn serves as a springboard to further action. The person wants to *understand.* Sometimes he seeks understanding because it may be useful. Sometimes he seeks it to satisfy such a catalyst as curiosity. From understanding, man strives toward wisdom. However, no rest awaits him, for from wisdom he moves toward unrest— thus completing one full turn of the endless spiral.

When speaking of arguing at the opinion level there are two key ideas. *First,* the word "arguing" does not refer to formal argumentation which is a part of logic, and sometimes demonstrated in courts of law. Rather it is disputation, often emotional, wherein the disputants (or at least one of them) uses any trick to prove his point. His reasoning may be shot through with intellectually dishonest tricks, and his generalizations are based on quite limited if any evidence. He gets away with all he can just to win the argument. One of the most common devices of the arguer is to cite his personal experience as proof. *Second,* the word "opinion" refers to unverified and often unverifiable opinion. It also embraces uninformed personal opinion.

In attempting to satisfy one's curiosity about how and why this habit of the mind is frequently encountered, we suggest that the reader talk to some individuals who have established this way of attempting to resolve issues, to solve problems, to find answers to knotty questions, and to meet controversies. Here is what was found in a modest survey.

1. Most of the individuals were not conscious that they were arguing at the opinion level.

2. Most of them were unaware that many of their opinions were unverifiable or uninformed.

3. Most of them did not realize that the tactics they used, just to win the argument, involved false reasoning and dishonest thinking.

4. It had not occurred to any of them that beliefs and opinions should be examined.

5. All but one immediately saw the need for discussion at the reflective level, if the disputation was to be fruitful.

6. Half of them guessed that part of the force that made them want to argue was their right to speak out, their right to free speech.

7. A few felt they were "pushed from inside" to assert themselves.

8. About three fourths of them expressed the general notion that now that they had been nailed for arguing at the opinion level, they might try to *discuss* at the *reflective* level. However, several of them were not hopeful because it "really requires some work" to become informed and to examine one's beliefs.

9. Within their statements was the unexpressed idea that they would feel restricted if held responsible for their opinions.

Most persons have done a good deal of arguing at the opinion level. They have not reflected on thinking responsibly during an argument. Typically, during an argument a person expresses himself much as he did when he was less mature, when his beliefs were insecurely based, and when his experiences were limited.

Discussion at the reflective level involves two key words: "discussion" and "reflective." In professional circles, discussion is characterized by the attempt to reach a solution, resolve an issue, seek the best possible answer to a question—not to prove a point! A reflectively conducted discussion also is characterized by the attempt to perform sound reasoning, reach verifiable generalizations, examine and reexamine each step of the discussion if necessary. It is marked by unemotional deliberateness. There is within this kind of discussion the willingness and encouragement to hear all the views from the other sides, and all sides should have a fair chance to be heard. In no other way can understanding and wisdom prevail. Not often is mere personal opinion injected into a discussion, and then it is so labeled by the speaker (or writer). The participants—and this is a major point—are *informed!*

There has been some loose thinking about the right to talk. There is no doubt that people in this country have the right to free speech, within the limits set by the law—and there are limits. However, among professional persons who are concerned with solving problems, resolving issues, meeting challenges, it is neither a sign of personal maturity nor professional responsibility for time to be taken at a meeting by persons who are not informed on the matter under discussion. (Obviously, a professional organization might arrange meetings designed for people to talk about things about which they know little.) However, to confuse the two purposes is misleading to everyone present. Questions, of course, are quite in order. Nevertheless, the uninformed person, maintaining his right to talk, seldom realizes it but there is a subtle inference that what he says is on a par with what an outstanding expert might say if given the opportunity. Often, there are many persons in the audience who are, admittedly, uninformed—that may be why they came to the meeting. They are in no position to distinguish fact from fiction. So often the informed expert does not push to be heard, and often is modest in his manner of presentation. He often shows to disadvantage with the emotional arguer. Thus, the uninformed audience may leave the meeting badly misinformed. The third type of person present who might be misled by the free-for-all disputation is the informed participant who gladly accepted the invitation to participate, thinking it would provide an opportunity to discuss the subject with persons who might disagree but were as well informed as he himself. The summarizer also has a dilemma when he must make concluding remarks on the meeting.

It is believed that as persons are more carefully and comprehensively prepared professionally, their example of reflective discussion will be catching. Part of this belief springs from the probability that the better qualified a person is for a given profession the more readily he recognizes and respects others who also are qualified, even though they may disagree with him. In fact, the mark of a mature discussant is that he maneuvers the discussion so that each person in the discussion has contributed his special information.

The tendency to argue at the opinion level is a pitfall well worth anticipating and avoiding. Solid ground is to be found in discussion at the reflective level.

False Similarity of Terms. Another pitfall is a basic failure to pay attention to certain words used. Most of us are careless in distinguishing between paired words that are sometimes used almost as synonyms, but that mislead the user and reader or listener alike. There are literally hundreds of such confusing words.

1. Assuming that enjoyment and excitement are closely related.
2. Assuming that uniformity and standardization are synonyms.
3. Assuming that absoluteness and universality are similar.
4. Confusing freedom with equality.
5. Assuming that equality and freedom are synonyms of liberty.
6. Failing to distinguish between desires and needs.
7. Confusing the meanings of motives and interests.
8. Assuming that authority and wisdom go hand in hand.
9. Failing to distinguish among riches, wealth, and a large amount of money.
10. Assuming that movement or change means progress.
11. Confusing such words as "meritorious" and "distinguished" (service).
12. Failing to distinguish among leadership, executive ability, and positions of prestige.

13. Thinking that reasons and causes are identical.
14. Confusing what is true with what is certain.
15. Confusing *theory of* with *philosophy of*.

Language is heavily peppered with other combinations of similar words which lead the journeying person into trouble. If one pays more attention to the words used in writing and speaking—especially when pursuing those elusive reasoned beliefs—straight thinking begins to be an accomplished goal.

Mistakes in Writing Out One's Discoveries. When one uses the written word to express philosophic discovery, the potholes have a way of becoming craters. Perhaps the single largest trap to foresee arises when pen is set to paper. In addition to the common errors found in most manuscripts (mistakes in English grammar, spelling, punctuation, and ambiguities in meaning), there are some mistakes that detract particularly from the written account of one's philosophy of physical education or any other discipline.

1. Lack of preciseness in selection of key words and terms.
2. Lack of clarity in statements portraying one's beliefs.
3. Failure to identify and take into consideration all assumptions that underlie the main areas of belief.
4. Failure to provide sufficient time for a careful, critical scrutiny of the rough copy and the final typed one, and for accurate editing of the manuscript.
5. Lack of consistency.
6. Undetected contradictions.
7. Evidence of faulty reasoning (consult a good book of logic).
8. Lack of organization and systematic presentation.
9. Failure to identify unusual usages of words and to give definitions if necessary for understanding.
10. Giving the reader a biased view of a discussion through over- or underemphasis of topics, and failing to otherwise write discriminatingly.
11. Permitting one's critical evaluation of one's own manuscript to be less incisive than when judging another's work.
12. Failing to remove extraneous words, phrases, sentences, paragraphs, and pages that detract from the quality of the manuscript.
13. Failing to write, rewrite, rewrite. . . .

The list is *not* exhaustive of the kinds of writing pits into which the novice is likely to tumble. It is only suggestive of the most common rough spots encountered in setting one's thoughts on paper. The philosophizing person should respect the difficulties in writing clearly just as much as he respects the difficulties in thinking clearly. Being good at one does not guarantee being good at the other. Being good at both—though much rarer than most think—yields a world-changing power indeed.

WHERE ARE WE NOW?

Our efforts have taken us to the quite foreseeable quicksand. Having been forewarned of the possible risks to be encountered, our adventuring philosopher can now forearm himself. He now realizes the need not only to look at (think through) the subject that interests him on his way toward reasoned beliefs, but he also now knows how important it is to *look at his own looking* so as to sidestep costly mistakes.

After alertness, perhaps the single most precious quality that will serve to forearm the inquiring mind against unnecessary exposure to predicaments, perils, and pitfalls is *patience*. We intend patience to be understood in a large sense, having at least two related meanings.

First, the patient philosophizing person will take the time and trouble to become informed. Whatever the issue, question, or problem, it is well to bother to become an informed person. Search out the facts. Examine the arguments closely. Study the reasons. Look for the proper causes. In short, become a student of whatever has captured your attention and needs tending to, by using the unmasking power of your mind. Understand. Analyze. Evaluate.

Second, we remind the philosophizing student that things take time. Not only is the journey through the philosophic process both difficult and discouragingly slow, but the changes such patient philosophizings are supposed to accomplish often do not appear. The haste and hurry by which most of us live tend to condemn us to listen only to the loudest voice, to try the expedient solution, to be in awe of the quickest to publish. Hurrying usually leads us to mistake frightful stupidities for absolute truths! Patience usually permits us to wait for the knowledge sought so as to see both the stupidities and the truths for what they are. We ought to remember the words of that famous resident television metaphysician Charlie Chan who said, "Patience is the sister of wisdom."

THE BEST WEAPONS AGAINST THE INFAMIES OF LIFE ARE COURAGE, AN INDEPENDENT MIND, AND PATIENCE. COURAGE STRENGTHENS, THE INDEPENDENT MIND AMUSES, AND PATIENCE GIVES PEACE.

—Hermann Hesse

Philosophy as Action

A PHILOSOPHY MERELY ACCEPTED FROM ANOTHER MAN AND NOT THOUGHT OUT FOR ONE'S SELF IS AS DEAD AS A MERE CATALOGUE OF POSSIBLE OPINIONS. PHILOSOPHICAL FORMULAS MERELY REPEATED UPON THE CREDIT OF A MASTER'S AUTHORITY LOSE THE VERY MEANING WHICH MADE THE MASTER AUTHORITATIVE.

—Josiah Royce

6

Discovering the "Soul" of the Philosophic Process

YOU WILL NOT LEARN FROM ME PHILOSOPHY, BUT HOW TO PHILOSOPHIZE—NOT THOUGHTS TO REPEAT, BUT HOW TO THINK.

—*Immanuel Kant*

To prepare the reader for an introduction to what the philosophers of old discovered by the philosophic process, namely, the *substance* of philosophy (see Part II), we must become even more certain as to exactly what the philosophic process is. Therefore, let us attempt to discover its "soul."

In 1822 William Hazlitt, in an essay entitled "On Going A Journey," wrote that the soul of any journey is *liberty*, "perfect liberty."[14] In the end, even the journey in ideas (or maybe, especially the journeying of our thinking) ought to be understood in this sweeping way. The practicing philosopher is liberated from prejudice, myth, superstition, fear. Philosophizing liberates the thinker for the peace of mind, professionally and personally, that is supposed to be realized in the discovery of the good life.

If we follow Hazlitt a bit farther on his journey, we find he is referring to the kind of journey common before the age of automobiles: walking in the country. Hazlitt, in writing about himself, his likes, and his dislikes, firmly informs us that he prefers to walk alone. He says he "cannot see the wit of walking and talking at the same time." He is for the "synthetical method on a journey, in preference to the analytical." Hazlitt is quite content to "lay in a stock of ideas then, and to examine and anatomize them afterwards." He states, "I want to see my vague notions float like the down of the thistle before the breeze, and not to have them entangled in the briars and thorns of controversy."[14]

Let us appropriate from Hazlitt his suggestion about the two ways of taking a journey. It is indeed clear that the philosophic process includes both *analysis* and *synthesis*. If the ultimate soul of the philosophic process is perfect liberty, then analysis and synthesis are the necessary actions through which such liberty is achieved. They are opposite poles of a unity, to wit, the philosophic process.

NO CONTENT WITHOUT PROCESS

The content of philosophy has always had to wait until someone produced the subject matter. This condition is as true today as it was at the dawn of philosophy. It is the *mental activities* of the philosopher that produce the substance of philosophy. The obviousness of this fact should mislead no one. The impact of the awe experienced by the early philosophers was not only what they wrote and were supposed to have said, but also that they used mental *activities in such ways* that this product ensued. As mentioned previously, Pythagoras, when giving a name to this noble enterprise, used first the word "philosophos" (philosopher), *not* "philosophy"? Must not he have been struck by the fact that a man was *doing* that which had not been done before, that man had gained a magnificent capability?

Philosophy, as the love or seeking of wisdom, involves not only wisdom, but the *requisite actions* involved. The discovery, identification, application and unification of these mental activities into the *philosophic process* includes this other kind of wisdom. There would have been no philosophic content without this process.

Let no physical educator, seeking an easy way out, imagine that the philosophy of physical education is formulated by reading about and applying the major philosophic positions and variants to his discipline. Such an effort may be educational and cultural, but it is not philosophic. The philosophy of any discipline—science, history, art, education, or physical education—comes as a result of *making use of philosophic operations*. Some of these are presented in the chart on page 74.

Modern scholars interested in the *peoples* of ancient civilizations point out that the Sumerians, Babylonians, and Egyptians of antiquity, with all their advances, missed the path that led to the flowering of wisdom that the Greeks experienced. They failed to develop men who wondered *enough*, were curious *enough*, doubted *enough*, asked why *enough*, and examined their thinking *enough*. Ordinarily, when one thinks of the wisdom of the Greeks, he does not stop to think that it emerged from this other kind of wisdom—this other part of our heritage—this *performing of philosophic actions*.

The philosopher within one's self would have one read about and learn the lessons from the bold ideas of brilliant minds from that other age. But if the inner voice is that of a *philosopher*, it will also tell one to seek further—to discover the *process* that produced these ideas. This concept was outlined by an advanced student in a philosophy of physical education class. "What more is it that I can do if I pursue wisdom? Would it help if I found out what it is that I really believe? I'd like to figure out for the first time just what my beliefs are and why I believe them. I doubt if a person in the room has taken the time to get down to bedrock in things like this. You've said that wisdom begins with knowledge and understanding and these are applied to living. Well, the way I live, everything I do, and the way I do it depend on my beliefs. Isn't it sort of natural to take most of your beliefs for granted, unless they run into a brick wall? Wouldn't it help me to gain a bit of wisdom if I took a good look at my beliefs before that happened? Wouldn't I stand a better chance of living a little bit more wisely if these beliefs of mine were submitted to some sort of testing? And, I'm not just talking about life. I'm thinking also about my profession. Wouldn't it help me to have a little more wisdom in my work in physical education if I knew where I really stood, if I knew where I am, if I knew why I do and say a good many things which I assume are okay? I don't want to be a philosopher but the old philosophers must have *done* something that I do not do. Did they do something I could just try my hand at doing? I can read what they wrote and were supposed to have said, but I'd like to know what they *did* to get their ideas, if that would help me."

It has been reactions like this which have led to the major emphasis in this chapter and in much of this book. There is, of course, one word of caution from *professors* of philosophy. This is that when one tries to philosophize one is apt to miss the key to the process. They say, "You are not *consistent* and *systematic* in viewing philosophy as a process. How much we wish that you were systematic in your beliefs and what you do to the beliefs and with them!" Recently, professors of philosophy have come to realize that learning about and attempting to apply the great ideas are not enough. They see that man, if he is to improve as a rational being, must learn to perform at least some of the philosophic operations described in the following pages.

PHILOSOPHIC OPERATIONS

We have tried to simplify the soul of the philosophic process accurately with the suggestion that the two basic actions necessary to the realization of this notion of perfect liberty (without which the process cannot go forward) are analysis and synthesis. Generally, these two actions include many other essential *functions* of philosophers. For example, one kind of function broadly conceived to be within the action we call analysis is *comparison.* The various functions apply to philosophic *areas* such as values, standards, purposes, hypotheses, assumptions, and others to

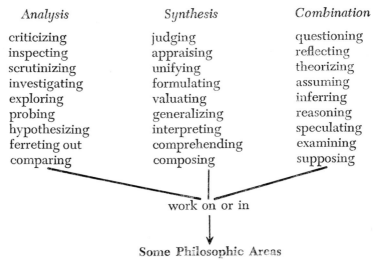

Some Philosophic Functions

Analysis	Synthesis	Combination
criticizing	judging	questioning
inspecting	appraising	reflecting
scrutinizing	unifying	theorizing
investigating	formulating	assuming
exploring	valuating	inferring
probing	generalizing	reasoning
hypothesizing	interpreting	speculating
ferreting out	comprehending	examining
comparing	composing	supposing

work on or in

Some Philosophic Areas

ideas, facts, experiences, objectives, goals, purposes, values, consequences, results, outcomes, relationships, motives, beliefs, convictions, opinions, reasons, aspirations, principles, assumptions, hypotheses, theories, interpretations, meanings, generalizations, conclusions, syntheses, standards, analyses, knowledge implications, inferences, ideals, ethics, morals, aesthetics, being, becoming

the action of a function working
in or *on* an area is applied to

Some Aspects of Physical Education

program and its parts, e.g., competitive athletics, dance, rehabilitative activities, intramurals, gymnastics, aquatics, and the like; and tasks or actions of the physical educator, e.g., facilities, equipment, and supplies; teaching and coaching; supervising, administrating, organizing; research, problem-solving; testing, evaluation and measurement; guidance and counseling; curriculum construction, program building; professional standards; professional conduct; professional and public relations; and similar professional tasks

PHILOSOPHIC OPERATIONS

be mentioned later. For example, as *values* and *standards* are *compared*, a philosophic *operation* lacks one step of being performed.

Furthermore, after one has compared values or standards, this action of a function (comparing) working on or in an area (values) usually is directed at the *aspects* or phases of physical education (viz., teaching, public relations, program). All these processes constitute what is called a "philosophic operation." When one *compares* (function) *values* (areas) of two *programs* (aspects or phases), one has performed a philosophic *operation*. Further examples can be drawn from the chart on page 74, such as *inspecting* the *theories* of *administration; interpreting* the *implications* of *research;* or *theorizing* about the *outcomes of sport, games,* or *exercise.* Most of the functions apply not only to one but to many of the *areas* shown in the chart, and many of these combinations of functions and areas may be applied to most of the aspects of physical education to form philosophic *operations.*

Thus, one may explore the purposes of teaching physical education or examine the values of teaching a given activity. One may ferret out the meaning of standards for professional behavior or scrutinize the principles involved in an ethical code. One may unify or generalize all the purposes of physical education into one master purpose or judge the validity of a knowledge test for beginning tennis players.

Scores of beliefs are about the program, for example. One task might be to examine (*function*) the relationships (*area*) between the physical education activities for seniors (*aspect*) and those for young adults (another *aspect*) offered by the municipal recreation department. Assume that this *operation* leads to beliefs about coordinating the two programs (still another aspect), but that you do not believe in this particular unification. Beliefs about this particular administrative coordination rest on and are supported by hearsay, guess, and perhaps a fact or two.

The chart shows an adequate list of philosophic functions, areas, and operations. It also illustrates the kinds of actions that philosophers perform as they consider the doubts, wonderings, curiosities, quandaries, confusions, perplexities, questions, and even the major problems of man and mankind.

Notice that the listing of philosophic functions appears under three different headings: *analysis, synthesis* and *combination*. Some functions are primarily analysis, others chiefly synthesis, and others are, strictly speaking, neither one nor the other, but a little of both.

It will also be noted in the chart that there are instances of two words appearing in both the function and area groupings which spring from the same root. An example is hypothesizing and hypotheses. More instances of this kind could have been shown than actually appear in the *function* and *areas* columns. This seeming duplication is not, in fact, what it appears to be. The action verb *hypothesizing* can be applied to

quite a number of the philosophic areas. For example, one might hypothesize with reference to some standards, principles, ethics, viewpoints, and
so on. Under the noun *hypotheses* quite a number of the philosophic
functions may work on and in this area. For example, one might ferret
out, formulate, and investigate certain hypotheses or a hypothesis.

Another word of explanation seems desirable. All the words listed (as
well as others) definitely refer to *philosophic* connotations and implications. Several of the words in both lists are used in other disciplines of
knowledge, but they have meanings unlike the philosophic meanings. The
word "standards" is an example. In science, standards refer to a dozen
different kinds of measurable phenomena. Many of these multi-meaning
words may be treated by the philosophic process. For example, one might
explore the value of establishing sanitation standards in a primitive community of nomadic, illiterate persons. This reference to the word "value"
suggests that some of the words in both lists refer quite definitely and
usually exclusively to the philosophic process. This generalization is based
on an invalid example! *Value* may be an unphilosophic term in economics! Purposes, reasons, and conclusions are more satisfactory examples.

THE ROLE OF CATEGORIES IN PHILOSOPHIC OPERATIONS

If one's philosophizing is to be reasonably systematic, it is necessary
to select a satisfactory family of categories. There must be homogeneity
or internal consistency among the categories. The main divisions of one's
philosophic statement cannot be a mixture of families of categories. Some
of the categories cannot deal with the kinds of programs (intramurals,
adaptive physical education), others with teaching, administration, and
the like, and still others with the different kinds of people involved,
such as parents and students.

At the bottom of the chart several phases of the program are given.
Beginning with teaching and coaching, most of the tasks or actions listed
are performed by the physical educator. As examples of the *persons* family of categories, besides parents and students, there are taxpayers, departmental associates, other members of the profession, and one's self.

1. If the family of categories selected is that of *persons,* how is it helpful
to the novice philosopher? *First,* recognize that the *functions* and *areas*
in the chart must be put to work in connection with the category. For
example, the philosophic *function* "examining" is applied to the philosophic *area* "ideas." Assume that the category is *students.* The philosopher
examines the ideas of students. About what? To answer this question,
select one element or idea or phase of physical education from the list
of elements or centers of belief on page 26. Suppose "objectives" is
selected. The task is to *examine students' ideas of the objectives of physical education* (or of this activity) (or of this lesson).

2. Suppose the family of categories selected to serve as the framework of one's professional philosophy is parts or phrases of the *program*. Assume that the philosophic *function* "ferreting out" is selected from the chart and applied to the philosophic *area* "values." From the bottom of the chart, the phase of the program chosen to be written about at a given spot in one's philosophy is "intramurals," thus, *ferreting out the values of intramurals*. But for whom? Suppose you decided to highlight *taxpayers* (the idea might be to show the taxpayer that intramural athletics, although costly, is more economical than interscholastic athletics). In addition, it would not be difficult to ferret out the value of interscholastic athletics for the average qualified youth.

3. Assume that the family of categories selected is the *tasks or action of the physical educator* himself. Again from the chart, "formulating" is selected as the philosophic function and "principles" as the philosophic area. "Teaching" is the professional task selected, "dance" is the phase of the program, and the "teacher" is the person. Thus, the novice philosopher would write about his *formulation of the principles of teaching dance as far as the teacher was concerned*.

The chart suggests the many combinations and intercombinations of *functions, areas, phases,* and *action-tasks* of the physical educator. When the different persons that might be involved are included, thousands of personal beliefs are possible. As some of the beliefs are compared, the philosophic *content* grows apace. If the thinker answers the philosophic question "why" for only his prime beliefs, the result is a still more enriched philosophic content.

One of the more valuable outcomes of engaging in the philosophic process is that the individual is led toward new beliefs and ideas. He extends his knowledge or understanding toward wisdom.

ANALYSIS AND SYNTHESIS

Now that you have a grasp of the basic structure of what is called a "philosophic operation," it is necessary to distinguish more specifically between the two major functions: *analysis* and *synthesis*. As mentioned, these opposite processes are essential to bring the soul of the philosophic process into view. The understanding of these functions will soundly prepare the philosophizing person for his lifelong philosophic journey.

One reason that a person's philosophy of physical education may reflect the incomplete and myopic view is his lack of perspective. From his vantage point the individual reflects what *he* sees. He may compound the error by failing to change his vantage point. This analogy permits the observation that had he used different points of view, what he saw might have been different. Thus, one advantage of advanced graduate study is that it often helps to bring the perspective needed to see *ever-larger wholes*. Great ideas, worthily expressed, are encountered.

One counterview to that being suggested is that lumping together all of life's or a profession's ingredients encourages the sacrifice of discrimination or the ability to distinguish. The claim here is that these two valuable philosophic techniques demand *analysis*, just the antithesis of synthesis. It is true that to distinguish between this and that and to be discriminating, one must be able to analyze. Comparisons are necessary between norms, standards, and perhaps values and purposes. Analysis is *necessary* in the forging of one's philosophy of physical education.

Does analysis stop with analysis? After analysis, if it is not a cul-de-sac, is there anywhere else to go in one's mental venture but to start to pull the parts together, unifying some of them with fragments of other parts of life or of the profession or other professions? Just as analysis produces words or symbols representing the parts spawned by the analyzing process, so words are the means by which the mind *synthesizes* ideas and experiences, expresses them and makes them known. It is with words that both the eminent and the novice philosopher are able to weave together ever-larger patterns. Thus, analysis and synthesis, although standing in opposition, combine to produce order, balance, harmony, and perspective.

Analysis

Hazlitt, you will remember, likened talking, on his country journey, to the analytic method of journeying. He said he preferred walking, "vegetating like the country," to "criticizing hedge-rows and black cattle."[14] For Hazlitt, then, walking is a synthetic act; talking is an analytic one. Talking is critical comment.

To analyze is to systematically criticize. It is not necessarily censure or faultfinding. However, it does imply close scrutiny. Usually we mean that there will be an effort to separate the subject matter, argument, or proposition (statement) into its various parts or elements. There is intention to decompose, to breakdown, to particularize, to fractionate.

Although there do not seem to be definite sequential steps in carrying through analysis, there do seem to be certain parts to keep in mind. Let us say that the novice philosopher wishes to analyze a specific statement. For example, suppose someone advances the proposition that sports build character. In our analysis of analyzing we find the following elements would be useful to apply directly to the statement (all the elements could, of course, be applied to the analyzing of arguments, position papers, short or book-length essays, and so forth).

Sports Build Character

1. Study the *statement* carefully to discover its meaning, clarity, coherence, and significance.

2. What do the *words in the statement mean?* Study each word, looking for ambiguity, multiple meanings, inaccurate grammar, and so forth.

3. Scrutinize the *purpose*(s) implied by the statement. Ask what purpose, if any, the statement could serve.

4. Incisively study the quality and quantity of the *supporting evidence* for the statement. Is the statement meant to stand by itself or does it require support? What kind of support is necessary?

5. Ask what *weaknesses* and *strengths* are implicitly contained within the statement.

6. Identify the *values implied* or taken for granted in the statement.

7. Question both the *reliability* (how generalizable) and the *validity* (how true) of the statement.

8. If the idea behind the statement can be verified, can the idea be put into action? In short, does the statement have an understood *applicability* or *feasibility?*

9. Study the intended *scope* of the statement. Does it presuppose some kind of echelon or hierarchy?

10. Identify the possible *consequences* of the statement, if it were shown to be a true statement.

11. Examine both the statement and its possible consequences for its *controversialism.* Determine as far as you can what elements in the statement make it controversial.

12. Determine what *relationships* the statement has to other aspects of the same general subject matter. Is the statement in concert or conflict with other things you know to be true or false?

13. Forecast the *probable effect* such a statement would have (if true) on present and future practices in physical education. What is the prognosis of the statement?

14. In the most general way, try to *state all the presuppositions* on which the statement depends. What needs to be true for the statement to be true?

We hope in the breakdown of this statement the novice has not suffered his own breakdown. Who would imagine that three little words innocently strung together (sports build character) could possibly elicit a detailed operation involving at least 14 parts? Indeed, criticism is not easy. Nevertheless, to criticize seriously is to perform these operations precisely.

Few philosophies would ever have been written if the philosophers critically analyzed *each* of their statements! It would take many years to read the philosophic writings of but one major philosopher if the reader critically analyzed *each* statement. Nevertheless, the degree to which at least a few of these tests are applied to the written expression of thoughts, and the carefulness with which all of them are applied to

most fundamental beliefs and strongly held convictions, to that extent
will this phase of philosophic ability develop. Even the length of the list
of elements is arresting enough to prevent ever using the term "analysis"
carelessly!

Synthesis

If analysis is criticism, synthesis is vision. Even Hazlitt (preferring
the synthetic method) wrote of the elbowroom, the few encumbrances,
the breathing space,

> "To muse on indifferent matters whence contemplation
> 'May plume her feathers and let grow her wings,
> That in the various bustle of resort
> Were all too-ruffled, and sometimes impair'd.' "[14]

Seeing life and seeing it whole is the familiar watchword of philosophy.
It points up the necessity of unifying life's experiences, ideas, feelings,
knowledges, aspirations, and understandings. If synthesizing is to be improved, then thinking, judging, and living in *ever-larger wholes* is the
personal challenge. You say life is bitter? sour? sweet? Sure! It could not
be life and be anything but sweet *and* sour, black *and* white, emphasizing
a facet of the watchword. It spells *whole* in such a way that unavoidably
we see clearly that the negative is included *with* the positive, the evil
with the good, weaknesses *with* strengths, as life is viewed and lived.
Life then loses some of its chaotic fragmentation.

The degree to which the individual is able to synthesize all of life's
ingredients—all that it is, all that it does, and all that it includes—to that
extent does he come to see life and see it whole. It is the partial vision,
the short look, the narrow slant, and the thin view that provide the basis
for his seeing life inaccurately, twistedly, limitedly. This skewed view of
life unfortunately may set the pattern for the individual's view of his
profession. His habits of thinking prevent his *seeing* his profession as
the whole it actually is. He may even miss the towering significance of
seeing the profession as inseparable from the life of the people, from
their way of life. The necessary task of thinking and seeing in *ever-larger
wholes* comes to an end for such an individual long before the task is
completed.

Nevertheless, the picture is not depressing for most physical educators.
A wide-angle lens yields a larger view, wherein an increasing number of
men and women in this profession are successfully and continually extending its perimeter, pushing its vision outward, increasing its depth.
Such a demonstration of growth of a discipline could not be effected
without increasing ability to unify physical education efforts and results
with those of other disciplines, and with life itself.

The charge given physical educators is to fashion and refashion, orient

and reorient, their best offerings so that they are available to and come alive for the American culture. This charge has been rather generally and successfully dodged in American physical education to date. It has been too *school* and *college* oriented. But the hope for change grows.

Synthesis Unifies Knowledge. Doubt, curiosity, and wonder move us to seek and attain knowledge. A synthesis of knowledges, then, is necessary if understanding is to follow. Moving mentally from understanding toward wisdom, a synthesis of understandings becomes necessary. Reference is made to synthesis of not only the understandings of the matter at hand, but also the understandings of life and living. The number of ideas grows apace and needs unifying.

Philosophers emphasize the need to *bring together* experiences, aspects of human behavior, ideas, beliefs, and, in addition, words that put professional knowledges in perspective as a synthesized whole. To go beyond keeping up with the news, and attending to professional responsibilities and domestic activities, to where one can see life and see it whole seems to be an impossibility. Thus, understanding lags behind as new knowledges leap ahead. The possibility of attaining wisdom seems ever to recede. Despite this frustrating situation, man does not say, "It's too much for me! I give up. Only a fool would delude himself into thinking he has a chance to move from knowledge toward wisdom. From here on I'm content to rest on my oars." Man cannot quit by default and remain *man!* Some men, yes, but not *man.* Life baffles all formulas.

The last man who is supposed to have known everything was Benjamin Jowett, great English university professor of the last century. However, the quest for knowledge is not the quest for wisdom. Wisdom demands a synthesis of knowledges or understandings and their application to living.

Recall some meanings of the word "wisdom." Wisdom is judging rightly the goals and purposes of life and the means of reaching them. More specifically, wisdom refers to judging rightly the means one uses to pursue worthy ends. It embraces judging rightly what is of value and what is good for man. Wisdom starts with the known, with facts, if possible, and moves toward understanding, as relationships are discovered, and then judiciously applies these to living. Another mark of wisdom includes the use of good reason and intellect in handling incompatible parts, in yielding gracefully and without rancor in the face of the unpreventable, the inescapable, the impossible. This is a long way of saying seeing life and seeing it whole. Some *knowledge* about kinds of conduct, kinds of goals, and so on, is basic, necessary. It underlies *understanding,* but it does not guarantee understanding. Certainly, knowledge of all areas of learning is quite an impossible and unnecessary feat today. It may have seemed necessary in the nineteenth century. Today, man is not content with merely amounts of knowledges.

4

Synthesis Leads to Understanding. Rapid expansion of knowledge, the inability to make understanding keep pace with knowledge, and modern man's relatively limited time for gaining understanding may be considered as sufficient rationalization for his failure to see the unity of life. Perhaps the case is more honestly implied above. Yet, are pointless distractions permitted to shorten the time actually spent on trying to understand? Does not permitting a thousand meaningless details to enter in prevent the discovery of a master purpose—and letting it function? Are not most persons prone to spend energy on quite silly pursuits and thus lack the energy, inclination, and patience to gain an understanding of more of life and one's fellow man? The case is far from hopeless. More and more persons are recognizing some of these situations, which accounts in part for the discontent and criticism of our current way of life in the West, perhaps not from an economic viewpoint but certainly from a philosophic one. Identification of situations such as this is the first step toward change. It is the man doing only little things who prevents himself from gaining understanding more rapidly or to a greater degree.

A facet of the effort to simplify in order to unify life somewhat more readily and surely is apt to slip by unnoticed. In unifying experiences, ideas, and the like, the joining together is possible when the individual *sees* where one experience may hook onto another, where one concept may hook onto another. This process is continued until a cluster is formed. This linking is, for most of us, a trial-and-error-trial-and-success process that must be done. The old saying that there is nothing more useless than an unattached fact is balanced by the saying there is nothing more dangerous than an unconnected idea. This same sort of thought applies to experiences and to human behavior. The philosopher residing in each man knows he should constantly look for places to make connections and interconnections as he goes about mental journeying. Finding them is never an accidental trifle.

One also should *seek* additional experiences and ideas to round out or fill in a cluster and an overall synthesis of the discoveries that make up a philosophy. So much a part of philosophy is this pulling together that the Institute of Philosophical Research under Mortimer Adler, with the help of a large research staff, is writing entire books about each one of 102 great ideas as a phase of the Great Books project.[1] Obviously, the entire task will outlast anyone now living. When the last of the books on the great ideas has been written, together with bringing them up-to-date, the master task will be to synthesize all of this information into some gargantuan concept.

In physical education the current tendency to fractionate the overall value of it makes such unification difficult, but more necessary than ever. Frequently, there is overemphasis on *one* aspect or *one* sport or *one* method of investigation. Not infrequently, those who fail to see the forest because of the trees are faddists who jump on a new bandwagon every year or two. One reason for this conglomerate of small views of some persons is the failure to have formulated an overall purpose of their profession.

The person who purposely seeks additional ideas with which connections may be made with presently held ideas is on the road toward deeper, broader understanding. In contrast is the individual who reads a book on a given subject or the student who takes a course in a given discipline and then concludes that he has acquired an *understanding* of the subject! If the individual permitted the book to lead him to read a dozen books about the subject, and if he permitted the course to push him to become really informed in the subject (not, *about* the subject), the chances for new ideas to be added to originally held ideas would be tremendous! Understanding cannot follow knowledge until ideas that are different from knowledge ideas have come to the individual. This is one of the most difficult concepts for even some advanced students to grasp. They conceive, at least in the beginning, that the doctoral program, for example, will give them more and more knowledge about their profession, instead of gaining a greater understanding of the deeper meaning, of the wider implications, of the farther reaches of their discipline, of the charm of the intangible.

The limited approach may occur in philosophy, or some part of philosophy, such as ethics or aesthetics. If a person reads only Dewey, he believes the difference between Peirce's and James's conceptions of the doctrine of pragmatism is the difference between particular and general consequences as the test of truth. If he reads other writers, he believes that Dewey's notion of pragmatism (instrumentalism, operationalism, experimentalism) became increasingly practicalistic, and that increasingly Dewey squeezed out metaphysics until none was left.

The point is not that turning to other sources necessarily will drive beliefs gained away from the first source. Rather, it is that the practice of basing a person's beliefs on the teaching of one man produces the narrow, short view, unless other teachings are available. A different kind of person is developed, a different kind of mind is developed, if the individual bases his beliefs on the teachings of several thinkers. This is true even though (and perhaps, particularly if) the thinkers disagree among themselves.

Better understanding comes when differing views are brought to one's mind. Such views drive one to scrutinize, examine, appraise, compare, interrelate, and then unify. Such a process lends quality to one's judgment. It provides some basis for increased understanding.

It should not be concluded that the views of one thinker should be rejected. For one thing, he may have thoroughly analyzed and appraised the views of his colleagues and produced a composite point of view.

This is precisely the sort of thing Democritus did in working out his theory of the atom. For another thing, one of the thinkers might have devoted a lifetime to the topic at hand. His views, on examination, stand above any of the others. However, if a background of many other ideas is to be gained so that clusters of ideas are filled out, thus facilitating the writing of a philosophy, one needs to consider the various proposals, contradictory though they may be. Nevertheless, this way of gaining a basis for a philosophy should be done sufficiently ahead of the writing of the philosophy to enable one to arrive at ideas of one's own. The borrowing of unexamined ideas from whatever the source is not the philosophic way.

Throughout the searching into the minds of others for differing and perhaps new ideas, one should not forget that the goal remains that of pulling together into larger and ever-larger wholes the ingredients of philosophy: ideas, experiences, human conduct, and the words that represent their meaning, without losing the art of doubting.

A part of the goal that occasionally occurs confuses some and intrigues others. Sometimes it becomes apparent that those who write interpretations of the works of a great thinker violently disagree as to what he meant here and there. This may even occur among his direct disciples. It is particularly interesting to see what happens to the master's teachings as time moves on, as the disciples' followers begin to write. Sixty seconds (or more!) spent conjecturing about *why* the master's original was skewed, diluted, or projected into almost unrelated territory is rewarding in terms of gaining perspective in viewing great ideas that have survived. A moment thus spent also may be fruitful in terms of gaining a clear realization that language is *not* an *exact* tool.

Using *one's own* interpretations as one reads the writings of Thomas D. Wood, Clark Hetherington, Jay B. Nash, Jesse F. Williams, Catharine Beecher, Luther Halsey Gulick, Dudley A. Sargent, Margaret H'Doubler, and a score of other innovators is apt to produce quite different ideas than their interpreters present.

Sometimes the varied interpretations, the mixing in of others' ideas, and the skewing of the original teaching enable a good deal of the great idea to survive. In fact, these changes may enrich the original, making it more applicable to more situations and enabling more ideas to hook onto it. Except for some rare instances, it appears that if an idea endures it must be capable of joining with other substantial ideas that emerge with *significant* changes in man's thinking. The rare exceptions are those ideas that have rightly interpreted human nature. As far as we know, human nature has not changed for a long, long time. If human nature is judged on the basis of recorded thought, the Egyptian who wrote the Memphite Drama over 5000 years ago could give a modern lecture on social welfare. The reader might enjoy browsing through Breasted's

Dawn of Conscience to come to closer grips with man's sameness when it comes to his inner nature.[6] de Chardin in *The Phenomenon of Man,* although not emphasizing the written record, makes a similar point from the biologist's viewpoint.[8] Biologists and anthropologists believe today's man is virtually unchanged in nature from the remarkable Neanderthal man. Nevertheless, all other aspects of man (which are modified with the changing times) require that laws, principles, theories, hypotheses, other beliefs, and facts become subject to the inevitability of possible change, and thus open to synthesis with new, different, or other beliefs, if they are to endure. Thus, synthesis serves as one function which keeps beliefs and their foundations and supports geared to the present. The more an idea, experience, belief, phase of human conduct, or word is linked with current ones, the more apt it is to endure in some form. Many parts of Whitehead's *Adventures of Ideas* are a rewarding source of ideas about ideas.[28]

Synthesis Demands Seeing Relationships. Assume that one's beliefs about the program of physical education, about teaching, and about guidance have been formulated. As one scrutinizes and analyzes these three *centers of beliefs,* he may find one or a few in each of the centers that are related at one or more points. This situation may not be recognized at first, but when discovered one can pull together these previously unconnected beliefs into a new (at least to him) and larger belief or a small cluster of beliefs. This same action may be extended to other clusters and constellations of beliefs. This process not only produces new and often larger and more meaningful beliefs, but also promotes the *seeing of relationships* within and between our experiences, beliefs, concepts, and so on.

Understanding is forever stopped until *relationships* are seen. For example, assume that good teachers believe in doing their *best* in selecting and applying activities in the program. Assume that these teachers also believe in doing their *best* while giving guidance to students who come to them. All these beliefs about *best* are different, as they are applied. That is, the teacher performs different kinds of actions in all three of these instances throughout the year. However, the idea of best also has similarities in all these situations. Assume that these same teachers believe that they should *improve* in each of these three major duties (teaching, program, and guidance). This idea of improvement, like the idea of best, is different in all situations and yet similar.

In still another phase of work, assume that these teachers believe that they should *strive,* put forth genuine *effort,* both to do their best and to improve. It is not unusual for three sets of beliefs like these to remain not only unidentified, but also unsynthesized. Once the desirability of unifying beliefs into larger wholes is seen and accepted, the teachers may acquire a large-scale belief: *Do your best to make the effort to improve.*

In fact, this idea is large enough in meaning and force for one of the great biologist-philosophers, du Noüy, to select it as the key to man's destiny.[9] Quite a number of individuals now hold this idea as their master purpose of human life, and others consider it as an ultimate value. In a sense, it seems incredible that the *synthesis* of only three quite common beliefs of good teachers could form such a large-scale idea and belief.

WHERE ARE WE NOW?

We have tried to capture the soul of the philosophic process. Throughout this and the previous four chapters we have sketched the barest outlines of the adventure of philosophizing. If the soul of the process is *perfect liberty*, then the student philosopher must understand the necessary articulation of the two polar opposites: analysis and synthesis. To realize the precarious balance between criticism and vision is to appreciate the philosophic process itself.

The second part of this book is devoted to exploring the *substance* discovered over the years by persons using the philosophic process. The novice philosopher should now be in a position to understand exactly how this content came to be. Moreover, the improving, beginning philosopher may actually bring the philosophic process to bear on the various positions and claims of professional philosophers presented in Part II. Thus, not only will the striving student of philosophy be treated to a collage of ideas and points of view, he will also be encouraged to think through, to follow the arguments of, these same ideas and views. There is nothing passive about Part II. The student will be active in sifting through and examining the wisdom of the ages. Let us press on!

THE UNIVERSE IS NOT TO BE NARROWED DOWN TO THE LIMITS OF UNDERSTANDING, WHICH HAS BEEN MAN'S PRACTICE UP TO NOW, BUT THE UNDERSTANDING MUST BE STRETCHED AND ENLARGED TO TAKE IN THE IMAGE OF THE UNIVERSE AS IT IS DISCOVERED.

—*Francis Bacon*

TO BELIEVE YOUR OWN THOUGHT . . . A MAN SHOULD LEARN TO DETECT AND WATCH THAT GLEAM OF LIGHT WHICH FLASHES ACROSS HIS MIND FROM WITHIN . . . NOTHING AT LAST IS SACRED BUT THE INTEGRITY OF YOUR MIND.

—*Emerson*

LET ME REPEAT ONCE MORE THAT A MAN'S VISION IS THE GREAT FACT ABOUT HIM.

—*William James*

References

1. Adler, M. J.: What Is an Idea? *Saturday Review,* November 22, 1958.
2. Anderson, H. H. (Ed.): *Creativity and its Cultivation.* New York: Harper and Brothers, 1959, pp. 51, 75, 86.
3. Barzun, J.: *The House of Intellect.* New York: Harper & Row, 1959, p. 34.
4. Beardsley, M. C.: *Thinking Straight.* Englewood Cliffs, N.J.: Prentice-Hall, Inc., 1956.
5. Bookwalter, K., and VanderZwaag, H.: *Foundations and Principles of Physical Education.* Philadelphia: W. B. Saunders Co., 1969, p. 5.
6. Breasted, J. H.: *The Dawn of Conscience.* New York: Charles Scribner's Sons, 1947.
7. Bryson, L.: *Science and Freedom.* New York: Columbia University Press, 1947.
8. de Chardin, P. T.: *The Phenomenon of Man.* New York: Harper and Brothers, 1959.
9. du Noüy, Le Comte: *Human Destiny.* New York: Longmans, Green and Company, 1947.
10. Dewey, J.: *How We Think.* Boston: D. C. Heath & Co., 1910, pp. 68–78.
11. Flesch, R.: *The Art of Clear Thinking.* New York: Collier Books, 1951.
12. Gardner, J. W.: *Self-Renewal: The Individual and The Innovative Society.* New York: Harper & Row, 1963.
13. Ghiselin, B.: *The Creative Process.* New York: The New American Library of World Literature, Inc., 1957, p. 29.
14. Hazlitt, W.: On Going A Journey. *New Monthly Magazine.* January, 1822. (Reprinted in Riverside Literature Series, *Selected Essays,* by Claude Fuess, 1914.)
15. Hesse, H.: *Reflections.* R. Manheim (Trans.). New York: Farrar, Straus and Giroux, 1974, p. 52.
16. Jaspers, K.: *Way To Wisdom.* New Haven: Yale University Press, 1954, p. 125.
17. Kelley, T. L.: *Scientific Method.* New York: The Macmillan Co., 1932.
18. Noyce, W.: *Springs of Adventure.* New York: The World Publishing Company, 1959.
19. Ortega y Gasset, J.: *Meditations on Hunting.* New York: Charles Scribner's Sons, 1972, p. 152.
20. Osborn, A. F.: *Applied Imagination.* New York: Charles Scribner's Sons, 1957.
21. Rugg, H.: *Imagination.* New York: Harper & Row, 1963.
22. Saint-Exupéry, A.: *Wind, Sand and Stars.* New York: Harcourt, Brace & Co., Inc., 1949.
23. Schweitzer, A.: *Out of My Life and Thought.* New York: Mentor Books, 1953, p. 171.
24. Straus, E.: *The Primary World of the Senses.* New York: The Free Press of Glencoe, 1963, p. 315.
25. Tze-chiang, C. (Trans.): *A Chinese Garden of Serenity.* Mt. Vernon, N.Y.: The Peter Pauper Press, 1959.
26. Verne, J.: *Around the World in Eighty Days.* New York: Dodd, Mead & Company, 1956, pp. 15–17.
27. Werkmeister, W. H.: *An Introduction to Critical Thinking,* (rev. ed.). Lincoln, Nebr.: Johnson Publishing Company, 1957.
28. Whitehead, A. N.: *Adventures of Ideas.* New York: The Macmillan Co., 1933.
29. Young, J. W.: *A Technique for Producing Ideas.* Chicago: Advertising Publications, 1940.

II

PHILOSOPHY
AS HERITAGE

II

PHILOSOPHY
AS HERITAGE

THAT WHICH THY FATHERS HAVE BEQUEATHED TO THEE,
EARN IT ANEW IF THOU WOULDST POSSESS IT.

—Goethe

Western man's philosophic heritage, despite some contrary evidence, is rich in matchless effort, worthy accomplishment, magnificent failure, bold versatility, and ever-hopeful potential. A scholar's patient pursuit indicates his deep appreciation of this legacy. Only the highlights of far-famed Western thinkers and their peaks of thought appear in these pages.

Chapters 7 and 8 examine the sources of human beliefs; the taproots and meanings of philosophy; the distinguishing marks of philosophy as compared with science, religion, art, and history; and the major parts of the formal content of philosophy.

The remaining four chapters in this part present concise reviews of idealism, realism, pragmatism, and still more compact discussions of some other ways of thinking such as personalism, analytic philosophy, existentialism, and others. Implications of these philosophic positions, methods, and approaches for physical education receive appropriate attention.

References for chapters in Part II begin on page 221.

7

Searching for the Sources and Meaning of Western Philosophy

IT IS ALWAYS THE ADVENTURERS WHO ACCOMPLISH GREAT
THINGS.

—Herbert

BEGINNINGS OF HUMAN BELIEFS

Let us recall with John Dewey one probable set of the beginnings of beliefs. Prethinking man *did* things. He did things as a result of and in reaction to his environment—trees, rocks, animals, the enemy, family, mountains, as well as wind, sun, rain, the seasons, and the other elements and processes of nature. Later, thinking man also did things, but there was a difference. Prethinking man remembered that this experience was like the one he had yesterday or when the moon was this same size last time. In relating experiences to his fellows, sooner or later they, too, had experiences similar to other tribesmen. Some of these repeated experiences became rather commonplace. Undoubtedly, the majority of his brothers came to know the ordinariness of having somewhat similar experiences again and again.

These ancient ancestors probably had short periods of work, at least in favoring climates. The periods of leisure encouraged, among other things, the telling of stories about what happened on the last hunt or when fishing yesterday. These experiences developed over a long period of time into endlessly repeated tales and then into legends. It is important to sense that accuracy in reporting facts was not the point in the repeated tellings. The story was the thing! Thus, imagination is added to memory. They were both used! They both developed.

As the skills of thinking developed along with more pedestrian skills, man increased control over his environment. Animals were better manipulated and controlled, even domesticated. They also played a greater role in the development of the stories.

Some experiences and observations became generally accepted legends. Pantomime, drama, and suggestions became traditions, rites, dances, cults, dogmas, and doctrines. In fact, as these activities intermeshed with the life of the tribe, *group* beliefs began. Offspring began to receive instruction in what to believe as well as the way to believe. Eventually, this socialization of beliefs became systematized and obligatory. Tribes that were most successful in extending their influence over other lands and tribes found good reason for developing loyalty to their group beliefs!

As oldsters died and younger men took their places, or as the ins became the outs, some of the rites, dogmas, and doctrines were modified. Some beliefs of conquered peoples also were incorporated into the conquering tribe's system of beliefs.

An overall extension of beliefs is another and quite different path to man's formation of beliefs. Picture the tribesman, with his imaginative recitations of an experience, and include the women of the tribe preparing a meal. The women are working near the fire or carrying water. They, too, are skillful in noting such practical facts of their lives as food, seasonal and night-day rhythms, use of club-shaped sticks, variously shaped rocks, and so on. Recall that among the gods of almost all known primitive cultures were some symbolized by fire. Here, then, is the mystic god fire. It is a thing to placate, to revere, to fear. It is a god!

It must have been one of the women who first began to have another kind of belief, another way of thinking. The men were away on a hunt. Some of the women were engaged in domestic duties. The woman stands near the fire. She is using the fire for cooking! She begins to muse as she looks into the flames and glowing coals. "Here is the god fire! Yet it warms me. It cooks the meat. It bakes the clay. It eases the painful joint!" What blasphemy! She dare tell no one of this perilous thought. However, she does tell her husband when he returns. The violent blow she receives from him does not drive out the idea! Yet, in her mind two compartments are formed. The one has to do with such things as rites, dances, and doctrines involving the god fire. The other, a body of facts about what fire does—both helpful and harmful, is the beginning of arts, crafts, and industry (and thus science), together with the knowledge, the skill, and the expert craftsmanship of working with metal, clay, wood, bone, rock. This is the beginning of a people who have two compartments in their minds as the factual body of beliefs develops side by side with the imaginative beliefs (founded originally through the stories of the imaginative tribesman).

The two sets of beliefs were *kept* separate for the most part, not only by the individual but also by the tribe. The two bodies of beliefs and ways of thinking eventually began to be represented by two different groups or classes within the society. On the one hand were those who held to the imaginative beliefs, traditions, and dogma. For the most part these persons were in authority and had social position and prestige. On the other hand were those without authority, position, and prestige—the craftsmen, artisans, and all others who worked with their hands.

Finally, the increased bulk and scope of factual beliefs enabled the latter group to come in open mental conflict with the content and spirit of the traditional and imaginative beliefs' group. This eventually led to the rise of the Sophist movement. Socrates attempted to bring the conflicting groups together, and in so doing defied the authorities, the traditionalists. He refused to agree to modify his method or message.

The Sophist movement, of course, was not the end of seeking for factual bases of beliefs, although many students of the history of science feel that the scientific spirit was dwarfed in Greece at the height of her external glory and influence. The spirit of inquiry still questions and thus undermines the old ways. Even in deep-seated controversies, if the questioners and skeptics win, all of the old is never discarded completely. If discarded at the outset, some of the old is always brought back. Changing cultures find it the better part of wisdom to preserve major values, for example, unless or until they have concocted alluring substitutes.

The reference to the conflict between imaginative and factual beliefs is not limited to that other day. The avoidance of compartmentalization of conflicting beliefs takes courage, but it leads toward developing ways of inquiry, ways of verification, and ways of getting at truths. The prevention of the interpenetration of beliefs, of course, not only perpetuates ignorance, but also precludes the individual from maturing.

SOURCES OF WESTERN PHILOSOPHIC THOUGHT

We turn now to the pursuit of wisdom through the past. Each time it is recalled that many of today's questions and answers have their matrix in voyaging minds of men who lived and worked and died over 2000 years ago, one's sense of respect and awe and debt is large. It was they who hammered out the matrix of philosophy as they fearlessly faced questions and forged answers in a manner that was new and strange to Western man. Most of the ideas of these mental noblemen seem to have emerged from audaciousness, not only in their questions and answers, but also in the weaving together of ideas, experiences, human behavior, and knowledge.

The mature student may find it rewarding to permit himself to speculate, while reading Chapters 8, 9, 10, 11, and 12, as to the possible sources of the ideas of these men of the mind. If he is experimentally minded enough to try this suggestion, let him be forewarned that the beliefs of these first philosophers were not the grand offspring of an impartial intellect. Rather, their beliefs were made of imagination, observation, memory, tastes, reaction of and to people, and even the weather!

The philosophy of the West sometimes is pictured as having begun about 2500 years ago when suddenly some fantastically gifted Greeks, with a good deal of leisure, began to think differently from the way man had thought before. This view is well-intended, romantic, and intriguing, but it is not accurate.

Without meaning to diminish the awe, respect, admiration, and credit long given to and deserved by these early thinkers of the West, it seems reasonable to take the view that the geneses of Western thought, in part, may lie in other times and places. Might it have been not a matter of an explosion but a change of direction of mental activity? This idea has support from mounting archeological evidence. It must suffice here to present a dangerously brief identification of some possible sources of Western philosophic thought.

Human Experiences. Beginnings of any philosophy must await the action and experience of the people as they observe and meet life, its activities, and their reactions—all in a universe as they sense it and believe it to be. When man developed *enough,* he became aware of questions, problems, and opportunities that lay outside the concrete and practical world. These were the sorts of experiences that challenged him. Not only must he have developed enough, but also he must have had leisure enough to reflect on what came to his consciousness through his senses. He also had to reflect on what his imagination conjured up, what he felt and had hunches about. Some of these things challenged him because of the driving thirst of his curiosity. Other things captured his attention because of his innate proclivity for improving his lot. This proclivity to accept the challenges toward improvement and the bent to be curious were two sources that thrust man in the direction of becoming a philosopher.

Oriental Taproots. One of the things that ancient Greek philosophers wondered about was the nature of reality; that is, what is real? This question, of course, is geared to the problem of the nature of the universe. Archeologists have found writings on this subject that date back to 4000 B.C. These writings have been found at sites in ancient Sumer, Egypt, and Mesopotamia. Such writings from the Indus Valley and China are more recent but still antedate the official beginnings of Grecian philosophy by several centuries. It also should be recalled that digs in the Far East have been relatively few to date.

Hebrew Influences. Although the evidence so far is lacking on a wide scale, and some of it seems to be to the contrary, there are those who believe that Hebraic philosophy—bits of it—could not help but have reached Greece. Wherever man has gone, there also have gone new ideas. Other new ideas came back with him.

Early Greek Sources. There is a tempting tendency to glance swiftly over the pre-Socratic philosophers, beginning with Thales. Nor do some college classes in formal philosophy explore the philosophy of Homer and Hesiod. Certainly, some rather well-formed ideas, credited to Grecian philosophers of the fifth, fourth, and third centuries B.C., must have had *prior* rootages in Greece. The atomic theory is an example, with Democritus receiving the accolade, whereas the previous work of Anaxagoras and Leucippus and of Empedocles is almost forgotten. Democritus *did* synthesize and extend their rightly guessed ideas.

Sources from the Classical Greek Period. After the prephilosophy period of Homer, the tracings are thin but it seems probable that the Greeks began to identify some major queries. Such a company of men cannot face such questions as "Who am I?" "Where am I?" "Why am I here?" "Of what value?" "Why?" without attempting to answer them. Here again, these seekers after wisdom proved to be unique among their Western brothers. They tackled such useless questions with imagination and with reason. Failing these tools, they guessed and speculated. Is it any wonder that by 600 B.C. the ferment was widespread and violent enough for Thales, the Greeks' first geometer, "the first true man of science," and a successful business man, to start the first school of philosophy.

Limitations of space prevent a full account of the contributions of the ancient Greeks to almost every phase of human life. Two acknowledgments must suffice. They are selected because of their relationships with the contemporary scene. Experimentation began long before the days of Archimedes. There are records of experiments performed among the early Pythagoreans at Croton in southern Italy. In fact, some modern Greek scholars believe experimentation began long before the days of Thales. They make no claim that these experiments were nicely controlled or that experimentation was conducted on a wide scale. Nevertheless, there appears to be good reason to believe experimentation, as a way of seeking wisdom and arriving at the factual truth, had tracings reaching back into the dimness of Grecian antiquity.

The other contribution selected by way of illustration is the atomic theory. At some time in the fifth century B.C., the Ionian Anaxagoras and Leucippus, founder of the school at Abdera, along with others, formulated statements about the nature of the world and matter. These efforts prompted Democritus (a half-century later) to synthesize these ideas, together with his own, into his now well-known atomic theory. He claimed no originality for his theory! We know of these earlier efforts because of a pattern set by a later Greek. The pattern was to review the works of those who previously investigated matters related to the problem about to be undertaken. This Greek's name was Aristotle!

Ancient Near East Sources. The attempt to trace beginnings of well-formed ideas is risky. In man's significant milestones, as he moved from prehistoric to historic times, was there the single *first* idea? Were there several simultaneous firsts? In some instances, was an idea lost for centuries and rediscovered in another place and at a later time?

James H. Breasted, eminent American Egyptologist, speaks of the vast debt owed Egypt by the ancient Hebrews. Again, man is seen taking his ideas with him as he walked the earth, or rode a camel or the waves.[13]

The Henri Frankforts, John A. Wilson, and Thorkild Jacobsen, of the Oriental Institute of the University of Chicago, lend support to Breasted's revealing interpretation of his translation of the Memphite Drama (3400 B.C.) as a rich treasure of the beginnings of a few philosophic ideas.[42] With rare insight, these writers make a helpful suggestion to those who have wondered how "all the wisdom of Egypt," her extremely long experience, and her beginnings in many fields, as well as her power and her size, could pass out of existence without a trace, as far as having transmitted much to the culture of the ages. It is the view of these eminent archeologists that the ancient Hebrews and Greeks had a vague, uncritical, and high appreciation of Egypt's contributions. This appreciation gave them "a sense of high value outside their own times and place," thus providing some historical setting for the ideas they were having. It also made them curious "about the more obvious Egyptian achievements. . . ." This curiosity led them to find earlier Egyptian intellectual and ethical advances. However, these accomplishments could be *valid* to the Greeks and Hebrews *only* in "terms of their own experiences, because they already were ancient history in Egypt." Thus, the ancient Hebrews and Greeks "had to re-discover, for themselves, the elements which had lost persuasive force in Egypt." We appear to have here one possible answer to the puzzling, persistent question of why nations seem never to learn lessons from the past experiences of other nations.

These four authors also recount values held by the ancient Egyptians of the Old Kingdom and of the Middle Kingdom, which provide unmistakable evidence of the beginnings of parts of idealism. Here are the roots of democracy, the worth of the individual, his freedom to aspire to his potential, and some appreciation of the intangibles of life (despite the fact that to these people of the Nile the good life was interpreted principally in terms of material goods).

The recent and continuing translations of the invaluable tablets from ancient Sumer promise still further inescapable evidence supporting the assumption that Western philosophic beginnings antedate even Egypt's rich and ancient store.

These reminders, brief and incomplete though they are, suggest some sources of beliefs and ideas. Anticlimactic though it may be, caution must be exercised in making an overly spacious estimate of the contributions of these remarkable frontiersmen of philosophy. It would be quite un-Greek to do other than to be rational about judging what they were and did and thought (insofar as the written word portrays thought). It would be quite unfair to judge these men and their intellectual products by any standards other than those that prevailed in their times.

For one thing, some of the astonishingly accurate guesses, speculations, and hypotheses of these men compatibly shared the same mental beds with the notions that were in ridiculous error. If we look at all they believed (any and all of these great personages) through today's perspective, they were, of course, far behind us. Just to *think that* is a source of discomfiture, because it is a little short of incredible that they, with their roving, exploring, courageous minds, "hit" so many ideas that are in agreement with the best that we know today—2500 years later.

One reason that these initiators of Western thought did not transcend even the far boundaries which they established is because most of them were philosopher-scientists. For some, their science hampered their philosophy. For others, their philosophy dulled their scientific efforts. It probably is a case of their not distinguishing between the two. At any rate, science was retarded by 2000 years because of this lack of distinction. It was ever thus.

WHAT IS PHILOSOPHY?

The philosopher within every man—like philosophers, ancient and modern—inquires deeply, frankly and humbly into such profound yet simple questions as "Who am I?" "Why was I born?" "Why am I living?" "Where am I?" Overcoming "the curse of ignorance," in the words of Socrates, became one of the pursuits of early Greek philosophers. However, philosophy is not limited to examining questions. What, then, are some meanings of philosophy?

There is no record of a word like "philosophy" in all of man's languages until a century after Thales started his school at Miletus. Even then (as stated on p. 2), Pythagoras first used the word *philosophos* (philosopher) *not* philosophy, as applied to himself. That is, he said that he was a philosophos—a lover of wisdom, a lover of truth, a pursuer of wisdom, a pursuer of truth (there is disagreement in the translation). Fuller and McMurrin infer that, thereafter, the word and its derivations, including philosophy, became a part of the language, meaning such things as "the love of thinking about things . . . the possession of a . . . reflective attitude toward life in general."[43]

The question "What is Philosophy?" seems to require that one identify certain of one's beliefs. Is it a formal subject of pristine academic concern, a program of philosophic activities, the amalgam of ethics, logic, and the like? Is it the process in which the great philosophers engaged to produce this amalgam (in the sense that great historians and scientists believe a process best characterizes their respective fields)? Or is philosophy the individual's hierarchy of systematic, personal beliefs about living and life?

Philosophy as a Process. Dr. Fung Yu-lan, in his *Short History of Chinese Philosophy*, wrote that philosophy means a "systematic, reflective thinking on life."[128] He stated that a philosopher "must think reflectively on life and then express his thought systematically." Thus, he sees philosophy as a *process.*

Dr. Joe Park, in *The Philosophy of Education,* asserted that philosophy is concerned with a study of "principles, underlying knowledge . . . a system of basic principles for guidance in practical affairs . . . attempts to answer intimate questions critically, after investigating all that makes such questions puzzling and after realizing the vagueness and confusion that underlie our ordinary ideas."[86] He gives Bertrand Russell credit for the latter part of this statement.

In a glossary, Earle F. Zeigler, in his *Philosophical Foundations,* stated that philosophy is "a science (*sic*) which investigates the facts, principles and problems of reality in an attempt to describe, analyze and evaluate them."[129] One would need an answer to the question as to the sense in which "science" is used here, before fruitful discussion of this definition were possible. Too, this definition appears to eliminate some of philosophy's broader, deeper reaches. (See Chapter 8 for the distinguishing characteristics of philosophy and science.)

Roger K. Burke, in the first edition of this book, stated that philosophy "provides a framework, a rational theory, a logical method, a penetrating explanation and universal guide for (dealing with) the problem of human existence."[23] In the same book, Minnie L. Lynn wrote, "philosophy proposes to bring logical clarification of the nature of things . . . attempts to find and to clarify the truths . . . of the contiguous world, thence out even to the ever-yielding boundaries of the universe . . . (as the philosopher) strives to apprehend in its entirety . . . concerns with the aesthetic, the spiritual, the moral intuition and humanity of man."[23] Still another writer in the same book stated, "Philosophy is the attempt to unify all possible aspects of life and the world into a satisfying whole (after analysis), and tentatively, to accept without dismay or irritation those incongenial parts that do not seem to fit into the whole."[23]

A Method of Pursuing Truths. Philosophy deals chiefly with the process of pursuing philosophic truths and speculating about this process. Philosophy is not so much concerned with answers and solutions. Nevertheless, philosophy may explore, examine, and identify elements of a situation in order that an answer or solution may be more readily gained.

It is helpful, of course, to consider the idea that there are different kinds of truth, represented by philosophy and by such disciplines as science, history, religion. Each can be seen using methods appropriate to its task as it pursues the special kind of truth with which it is concerned. Nevertheless, it is no more incongruous to use scientific methods in pursuing philosophic or historic truths than it is to use philosophic or historical methods in pursuing scientific or theological truths. The trouble has been that in the preparation of its workers no field has found it convenient or feasible to train them in truth-seeking methods used in all other major disciplines. Only a few men, for example, Alfred North Whitehead, have educated themselves in more than one field's methods of pursuing truths.

A Reflective Attitude. The philosophic attitude consists of the insatiable desire and the intrepid persistence to strive to enlarge one's understanding, to find justifiable bases of convictions and beliefs for all personal thought, together with anticipations of the consequences of such convictions. Philosophy as a process insists that *thought moves on.* It considers The Rule (inflexibility) as the "Sepulcher of the Prophets." Mary Carolyn Davies, with a poet's rare touch, put it this way, "youth and maid who, past my death, . . . break the rules that I shall make."

Philosophy asks one to look beyond the obvious and the known, beyond that which appears to be fact or final truth, beyond expectations, beyond excellence. These are but springboards to enticing unknowns for philosophy as a process. Philosophy amalgamates memory, common sense, reason, imagination, and intuition, enlarges on them, and interweaves them into a blended process.

Philosophy readily acknowledges it has no practical utility. Nor is it ashamed of that part of the process characterized by the arm-chair meditative kind of thinking. William James looked at the matter this way: "Philosophy is pledged to transcend every provincialism of time and space and point of view . . . philosophy is speculative; that is, it questions assumptions, breaks habits, accepts no 'is' without wondering what 'it might be.' "[57]

An Attempt to Understand Life's Problems. Philosophy's environment and enlargement of life are not typified by material contributions such as typically emerge from science. Rather, its contributions are to such struggling efforts as man's understanding of meanings, values, and purposes.

Philosophy, at its circumference, not only embraces some of the processes of science, but also the disciplines of history, art and religion, as it searches to evaluate and explain, and strives to synthesize and interlace them into the fabric of life—the whole of life. Concluding that philosophy is the final goal of all development, Hegel observed that "art renders the infinite visible, religion symbolizes it more than art, and philosophy brings it under the mastery of thought."[2]

The previous comments and quotations form no pretentious claim of completeness. They are but a few examples of beliefs and ideas about some meanings of philosophy. They should suffice to illustrate the point that some fruitless arguments about what philosophy is may be avoided if disputants would first identify and clarify their beliefs related to the matter. Furthermore, needless disagreement among discussants about some other philosophic matters may be avoided if identification and clarification of basic philosophic positions first are brought into the open before beliefs, which grow out of them, are expressed.

PHILOSOPHY BEGINS IN WONDER, AND, AT THE END WHEN PHILOSOPHIC THOUGHT HAS DONE ITS BEST, THE WONDER REMAINS.

—Alfred North Whitehead

8

Exploring the Formal Content of Philosophy

WHEN YOU READ PAST PHILOSOPHIC AUTHORS ONE OF THE
FIRST THINGS WHICH LEAPS TO YOUR EYE IS THE AMOUNT OF
NONSENSE THEY ARE WRITING. . . . LEARNED WORKS ARE
NOT FREE FROM SILLY NOTIONS.

—Alfred North Whitehead

As the rank beginner in philosophy undertakes to storm what appears to be the stronghold of formal philosophy, as in any discipline, he encounters some unfamiliar terms. He is confronted with new technical words that seem obscure, and without necessary expositions of these terms that hold no personal interest. As one mature student of physical education (but a neophyte in philosophy), describing the problems he had encountered in the reading of philosophy, stated: "I feel like the disliked courtier of the King of Siam who was given a beautiful white elephant. The miracle beast deserved such ritual that to care for him properly meant ruin. Yet to care for him improperly was worse. It appears the gift could not be refused. The gift, philosophy, cannot be refused, yet it is a beast. Reading the arguments of some of the philosophers is like listening to two astronomers discussing the difference in the appearance of the constellation Andromeda, when all I can see are stars. And to grasp the ideas of philosophy is something like a one-year-old child trying to grasp a ball six feet in diameter."

Milton, long ago, mentioning philosophizing as one of the "pursuits of hell," described a group of devils debating over "Fixed fate, free will, foreknowledge, absolute, and found no end in wandering mazes lost." Most bona fide philosophers acknowledge that in the minds of other philosophers they do not write with clarity. They feel it is necessary to use words in their own special ways because of the limitations of most languages in the area of philosophic thought. The recurrent outbreaks of skepticism and debate among philosophers remind Bowne, in describing the instability of the philosophic structure, that "Many a navigator has sailed away over the misty seas of speculation and never come back. . . ."[11] Nevertheless, to most eminent philosophers, the coming back is not necessarily important. Theirs is the life of intellectual speculation, exploration, search, adventure, and pressing forward. The quest is the thing.

Students also complain that some professors of *educational* philosophy fail to clarify obscurities found in philosophic readings. This condition moved Tomlin to write that one of the curses of philosophy is that many books have been "making difficult problems more difficult still: or, worst of all, obscuring the comparatively simple problems, with which philosophy begins by a parade of conundrums, paradoxes, pseudo-problems calculated to put the innocent reader into a state of alarm or despondency."[112] Those who write books of philosophy might be cautioned by the words of Socrates when he criticized a budding young poet:

> As to the sentiments I submit to your judgment. As to style—he repeated himself two or three times, either from want of words or from want of pains. And he seemed to me ambitious to show that he could say the same thing over in two or three ways.[47]

Despite some initial difficulty, one quite unfamiliar with reading philosophy must use the disciplined hand, when coming to grips with technical terms,* should he wish to gain at least a passing familiarity with its formal content or subject matter. He then may begin to gain a fingernail grip on some of the philosophic ideas of dominant personalities in this discipline.

There are three areas about which some explanation may be helpful for the rank beginner as he continues his journey in the exploration of philosophy. These areas, which concern the relationships of philosophy, philosophic positions or schools of thought, and philosophic terminology, are explored in the following sections.

THE SEARCH FOR SOME RELATIONSHIPS OF PHILOSOPHY

Some possible disciplines with which philosophy may have noteworthy relationships are science, history, religion, and art.

In what ways can these disciplines be identified? How can they be distinguished from philosophy? The concern in the next few paragraphs is not to deal with, for example, the science of history or the history of science, but with establishing the interrelationship between philosophy and some adjacent disciplines, with philosophy as the base.

Science. Philosophy's most eminent daughter, of course, is science. Philosophy, being essentially subjective, allocates verification or check-

---

* Also see Glossary.

ing and testing to the scientific process. Science provides concrete, precise kinds of knowledge. Science uses relatively exact ways of solving problems which are amenable to such methods. It searches after scientific truths, produces tangible results, contributes to material happiness, attempts to master the external world, and provides certain kinds of practical and useful facts. There is no doubt that scientific methods are the ways some of the world's peoples can hope to gain the basics of life, for example, freedom from hunger. Gargantuan, revolutionary products are spawned every hour of every day as the outcome of the scientific process. Thus science and technology are tools. How are they to be used? toward what ends? for what values? These questions, these key matters, are the concerns of philosophy.

There is no doubt that modern science creates vast problems it cannot solve—thermonuclear war, overpopulation, automation, energy depletion. Science's avowed objectivity, so far, has enabled the scientist to avoid responsibility for the impact of his science on earth's human beings and possibly its impact on areas beyond this spatial speck. The importance of these factual endeavors is a philosophic matter.

The clarification and interpretation of values are not scientifically demonstrable. For example, some questions that science cannot answer include What are the meanings of democracy? Are the consequences of democracy good or evil? What is happiness? Are the means of happiness worthy? What is just, beautiful, good? What is man? Why is he here? The kinds of knowledge related to philosophy are those that are used to give perspective to, direction for, and valuation of the pathway of life—toward the best ends that man can visualize.

Although philosophy and science are related, philosophers are cautioned against being pressed into imitating scientists, into being researchers producing reliable knowledge in the mode of science. Barrett, in his *Irrational Man,* made the point that philosophers, feeling guilty about not being scientists, concern themselves with the technique, logical and linguistic analyses, syntax and semantics, and the "refining away of all content for the sake of formal subtlety."[9]

Over the centuries, the philosopher's path of specialization, Barrett observed, now and then has led away from the urgent and the actual toward remoteness from man's day-to-day life. Thus, philosophy periodically loses its mission and momentum as it becomes a process concerned primarily with itself, as a tool in the hands of professional philosophers concerned with their own nest of eggs. Just as self-thoughts unmake the man, self-thoughts unmake philosophy. Today, philosophy needs to find itself by more and more philosophers becoming concerned, profoundly and sincerely, with the failures, fears, doubts, conflicts, confusions, and wonderings of man as man, and of mankind.

Religion. Not since Pythagoras has philosophy been a religion. Despite this, the main concerns of religion are philosophic. Philosophers, for the most part, deal with the concept of God and the relation of God to man. Some problems involving religion face man, but they cannot be solved on a religious or a philosophic basis alone. Nonetheless, the roots and trunk of ethical behavior form more than a fragment of religion.

The philosophy of religion investigates the elements of religious consciousness, the theories that religion has evolved, and takes account of religious practices as illustrations of the vitality of beliefs. Types of philosophies of religion concerned with God and man's relation to God may be distinguished in all historic religions, including Christianity in its two principal forms of Catholicism and Protestantism, the numerous religions of Judaism, Hinduism, Mohammedanism. Concerning the concepts of God, a specific philosophy of religion may be a theism with its many forms, or may fall into general classifications, for example, transcendentalism, absolutism.

As a process, religion today in the West is aware of its need to embrace some problems of secular life and thought. Religion acknowledges that it is subject to attack and protest from nonreligious sources. For one thing, people disagree as to what the church should do, what its purpose should be. Man has placed a high value on justice for at least as long as his first written thought. It is a reasonable expectation to find it as a part of his philosophy. How commonly is justice pursued as a practicing part of the world's religions? How commonly does the church tackle ethical and moral problems? This implied intimate relationship with the workaday world need neither diminish the goals nor dim the ideals of religion. This part of the religious process enables most human problems to have a religious side. Thus, both religion and philosophy have the ways of rediscovering themselves. Each is author of its own process of ways to evaluate itself.

As was noted earlier, philosophy is supersensitive to science. Such is the case with religion also, and with what results? Is it true that "Our cyclotrons and launching pads have become our cathedrals and temples"? Science, for one thing, asks about the nature of personal beliefs, including spiritual beliefs. Science has made every man aware of scientific truths. Should religion feel guilty about its lack of scientifically demonstrable facts? Should the results of science be subjected to religious and philosophic modes of thought? Philosophers recognize that the solution of the problems of human destiny presupposes a clear conception or a clarification of what matters most in the lives of all of us—the values man lives by.

Art. The problems of man's artistic experience are complex, not only in terms of principles, but also in terms of personal expression, the creative process, perfection, form, the spectator. Such questions as "What makes a work of art beautiful?" "What is beauty?" "How may its principles be applied to the conduct of life?" have produced volumes written in the hope of coming to grips with this elusive quarry.

The responses to such questions, however varied, are infused with questions of value, thus becoming philosophic concerns. Nature herself boasts a great fund of knowledge for the aesthetic philosopher. Some people contend that nature embodies an ideal rightness, beauty, art. Perhaps they see through Tennyson's eyes, "If I could understand what you are, root and all, and all and all, I should know what God and man is." Other people contend, perhaps like the "emotionless" scientist, that nature is indifferent, strictly utilitarian, and that it is an illusion to think that nature strives toward beauty. Perhaps it is they who disagree with Wordsworth's idea that in the meanest flower that grows there is "a thought too deep for tears." Obviously, then, the goals of philosophy, those of understanding and meaning, are irrevocably related to man's experience in art and in beauty.

Art pursued as a process, like processes of philosophy, science, and religion, enables man to come closer to knowing himself, to come closer to grasping the meaning of the universe, and to come closer to projecting his views of the world through the artist's touch and feel. Dewey implied that art must begin in the events of man, arousing man's interests and affording him enjoyment as he listens, sees, tastes, smells, or feels.[27] In contrast with the scientist who works with symbols, words, and mathematical signs, the artist's thoughts are embodied in the object of art he is creating. Art carries the observer forward, not restlessly desiring to arrive at a final solution, but by the pleasurable activity of the process itself.

As noted in philosophy, religion, and ethics, art experience, too, suffers from a dreary prejudice against the subjective. Perhaps art also experiences supersensitivity to scientific description and control. Santayana stated that "philosophers seem to feel that unless moral and aesthetic judgments are expressions of objective truth, and not merely expressions of human nature, they stand condemned of hopeless triviality."[101] Santayana made the sagacious observation that a judgment is not trivial because it rests on human feelings; on the contrary, triviality consists in abstraction from human interests. Inner feelings, according to Santayana, about the great external world are the means through which man knows his existence, and from which it derives all its values.[101]

History. Because there are different types of historians, different types of histories are produced. *First,* there is the *reformer* who, in his use of the historical process, focuses on that which represents man's mistakes, his weaknesses, and his lack of judgment. *Second,* there is the historian who examines and presents that which lends support, sanctions values, and cherishes the *past.* Still a *third* type of historian presents the past as a *time of growth, of endless change.* A *fourth* type uses the historical process to *provide a backdrop for the present* so as to make the present understandable, to explain it. A *fifth* type of historian presents the past in such a way as to *analyze, describe,* and *explain how things used to be* (the history of philosophy helps one to understand how philosophy was). A *sixth* type of historian presents a *road map of the past*—interesting for its own sake—showing what man and the world were like.

Thus, history's subjectivity is unquestionable, but accepted unashamedly. What the historian selects to write about is quite as subjective as the interpretation of that which he selects. This means that the historical process can be made a disservice. Carelessly selecting and carelessly interpreting the facts can make history into intolerant prejudice, into partial-truth or propaganda.

History, as a process, pursued carefully like the processes of science, philosophy, and religion, enables man to learn of the experience of others, and it may help to develop, broaden, and educate the doer. The reader of history, like the reader of philosophy or of science, may gain knowledge. He also may gain perspective. He may even learn lessons from the past.

History is related to philosophy in two ways. *First,* formal philosophy actually is the history of the subject matter of philosophy. *Second,* there is the recognized study called "history of philosophy." The subject matter of this discipline, in most college courses, remains an accounting of the men, events, and beliefs of philosophy as they occurred through the millennia.

History is also related to science. There is, as there is in philosophy, not only the history of scientific discoveries, but also the history of science as a process. The latter is well documented. It was recognized early that the process of science was on-going and easily identified. There also may be said to be scientific aspects of history, not quite a science of history, but scientific methods applied within the historical process. However, even the most scientific historians need to select and to interpret.

IDENTIFYING PHILOSOPHIC POSITIONS

As taught by some *professors,* philosophy is a recounting, often chronologically, of Western philosophic thought, systems, schools, positions, approaches, stances, methods, and slants. This historical treatment also applies to these professors' discussions of famous past philosophers who initiated or supported these systems. Many college courses of general philosophy lack an accounting of the ideas and beliefs of earlier Eastern philosophers. This unfortunate abyss also leaves the student quite unaware that he has explored but a part of general philosophy.

Only after graduation do some former college students come to appreciate that even some textbooks purporting to cover formal philosophy are obscure, propagandistic, or inadequate in vital areas.

Anyone, who is neither an authentic philosopher nor a professor of authentic philosophy, and who attempts even superficial explanations of major philosophic systems, may be considered rather presumptuous, including the writers of this textbook! Numerous philosophers and other scholars have devoted their entire professional lives attempting to translate, interpret, elaborate, and state more clearly certain philosophic matters. Even the classification of philosophies for most philosophers has not been performed satisfactorily so far. The solution will not be attempted here. Nevertheless, a few of the ways in which philosophic concepts, ideas, and points of view have been organized and classified in a dangerously brief manner, together with some of the attendant problems, are attempted in the following paragraphs.

Some fundamental philosophic amalgams of concepts have been classified as philosophic schools, positions, or families, for example, idealism, realism, and pragmatism. Obviously, however, injustice may be done to any philosophy or philosopher should one hazard to categorize it or him under one label. An idea could be labeled Aristotelian and yet fit into a pragmatic theme. For example, a physical educator could think that a program should be orderly, even as nature is orderly, and be totally unaware that the *test of a program* for him had become whether or not it was orderly, that is, whether or not the students carried it on in an orderly, systematic way. Plato could be labeled a realist, as well as an idealist. Some eminent physical educators' writings and teachings might be said to reflect Platonic idealism in their emphasis on such objectives as the development of personality, intellect, character, yet they also may be identified with the pragmatic slant of Dewey in their emphasis on social objectives.

Further perplexity may result from the attempt to categorize the schools of philosophy. There is a lack of agreement among authors of textbooks on formal philosophy as to what constitutes the boundaries of a given school. These writers may disagree among themselves about the various classifications of the main stem: realism, for example, including scientific realism, naturalistic realism, and the like; or they may reclassify the old terms "idealism," "realism," and "pragmatism" under new headings—essentialism or progressivism—whatever their motivations and penchant for certain words.

Other authors have complicated the discussion of classifications of philosophies by pairing words such as supernaturalism and naturalism, rational and empirical, absolute and relative, traditional and modern. According to Burns and Brauner, Earl C. Cunningham explained two general positions in philosophy (the Aristotelian and the operational) by broad outlines: (1) a *rationalistic* set of first principles drawn from the thought of Plato, Aristotle, St. Thomas Aquinas, and Jacques Maritain, and (2) an empirical set of first principles drawn from Heraclitus, Francis Bacon, David Hume, and John Dewey.[17]

Although one may subscribe to methods of classification, such as identifying philosophies as rational or empirical, this classification becomes slippery because "no rational philosophy denies the uses of experience and no empirical philosophy denies the uses of reason," according to Burns and Brauner.[17] However, one *approach* to philosophy, existentialism, is based in part on an attempt to reject both rationalism and empiricism in philosophy.

Similarly, Brubacher courageously attempts an exposition that epitomizes philosophic positions in education for the most part under two headings: progressive and conservative. Nevertheless, he admits that this dichotomous classification, although useful for analyses of some specific issues, will not suffice when large-scale viewpoints must be summarized, and this latter is one of philosophy's major processes.[15]

Obviously, the attempt to categorize major philosophic divisions may serve as a Procrustean bed in the sense of the attempt being too harsh or inflexible in fitting the person or philosophy to a preconceived system or set of preconceived concepts. It is neither fruitful nor realistic to deny or avoid the inertial and traditional forces of formal philosophy—the basic heritage of what has come to be known as formal philosophy. Yet, the reader is forewarned that *these forces may act unbeknown to the one attempting to philosophize.* The thinker who consciously recognizes them must inevitably incorporate them into his philosophy. Through the ages a few men have struggled to originate and systematize their own philosophic systems in order that values, purposes, and man's choices might be organized and synthesized, and then guided, interpreted, and applied to daily living.

EXAMINING PHILOSOPHIC TERMINOLOGY

As the beginner in philosophy explores the ideas of eminent philosophers, a more error-free interpretation may be made if the basic categories or major ingredients of philosophy are understood. Some of the terms commonly found in the writing of philosophers and those who refer to their works will be explained briefly.

Metaphysics

One question that has always challenged man is "Of all the things in the world and in life, what is real?" If the record were known, the first of the Homo sapiens to ask this question was, probably, Greek. But one can speculate that many men before him wondered about what is known as reality, as evidenced in myths, legends, and magic. According to the

Oxford Universal Dictionary, "real" (in philosophy) means "that which is fact and not merely in appearance, thought or language." The wording used by philosophers is "The immediate object of that which is true."

Questions concerning reality were placed by Aristotle under the label of metaphysics. Although distinctions within the realm of metaphysical speculations are largely those within the traditional philosophies (idealism, realism, and pragmatism), and thus distinctions of diminishing importance in the realm of philosophic inquiry, the reader will nonetheless encounter these distinctive viewpoints as he reads the ideas of many eminent philosophers.

Answers to the question *"What is the nature of the universe* (or cosmos)?" and explanations of its origin and development center around the distinctive views of *evolutionism* (the universe evolved by itself) and *creationism* (the universe is a result of a creative cause or personality). Conceptions of and about God are related to these views of the universe. To illustrate, atheism is the view that there is no reality in or behind the cosmos which is God, Person, or Spirit. Theism places ultimate reality in a personal God who is more than the cosmos but through whom the cosmos exists. The existentialist and realist, for example, may be theistic or atheistic, whereas for the idealist there is spiritual reality. The pragmatists may find the concept of God, for which there is no common name, as emerging, evolving, within the cosmos, an end toward which this universe is moving.

"Teleology" is the term given to considerations relating to the question *"Is there purpose in the universe?"* Idealists and spiritual realists hold that there is purpose in the universe. A nonteleologic position is that of the atheistic existentialist who holds that the world is what it is because of chance, accident, or blind mechanism. Experimentalists do not find purpose inherent in the universe, but by purposeful activity seek to impose purpose on it!

In answer to such a question as *"Is reality one or many?"* the unitary view is that everything in the universe eventually reduces many "things" to some single, unitary world stuff, such as ideas in mind, or matter in motion, energy, or will. This was known as a *monistic* view of reality. Other men described reality in terms of two kinds of world stuff, such as mind and matter, or God and nature (dualism). Plato's ideas of form and matter, for example, represent a dualism in metaphysics, as does St. Thomas Aquinas' dualism of God and nature, or the Cartesian dualism of mind and matter. Still other pioneering thinkers took the position that reality is composed of at least three or more kinds of stuff such as minds, things, materials, energies, laws, processes, all equally real and somewhat independent of each other (*pluralism*).

Answers relating to the question *"Is there constancy, or lack* of it, in reality?"* are described in two terms: absolutism (reality is considered constant, unchanging, fixed, dependable), and *relativism* (reality is regarded as a changing thing, so-called realities being relative to something or other). Absolutism is identified with the philosophies of idealism and realism. Man also began to be concerned with such questions as "*What is the nature of man?*" as one important aspect of reality.

Often the term "ontology," or the nature of existence as such, is used as a synonym for metaphysics, or at least is often included as part of metaphysics. One of the questions concerning the nature of man and existence relates to freedom: "*Does man have free will or are his actions determined?*" Answers are presented in the alternatives of *determinism* (all man's actions are determined by forces greater than he is); *indeterminism* (man has the power of choice); and a third alternative, for which there is no name, proposed by the experimentalists, that man's responses are neither completely automatic nor free but can be reconstructed to give a new direction to subsequent activity.

The fundamental question "*What is the relationship of body and mind?*" has perplexed man throughout the history of philosophic thought. Answers to this question are interwoven with queries regarding such matters as the nature of the universe and the nature of reality. As suggested previously, idealism and spiritual realism hold that self is a soul, a spiritual being, and that mind and body are two different kinds of reality in which body depends on mind. The body–soul relationship is described by Plato in his *Phaedo*. This idea continues with Descartes' ("I think, therefore I am") and other idealists who extended the concept of the dualism or a separation of body and mind or soul. Later, sense empiricists (physical realism and naturalism), rejecting idealistic rationalism or mentalism, asserted that self is essentially the same as the body. This gave initial credence to the importance of the body (senses) to man's ability to know. Pragmatists or experimentalists, holding that existence is a category that is not valid in any ultimate sense because everything is in flux or change, view self as a social-vocal phenomenon.

Long-standing approaches to questions of reality, including the problem of mind–body relationships, have been subjected to attack from contemporary existentialists and analytic philosophers. Although existential philosophers have not given much attention to metaphysical speculation about reality, their central concern is ontology—the nature of being or existence. They are primarily interested in man's quest for being or essence. They take the view that reality lies in subjective human experience—through existence man is given essence. Rejecting dualistic views of mind and body, they view the body as the *primary* self, one's mode of being in the world rather than as an instrument of the mind or as an object or vehicle for receiving sensation. Devotees of analytic philosophy reject entirely traditional metaphysical speculation concerning "What is real?" and concern themselves primarily with epistemology. They are interested in supplying philosophy with a methodological tool, that of language analysis.

As one grapples with metaphysics, in the study of the ultimate reality of all things, one encounters questions concerning the processes of perception and knowledge. Thus, the term "epistemology" becomes a part of one's journey through the content parts of philosophy.

Epistemology

Will Durant believes that "epistemology has kidnaped modern philosophy, and well nigh ruined it."[37] Until the time, hoped for by Durant, "when the study of the knowledge process will be recognized as the business of the science of psychology," the reader cannot avoid its vocabulary, however puzzling it may be, in studying the writings of some vital philosophers. A few brief descriptions of the nature of the knowledge process may help clarify meanings and words.

The general definition of the term "epistemology," although not known as such to the first philosophers (it was first used in English in 1854), is "that aspect of philosophy dealing with the origin, structure, methods and validity of knowledge." Epistemology seems acutely crucial in educational philosophy because of its concern with such central questions as *"Where does knowledge come from* (the sources of knowledge)?" *"What is the human mind capable of knowing and what beliefs are true* (the validity of knowledge)?"

Sources of Knowledge. Main sources of knowledge are generally acknowledged to be testimony or authority, the senses, or concrete experiences, thinking or reasoning, intuition or insight. Each of these sources of knowledge has its acknowledged values and shortcomings.

Testimony or authority, characteristic of most traditional philosophies of idealism and spiritual realism, may be said to include custom, revelation, myth, faith, hunch, bias, and words that encompass man's experience throughout the ages. Although not a primary source, this source of knowledge or method of searching for it does provide a summary of the wisdom of others which cannot be experienced for oneself. Critics of this method of acquiring knowledge point out that it permits one to believe in spite of the evidence, and they recount the dangers of blind acceptance and the surrender of independent judgment.

Experience or finding out what one sees, hears, touches, feels, tastes, and smells constitutes a first-hand source of knowledge of facts and relationships. On the other hand, experience is personal. Therefore it is fickle, subject to distortion, prejudice, misinterpretation, and emotional coloration. *"Empiricism,"* which is the term used to designate knowledge gained through the sensations and experiences (knowledge labeled "a posteriori"), has taken many forms throughout the history of philosophic thought. For example, John Locke's eighteenth century idealistic theory of the mind as a blank tablet (tabula rasa) on which the world writes its impressions is regarded as a narrow *sensationism*, because it asserts that there is no knowledge other than that derived from the senses. More recently, *pragmatism*, a form of radical empiricism, stresses the changing world of experience. Existentialistic philosophers refer to experiencing as the essence of knowing—the process by which one can become aware of oneself and the world.

Another source of knowledge is obtained by comparing ideas, which is made possible by man's power of *thought* or *reason*. *Rationalism* regards the mind as central, that there is *a priori* knowledge or knowledge which is self-evident, as seen in such disciplines as logic and mathematics, not directly derived from experience. Extreme rationalists, contending that the mind has certain innate principles of operation, interpret these principles discovered by thought as irrefutable, or as genuine or absolute knowledge. Such medieval Schoolmen as René Descartes, as well as Berkeley, Kant, and most idealists of the past, are regarded as extreme rationalists or proponents of mentalism. Their critics contend that the danger of extreme mentalism (which substitutes deductive reasoning for empirical observation) may provide some logically consistent system, but one having little relevance to the world in which one lives.[110] Plato's dialogue *Theactitus* is said to have marked the initial epistemological debate between *rationalists* and *empiricists*. The debate between these two protagonists has been going on for more than 2000 years.

Another acknowledged possible source of a kind of higher knowledge, or present to some extent in all knowledge, is *intuition*. Intuition may be regarded as a supersensory knowledge present in awareness, feeling, imagination, insight into the total situation. Although intuition is not the direct result of reasoning or experience, it is regarded as a supplement to the senses and efforts of the intellect. Although feeling–knowledge, in the emotional sense, may give essential elements of truth to meet various life situations (choosing a friend, deciding on one's major college field, enjoying a work of art, and so forth), critics contend that it is not a safe method of knowledge by itself, unchecked by the senses or reason.[110]

Several philosophic writers stress that the various sources of knowledge are not in conflict but rather are complementary, each having contributions, and each being superior to others in some areas. W. P. Montague in *The Ways of Knowing* describes the "federation of methods." Titus writes that knowledge does not come in neat packages easily traced to separate sources. Joseph Wood Krutch, writing "In Defense of Prejudice" (*And Even If You Do*), puts the word "prejudice" alongside the word "preference." He suggests that the scientist must resume interest in *other* aspects of truth and *other* methods of searching for it, than are found in the objective neutrality of the laboratory, even though he may call them merely human prejudices.

The Validity of Knowledge. Attempting to determine what is truth or what is true knowledge, philosophers have relied, for the most part, on three tests of truth.[110] The *correspondence* theory proposes that truth is that which corresponds with the facts or the actual situation. This theory is identified most generally with the philosophic position of realism, wherein will be found such characteristic words and phrases as objective tests, scientific data, empirical investigation, and the like. Critics of this test of truth (generally idealists and pragmatists) point out that man's sensory perceptions are not always accurate or complete, and that there are ideas in human thought (e.g., logic, ethics) that have no objects to which comparisons can be made in checking for correspondence.

The *coherence* or consistence theory presents truth as that which is logically consistent with or in harmony with what has already been discovered or accepted to be true. Idealists, in general, are proponents of this theory of truth, believing that immutable ideas and theories in the whole of reality—religion, economic life, science—have worked for a long time. The reader will find in Plato and in the more contemporary philosophers of idealism, such as Hegel and Royce, principles of coherence, wherein an idea or theory or hypothesis works because it is true. Critics of this test of truth (generally, pragmatists) declare that it is formal and too intellectualistic, dealing mainly with logical relations and failing to provide a basis for judging everyday experience.

The test of utility or pragmatic theory of truth proclaims that truth is that which works in practice or leads to satisfactory results. The test of utility or workability is utilized by the pragmatist who repudiates claims about ultimate realities in his interpretation of the flux of experience. For the pragmatist, that which is true can be experimentally verified, it is active, relative to the situation, aids us in the everyday struggle, satisfies our purposes. Critics of this test of truth claim that such *relativism* may not conform to the facts or stand the test of time, and simply may be a concession to our subjective emotions and prejudices.

In addition to these three main tests of truth which have appeared in the literature of philosophy, other positions regarding the possibility of knowledge should be acknowledged. *Skepticism,* or the view that nothing can be known, is associated with early Greek Sophists and in more recent times with the well-known skeptic David Hume. *Agnosticism,* meaning "unknown" or "without knowledge," refers to man's ignorance of such ultimate realities as matter, mind, and God. Skepticism, which takes many forms, perhaps is self-refuting, as Titus points ont, because "if nothing can be known, then how does the skeptic know that his position is a valid one?"[110] On the other hand, a certain amount of skepticism, from the type presented in the questioning attitude of Socrates to any individual's rejection of dogmatism, may serve a worthy purpose.

In summarizing the ways of knowing, it may be said that they are many rather than one, and that there are many truths rather than one simple truth that may need to be approached by many methods and many minds. Such has been and continues to be part of the task of philosophy. As Will Durant, even with his disdain for epistemology's "weary exploitation," so aptly stated, "God knows there is no short cut to knowledge."[37]

Axiology

Further decisive questions about life concern man as he attempts to deal with values. Although "axiology," the term used to designate value-oriented concerns, is connected with metaphysics and epistemology (because values are based on one's view of reality and truth), there are, of course, some additional terms and meanings connected with the study of values which confront the student interested in grasping the writings of eminent philosophers and thinkers.

The question *"What is the worth of living?"* gives rise to various alternatives designated by the terms "optimism" (existence is good and life is worth living), "pessimism" (life is not worth the struggle and we should escape it by some means), and "meliorism" (conclusions as to the goodness or evilness of existence cannot be made final, but human effort may improve the human situation). The question *"What is the ultimate objective in life, the highest good or summum bonum?"* is answered in such positions as *hedonism* (the highest good is pleasure), *utilitarianism* (the greatest happiness of the greatest number), *perfectionism* (perfection of the self or self-realization). From one's conception of the highest good there follow certain *criteria of conduct* or practical principles for living. Morals usually covers the codes of conduct of an individual group, although some writers use it as a synonym for ethics.

Ethics is said to be concerned with "those judgments, on the one hand, of goodness–badness, desirability–undesirability, and on the other hand, judgments of rightness–wrongness, obligation, and/or wisdom–foolishness. . . ." There are two main directions that this study, or concern, may take: (1) a concern with psychologic and sociologic analyses and explanation of ethical judgments, showing what our approvals and disapprovals consist of, and why we approve or disapprove of what we do; and (2) a concern with establishing, or recommending, certain courses of action, ways of life, or ends, as wise, good, virtuous, or their opposites. Herein, the concern is more in action than in approval, more in guidance of action than in explanation.

Some philosophers attempt to combine the two directions that ethics may take. However, in any study of ethics, the meaning of ethical statements, their truth and objectivity (or their opposites), and the possibility of systemizing these statements under one or more first principles are synthesized.

Some men have developed the view that goodness or rightness is not dependent on people, but that people are obligated to behave in certain ways because they intuit it. According to this theory (known as the existence, intuitive, objective, or indefinable theory), values have an existence in their own right. The idealist is committed to the rational solution of moral problems and takes the position that certain immutable moral principles are part of the heritage of mankind. Kant's categorical imperative, for example, is that one should act on those principles that he is willing should become universal moral laws. The realist, believing that the world of material objects is the real world, concludes that values derive from natural laws. Spencer's principle, for example, is that action to be right must be conducive to self-preservation.

The theory of the experimentalist is that whatever is of value is that which yields a greater sense of happiness in the present, and opens the way to future goods and experiences. Dewey's principle is that one should go through an imaginative rehearsal of the possible consequences of what he is considering doing. Still others believe that ethical concepts, rather than being objective facts, merely express feelings and persuasions of people (known as interest, emotive, or subjective theory). Some existentialists, rejecting set systems of values or definite value positions, assert that the individual should choose what he values in being an authentic self—do your own thing—regardless.

Another dimension of the general category of axiology is *aesthetics*, which deals with questions regarding the nature of values found in the feeling aspects of experience—beauty, taste, the aesthetic experience, enjoyment and appreciation of the arts, and the like. Although there is a question whether aesthetics ought to include the study of values in the realm of beauty and art, questions concerning the nature and purpose of art, for example, when placed within the framework of the moral problems of man, become part and parcel of an ethical inquiry. The philosophy of beauty, as Santayana put it, is a theory of values. Some philosophers may consider the purpose of metaphysics as a proposal to make life an art.

The various points of view regarding what beauty (or a thing of aesthetic worth) is and standards for the evaluation of its quality mainly correspond to the major philosophic positions. The statement that beauty is in the eyes of the beholder expresses the position that beauty is relative, never absolute. Dewey, espousing the experimentalist position, emphasizes the functional or utilitarian aspect of art. Art cannot be separated from everyday experience. It is a quality that permeates an experience. Thus, art as experience carries the observer forward by the pleasurable activity of the process itself. The idealist would consider beauty to be an unchanging perfect ideal and would evaluate beauty according to certain immutable standards evidenced in the best of the past. He would conclude that beauty exists even if there were no eyes to behold it.

The realist considers the laws and order of nature as man's most reliable guide to what is beautiful; thus, with Whitehead, he contends that the sheer harmony of a properly functioning body is a thing of beauty. The existentialist points to another view of aesthetics which may be placed in the context of Buber's "I-Thou" relationship. The implication here is that the essence of the work of art is the relationship between the person and the work of art, a relationship that is an aesthetic moment, a moment to be encountered in its present, timeless aspects.

Logic

Philosophy also depends on the use of certain intellectual tools. That branch of philosophic thought concerned with the way man thinks is known as logic. It attempts to determine such inquiries as what kinds of thinking lead clearly and in orderly sequence to correct conclusions.

There are many types of logic, deductive and inductive being only two of them. *Deduction* is a form of reasoning from the general to the particular, from the universal to the individual, or from given premises to their necessary conclusions. Aristotle's classification technique is cited as the first illustration of deductive logic. Aristotle's syllogism ("All men are mortal. Socrates is man; therefore, Socrates is mortal.") represents reasoning from the general to the particular. An illustration of more recent application of deductive logic may be found in several articles concerning sport and play that appear in Ellen Gerber's book, *Sport and the Body: A Philosophical Symposium.*[45a] In an article by Eleanor Metheny, "This 'Thing' Called Sport," the characteristics or particulars of sport (their common elements) are deduced from the generalized idea or definition of what is the nature of sport. *Induction* is the method of reasoning that involves the forming of generalizations or conclusions from specific instances or certain particulars. Bacon introduced the idea of establishing generalized principles after making observations and collecting facts. A more recent illustration of the application of inductive logic may be found in H. Graves' article "A Philosophy of Sport," in which an all-embracing general definition of sport is induced from a list of specific activities accepted as sport.[45a]

Logic establishes criteria such as the *principle of self-contradiction* by which one can assess consistency of statements. Some contemporary philosophy has been devoted to penetrating language analyses to try to determine with greater precision the criteria of meaning. Logical positivism attempts to drive home the demand for criteria for judging meaning and truth. Since the days of Aristotle and the beginnings of formal logic, the new tools of deduction, however foreboding they may appear to the neophyte in philosophy, make possible an exactitude in logical proofs heretofore possible only in mathematics. Philosophers of logical positivism (language analysis) utilize a different system of logic than that represented by defining, which is basically an application of inductive reasoning, or by characterization or classification, which is basically an application of deductive logic. Logical positivists in analyzing sport, for example, assume it has no ultimate nature or describable essence, but is as language has used it. Thus, they refer to the thing "sport," as a sum of its qualities or attributes as they are evidenced in the verbalization (ordinary language usage) of individuals who experience it. Wiggenstein, in "Language—Games" (1958), provided a taxonomic model of linguistic analysis. More recently, other writings, such as Fogelin's "Sport: The Diversity of Concept," may be considered as utilizing the analytic philosophic model.[45a]

These over-simplified definitions and discussions are intended only to suggest the scope of basic aspects of philosophy. There are disagreements among philosophers and within their philosophies concerning the validity of such definitions and their implications. Neither this chapter nor the entire book could attempt comprehensively treated definitions, serve as a complete outline, or even claim to be an adequate summary of the branches of formal philosophy. For such an adequate coverage the student should take at least one college course in general philosophy, and preferably more. Even then, the formal content (categories) of philosophy is only "the parts of philosophy," *and* as Will Durant stated, "but so dismembered it loses its beauty and joy. We shall seek it not in its shrivelled abstractness and formality, but clothed in the living form of genius."[37]

Perhaps the first task, then, is to examine formal philosophy as completely and critically as a necessarily limited treatment provides. The following four chapters serve this purpose. Because there is general agreement about the long-established *fundamental* positions of idealism, realism, and pragmatism, these philosophies will be explored in Chapters 9, 10, and 11. Chapter 12 deals with other vital modes of thought or existing *variants* of the more established philosophic positions.

The beginning student of formal philosophy may be dismayed to find conflicting accounts of what the major slants of philosophy are supposed to include. We do not wish to confuse the reader by reporting well-known differences. There are not only many differences, but some of them may appear to be trivial. The descriptions of philosophic positions that follow include those elements and interpretations which seem to be most meaningful today to physical educators.

Because we believe that neophyte philosophers may understand philosophic discussion better if it is presented as the ideas of certain individual philosophers, some of the eminent philosophers and their fundamental positions are identified in the following chapters. As a student of physical education looks at the philosophic positions, he might well examine each of them from vantage points suggested by such questions as:

1. What are the different "flavors" or "colors" of materials given to the physical education story, as seen through the telescope of a particular philosophic position?
2. What in a particular philosophic position should one know that would help one in writing a personal philosophy of life or a professional philosophy?
3. What aspects of physical education seem to escape ready application of a given philosophic position?
4. To what extent should a given philosopher's ideas or a given philosophy influence the novice searching for his personal philosophy?

LET US NOW PURSUE OUR ANCIENT AUTHORS, FOR OUT OF THE OLD FIELDS MUST COME THE NEW.

—Edward Coke

9

Idealism*

MAN, BEING BORN TO ACT, WAS A PREDESTINED IDEALIST,
SINCE TO ACT IS TO AFFIRM THE WORTH OF AN END, AND
TO PERSIST IN THE AFFIRMATION IS TO FRAME AN IDEAL.

—*Oliver W. Holmes*

The roots of idealism reach down into antiquity. Springing from the prephilosophy thinking of the Sumerians and Egyptians, the identifiable roots of idealism began with Socrates and Plato. Although idealism did not receive its name until about two and a half centuries ago, Plato is considered to be its founder. It was he who first and most earnestly presented idea-ism as he elaborated on the concept that ideas are the true reality. Idealism later received strength from the Judaic-Christian concept of God, and was notably exemplified in later centuries by such men as Berkeley, Kant, and Hegel. Other idealists may be added to the list.

Plotinus (third century B.C.) developed the idea of free will and moral responsibility (individual responsibility). René Descartes and Berkeley in the seventeenth century were regarded as proponents of mentalism, that idealistic tenet proposed in Descartes' famous words "I think, therefore I am." The trend of thought concerning the distinction between mind and matter also started with Descartes, and thrust to the forefront the mind–body issue and the interpretations of the relationships between them.

The philosophy of Baruch Spinoza (1632–1677) is a modification of Descartes' position. Like Kant, Spinoza regarded mind and body as two aspects of one reality. For Spinoza, that one reality was God. If God is the significant fact, then moral and religious values have importance in existence.

*The Glossary (p. 315) may be helpful in reading Chapters 9 through 12. Chronological Perspective (Appendix B, p. 313) also may be of interest to the reader.

One can find almost every kind of idealist, so many ideas can be made *idealistic.*

Of the philosophic positions presented, idealism is the oldest. It is also the strongest in terms of the numbers of persons the world over who believe in some of its tenets.

Idealism views man's mind, that which he is and that which he makes, as an imperfect replica of the idea of perfect mind, perfect self, perfect thing. In each instance, this idea of a perfect something remains as the one unchanging perfect model of that something for all time. Examples of the major qualities of which perfect ideas could be found in man's mind are truth, beauty, and good. That which man thinks, sees, does, and so on, are but imperfect reflections of the eternal, the absolute, the universal. The world as portrayed by our senses is characterized by imperfections, restrictions, limitations, problems, difficulties, and the like.

It was not a long step to believing that the world of ideas (the perfect models) was "higher" than the world of imperfect things that the senses brought to man's mind. Near the beginnings of philosophic schools of thought, a dualism was formulated. In passing, it might well be repeated that scholars of both East and West believe that Plato probably spent some of his 12 "absent years" in either India or China, or both. Oriental teachings (that began more than a century before the time of Socrates) would account in part for Plato's emphasis on the inner self and on the importance of the unworldly.

In the following pages brief discussions of the philosophies of Socrates, Plato, Berkeley, Kant, and Hegel are presented as representative of the roots of earlier branches of idealism.

Early Idealists

Socrates (469–399 B.C.)

Socrates is considered to be one of the greatest forces in the evolution of human thought, although he committed none of his thoughts to paper. Without the writings of Plato, Xenophon, and to a certain degree, Aristotle, little if anything would be known about Socrates.

Plato, making Socrates the central figure of his dialogues, gives the philosophy of a man who professed to know nothing himself. A vivid picture is portrayed of a man whose personality revealed independence of spirit, imaginative subtlety in debate, uncompromising frankness, blistering irony, and yet, as the familiar quotation stated, "so wise in judging good and evil he was never at fault, in a word, the best and happiest of men."

Believing he lacked wisdom and not wanting to disbelieve the oracle at Delphi who said he was the wisest of men, Socrates concluded that the god Apollo had imposed a mission on him. Throughout his life he believed he was inspired by this divine voice (daimon) commissioning him to search for truth and lead men to the virtuous life. He constantly stressed the need for critical self-examination. "Know thyself" and "The unexamined life is not worth living" are parts of his modus operandi.

Socrates was not an originator of the search for knowledge. The method of his search, however, was unique. He sought to uncover error by the question–answer method (dialectic), frequently feigning ignorance himself in order to elicit truths latent in the minds of others.

Although he never formulated any specific metaphysics, apparent harmony in the universe led him to believe it is ordered by a Divine Spirit, and that the soul is immortal.

His deepest concentrations were with ethical questions—what makes a good citizen a good man. He was interested in discovering not only the kind of life most worth living, but why one way is more worthy than another. Happiness does not consist in material rewards or pleasures. For Socrates, "to want nothing is divine." Happiness to him was synonymous with virtue.

Socrates believed that without right knowledge, right action is impossible. No one is deliberately wicked. "Knowledge is, therefore, always the strongest power in man and cannot be overcome by passion."[130] What was good for one was good for all; there was no room for relative morality. Tomlin made the point that for Socrates there exists within each one a "universal conscience," a moral imperative that needs only to be uncovered and put to use.[112] To this aim, education should be dedicated.

Although he did not force his convictions on others, but examined theirs, Socrates was uncompromising in his personal and civic life, and in his teachings. The last days of Socrates in prison are poignantly dramatic in Plato's *Phaedo*. He refused to compromise with principle during his trial for impiety and followed the ideal that citizens owe complete obedience to the law. The fatal cup of hemlock demonstrated the depth of his conviction.

In Plato's *Symposium*, as related by Alcibiades, Socrates was a man of rigid self-control, showed an amazing capacity for endurance, and was unaffected by the rigors of climate or hardships. As Gardiner pointed out, for Socrates "no citizen has the right to be amateur in the matter of physical training: it is part of his profession as a citizen to keep himself in good condition to serve his state at a moment's notice."[44]

Although preparing the body to endure the tortures of war was uppermost in this period of Greek history, Socrates indicated reasons for complete physical training that extended beyond the battlefield: "what a disgrace it is for man to grow old without ever seeing the beauty and strength of which his body is capable."[44]

Plato (427–347 B.C.)

Omitting the metaphysical or epistemological detail of his philosophy, Plato's famous theory of ideas, by which reality is seen to be idea-(1)-istic, is essentially that the transitory world experienced through the senses is changing, unreliable, a shadow, or an imperfect copy of the real world. The "real" world, which is an unseen realm of essences of forms or ideas (Plato used idea and form interchangeably), is constant, eternal, unchanging, perfect, therefore ideal. In the real world, which is a world of ideas, a world apprehended by the mind, can be found the ideal of everything (e.g., justice, truth, beauty) to which particular things or practices of the world man experiences can be compressed to fit. Plato did not deny the existence of matter, but he elevated things of the mind and spirit to a higher degree in the hierarchy of importance. Such a view of ultimate reality teaches that truths are in the mind rather than in the world, that all that is really real is good, that the highest form is the idea of good.

In his rationalistic theory of knowledge, Plato argued that the soul comes into the world with true, innate ideas stored in the mind from a pre-earthly existence. Man can know, therefore, because he is rational, and his ability to reason is inherent in him.

Platonic idealism combines epistemology and ethics because Plato equated virtue with knowledge. For him, morality rested on true knowledge of the good with its special forms, the true and the beautiful, and their species, temperance, harmony, spiritedness, wisdom, justice, and the like. It would be impossible to draw implications from Plato, as the greatest symbol of perennial idealism, apart from the glory that was Greece.

Above all other available examples, the physical education of early Athens is idealistic and is rather thoroughly consistent with the philosophies of both Plato and Aristotle, although they lived in the *succeeding* period often called the "golden age of Athens." However, even in that bitter period preceding Plato during the fall of Athens, Thucydides, the commanding historian of the time, gives full place of honor to the splendor of Greek games.

Through the dialogues of Plato moves the figure of his great teacher Socrates, and both held up a mirror of the Greek way—the spirit of inquiry, the ideal of the excellent in mind, body, and spirit—which has never been surpassed.

To these Greeks, the beautiful was inseparable from the true and the good. All were related to everyday life—politics, learning, religion, art, sport. Men were composite creatures made up of soul and body, mind and spirit. Disregard of any one for the other meant a human being partially developed. Such a view encouraged man to participate fully in life, including a love of reason, a delight in the use of the body, and a trust in his highest aspirations in all things.

Being a pupil of Socrates, who commended bodily exercise, and being a participant in military expeditions, Plato spoke with authority on the subject of Greek athletics and military gymnastics. His name, originally Aristocles, was changed by his wrestling teacher to Plato (broad-shouldered). Although in *Phaedo* he pictured the body as merely a prison for the soul, his writings make clear that the bodily condition should be as perfect as it can be through severity and simplicity in physical education as opposed to luxurious ways of living and eating. In *The Republic,* Plato emphasized that "anyone who can produce the best blend of the physical and the intellectual sides of education and apply them to the training of character is producing harmony. . . ."

Until the age of twenty, Plato believed the principal subjects in education were gymnastics and "musical" training because they "constitute the first stage to knowledge of Ideas, for the harmonious soul and the beautiful body in the concrete individual are copies of the Ideas."[90]

If given the elevation of Platonic idealism as a whole, physical education programs would hold high the objectives of character education, beauty, harmony, versatility, moderation, excellence.

George Berkeley (1685–1753)

Berkeley (pronounced barkley), Irish philosopher and bishop, is among the greats in philosophy, particularly because of his *Treatise Concerning the Principle of Human Knowledge.* His philosophic position is best seen in contrast with that of John Locke (*Essay Concerning Human Understanding*), who was the proponent of the great scientific achievements of the seventeenth century. Berkeley, reacting vigorously against the scientific, which he called an atheistic world view, preferred the word "immaterialism" for his philosophy.

Locke believed in the reality of matter, spiritual substance, and ideas separating the substance of matter into primary qualities (e.g., form, motion, number) and secondary qualities (e.g., color, taste, odor, sound). Primary qualities were in the outer world, secondary qualities in the mind. Locke proposed that ideas are the only objects of direct awareness, that we cannot know what ordinary objects are or that they even exist, that such things as color or motion are separated from the object.

Berkeley regarded sense experience as the base for epistemology, and asserted that there can be no object without a knower, that the mind creates its object. In Berkeley's subjectivism, or what is called "epistemological idealism," objects perceived through the senses do not exist independent of consciousness of them. Secondary qualities such as color, size, shape, and motion exist in the mind and cannot be separated from an object. The same arguments can be applied to primary qualities which are also in the mind.

From the belief that a physical object exists only as it is experienced came Berkeley's dictum "to be is to be perceived." But an important companion proposition is that the human mind does not create its perceptions. Berkeley's *to be* had reference to the existence of an ideal in the mind of God. That which produces perceptions behind the objective world is spirit, not matter. Furthermore, knowledge of self and God is implied, not directly received. In short, ideas are the product of mind. Mind is the product of the perfect subject or mind, called God.

Objectivists or epistemological realists, of course, reject this view. They insist that there is a reality independent from mind. Kant, according to some writers, takes a position between subjectivism and objectivism—that man can know only phenomena, not ultimate reality. Idealists such as Plato and Hegel, and many of those on the contemporary scene, reject this subjectivism or mentalism which admits no reality other than the world of thought.

According to Butler, an idealist axiology paralleling Berkeley's can be formulated, assuming that epistemology to be valid: "Values exist only for the individual person when he works out those adjustments which realize value for him, and when he has the emotional experience which is the enjoyment of value." Nevertheless, all values reside in God, and "in Him is that perfection in which all possible positive values are fully realized and enjoyed."[8]

Immanuel Kant (1724–1804)

Kant was a German philosopher who taught logic, theology, mathematics, physics, and anthropology, as well as philosophy. The philosophy of Kant dominated the thought of the nineteenth century, and his great writings have become classics in philosophy.

Kant's critical idealism developed from his analysis of knowledge, the aim of critical philosophy being concerned with the distinction between the world of sense and the world of understanding. He postulated two worlds: the unknowable world, or the thing-in-itself (noumenal), and the knowable world of experience (phenomenal). Opposing Berkeley's subjectivism (that material objects exist only in the mind), Kant asserted that the natural world exists but man cannot know the world lying outside the realm of his own thought. For example, man perceives the tree because of his mind, but he cannot know the cause of the sensation he receives. Kant insisted that mind never perceives things in isolated bits but always in the forms of Gestalts. One relates all sensations passively received by the mind by locating them in categories of perception and by relating ideas logically (reason). According to this *coherence theory,* then, an idea is tested for its truth by comparing it for fit with ideas already known to be true.

Crucial questions of critical philosophy arose also concerning moral laws. In an "Age of Reason," in which the inquiry into the nature and sources of knowledge ceased to be a support of religion, Kant was roused from what he called the "dogmatic slumber" (he had assumed religion and science without question) in an attempt to save them. Bacon had inspired Europe with confidence in the power of science and logic to solve all problems. Spinoza's "faith in reason had begotten a magnificent structure of geometry and logic." In Hobbes the rationalism of Bacon had "become an uncompromising atheism and materialism." Locke, Berkeley, and Hume had paved the way for such a critical examination of the worship of the goddess of reason but apparently they were too hostile to religion.[37]

Locke, although arguing for "The Reasonableness of Christianity," could not accept the supposition that innate ideas (e.g., God) were inherent in mind from birth, prior to all experience. Rather, all our knowledge is derived from sensation—the mind at birth is a clean sheet, a *tabula rasa,* and sense experience writes on it. Bishop George Berkeley, refuting Locke's analysis, attempted to show that matter does not exist except as a form of mind, the ideas derived from these sensations; the only reality we know directly is mind. To this argument of the Enlightenment, that reason makes for materialism, Berkeley had answered that matter does not exist, which in turn led David Hume to respond that by the same token neither does mind exist.[37]

Although Rousseau, too, had opposed the materialism and atheism of the Enlightenment ("above the logic of the head is the feeling in the heart"), it was the mission of Kant to thread together the ideas of Berkeley and Hume with the feelings of Rousseau, to save religion from reason and science from skepticism.[37] Kant's *Critique of Pure Reason,* written in 1781, was the beginning of a "critical philosophy" which has ruled philosophy in Europe since that day. It was an eloquent argument that the "objects of facts—a free and immortal soul, a benevolent creator— could never be proved by reason." His *Critique of Practical Reason* was an attempt to change the base of religion from theology to morals. It was an argument that pure reason can be practical in that it can determine the will independent of sense experience. The moral sense is innate—our inescapable feeling that legislates a priori all of our behavior regarding right and wrong.[37]

Thus, Kant believed that in every person there is an "innate imperative" that orders his conduct toward good. Kant's criterion of conduct was to act only on those principles that one is willing should become universal moral laws.

Butler summarizes Kant's principles exemplifying the ethical values of idealism:[18] (1) He believed that there are universal moral laws. (2) He believed that man has a feeling of obligation to obey these laws and this sense of duty is rooted in reason just as the categories of perception and conception are; therefore, it is called a *categorical imperative.* (3) He believed in freedom; it is possible for one to do good out of desire or intent free from dependence on experience. (4) He believed in the immortality of the soul. (5) He believed in the existence of God. The categorical imperative and lack of moral guarantees in the world make God necessary.

Kant saw the goal of education as being the enlightened moral person. Some of the processes of this education are (1) to restrain the natural wildness of the child through discipline, (2) to cultivate the child's mind, and (3) to assure his moral development through the proper conditioning of the will.

Georg Wilhelm Friedrich Hegel (1770–1831)

Hegel combined conceptual themes from the philosophies of Kant, Aristotle, Plato, and Christianity. In common with other post-Kantian German idealists, Hegel built on Kant's analyses of knowledge and of reason. Rejecting Kant's two-world dualistic view of reality, however, he argued that Kant's noumenal (unknowable) world had no real existence. From Hegel's point of view, the only real world is the world that thought constructs, that experience observes, and that constitutes life and its meaning. His concept of experience (restricted by Berkeley to sense experience) included consciousness, imagination, reason, perception, everything. Reality is experience, broadly conceived, unified, whole, absolute. Reality is mind or idea out of which develops the processes of nature and human history.

Other characteristic features of Hegelian doctrine are, especially, his dialectic method and his theory of the absolute. From any situation (thesis) grows a contradictory situation (antithesis), and the struggle between these two opposites resolves into a new situation (synthesis). All life and thought consist of a series of movements determined by the dialectic process (a procedure of which some of the dialogues of Plato give instances). Truth, according to Hegel, comes through immediate experience (and this is the justification for empiricism in philosophy). In order to make immediate experience meaningful, one classifies, divides, and forms generalizations, and so connects experiences into concepts through the activity of thought. Understanding is involved in the contradictions which inevitably follow, and truth is the synthesis of various points of view. Thought must take things in connection with their origin and in relation to other things with which they are competing. The true is the whole, a totality that is never reached but that drives thought on endlessly.

According to Butler, Hegel's realm of morals is also amenable to this dialectic movement.[18] One way Hegel stated this trial in ethics is to set innocence against evil, then find the synthesis in virtue. Evil, then, is a necessary aspect of the realization of good.

Like other monistic idealists, Hegel thought of God as universal mind or spirit or absolute, a perfect all-inclusive reality.

Marx and Engels, although rejecting Hegel's emphasis on mind or idea, accepted his dialectic method almost completely. Theirs became the famous dialectic materialistic philosophy of history.

Idealism in Eighteenth and Nineteenth Century Europe

Idealism following the periods of Berkeley, Kant, and Hegel was represented in Europe by such figures as:

England

    Samuel Taylor Coleridge (1772–1834)
    Joseph Henry Green (1791–1863)
    Thomas Carlyle (1795–1881)
    Benjamin Jowett Morrison (1817–1893)
    James H. Stirling (1820–1909)
    John (1820–1898) and Edward (1846–1924) Caird
    Andrew Martin Fairbairn (1838–1912)
    Francis Herbert Bradley (1846–1924)
    Bernard Bosanquet (1848–1923)

France

    Henri Bergson (1859–1941)

Italy

    Benedetto Croce (1866–1952)
    Giovanni Gentile (1875–1944)

Germany

    Johann Friedrich Herbart (1776–1841)
    Friedrich Froebel (1782–1852)

Bradley and Bosanquet of England probably are the names most often heard in present-day discussions of idealism. The writings of Coleridge and Carlyle of England were widely read and influential in the early idealistic movement in America, particularly that of the New England transcendentalism expressed in the writings of Ralph Waldo Emerson. Similarly, the influence of German idealists spread to America. Such

German scholars as Carl Follen (1796–1840) and Francis Lieber (1800–1872), proponents of German gymnastics in America, did much to influence early physical education programs.

An adequate history of idealism includes two other idealists. One is Johann Gottlieb Fichte (1762–1814), a disciple of Kant, who wrote on some phases of Kantian philosophy not then worked out by Kant, and probably the most important figure linking Kant and Hegel. The other was Arthur Schopenhauer (1788–1860) who became one of the world's famed pessimists.

Idealism is indirectly connected with the vast socialist revolution in Russia, according to Butler.[18] The dialectical materialism of Ludwig Feurbach (1804–1872), Karl Marx (1818–1883), and Friedrich Engels (1820–1895) "was developed as a counterthrust to idealism," not because the official philosophy of the USSR is idealism. The dialectical materialists embraced the dialectic of Hegel, but substituted a materialistic metaphysics for Hegel's idealistic metaphysics.

As Kant, who started German idealism, has been called the philosopher of the Reformation, perhaps Herbart and Froebel may shoulder the mantle of idealistic educators. For this reason, the views of Herbart and Froebel are presented as representative of roots of idealism among early educational theorists.

Johann Friedrich Herbart (1776–1841)

Herbart, successor to Kant in the chair of philosophy at Koenigburg, was one of the first trained philosophers since the time of Plato to give serious attention to education. Herbart believed that the mental process is the material of education, and objected to the attempts of Comenius and Pestalozzi to "practicalize" educational theory. Herbart's educational theories were characterized, therefore, by the intellectualism of scholarly discipline and attentive compliance of the learner by force if necessary. For Herbart, knowledge was acquired by the mind by means of association of new ideas with ideas already in the mind (theory of apperception).

Furthermore, the aim of education for Herbart was the development of moral character but, because the soul cannot be divided into faculties, education cannot be divided into intellectual and moral instruction. True morality is not something imposed from without; the truly moral man is self-commanded.

Herbart analyzed the importance of interest to learning perhaps more than had been done previously. He believed knowledge is not innate, interest needs to be instilled, and learning is a function of experience. Thus, for Herbart, it was the teacher who was of utmost importance in setting the environment for the development of the child's mind and character.

Friedrich Froebel (1782–1852)

Although a teacher and learner for several years in Pestalozzi's school, and although he drew his three-point theory of natural development (play, activity, and social cooperation) from the romantic naturalism of Rousseau, Froebel turned to idealism for the postulates on which he based his educational theories. The one continuous purpose throughout education should be the development of the full powers of the human individual as a child of nature, of man, and of God. "God-likeness is and ought to be man's highest aim in thought and deed." Knowledge should help man attain his destiny of earthly perfection. He believed that the child's education should be threefold, taking into account the mental, spiritual, and physical natures. According to Froebel, games educate the boy for life, for civic and moral virtues. He stressed that memory can be improved through such activities as ball playing. Education should be a spontaneous growth or development from within, not a prescription from without. To Froebel, the teacher helps the child realize all his God-given capacities, just as the gardener helps the flower unfold its potential realization; thus, the analogy kindergarten (the children's garden).

Recent and Contemporary Thought in America

Those who are regarded as figures in the idealist succession in America are:

America
  Ralph Waldo Emerson (1803–1882)

St. Louis Philosophical Society
  Henry C. Brokmeyer (1828–1906)
  William T. Harris (1835–1909)

University of California
  George H. Howison (1834–1916)

Boston University
  Borden Parker Bowne (1847–1910)

Harvard
  Josiah Royce (1855–1916)

Cornell
  James Edwin Creighten (1861–1924)

Wellesley
  Mary Whiton Calkins (1863–1930)

Harvard

William E. Hocking (1873–1966)

New York University

Herman Harrell Horne (1874–1946)

William T. Harris, editor of the first American philosophical journal, is said to be the fountainhead of the American idealist movement, and Josiah Royce probably the greatest single exponent of idealism in America.[18]

Despite the fact that contemporary American culture is predominantly materialistic, secular, and empirical, and despite the fact that a writer such as Hansen described a new philosophic orientation in which traditional philosophic idealism is said to be obsolescent,[48] idealism still is an important and vital philosophy in the United States. With regard to the idealistic spirit in the history of human thought as being a "permanent triumph," Royce wrote, "Modern Idealism, like that of former rationalism, is a sort of universal and often secret infection. Whoever contends against it shows that he is already its victim."[96] The most radical empiricism is therefore, according to Royce, full of idealistic motives.[96]

Twentieth century idealism finds its origin in three sources: (1) historic idealism; (2) the cultural inertia of the "Greek tradition" of classical humanism; and (3) the doctrine of the Christian churches. But tradition alone cannot support a dynamic philosophy, there must also be a coexistent raison d'être. In the case of contemporary idealism, the coexistent force is a conservative reaction against current extremes of scientific empiricism, modern social theory and social reform, socialism, secularism, progressive education, behaviorism, and relativistic psychology.[23]

Characteristics of Twentieth Century Idealistic Philosophies. A short and generalized discussion must necessarily take some liberties with specific idealistic philosophies of which there are many current varieties. A few of the most common and representative principles can be listed, after which the important distinctions among some of the more important philosophies will be indicated.

Perhaps the most notable of the characteristics of contemporary idealism, as pointed out by Burke, is the reaffirmation of the principle of dualism between man and nature, and between body and mind.[23] Ideas, mind, and absolutes are held to be the realms of ultimate reality, in the Platonic tradition. To the extent that material things are considered to be real, they are subordinate.

A *second* characteristic is the philosophic position that values and moral standards are absolute and permanent, rather than relative and changeable.

A *third* characteristic is the espousal of a "faculty psychology." Man is considered to have a discrete faculty or quality of intellect uniquely capable of grasping truth and knowledge. The educational process aims at the training or disciplining of this intellectual faculty. A liberal education is one enabling man to learn to think, to reason, to make judgments, to perceive truth and beauty, and to identify eternal moral values. These intellectual ends are pursued, whereas crassly practical learnings, purely vocational studies, and narrow professional specializations are minimized.

In the *fourth* characteristic, man is placed above nature. He is pictured not merely as a bundle of reflexes and a complex biochemical mechanism, but as a creature with a superimposed spark of the divine. This spark is something above and beyond any evolutionary product.

Although modern idealists reflect definite individuality of points of view, according to Antz, among American idealist philosophers of education probably the greatest difference is in the degree to which theism and personalism do or do not influence their thought.[17] They largely accept "the theory of Berkeley that *to be* is to be for a mind; . . . the theory that God both transcends the universe and is imminent in it; . . . the Personalist conclusion that the human self is the best key we have to the nature of that of which we are a part."

In contrast with many American pragmatists, the modern idealist accepts metaphysics (the study of the nature of existence, or the nature of the world) as an integral part of philosophy. The idealist also believes that it is part of the responsibility of the scientist to admit that his account of the world is built on man-made assumptions and hypotheses. The idealist does not reject science, scientific methods, or scientifically determined facts. It is true that he places a different kind of use and value on them than does the realist or pragmatist. The idealist regards these as important because they help to provide surer bases for knowing more about the world. Science helps man see and better understand the world as a demonstrated work of a Supreme Mind, which also keeps the stars in their courses and thinks eternal, universal thoughts.

The question of whether there is purpose in the universe finds the idealist on the affirmative side. This belief is consistent with the idea that man's mind is the microcosm and the Perfect Mind is the macrocosm. It also is consistent with the idea of man's striving toward perfection.

The modern idealist also is interested in the development of man's attitudes, feeling, insights, motives, vision, body, emotions, social self, and the spark of the divine within him.

Philosophy, through its branches, eventually sets the quality and the level at which human behavior operates, and human behavior governs the quality of human living. The idealist views his major concerns as intimately and constantly connected with such aspirations.

Implications of Idealism for Physical Education*

Actually, idealistic philosophy embraces principles under which physical education programs can be actively promoted. *First,* there is the classical Greek example, which current humanists revere. *Second,* there is the emphasis on transfer of training, on which the faculty psychology strongly depends for its justification, and with this there is the additional emphasis on the cultivation of moral values—all of which lead to the deliberate inauguration of sports participation to obtain the high ideals of sportsmanship, courage, individual initiative, justice (fair play), and aesthetic appreciation. *Third,* individualism and self-discipline also appear both as philosophic ideals and as outcomes of physical education programs. *Fourth,* the idealistic emphasis on things of the spirit does not require, logically, a negation of interests in the body, so long as the levels of importance are defined. *Fifth,* the idealistic push toward perfection (one's highest potential) is reflected in that part of the physical education program emphasizing competitive athletics. *Sixth* is the persistent striving again and again for the highest achievement after each failure and, for that matter, after each successful endeavor—a setting of a higher goal toward which to strive. Inherent in the athletic program is this built-in set-up for idealism. One never masters a sport, for always lying ahead is the perfect performance.

The writings of Herman Harrell Horne are somewhat expressive of contemporary idealistic thought regarding physical education. Horne has been classified both as an idealistic theist and as a personalist (a philosophic variant presented in Chapter 12).

Horne's definition of idealistic education is that "Education is the eternal process of superior adjustment of the physically and mentally developed, free, conscious human being to God as manifested in the intellectual, emotional and volitional environment of man."[54]

Physical education for Horne would be a necessary element in education, "Because of the influence of the body on the mind . . . because of the constant attention the body and brain should receive . . . and have received in the past. . . ." Horne pointed out that self-activity leading to self-development is not an abstract process that has little relation to bodily or temporal factors. "To develop the self certainly includes development of the body and fully embraces physical education."[54] For Horne, play is the method the individual takes in preserving himself and his freedom.[54] Further implication of the objectives of physical education is made in his declaration that the educated individual should be "physically fit," be able to "play with his children and have a truly fine time,"

* We are grateful for the permission given by the William C. Brown Company to use considerable material in this section taken from *Philosophies Fashion Physical Education* (currently out of print).[24]

should "live near the maximum of his efficiency," and should have "a body which is the ready servant of his will."[53] Although he would put these qualities of "good health" at the bottom of the hierarchy of educational values, Horne would "yet esteem it (health) highly as a basic value for all others, enhancing the richness of each and all of them."[52]

The following brief expositions bring together a few additional basic threads indicating what the idealistic philosophy means in general and in physical education in particular. At the same time, it seems necessary to remind ourselves that some idealist may find some statements to which he does not give assent.

Objectives of Education

The idealist has a spiritual destiny to fulfill and the objective of education is to help him do this. Horne, affirming the ultimate worth of the personality, said that "there is nothing higher or more valuable than selfhood or personality."[52]

Because the personality has ultimate worth (self-realization), achievement of a superior life is the objective for the individual. Every opportunity is opened for the person to grow to his full stature physically, intellectually, morally, and mentally.

Greene, believing that the school is the only agency whose primary responsibility is to stress knowledge and the development of the mind, urged the schools not to become involved in too many tasks that are functions of other institutions.[46]

Idealistic objectives are most likely to be met in liberal arts studies and in the liberal pursuits thought of as exercises of mind, of reason, of reflection. Physical education may be suited for inclusion in a liberal education. As described by Williams, John Henry Newman (Catholic idealist) pointed out, "There are bodily exercises which are liberal, and mental exercises which are not so." A physical education activity has the capacity for being liberal in Newman's description to the extent that it is undertaken for its own sake, for the sake of the perfection which belongs to the activity itself, for the knowledge imparted, rather than being engaged in for such utilitarian reasons as to be amused, refreshed, put in good spirits.[125]

Horne suggested that the body cannot be developed without touching the mind at many points. Because man reflects an absolute whole, he is developing the whole of man many times when at vigorous play. As Horne stated the matter, "The spontaneous physical expression of individuality is play."[54]

The outcomes of physical education, therefore, are viewed as values if they are good to and for man. Health is esteemed in the hierarchy of idealistic values because it enhances and makes surer and richer the realization of the social, moral, and spiritual-mental aims.

Values

Idealists declare that major values are permanent or unchanging, not man-made, but rather a part of the universe.

Values are of unique importance and provide the first occasion for reflective decision. The school, therefore, has a responsibility to provide opportunity freely for the consideration of values.

The spiritual-mental ideals in idealism, such as truth, beauty, and good, are the true objectives of education. Such essential realities (or ideals) call for exposing each pupil to the best of the past, man's finest thoughts, the accumulated superior heritage of the race.

Thus, the idealist is basically a traditionalist in physical education. As elsewhere, he believes in the tried and true. Physical education under idealism, like any other subject matter or activity, is a means of providing for the full development of the individual's intellect, creative powers, and moral values that are in harmony with highest ideals. Physical education, therefore, is concerned with the production and enjoyment of the beautiful and with the acquisition of such ideal virtues as understanding, cooperation, self-sacrifice, courage.

Students are directed toward the wisdom of the race, accumulated since time immemorial, and permitted to recreate truth, beauty and goodness in their thoughts, feelings, and actions. The teaching of such values as fair play, respect for others, integrity, and character is not left to chance or imitation. Provision is made for self-activity of the student through discussion, analysis, decision-making, and selection in the areas of moral values and ethical behavior. The individual, the ultimate moral *end,* is never treated merely as a *means* for another's self-gratification, selfish ambitions, and personal gains.

Curriculum or Program Building

The curriculum, for the idealist, is built to consider the abilities and needs of the learners, the legitimate demands of society and the universe. The curriculum would be stable, include the tried and true, and the learner would not be exposed to fads and frills which reflect irresponsible change. Because such changes do not represent the best of the past they often lead to blind alleys.

The curriculum includes essential disciplines (for most idealists this means the fine arts and the practical arts, as well as language, logic, mathematics, science, philosophy, history, geography). These areas interweave to provide a stimulating and cultural education. As pointed out previously, a narrow view of liberal education would be inconsistent with the philosophy of a Catholic idealist such as Newman. He proposed that "manly games or games of skill" are accounted liberal if they are pursued for their own sake and aim at achieving a "habit of mind . . . of which the attributes are freedom, equitableness, calmness, moderation, and wisdom."[46] No distinction is made between curricular and extracurricular activities because such distinction is inconsistent with total personality.

Curriculum planning is done by teachers. Because achieving the ideals of man cannot be left to chance, students have only a limited part to play in curriculum planning.[52]

The curriculum is ideal-centered with emphasis placed on the development of self toward perfection, leading the learner toward his ultimate potential. It would involve objective content and book learning. The emphasis on self-improvement means that the program is expected to provide students with opportunities to develop self-reliance, self-responsibility, self-direction, self-examination, and the like.

As the idealist physical educator considers the best development of the student's personality, he often makes certain that the student actually makes connections between a program of selected activities and important aspects of living. He also helps the student seek balance and breadth in a program of muscular activity. The kind of perfection that he envisions includes the individual's being aware of, appreciating, and feeling such attributes as beauty and grace; seeking that which is true and genuine; striving toward the good for others and self; and promoting and practicing justice.

The Learner and the Learning Process

The nature of learning to the idealist is considered to be an unfolding and transferring of personal innate absolutes by reflective thinking to a way of living. The idealist sees the importance of learning as enabling the student to develop himself to his highest potential.

The learner is considered to be a spiritual-mental-physical whole. He is mind-body-soul, constituting an organic unity of self. He is not merely a biologic organism responding only to the natural environment. Because man is the kind of a whole that he is and the human center of the universe, learning takes place within the self of the learner. This self contains the momentum for its own growth. Only through a voluntary act of will can the individual educate himself.

The body is the physical expression of the nature of the soul and is responsive to the will. In physical education, therefore, the development of strength, fitness, skill, posture, physique are not *ends* to be developed for their sakes; rather they are *means* that contribute to spiritual-mental ends.

The Teacher and Teaching

The idealist teacher is more important than facilities, equipment, or any physical thing. He occupies the central position as the representative and purveyor of all culture. He plays the major role as the source and symbol and force behind such services as selection and interpretation of the best of that which is known, setting the stage and climate for learning, selecting subject matter, and leading students into higher levels of attainment, insights, maturities, and broader knowledges.

The idealist physical educator must be worthy of imitation, inspiring effort toward greater achievement by his personal example of wholesome, vigorous living, and as a personality. He is firm, yet friendly, with a thorough knowledge of his subject and of his students. Thus, the idealist teacher also becomes the student, the seeker after true and comprehensive knowledge. The real challenge for him and his students is the best use of every appropriate resource—past and present, within and without—in the effort to actualize the ideal.

How subjects are taught is at least as important as what is taught. The idealist, believing he is responsible for his effectiveness, does not feel confined to one way of teaching. He may select several differing methods —the best methods. He strives to use them with finesse. For example, he may create a slight feeling of suspense that leads the student to self-activity. Some methods most common to the idealist teacher include questioning and discussion (informal dialectic); the lecture in which precepts, beliefs, and interpretation are offered, not merely a recitation of facts; and the project method employing constructive and creative work.

Although the idealistic tendency is to stress the personality rather than the subject taught, increasing the student's store of knowledge also is regarded as of consequence. For the idealist, this knowledge is true knowledge. Facts, too, are *means* to fuller self-development in helping the student reach the ideal of complete knowledge. In physical education, in the idealist custom, the student is helped to see and appreciate the *word* side, the *idea* side, and the *knowledge* side of physical education, and formulate concepts of skills into words.

Traditionally, the lecture method and assigned readings are usually associated with idealism. Through such media the student learns, if he will, such essentials as sociomoral standards and conduct.

Use also may be made of group discussion, the question–answer way of arriving, or attempting to arrive, at truth. Physical educators, too, make use of the question technique in revealing sources and degrees of student understandings. Student questions are encouraged and serve as an index to ethical development, personality improvement, completeness of knowledge, and degree of insight into that which is being learned.

For the idealist, direct, personal experience of the student needs to be augmented and enriched. Nor is time wasted in needless trial and error. It would not be sensible for the student to learn *through experience* things that are not good for him. Let him follow the path well blazed by the best of the past. Students are, in contrast with experiencing everything directly, surrounded by positive influences and their attention focused on worthy eminent persons and inspiring literary works, and are provided with opportunities for self-initiative and self-direction.

Idealists favor freedom and authority as opposed to authoritarianism and permissivism. Students are challengingly confronted with difficulties to force their efforts and to gain disciplined achievement, through freedom to do something not freedom to do anything. Interest is utilized to evoke effort, but external discipline may be employed to stimulate effort leading to interest and to establish the habit of self-discipline.

Evaluation

Evaluation to the idealist is not concerned with the mechanics of activities, specific knowledges, quantitative measures of success, but rather with changes in self. Outcomes in physical education, as in any other area of education, are evaluated in terms of the self-education developed.

Part of the concern of any idealist in physical education pushes to the fore an emphasis on the intellect. He also is concerned with character development and related matters, which in turn generate concern about personality development and temperament formation. These, then, are some of the items that the idealist wants to evaluate and grade.

Whenever possible, the idealist also prefers to compare a student's abilities with national norms. He finds it challenging to compare a student's abilities with his (the teacher's) estimates of what these abilities ought to be. His interest includes not only that which the student does but also that which he knows, thinks, feels, and is. In addition, he wants to evaluate and grade such elements as student behavior, citizenship and sociomoral conduct, with highest standards as the basis of comparison. He is not fearful of the subjective grading of subjective phenomena.

Because the idealist wants to see things in perspective, he seeks to find out how the student envisions physical education's fitting into the educational matrix. In fact, how well does the student see physical education's fitting into the whole of his life and into the life of a people? In similar fashion, how well does the student see his present status? How well does he see it in comparison with his best self, with his highest potential?

Not all the idealist's concerns are abstract. Part of the student's grade comes from how well he retained what he read and studied. Another part comes from respectable written assignments. Still another part of the grade may be an estimate of the student's ability to synthesize the avowed purposes and actual outcomes of his physical education experiences. How well has the student caught the values of physical education? What of his beliefs, ideas, and expectations of physical education?

The Administrator and Administration

The acid test of effective administration for the idealist administrator is whether or not those under him (including students) grow and develop toward increased self-fulfillment. His concern for their growth means that he deals personally, humbly, and understandingly, yet firmly, with those under him. He is apt to talk things over with teachers, but is not reluctant to make his own decisions and carry out his self-appointed tasks. He does his best, observes the results, and if necessary, modifies his method.

He selects teachers on the basis of personality, high ideals, knowledge of subject. Promotion or salary increase is determined on the basis of merit rather than an across-the-board remuneration.

In terms of curriculum improvement and similar concerns, he considers that the school personnel, rather than the community, knows best.

Teacher Preparation

The idealist's concern in professional preparation is to help the student discover his inner sources of talent, to help him unlock himself, to help him make the effort to improve, to give of himself in whatever he is doing. "It is not necessary to live, it is necessary only to sail the seas" is the Hanseatic League vision held out for the student. "But what is your best?" is the question with which the student would be confronted.

The idealist physical educator does not play a part in keeping tomorrow's physical educators narrowly educated. He emphasizes the importance of a broad education and quality of human living. The sustaining nutriment more important than skills development, knowledge of facilities, and the like is to encourage such marks of excellence as self-direction, dedication, the ability to think reflectively, the ability to communicate, the ability to analyze, synthesize, and discriminate.

Trying to prod thinking or to stimulate feelings, of course, escapes the walls of course content, being satisfied with letting students merely know about, or permitting students to pursue only their interests and pleasant ways. Most professional preparation is not factual. Rather, it is very much a matter of such subjective phenomena as judgments, relationships, beliefs, and values. Teacher education should provide perfect models by exposition, by assigning intensive study or wide reading, and the like. The professional responsibility is to challenge, test, and apply these ingredients in new combinations in all experiences which the student is charged with mastering or striving to surmount.

Comments and Criticisms

The strength of idealism may be said to lie in its respect of man's infinite potential for growth, its stress on emotional and spiritual experiences that transcend the materialistic aspects of life, and its provisions for total personality development—cultivation of powers of the mind as well as development of strong bodies and beautiful souls.

Especially significant in idealism is the concept that the personality has ultimate worth. Such a concept of man has a hearty positivism. Man is a self that can rise above misfortune and win without external aid, he can aim for the stars, and he can make the most of himself. The companion feature of selfhood, that the self is invisibly linked to other selves and the whole universe of being, offers many persons a clear insight into the spiritual and moral dimensions of life. The method of thinking characteristic of philosophers of idealism, the so-called dialectic or antithetical method, derived from Socrates, elaborated in Platonic dialogues, and gradually developed and revised by later idealistic philosophers, when used within limits will always remain a valuable instrument of philosophic thought.

For some contemporary thinkers, the philosophers and theories of idealism seem hopelessly remote, inflexible, and obsolete. Kant's ethics—his theory of innate *a priori* absolute moral sense, his advocacy of duty for duty's sake—was dealt with harshly by some nineteenth century critics.[37] Hegel's concept of strife—the idea that a man reaches his full height only through responsibility and adversity—is declared by some critics to be a truth just for Hegel's time. Of Plato it was observed that he lacked a sense of flux and change, his "moving picture of the world becomes a fixed and still tableau. . . . He loves order exclusively . . . his state is static . . . it worships the name of beauty. . . ."[37]

Some critics repudiate the idealistic appeal to a transcendent being or process. The current exhortation to "do your own thing," the idea of a divine authority who alone knows what is good or true seems to be outmoded dogma. Yet in an idealistic vein, it is contended that the world suffers from a spiritual crisis within the soul of man and that the search for spirituality is everywhere. The current drug culture, the interest in the occult, and the newest of the various techniques of pursuing self-awareness are cited as indicative of the attempt to find some sort of religious experience. Even sport is regarded by some persons as a current substitute for religion, the opiate of the masses. Whether or not these so-called substitutes do justice to human aspiration, the idealist belief is that religious faith is the substance of things hoped for, and belief in an Ultimate Person is a unifying principle providing drive and direction to life's efforts.[63]

Certainly in today's increasingly permissive society with its open marriages, legalized abortions, wide use of drugs, pornographic literature, and X-rated movies, a number of arguments are presented against reliance on immutable moral codes. The basic claim is made that as long as those involved share of their own free will, moral absolutes are of no consequence. Reasonable idealists emphasize, however, that, although idealism emphatically insists on the freedom for self-determination, self-activity should lead to ever-higher, ever-richer experiences.

As Durant points out, "after a century of reaction against the absolutism of Kant's ethics, we find ourselves again in a welter of urban sensualism and immorality, of ruthless individualism untempered with democratic conscience or aristocratic honor; and perhaps the day soon will come when a disintegrated civilization will welcome again the Kantian call to duty.[37] Durant also acknowledged that although Plato described an ideal Utopia difficult to attain, "he answers that there is a value in painting these pictures of our desire; man's significance is that he can image a better world, and will some part of it at least into reality. . . ."[37] Durant himself asserted that perhaps more needed than ever in a world besieged by violence and chaos, the horrors of war, the neglect of ecology, and the swallowing up of economic surplus is the consolation of religious hope, an alleviating vision of man striving for a vaster life.

Idealism's emphasis on improvement toward the perfect self has led some critics to observe that the idealist would eventually become a defeatist, because perfection is never attainable. Strange as it may seem, the idea that the ideal is there not only constantly draws the idealist on and motivates him, but also represents a kind of stability because of his belief that his own mind is but a transient replica of the Perfect Mind.

Physical educators and participants in sports, as well as others in the performance arts, readily understand reaching toward perfection. In spite of the discomfort of failure, the quest for a better performance goes on. Never has the Hegelian concept, that struggle is the law of growth, assumed a loftier place than in modern Olympics where aiming high and striving hard, even in the face of overwhelming obstacles, are themes that dominate the contest. Seemingly, in the words of Phillip Brooks, "The ideal life is in our blood and never will be still. We feel the things to be beating beneath the things we are."

Other critics avow that idealism's emphasis on the individual self lacks a social consciousness, it neglects the importance of others. On the contrary, the idealist regards sociomoral standards of conduct as outcomes of the individual's highest capability, in terms of both his inner relationships and his social relationships. Although idealism insists on the freedom for self-determination, it emphasizes that such self-determination take place within a matrix of social concern.[24] Kant declared, "Act so that in your own person as well as the person of every other you are treating mankind also as an end, never merely as a means." The idealist teacher believes in the importance of passing on the social and cultural heritage as a way of handling perennial social problems and improving society, not just as a means of preserving culture. Infusing students with a "passion for social justice" through stressing knowledge and development of the mind is the role of the school in society.[46]

One of the features of idealism that perplexes many physical educators is the dualistic view of man. They see the dualism of mind and body as exerting a detrimental effect on physical education—the body is sent to the gymnasium and the mind to the classroom. Although physical educators may be dissatisfied with the idealistic hierarchy of values, which places physical education on the low rung of the educational ladder, they may gather solace from the explanation that idealism does not negate the importance of physical fitness and sound health. It merely places them somewhat lower in a hierarchy of desirable aims in life—bodily development is a means to the end of truth, beauty, and goodness.

Early Christianity, with the ascetic concept that ultimate salvation is made possible by elevating the mind (soul) through punishment of the evils of the body, certainly helped to promote the idea that play is wicked; thus, physical education might be regarded as catering to demands of the flesh or lower self. This early influence, however, has been negated by more recent Christian churches and church-related institutions. Health, physical education, and recreation are today an integral part of such organizations as the YWCA and the Church of Jesus Christ of Latter-Day-Saints. Several organizations and groups are voices for the Christian idealistic life in sports, physical education, and recreation. The role of sports, as a medium of spiritual and moral enrichment, has led to the establishment of the Fellowship of Christian Athletes (FCA). This group, conceived of by a physical education student and now supported by religious leaders and sport stars, has made considerable gains in membership and in impact on the lives of coaches and athletes. In the idealistic tradition, emphasis is placed on the importance of outstanding personalities to awaken the dormant potential of the young. It is the belief of supporters of the FCA that the hero worship accorded coaches and athletes by millions of people "is inherently neither good or evil but a medium out of which either may come!"[26a]

Sports, games, and play activities have been variously perceived by many persons as playing a leading role in developing the ultimate personality—the ideal virtues of self-sacrifice, courage, sportsmanship, and the like—and the basic values of the good life—health, skill, beauty, knowledge, noble achievement, and the like. The standard recital of benefits of competitive athletics to participants, spectators, community, school, and nation is equally familiar and shot through with idealistic motives and goals. Unfortunately, in some quarters the problems that beset contemporary athletics provide disconcerting thought for those who seek high standards of morality in sports. In many areas where sports have become big business, the materialistic goals mitigate against any *a priori* ideal of building character and other desirable personality values. Results of inquiries point to such moral and ethical excesses as exploitation of the athlete, competitive overemphasis, overzealous recruiting, unhealthy pressure for victory, commercialism, drug abuse.[47a] The win-at-all-cost philosophy even infected the Soap Box Derby, and the anti-hero antics of some athletes, who put aside moral obligations, as attested by the vast literature in the world of professional sports, seem to suggest that idealism in sport is dead. Perhaps now more than ever, there is need to get a regrip on idealism, which preaches the ennobling worship of heroes and to, as did Schopenhauer, "force philosophy to face the raw reality of evil, and . . . point the nose of thought to the human tasks of alleviation."[37]

IF HE IS INDEED WISE HE DOES NOT BID YOU ENTER THE HOUSE OF HIS WISDOM BUT RATHER LEADS YOU TO THE THRESHOLD OF YOUR MIND.

—Kahlil Gibran

10

Realism

LET US SUPPOSE THE MIND TO BE, AS WE SAY, WHITE PAPER
VOID OF ALL CHARACTERS, WITHOUT ANY *ideas*. HOW COMES
IT TO BE FURNISHED? WHENCE COMES IT BY THAT VAST
STORE WHICH THE BUSY AND BOUNDLESS FANCY OF MAN HAS
PAINTED ON IT WITH ALMOST ENDLESS VARIETY? WHENCE
HAS IT ALL THE MATERIALS OF REASON AND KNOWLEDGE?
TO THIS I ANSWER, IN ONE WORD, FROM EXPERIENCE; . . .

—*John Locke*

Early Realists

Although Aristotle is considered by some to be the father of realism, and although others regard Plato as the first to explicitly set forth concepts that Aristotle developed, the nuclei of scientific thinking began centuries before either was born. Egyptians observed the annual flooding of the Nile as Mesopotamians noticed the rhythmic cycles of the stars. To both, nature was orderly, dependable, systematic. She operated according to plan. Such a plan could be found by man. Thus, man discovered nature's laws. This led to the conjecture that nature must have laws that fitted other phases of life. This quest suggested the possibility that there might even be laws governing man's affairs, all within the basic framework of nature. Ancient Grecian scientist-philosophers and philosopher-scientists of the sixth and fifth centuries B.C. also noted many recurring events in nature.

It took the kind of mind which Aristotle later evidenced to formulate the beginnings of realism. The Pythagoreans, ancient Greeks, and, later medieval Schoolmen, the foremost of whom was St. Thomas Aquinas, nurtured and passed along these seeds of science.

Two representative initial roots of realism—those epitomized by Aristotle and Aquinas—are sketched in the sections immediately following. Then the development of their common, major philosophic position, cate-

gorized into three eras (Middle Centuries, Early Modern, and Recent
and Contemporary Realistic Thought) is discussed. This development is
accomplished chiefly by giving point to the major beliefs of a number of
primary and secondary realists selected from the fifteenth to the twentieth
centuries. Finally, the implications of realism for various facets and
aspects of physical education are presented for consideration and study.

Aristotle (384–322 B.C.)

Aristotle, Plato's pupil and subsequent rival, is important in the history of idealism, as well as in that of realism. Perhaps he was a realist
more in scientific attitude than anything else because of his initial instruction. After he gained his own momentum, Aristotle organized and advanced substantial investigations in natural history, biology, and speculative physics. His work in logic, although limited narrowly to syllogism,
became both his glory and later condemnation. Reason to Aristotle was
the highest virtue. Although Aristotle's contributions to philosophy are
outstanding, his deductive logic unfortunately led to arbitrary assertions
and to the deification of pure reason.

Aristotle rejected Plato's metaphysics, differing most fundamentally on
the separation between the ordinary, sensed world of experience and the
other world. Unlike Plato, there seemed to be nothing otherworldly
about the world to Aristotle. For Plato, ideas were eternal forms whose
real existence was in another realm. For Aristotle, forms existed in things
or in the world, although he considered forms to be unchanging and the
proper object of highest thought. The regularity and orderliness of the
world were due to the presence of mind, pattern, and eternal purpose.
The use of the mind or reason was, for Aristotle, the highest function of
the soul.

Another idea of significance, which the West inherited from Aristotle,
and which differed mainly in emphasis from that of Plato, was presented
in his treatise on ethics (*Nicomachean Ethics*). Aristotle's idea of the
good life was the life of happiness (eudaemonia). Gathering together
strands of traditional thought (the materialism of pre-Socratics and the
idealism of the Socratics), Aristotle's own philosophic thought regarding good was the doctrine of the golden mean: "Nothing in excess."
Unlike Plato who felt that goodness was absolute, Aristotle believed that
goodness was different for each man and that there could be many
different goods of good lives. It was the concept of good as a *relative*
virtue. To achieve eudaemonia (the closest synonym in English is happiness), for Aristotle, was to succeed in living the good life. Again,
unlike Plato who was inclined to think of eudaemonia as a personally
inner condition, Aristotle regarded the good life in terms of good conduct in relation to others, a public affair. Because of the influence that
he had, which was later enormously expanded, Aristotle turned Western

thought into a channel that led away from the direction first given to it by Socrates and to which Plato gave assent: a deep concern for the inner man. In fact, only by faltering, slipping steps is the West today moving in the direction which Socrates gave philosophic thought and a way of life. Thus, in a sense, Aristotle went back to the pre-Socratics and built on the structure they started to build.

Aristotle's golden mean, or moderation, meant the avoidance of all extremes in all things. Courage, for example, was the mean or ideal balance between the extremes of cowardice and foolhardiness. Moderation, however, did not mean mediocrity. The maximum development of human potential was in keeping with Aristotle's belief that material things had an innate striving toward *arête,* an ultimate goal or ideal destiny. "Excellence much labored for by the race of men" seems to sum up Aristotle's idea of constant striving for an absolute pure form. Again, the borrowings by Aristotle and the Greeks' borrowings from prior persons and times should be acknowledged. The idea of excellence in many things goes back over 400 years to Hesiod, the peasant poet.

What do the foregoing concepts have to do with physical education? It may be assumed that in the practice of physical education, as in the pursuit of other processes of life, Aristotelian concepts of inseparability of mind and body, the avoidance of extremes, the striving for arête or excellence are typical. Moderation is implied in Aristotle's *Sane Comments on Athletics.* What is wanted in education of the body is "not the bodily condition of an athlete nor . . . a valetudinarian and invalid condition, but one that lies between the two." Statements by Aristotle, as well as Plato, often justify physical education merely on the basis of practical and worldly exigencies.

It appears that both Plato and Aristotle endorsed the idea of the contribution of a physical education to the total education and high moral destiny of man. From ages seven to fourteen, the schools, according to Aristotle (*Politics*), were to be primarily concerned with developing moral character through light gymnastic exercises and some literary instruction. Aristotle stated, "The education of the body must precede that of the intellect, it clearly follows that we must surrender our children in the first instance to gymnastic and the art of the trainer." Aristotle, along with Plato, stated what has come to be known as the cathartic theory of physical activity: that preoccupation and expenditure of energy in physical activities help to extirpate vice and direct animal spirits toward constructive, rather than immoral, ends.

St. Thomas Aquinas (c. 1225–1274)

The philosophy of scholasticism or Thomism emerged in medieval times. The Scholastics, also known as the Schoolmen, consisted of a group of Catholic philosophers. Aquinas became the most influential of them. He was interested in reconciling the beliefs of the Greek philosophers (chiefly Aristotle) with the theological beliefs of the medieval church. According to Aquinas (and Aristotle), truth could be discovered through the activities of the mind, but in the Christian tradition truth is the revelation of God through faith.

Aquinas drew heavily on Aristotle, whom he called "The Philosopher." For Aquinas, as for Aristotle, the universe was composed of matter and form. In Aquinas' hierarchy, God was ultimate reality and below Him were the angels, saints, humans, animals, inanimate matter.

Where Plato had used the word "ideas" and Aristotle "forms," Aquinas used "universals." Aquinas argued that universals were real and manifested their existence in particular objects. For example, a tree has merely external manifestations ("accidents") such as size, shape, weight. That which indicates the relationship, however, of a birch tree with a maple tree is a universal (essence) of "treeness." Although the senses can receive the particulars (birch, maple), it is the intellect (mind) that has the intuitive power to separate the essential qualities of the universals or essences from those brought in by the senses. At the same time, there are other knowledges of such things as God, angels, or moral principles which do not come through the senses, as do particular objects such as trees. According to Aquinas all universals exist first in the mind of God, who created the world of universals and matter together to produce things which man can know.

The educational implications of the Thomist position led to a belief that certain basic religious truths are important as knowledge in their own right, and assert a fundamental aim in terms of shaping the human being.

Several contemporary writers have turned to an interpretation of the Scriptures in order to discuss what they consider to be a relationship between Christianity and physical education.[8] Also, Davis drew from the Scriptures five concepts which he calls the biblical basis of physical education.

1. The body is an integral constituent of human personality;
2. the body of man is good;
3. the welfare of the body is essential to the welfare of the human personality;
4. the physical condition of the personality is secondary in importance to its spiritual condition;
5. motor experiences provide the individual with normal instruments of expression and find their highest value when used for the achievement of the abundant life.[25]

The famed English churchman John Henry Cardinal Newman, in *The Idea of a University*, suggested the bold proposition that "manly games or games of skill" can be accounted liberal in the sense that such bodily exercises are undertaken for their own sake, that they form and cultivate the intellect, rather than being pursued for utilitarian reasons.[125]

The Thomist position also appears to allow for intellectual aspects gained through physical education. Thomism's insistence on psychosomatic unity, as Rachel M. Goodrich stated, "Results, incidentally, in a proper appreciation of physical education interpreted not only as Gymnastics and Athletics; but also as the training of physical and aesthetic skills, and the perfecting of sense experiences as the gateway to knowledge."[17]

Perhaps typical of the Thomistic position concerning physical education are some of the views of more recent Catholic leaders and the cooperative, receptive attitude of the Protestant churches. For example, Pope Pius XI in his Encyclical Letter of 1961 stated: "We condemn only what is excessive, as for example . . . exaltation of athleticism, which even in classic pagan times marked the decline and downfall of genuine physical training."[17] Commenting further on the world and its dangers for the adolescent, Pope Pius XI warned of the necessity of "providing for occasions for good in his recreations."[17]

Realism in the Middle Centuries

The Renaissance of the fourteenth and fifteenth centuries, the Reformation of the sixteenth century, and the Enlightenment of the eighteenth century gave considerable impetus to realistic thought. What were the forces that powered the apparent trend from idealism toward realism during the Renaissance?

On the one hand, realism developed as a negative reaction to the increasingly rigid organization of humanism around the literary phases of the classical subjects such as Latin grammar or mathematics, and to the doctrine of the mental discipline believed to be automatically developed by study of these subjects. On the other hand, realism, now in a stage of vital growth, developed as a positive reaction to the findings of science. In addition, many other cultural forces were active, for example, the manifold influences of the society of the time, and the school's responsibility in shaping the individual to society.

Philosophers who clearly demonstrate the transitional humanist-realist position include the Spanish noble Juan Luis Vives (1492–1540); Francois Rabelais (c. 1483–1553) the French monk-turned-physician who advocated a reformed educational system by describing the education of his mythical characters, Gargantua and Pantagruel; the scholarly English philosopher-poet John Milton; and the French essayist Michel de Montaigne.

Francis Bacon was one of the first spokesmen of modern scientific methods. In keeping with the spirit of his philosophy were the statements of the sense realists, who were impressed with the potential values of broad sense experience and the inductions which could be fashioned from them. In the group of sense realists were two outstanding educational philosophers: the famous English headmaster Richard Mulcaster (c. 1531–1611), and the Czech educational reformer John Amos Comenius.

In the following pages brief expositions are presented of the ideas of Bacon and Comenius as representatives of the sense realists, and of Milton and Montaigne as representatives of the humanistic realists.

Michel de Montaigne (1533–1592)

The French essayist Montaigne, although following the humanists by representing the aristocratic tradition and by endorsing the principles of liberal education in the classics, demonstrated the influence of realism by his advocacy of education for participation in the world of affairs and by his disavowal of extreme mind–body dualism.

His essays *On the Education of Children (De l'Institution des Enfants)* and *On Pedantry (Du Pedantisme)* express surprisingly modern educational views. For Montaigne, the physical, intellectual, and spiritual aspects of man's life were closely interrelated. Physical education, therefore, received important consideration as a prerequisite for a healthy, thoughtful and moral individual, because "the soul will be oppressed if not assisted by the members. . . ." Montaigne advised, "our very exercises and recreations, running, wrestling, music, dancing, hunting, riding, and fencing will prove to be a good part of our study. I would have [the student's] outward fashion and mien, and the disposition of his limbs, formed at the same time with his mind. 'Tis not a soul, 'tis not a body that we are training up, but a man, and we ought not to divide him. And, as Plato says, we are not to fashion one without the other, but make them draw together like two horses harnessed to a coach."[48a]

Rejecting the medieval idea of neglecting the body in favor of the soul, Montaigne observed that it was not enough to toughen the spirit, the muscles also must be made strong. ". . . for the soul will be oppressed if not assisted by the members, and would have too hard a task to discharge two offices alone."[48a]

Francis Bacon (1561–1626)

Francis Bacon, an English statesman, philosopher, and essayist, profoundly influenced the next generation of English realists. The traditional view of Bacon is as the primary investigator of modern scientific progress and the leading exponent of the revolt against the Aristotelian and Scholastic traditions. He is recognized for his formulation and presentation of the new induction, in which the syllogism (deduction) of Aristotle gives place to inductive reasoning. In the *Novum Organum,* the new instrument of inductive experimental method, Bacon discussed the uselessness of older philosophies, advocating that men's minds must be cleared of idols (prejudices, customs, words, great names) involuntarily worshipped. He proposed that experimental methods be encouraged. Because senses can be deceived, perceptions must be controlled by experience. Although Bacon believed the observer should keep his own personality under subjection, he advocated "a marriage between the empirical and rational." Inductive thinking (establishing generalized principles after making observations and collecting facts), as publicized by Bacon, promoted new concepts in seeking knowledge and consequently, considerably influenced teaching methods.

In *Advancement of Learning*, Bacon set forth the ideal of human service as the goal of scientific effort. In ethics, Bacon's distinction between individual or "self-good" and "good of communion" is believed to have pointed forward to the doctrine of later utilitarians.

Van Dalen and co-workers, quoting from Bacon and other sources, present Bacon's views regarding the physical aspects of education.[115] Bacon wrote about the body as being the tabernacle of the mind: "there seemeth to be a relaxation or conformity between the good of the mind and the good of the body." Dividing the good of the body into "health, beauty, strength, and pleasure," Bacon observed, "there is scarcely any tendency to disease which may not be prevented by some proper exercise."

Bacon's ideas stirred the thinking of many educators among whom was the Englishman Richard Mulcaster, who wrote two volumes on education: the *Elementaire* and *Positions*. In *Positions* he declared that it is as necessary to train youth for "health in their bodie" as for "skill in their booke."

John Amos Comenius (1592–1670)

A Czech theologian and educator writing his educational theories in the seventeenth century, Comenius gained widespread popularity. Comenius built on Plato's theory of implicit ideas and Aquinas' theory of man's inherent potential to know. Comenius anticipated Pestalozzi's "germ possession" theory over a century before Pestalozzi was born. Comenius held that there is nothing in the universe (i.e., knowledge, morality, religion) "which cannot be compassed by man endowed with sense and reason." From such a theory of man, Comenius developed postulates for education which he asserted to be in harmony with the universe and the natural inclinations of the learner.

Lawson and Silver point out that "Comenius believed that the end of education is the comprehension of all nature ('pansophia') through reason, the senses and revelation, and that education should be extended to everybody through a system of graded schools. . . , using reformed teaching methods and textbooks."[74] His educational theory emphasized the nature of the child and sense-perception instead of the usual authoritarian teaching methods and rote memorization. To facilitate learning through the senses, Comenius wrote *Orbis Sensualium Pictus* (1658), which may well be the first *illustrated* school book. The treatise, which contains both a Latin and vernacular text, includes a number of drawings depicting objects to be found in the child's environment. Among the pictures is one entitled "Boyes Sports," which shows boys in contemporary costume playing a variety of games and using equipment like stilts, tops, and balls.

Comenius' writings reveal an attempt to make a science of education by approaching it through the same methods used by the physical sciences.

Comenius departed widely from the traditional Christian concept of body–mind dualism. The following quotations, cited by Van Dalen and associates, give some insight into his ideas.[115] "Nature is God's work, and is an enemy of man only in so far as he does not know it. He must, then, be taught to know Nature; and to know himself." "It is better to play than to be idle, for during play the mind is intent on some object which often sharpens the abilities. In this way children may be early exercised to an active life without any difficulty, since Nature herself stirs them to be something." An educationally progressive sense of freedom and of social humanitarianism was expressed when he wrote, "When they play together children of about the same age, and of equal progress and manners and habits, sharpen each other more effectually, since the one does not surpass the other in depth of invention; there is among them neither assumption of superiority of the one over the other, nor force, dread, or fear; but love, candor, free questioning, and answers about everything; all these are defective in us, their elders." Comenius reminded parents that "a joyful mind is half health. The joy of the heart is the very lifespring of man." The tendency of a philosophy of sense-realism to promote physical education programs was indicated by Comenius' statement, "Although the parents and attendants may be of great service . . . yet children of their own age are of still greater service . . . consequently, boys should meet daily and play together or run about in open places; and this ought not merely to be permitted, but even provided for, with the precaution, however, they do not mingle with depraved associates." Going beyond the aim of exercise for hardening and discipline, as advocated by the humanists, Comenius believed that the health of children should "sustain no damage from bruises, from excess of heat or cold, from too much food or drink, or from hunger or thirst."

John Milton (1608–1674)

John Milton, English poet and a Puritan, was among the noteworthy scholars of the Renaissance. He has been labeled an exponent of verbal realism and a progressive humanist. Verbal realism, like humanism, voiced belief in the worthiness of classical languages and literature, but condemned the shallow goals of humanistic study, in which the study of the classics was limited to such functional concerns as style and form at the expense of meaning.

In his *Tractate on Education,* Milton associated a form of bodily exercise with mental and moral training. (Milton's convictions regarding morality and religion were strong and often revealed in his poetic masterpieces, e.g., in *Comus and Lycidis* and *Paradise Lost.*)

Drawing from the various writings, Van Dalen and co-workers present Milton's views regarding the importance of developing the body as well as the mind.[115] Milton's classical definition of education recalls this theme: "I call, therefore, a complete and generous education, that which fits a man to perform justly, skillfully, and magnanimously all the offices, both private and public, of peace and war." Milton urged the magistrates of the commonwealth to "take into their care . . . the managing of our public sports and festival pastimes . . . Such as may enure and harden our bodies by martial exercises to all warlike skill and performance. . . ." His program, almost exclusively a military training program, proposed "The exercises which I commend first, is the exact use of their weapons to guard, and to strike safely with edge or point . . . they may be also practiced in all the locks and grips of wrestling. . . ." Believing that physical training of youth was to keep them "healthy, nimble, strong and well in breath . . . and to inspire them with a gallant and fearless courage, which will turn into a native and heroic valor . . . ," Milton proposed that, in an academy providing education for boys between ages 12 and 21, the day's work be divided into studies, exercises and due rest: "about an hour and a half ere they eat at noon should be allowed them for exercise and due rest afterwards. . . ." The boys were to be further engaged in military drills for two hours before supper. Milton further observed, "the spirit of man cannot demean itself lively in the body, without some recreating intermission of labour and serious things."

Early Modern Realistic Thought

The thought of the Renaissance and Reformation periods was gradually blended with and assimilated into early modern philosophic thinking.

From such thinkers as John Locke and David Hume (1711–1776), there developed, especially in England, during the eighteenth century an empirical movement that was critical of speculative thinking and metaphysics.

In the eighteenth century a significantly different naturalistic philosophy, containing crucial and revolutionary implications for education and physical education, was proposed by Jean Jacques Rousseau. This naturalism is embodied in both the philosophy of realism and that of pragmatism.

The realism of Francis Bacon was enlarged and extended by Auguste Comte (1798–1857), John Stuart Mill (1806–1873), and Herbert Spencer. The general trend of these philosophies may be termed "scientific realism," growing out of Newtonian physics, the Darwinian theory of organic evolution, and other developments of science. Later, scientific realism built heavily on the new psychologic theories of Thorndike, Terman, Watson, and others.

The idea held by most realists into the nineteenth century, which gave them a common bond, was their opposition to the belief that the classics held the sum of all knowledge, showed the way of knowing, and provided the directional force for living. The realists of this era attempted to put the curriculum on a scientific footing, one that was related to the realities of life.

Brief expositions of the philosophies of Locke, Rousseau, Pestalozzi, and Spencer are presented as representative of forms of early modern realistic thought.

John Locke (1632–1704)

Locke, an Oxford graduate, lecturer, student of medicine, and a physician in the household of Lord Ashley, produced writings in philosophy, economics, finance, theology, and education. His writings on the individual's right to life, liberty, and property had considerable impact on the writers of the Declaration of Independence and of the Constitution of the United States.

Locke denied the existence of innate ideas, an assumption that had remained unchallenged from Plato to Descartes. The movement of thought from Descartes to Kant during the seventeenth and eighteenth centuries was mainly idealistic, centering attention on the knower. The position of John Locke, however, represented an empirical movement, holding that knowledge comes by means of sense perception. In opposition to Leibnitz (personalistic idealism) and others who regarded the self as self-propelled, Locke argued that the mind of man begins as a blank tablet (tabula rasa) on which the world of experience writes its impressions—"there is nothing in the intellect which was not previously in the senses." (This idea was originally expressed by the Pythagoreans.) Locke reintroduced the early Greek distinction between primary qualities (solidarity, form, number) and secondary qualities (color, odors, sounds, tastes) of external objects. This distinction occupied an important concern in all later philosophic thought.

Empiricism received support in the nineteenth and twentieth centuries starting with the rise of science. It gradually led to the attention of linguistic (language analyses) philosophers. Locke's *An Essay Concerning Human Understanding* usually receives an important place among the great works of philosophy.

Locke's *Some Thoughts Concerning Education* was published in 1693. This work, which is based on a series of letters which Locke had written earlier to Edward Clarke regarding Clarke's son, opens with the famous lines: "A Sound Mind in a sound Body, is a short, but full description of a happy State in this World." He summed up his rules concerning the body and health as: "Plenty of *open Air, Exercise,* and *Sleep,* plain *Diet,* no *Wine* or *strong Drink,* and very little or no *Physick,* not too warm and straight *Clothing,* especially the *Head* and *Feet* kept cold, and the *Feet* often us'd to cold Water, and expos'd to wet." The body was to be kept in "strength" and "vigor" so that it would be able to obey and carry out the orders of the mind.[75] Locke also wrote to Mrs. Clarke regarding a similar regime for her daughter Elizabeth.[3]

As an empiricist who believed that the senses were the source of knowledge, it is understandable that Locke would be concerned with the body—a concern which may have been strengthened by his own irregular health, his medical training, and his friendship with Thomas Sydenham, the great clinical physician of the seventeenth century. (Before Sydenham's influence, medicine had for centuries relied heavily on speculation rather than direct observation of the patient.)

For safety and health's sake, Locke advised that children must learn to swim. Dancing he regarded as "that which gives graceful motions all the life, and above all things, manliness and a becoming confidence. . . ." Fencing and riding were looked on as necessary parts of breeding in peace and war, although Locke would rather have his son be a good wrestler than an ordinary fencer.

Locke's views concerning health, physical education, and active recreations had an enormous influence on writers on these topics throughout the eighteenth century and into the nineteenth century. References to Locke appear frequently in the works of authors from several countries. Notwithstanding several criticisms which he has of the English philosopher's ideas concerning education, Rousseau refers to him as "the wise Locke." Locke saw "recreations" as a valuable educational tool: *Recreation* is as necessary as Labour or Food. But because there can be no *Recreation* without Delight, which depends not always on Reason, but oftener on Fancy, it must be permitted Children not only to divert themselves, but to do it after their own Fashion, provided it be innocently, and without Prejudice to their Health; . . ." In a well-regulated educational program, Locke believed, the child would have no reason to go to excesses and could, therefore, usually be allowed to follow his own inclinations. Parents and tutors should endeavor to use such opportunities to foster the child's development: "the useful Exercises of the Body and Mind, taking their Turns, make their Lives and Improvement pleasant in a continu'd Train of *Recreation,* wherein the weary'd Part is constantly reliev'd and refresh'd." It is in children's recreations that they are most likely to "shew their Inclinations and Aptitudes, and thereby direct wise Parents in the Choice both of the Course of Life and Employment they shall design them for, . . ." It is through what parents learn of their children in their recreations, also, that "whatever Bent of Nature they may observe most likely to mislead any of their Children . . ." may be remedied.[75]

Jean Jacques Rousseau (1712–1778)

Elements of the philosophy which Rousseau espoused may be found in the writings of his predecessors and contemporaries. Naturalism, in its literal sense, is the key to Rousseau's philosophy. As a follower of naturalism, he can be linked to some of the most ancient philosophers. In the twentieth century both realism and pragmatism borrow from naturalism, and are considered by some professors of philosophy to come under that categorical heading.

Rousseau reacted violently to the extremely mechanistic concept of the universe, and likewise attacked the dictatorial and highly organized control of aristocratic civilized society. Man was not a mere machine, according to Rousseau, and should not be shackled by the bonds of a mechanical philosophy of science. Instead, he emphasized the human, feeling, sentimental natures of man. He advocated a "return to nature." As against the rigid controls of science and of aristocratic society, Rousseau championed the essential free spirit and individualistic worth of man. He was reacting against the stilted and artificial social and political systems of his time. Where the traditional Christian view depicted man as full of original sin, Rousseau saw man as a naturally pure, good, and right being, unless he became contaminated with societal influences which would make him selfish and evil. The educational implications of these ideas were revolutionary, and their effects on actual educational practice have been monumental.

Rousseau would have the child develop in freedom, naturally, according to his innate tendencies and inclination. For the first four years of life, Rousseau believed, a child's education should be devoted to physical development. Sense training through play, through freedom to follow natural curiosities, and through the stimulation of the natural environment should occupy the child from ages five to 12, during which time he would be protected and isolated from the artificialities and evils of organized civilization. Intellectual and moral training would be started later.

Children should be allowed to be children before they are men. Efforts to invert this order produce "precocious fruits which will have neither maturity nor flavor, and will speedily deteriorate; we shall have young doctors and old children. Childhood has its own way of seeing, thinking and feeling, and nothing is more foolish than to try to substitute our own for them."[95] Physical activities can be used to teach children such things as how to judge distances, heights, weights, use mechanical levers, and a variety of other skills that depend on sense experience. When such things are learned as a part of pleasurable activities, the knowledge will remain with children longer, Rousseau believed. Physical activities can also be utilized to help children develop self-sufficiency and positive moral attitudes. Rousseau's extremely liberal views on education did not extend to girls, however. Having decided that nature intended women to be "passive and weak," Rousseau concluded that "they ought not to have the same education." He believed that the two sexes had quite different interests, and although Rousseau would have girls take exercise, it was intended primarily to make them attractive wives and strong mothers.[95] As a boy passed into the period which Rousseau identifies as ages "twelve to fifteen," he would continue to engage in physical activities, often being challenged to surpass his *own* previous achievements: "Let us see what you can do now (the ditch which was jumped or the load that was carried). In this way I excite him without making him jealous of any one. . . . I see no harm in his being his own rival."[95]

Rousseau's ideas provided a rational foundation for the child-centered school and for truly naturalistic education. Many found immediate expression in a few schools. Teachers and schools, such as Basedow of *The Philanthropium* and Guts Muths of *The Schnepfenthal Educational Institute,* became influential pioneers in modern physical education.

Rousseau's educational plan was distinctly compatible with several important social and economic movements, for example, secularism, sense-realism, laissez-faire capitalism and the Jeffersonian type of democracy.

Johann Heinrich Pestalozzi (1746–1827)

Often celebrated as the intellectual father of modern education, Pestalozzi, Swiss educational reformer, has been labeled a philosophic realist and romantic naturalist. His ideas were considerably influenced by Comenius and Rousseau. Pestalozzi's "germ possession" theory held that the child is created by God and comes into the world possessing, in germ, all the moral, intellectual, and physical powers which should be developed fully by natural means. Along with Comenius, Pestalozzi's theory of man has been considered as a psychophilosophic theory and an early contribution to educational developmentalism, which later was given impetus by such men as G. Stanley Hall in his "science" of adolescence and in the behavioral psychology of Thorndike and others.

The principle of Pestalozzi's method was that of communicating all instruction by direct appeal to the senses and understanding, calling all the powers of the child into exercise instead of merely making him a passive recipient. This method would usually begin with the teacher presenting an object to the learner. The empiricism of Pestalozzi's "Object Lesson" had considerable appeal. His principles are substantially the basis of the normal school system of Europe. The campus of New York's Oswego State College today has a statue to Pestalozzi, a child on his knee and an apple in his hand in symbolic memory of the object lesson.

Pestalozzi put great emphasis on the training of the body in physical education to help the student develop skills and strength that would be useful in his future occupation.

Although believing that the physical advantage of gymnastics was "great and uncontrovertible," Pestalozzi, in his book *Letters,* contended that the moral advantage was as valuable, contributing "not only to render children cheerful and healthy" but also to promote "habits of industry, openness and frankness of character, personal courage, and a manly conduct in suffering pain. . . ."

Gerber reports that Pestalozzi recommended the development of a variety of special exercises for every part of the body, and that specific movements were devised and carried out at his Yverdon school. Children were also provided with hiking, swimming, skating, sledding, various games, and for those whose parents could afford it, dancing and fencing lessons.[45]

Pestalozzi believed physical education must be turned into an art; it must not be left to chance but must proceed according to rules and in a definite order so that it may bring man to the full height of physical capacity of performance. Physical activities must be arranged continuously from the simple to the more complicated.

In the first three decades of the nineteenth century, Pestalozzi's educational theories were brought to the United States by a number of his disciples. One of these was Joseph Neef, who had taught gymnastics and military drill at Pestalozzi's Yverdon school. Neef, a firm believer in healthful exercise and gymnastic activities, authored one of the earlier textbooks on education printed in America. It contained a substantial section devoted to the importance of physical exercises and games, and instruction for teachers to provide these for their pupils. Neef, like Pestalozzi, stressed the educational value of play.[84]

Herbert Spencer (1820–1903)

Today Spencer is usually classified as a humanist and realist. He called himself a "transfigured realist." The term "agnostic realism," closely related to skepticism, has also been connected with his name. Influenced by the many scientific discoveries of his day, he popularized the concepts of evolution with its emphasis on natural selection and survival of the fittest. His *Synthetic Philosophy* gave expression to the implication of Darwin's *Origin of the Species.*

Spencer's writings influenced the thinking of the twentieth century, which is the time of the development and unfolding of the new realism.

In *Education: Intellectual, Moral and Physical,* published in 1860, Spencer developed themes of great interest to physical educators to this day. Quotations cited by Holbrook in *Philosophies Fashion Physical Education* highlight Spencer's views.[24] In a modern realistic note, for example, Spencer wrote about providing opportunity for children to develop all their faculties for self-preservation and safety: "the training of children should be carried on, as not only to fit them mentally for the struggle before them, but also to make them physically fit to bear its excessive wear and tear." He continued in the precise vein of realism with: "Learning the meaning of things is better than learning the meaning of words"; and "Whether for intellectual, moral, or religious training, the study of surrounding phenomena is immensely superior to the study of grammars and lexicons." He favored physical activity for girls, "For if the sportive activity allowed to boys does not prevent them from growing up into gentlemen, why should a like sportive activity prevent girls from growing up into ladies?"

Recent and Contemporary Realistic Thought

Contemporary realism does not carry the same meanings as did realism in the middle centuries. The rise of realism at the beginning of the twentieth century was in part a revolt or reaction against various movements which tended to magnify the power of man in knowledge and reality. The humanists, regarded as rationalists, placed great value on the authority of human reason, in many cases giving it more value than faith as a source of truth. For this reason, humanism is sometimes defined as "emphasis on things human rather than things divine." The modern realists went further, although they still retained a great tendency to respect sense experience above pure human reason. To the extent that they did this, they may be called empiricists. Faith and tradition ranked below both pure reason and sense experience in the hierarchy of the realists.

In the twentieth century, natural realism led to two American schools known as neorealism and critical realism. The movement known as neorealism or new realism was developed by 1910 when six teachers of philosophy in the United States (Edwin B. Holt, Walter T. Marvin, William Pepperell Montague, Ralph Barton Perry, Walter B. Pitkin, and Edward G. Spaulding) formed a group, and in 1912 published a cooperatively written book called *The New Realism.* Bertrand Russell (some of Russell's views are presented under Analytic Philosophy) and Alfred North

Whitehead also have been classified as neorealists by some writers in the discipline of philosophy. According to Titus, the new realists rejected all mystical philosophies, and the view that things are either created or modified in any way by the knowing mind, claiming that "The outer world is actually present and is directly experienced; . . . The world is pluralistic . . . knowledge of an object does not change the object known. Some particular things and some universals or essences (Platonic realism) are real, whether we are conscious of them or not. . . ."[110] Apart from these basic convictions, the new realists claim there is neither a single realistic philosophy of life nor one inevitable answer to questions regarding mind, freedom, purpose, and the good.

Critical realism developed during the period 1910 to 1920. Members of this group included Durant Drake, A. O. Lovejoy, James B. Pratt, A. K. Rogers, George Santayana, Roy W. Sellars, and C. A. Strong. Titus pointed out that just as the new realism was an attack on idealism, critical realism was a criticism of both new realism and idealism: "The critical realists while maintaining substantial agreement in the area of the theory of knowledge, differ widely in their metaphysical views. Their views range from the naturalisms of Santayana and Sellars to the metaphysical spiritualism of Pratt."[110]

Contemporary neorealists and critical realists in the naturalistic tradition include Frederick S. Breed, Harry S. Broudy, William O. Martin, and John Wild. Among spokesmen of realism in the classical tradition of Aristotle and St. Thomas Aquinas are G. Watts Cunningham, Etienne Gilson, Robert J. Henle, William J. McGucken, Jacques Maritain, John D. Redden, and Francis A. Ryan. American exponents of the educational implications of classical realism include Mortimer Adler and Robert M. Hutchins. Their views are discussed under Aritomism or Perennialism.

In addition to those associated directly with specific movements of realism as discussed herein, there are other realists who vary from these positions, some leaning toward empiricism and others toward rationalism. It is probably safe to say that most realists, although having a profound respect for science, are opposed to the acceptance of any completely mechanistic or physical deterministic view. *The one realistic idea held by realists in general is the metaphysical belief that there is a physical world that exists independent of the minds of men.* Also, realism today appears to be not so much an attack on idealism, as it is an effort to begin to consolidate some positives of its own.

It would be impossible to select one person as being representative of *all* of contemporary realism. The views of four individuals (Whitehead, Santayana, Ryle, Broudy) whose works reflect various emphases of contemporary realism are presented in the following paragraphs. These views were selected because they seem pertinent to several of the questions which frequently confront the physical educator.

Alfred North Whitehead (1861–1947), who with Bertrand Russell wrote *Principia Mathematica* (1910–1913), is one of the best-known and widely read realists of the twentieth century. Whitehead also has expressed some general ideas related to physical education. Holbrook quoted Whitehead from his *Modes of Thought* and *Science and Philosophy*.[24] His writings are filled with references to the importance of the body: "our feeling of bodily unity is a primary experience. It is an experience so habitual and so completely a matter of course that we rarely mention it. No one ever says, 'Here am I, and I have brought my body with me' . . . The body is the basis of our emotional and purposive experience. It determines the fact that we enjoy the sense."

Whitehead emphasized the physical side of man in other ideas, such as "Our sense-experiences are superficial, and fail to indicate the massive self-enjoyment derived from internal bodily function. Indeed, human experience can be described as a flood of self enjoyment, diversified by a trickle of conscious memory and conscious anticipation."

In a number of books and in his philosophy of organism, Whitehead criticized the separation of matter and life, body and mind, nature and spirit, and denial of goodness, beauty, and religious values which he believes are essential for any high civilization. He said, "Men are driven by their thoughts as well as by the molecules in their bodies."[121] Criticizing the neglect of the body, he stated: "in teaching you will come to grief as soon as you forget that your pupils have bodies. . . . But nature can be kept at bay by no pitchfork; so, in English education, being expelled from the classroom she returned with a cap and bells in the form of all-conquering athleticism."[122]

Writing about relaxation in recreation, and in a realistic vein, Whitehead wrote: "The normal recreation should be a change of activity, satisfying the cravings of instincts. Games afford such activity. Their disconnection emphasizes the relaxation, but their excess leaves us empty."[122]

The Spanish-born American philosopher George Santayana (1863–1952) has been characterized as a realist, Platonist, and one of the most eminent of the contemporary naturalists. The essence of Santayana's philosophic thought as reported by Cory is "What I have yearned for all my life is not so much cosmic unity—like Whitehead, but simply 'completion'. If I see a circle half-drawn, I yearn to complete it."[100] It was Santayana's desire that everything fulfill its inherent potentiality, and this could be achieved through increasingly living a "life of reason."

For Santayana, matter exists independently of consciousness; it is consciousness that reveals the nature of reality. He places "mind" squarely within a biologic context. Human reason, Santayana held, is born into a wonderfully organized natural world. The function of reason is to render the instincts and sensations of the highly adaptable body—a body possessed of its own organic equilibrium—". . . harmonious with one an-

other and with the outer world on which they depend."[100] **Perfection of**
the physiologic functions of the body, he believed, was extremely important to the *value* of human existence: "They constitute health, without which no pleasure can be pure. They determine our impulses in
leisure, and furnish that surplus energy which we spend in play, in art
and in speculation."[101] Acknowledging the usual view of work being that
which is necessary or useful for life and play being useless action, Santayana points out that there is another way in which to view play: "there
is an undeniable propriety in calling all the liberal and imaginative
activities of man play, because they are spontaneous . . ."—done for their
own sake. The degree of happiness and civilization which any society
has attained can be measured, he contended, "by the proportion of its
energy which is devoted to free and generous pursuits, to the adorn-
ment of life and the culture of the imagination. . . . Play, in this sense,
may be our most useful occupation."[101]

The contemporary British philosopher Gilbert Ryle has been referred
to as a direct realist[76] and an ordinary language philosopher.[87] There
are some who would be more inclined to include Ryle under the general
heading of analytic philosophy (Chapter 12). The publication of Ryle's
book *The Concept of Mind* (1949) had an important impact on philosophic discussions of mind. Ryle took the position that traditional theories, which held that there is some mysterious entity called "mind"
which exists within the body, are insupportable. This theory of a visible
body and a mysterious invisible mind he calls "the dogma of the Ghost
in the Machine." The fundamental error arose when Descartes postulated two separate entities, mind and body, and the resulting dualisms
have affected philosophy ever since. The grammar that we use when we
talk about mental activities and bodily activities, Ryle contends, misleads
us into believing that these are two independent entities. Matson describes how Ryle believes this theory of two separate entities results
from a "category mistake"—when we represent the facts as belonging to
one "logical type or category (or range of types or categories) when
they actually belong to another."[79] Because of this category mistake we
have become accustomed to calling the operations of mental processes
by the wrong names. The mind's operations should really be regarded
as *dispositions to act*. To say that a man knows something is really to
say that under certain circumstances he is likely to perform in certain
ways. In addressing the so-called problem of how we can know that
other people have minds, Ryle claims that when I follow your arguments I am actually observing your mind in action. Ryle's thesis, Warnock points out, implies, at least in principle, that "everything about
every individual could be known by sufficiently protracted observation
of his bodily doings."[119]

To help explain his theory, Ryle (a former Oxford oarsman and row-
ing coach) uses the example of a foreigner watching his first cricket

game. Having seen the batsman, the bowlers, the umpires, and so on, the foreigner asks where is the person who contributes the famous British "sportsmanship." It has to be explained to him that sportsmanship is not another operation of the game of cricket; it is, roughly speaking, the "keenness" with which the various tasks of cricket are performed. Performing a task keenly, Ryle holds, is not the same thing as performing two separate tasks. If his thesis is correct, Ryle believes, the traditional dualism of unobservable mind and observable matter will be corrected: "It is perfectly proper to say, in one logical tone of voice, that there exist minds and to say, in another logical tone of voice, that there exist bodies. . . . They indicate two different senses of 'exist', . . ."[9] To the objection that his theory of mind is too behavioristic, Ryle responds that he has, at least, exposed the persistent dualisms which have caused such difficulty for Western philosophy.

Although their full impact may not yet have been felt, Ryle's theories have engendered considerable discussion among members of the physical education profession, especially in Great Britain. It is possible that Ryle's theories may have something of consequence to tell the profession about the kinds of statements which allege a connection between "intelligent intentions" and "successful actions." Here Ryle's own example is helpful in clarifying the point: "Whether or not the boxer plans his manoeuvres before executing them, his cleverness at boxing is decided in the light of how he fights."

Another important contemporary spokesman for realism, especially as it pertains to education, is Harry S. Broudy. Broudy's realism has been called a variant of the general position of essentialism and a realism in the Platonic-Aristotelian-Thomistic-Whitehead tradition. His educational realism, he says, depends on a realistic epistemology that there is truth to be discovered and learning consists in discovering truth. He is deeply concerned with education's role in promoting human good. His specific list of values includes bodily, economic, recreational, associational, character, intellectual, aesthetic, and religious values. In considering play as a carefree activity necessary to modern man's worthy use of leisure time, as Broudy viewed it in *Building a Philosophy of Education,* general education is an education for leisure and should provide activities that are truly recreational as well as a source of physical exercise.[14] One requisite, however, is that the performer be required to attain at least enough competence to assure continuation of participation. Nevertheless, the need and demand for such activities should not result in the idea and practice of play "being lost to the good life."

Synthesis of Views of Realism

Placing ancient Greece as the original home of realism may be a somewhat more accurate focus than was possible in the case of idealism. In the beginning realism was a revolution in thought, a revolt against the theory of idealism, although realistic postulates are also found in the idealism of Plato. It was an attack against the belief that a thing exists more in the perception of it than in itself, a thrust against archaic tradition, inflexible authority, and ideas being threatened by practice, experience, and the new sciences.

Like idealism, realism today is a multiple mixture of the old and new. It is a broad philosophy ranging from materialism at one extreme to a near-idealism at the other extreme. James B. Pratt, in his *Personal Realism,* and others represented a form of realism which may be identified with objective idealism. Two realists may disagree more between themselves on some matters than either would disagree with an idealist or with a pragmatist. Almost all modern idealists agree with realistic criticism of extreme forms of idealistic mentalism (no reality other than the world of thought).

Realism emphasizes objective and speculative aspects. It is the doctrine that the objects of our senses are real and they exist independent of their being known or related to mind. Furthermore, for the realist, the objects speak for themselves rather than being accommodated to our ideas, sentiments, or wishes.

One writer pointed out that John Wild accents the tenets of realism that are helpful guides to identify the characteristics of realism.[24] *First,* the world exists even as man sees it, and it is not man-made. *Second,* the human mind can know this existing world through the senses. *Third,* this resulting knowledge is man's most reliable guide to his social and individual conduct.

The first and second tenets are appealing to many physical educators. The real world is something with which people are familiar. It is not something intangible like Plato's ideas. All one has to do is to look and listen. What the senses bring in is the real. Understanding this real world begins both as the products of the senses channeling one's experience, and as personal experiences are connected with the functioning of the senses.

Rules, guides, principles, hypotheses, and tenets, to the orthodox realist, are based on knowledges brought in from nature by his senses, aided by the tools of science. This great source (nature) led the realist to believe that the universe consisted of forces, parts, processes, particles, and qualities which are in the universe whether man knows it or not. They are there to be discovered. Thus, the realist's chief concern is to find out what nature is, what it consists of, how it works, and be guided by it so as to know how to react and adjust to the environment and to life.

Alfred North Whitehead worded it in this fashion: "Man, who at times dreamt himself as a little lower than the angels has submitted to become the servant and the minister of nature. It still remains to be seen whether the same actor can play both roles."[123]

W. E. Hocking gives an idealist's view of realism, but one which is essentially in agreement with the realistic position of Whitehead and a contemporary British realist John MacMurray. Hocking stated: "If we can say of Idealism that it has the tendency to read the mind into nature, realism is its precise opposite . . . realism is inclined to depersonalize or de-mentalize the world, to see things starkly and factually . . . at once more objective and more scientific than that of Idealism."[51]

Such a large number of qualifying terms have been associated with realism that one must exercise caution to avoid becoming confused. Among the many terms associated with realistic philosophy are rational realism, classical realism, religious realism, natural realism, scientific realism, romantic realism, new realism (*neorealism*), humanistic realism, sense realism, verbal realism, empirical realism, social realism, scholastic realism, critical realism. The three points referred to earlier as helpful guides to identify characteristics of realism are worth recalling.[24] These three fundamental characteristics can be summarized as follows: (1) the belief in the reality of matter—the belief that the external world exists as man sees it, independent of any apprehension by human minds; (2) the belief that experience is a highly dependable means for coming to know about this external world, and that communication with this external world is achieved through the physical senses; (3) the belief that knowledge derived through sense experience is the most reliable (for some realists the only) means for man to guide his conduct.

Implications of Realism for Physical Education

Because there are so many varieties of philosophic realism, it is not surprising that varying emphases would be reflected in the kinds of physical education which realist thinkers would advocate. Among those elements which might be found would be an emphasis on studies that stress learning by doing and an environment that provides for a wide range of physical activities and ample equipment and facilities. Individuals inclined toward a natural realism would encourage purposeful out-of-door activities. Because the senses are important to learning, the realist would have children begin active physical activity at the earliest possible age. A structured program of perceptual-motor activities which emphasize the use of all the senses in learning would be deemed desirable. Older students would be provided with a varied program of activities, and teachers would encourage them to learn about their own bodies, the application of force, buoyancy, and similar principles as a part of their games, gymnastics, aquatics, and other activities. Physical education major programs would give precedence to such studies as anatomy, physics, physiology, biomechanics, tests and measurements. Laboratory sections would accompany most lectures. The environment, whether in the gymnasium, on the playing field, or in the classroom and laboratory, would include a wide assortment of sensory objects. Research would be encouraged, especially in the so-called scientific studies.

We turn now to a more detailed consideration of realistic implications for physical education, organized under familiar educational headings. *Philosophies Fashion Physical Education* is drawn on extensively in identifying the implications under consideration.[24]

Objectives of Education

Consistent with realism is the rational humanistic belief that man has a unique faculty of reason which education must develop. Consistent with naturalism, and the biologic "organismic needs" concept, the realist emphasizes the natural states or needs (e.g., the need for activity) within the individual which education must aid in satisfying.

In general, for the realist the goal of the good life, the good society, and the good school is for man to become a rational master of himself and of his environment. The realistic educator builds competencies that will enable the student to understand and to make adjustment to the real, external world. Realistic education, therefore, emphasizes verified truths and the means by which truth is obtained. It aids students in the adjustment to adult life and its new experiences. It transforms human capacities for rationally willed behavior into self-sustaining habits of action, feeling, taste, and thought. Because skill is an ingredient of habit, it follows that motor skills are as important for complete living and for building a vigorous human, capable of withstanding environmental stress, as are intellectual and moral skills.

The Learner and the Learning Process

Realists may differ among themselves in their conception of man, although there are many similarities or overlapping points of agreement. Natural realists view the individual as a biosocial organism whose supposed mental or spiritual activities form an intricate physicochemical process as yet unexplained by science. Free will is denied by most natural realists. Rather, the individual is a product of the impact of environment on his inherited structure. Catholic or religious idealists regard man as a spiritual being. Man has free will and is responsible for his actions. Classical rational realists (sometimes known as rational humanists) reject the view that man has been divinely created and maintain that his highest attribute is his rationality.

Realism looks for the finite, the concrete—things that are tangible and measurable. The realist wants the learner to experience the world as orderly and systematic, something the learner can touch and see and feel, for he is considered to be a sense mechanism. That which is to be learned—the learning experience—will be selected with this in mind, and the learning environment will be shaped toward this end. The process of learning also is planned so that it is orderly and prescribed and works smoothly, as nature works smoothly. If the curriculum is this way, if the teaching methods are aimed toward this end, if the process of learning is fashioned this way, and if the environment is made to foster the natural smooth-running clockwork exemplified by nature, learning will be properly channeled and orderly thinking will follow orderly action.

Most realists believe physical education and other appropriate branches of education should be synchronized with the natural rhythms of growth and development. Educators are encouraged to make use of the spontaneous play and sport activities, the motor movements seemingly related to man's racial inheritance as well as his physical makeup.

The naturalistic realist, who is a physical educator, denies the reliability of the behavioral sciences (psychology, sociology, anthropology) in the learning process, advocating instead the use of more scientific methods in learning. Classical realists give priority to reason and its cultivation and tend to be traditional in choice of learning methods. For the realistic physical educator, in general, exciting student interest and curiosity is good but students' desires are not of primary concern. Intelligence demands discipline and discipline is imposed by students' awareness of the limits of their abilities.

Values

Value, for the realist, is inherent in that which motivates man in the successful adjustment to his surroundings. A thing is good, right, or beautiful if it conforms to the laws and order of nature. For realists, objectives must be especially selected for their value.

Realists, in general, agree that values are permanent and objective, and that education should teach well-defined values, although they differ in their reasons for thinking so. Realistic values vary somewhat depending on the type of realist. The naturalistic or scientific realists deny supernatural sanction of values. They would teach that right and wrong come not from religious principles but from understanding the basis of nature. Morality is based on what scientific evidence shows to be beneficial. Classical realists of the Aristotelian variety believe that there is a universal moral law established by God which man can discern through his reason.

The realistic physical educator would be among the first to identify, accept, teach, and emphasize values related to man's body and its movement. Health, for example, is a value and a means of improving the environment, a basis of establishing good health habits, and a reason for teaching basic health knowledges. It is the realist who is apt to regard strength and endurance as intrinsic values, whereas the idealist regards

them as extrinsic. Of course, the bona fide realist does not place value
in the physical activity itself. Rather, it is those processes and outcomes
related to man and nature which harbor the values which he sees and
feels. It is *in* the vigorous movement, the competition, the overload principle, and the like in which the realist finds value.

The realist approves of the interscholastic athletic program, insofar as
it is extracurricular and teaches desirable social behaviors. Recess or
after-school recreational play is of value in that it provides release for
pent-up emotions and surplus energy, and equips the student with leisure
skills.

Curriculum or Program Building

A realistic physical education program could be expected to be based
on some authenticated health knowledges and on established forms of
physical and recreational skills. Such sources provide bases for new experiences. Such a program would contain activities helpful in preparing
students for life. A conscious attempt is made to develop the program
on scientific bases.

From the standpoint of the naturalistic realist, play and sport activities which spring from the natural interests of the child are the best
materials on which to build desirable habits of action, feeling, taste, and
thought. Consideration also is given to those activities that directly lead
to maintenance and self-preservation, and that make for a more rugged
human who is able to bear the excessive wear and tear of living.

There are two excellent examples of realistic programs in the history
of American physical education, namely, the Swedish and German systems. That last word is a cue. The Swedish *system* with its conscious
linkage with human anatomy, the nicety of its Day's Order, and Ling's
principles, all form excellent illustrations of realistic traits.

The Natural Program, initiated by Thomas D. Wood in 1909, also was
prompted by a realistic concept (that the program of physical education
should be fashioned to fit natural man, that which man did naturally and
that which man did since time immemorial). One of the examples of
the profession's former lack of being philosophy-oriented is the over-
sight of historians of physical education to see that the Natural Program
of physical education (so bitterly opposed by the supporters of both
the Swedish and German systems) also sprang from a matrix of realism!
The reader should recall the observation made earlier in this chapter
that realism is a broad philosophic position that provides room for a
variety of approaches.

Another realistic influence is found in the selection of activities typically based on kinesiologic, anatomic, and physiologic consideration. Still
another influence of realism is the preference for and design by many
physical educators for objective tests. Some of the adjustment-to-life

emphasis in physical education is found in realism as well as in progressivism.

The realist would be expected to provide more time for drills than either the pragmatist or the idealist. Through such exercises, the realist would hope to develop habits and automatism in student responses. The realist hopes that this in turn will lead to correct responses in game situations, right movements to prevent injuries, and right conduct on the challenging field of play.

Although realism could accept the use of the man-is-a-machine concept in order to condition the performer to act and react correctly, realism also permits use of the concept that the student should be taught to think as he sees, establishes, and appreciates the facts of nature, particularly scientifically determined facts.

The Teacher and Teaching

The realistic teacher chooses to aspire to be the "voice of science": clear, objective, and factual. Realists also are apt to be more impersonal than idealists in their relationships with students, carrying out the idea of being objective like the scientist. However, in emphasizing the spirit of discovery, their enthusiasm and encouragement point to good rapport with students. This does not mean that the realist goes as far as the pragmatist to let the student learn through his own discoveries. The realist makes certain that the student is provided with an opportunity to gain some background. There needs to be something with which to think and work. Furthermore, there needs to be an opportunity to try out some learnings in preparation for the experience which follows.

In his efforts to be exact, objective, make use of facts, seek for further facts, and bring the real world into the school, the realist would expect and encourage the student to use sensory aids to augment his senses.

One of the realist teacher's favorite methods is the project—definite, measurable, and well organized. Concrete, tangible units of work are indicated. This way is like nature's way.

As teaching machines, videotapes, and future mechanical aids prove to be helpful to the physical education teacher, it will be realists who will conduct the necessary initial experimentation. It also will be realists who will make most frequent use of such mechanical aids.

The physical education teacher with an inclination toward realism would seek the support of science and technology. Teaching would be viewed as a process that operates according to rules. The realist likes things that can be arranged neatly. He likes sequences and classifications. He likes step-by-step progressions. He wants his teachings dependable, as nature is dependable.

The realist is not satisfied with the student's getting the general idea. Demonstration, one of his favorite techniques, is performed after careful planning. It is performed usually so that specific and needed movements are featured. It would be the realist rather than the idealist who would have someone else perform a demonstration of how a skill is to be executed. He eschews the central role which the idealist teacher typically plays. The realist makes certain that the student tries out the established ways, and points out that these in turn may lead to still other ways of performing, augmented by the findings and implications of research. In all this teacher–student activity, the realist sees that what is to be learned occupies the central position. It becomes the means through which the student reaches happiness.

Evaluation

It would surprise no one to find the realist following the scientist when it comes to preferring an emphasis on measurement rather than on evaluation. The realist is apt to believe that the phenomena most worth grading and appraising are those that are tangible and measurable. He wants to translate performance into scores. He also may want to analyze that which the student does and shows so that small measurable bits are there for observation, recording, and grading. He prefers to avoid subjective items in the grading plan. When he works in a school system using anecdotal statements instead of numerical or letter grades, the realist usually will be found gathering all possible data that are objectively collected and as valid and reliable as possible before he formulates anecdotal statements. Furthermore, the realist would be expected to treat his scores statistically. If the number of students justify it, he probably will prefer to grade on the curve. The realist and idealist both favor the devising of standards of performance for various groups in suitable activities. It is true that the followers of the two philosophic positions make different uses of these standards and place differing values on them.

Teacher Preparation

As a realist, the teacher would be expected to make the undergraduate major curriculum in physical education as scientific as feasible. Scientific as used here is a catchall word. It includes such operations as carefully following the criteria and recommended steps in curriculum construction; using essential kinds of analyses of students; using examinations of the professional curricula of the past; and conducting studies of the duties, difficulties, opportunities, and expectations of teachers on the job. Scientific here also includes such considerations as justifying all required courses for undergraduate major students and deciding which courses in the sciences should be required. So important to realists is this scientific concept and its applications that some speak of physical education as being an applied science, and some even like to refer to it as a science.

A realistic curriculum for major students would be expected to emphasize principles of physical education. High value would be placed on facts. Even though many aspects of the professional curriculum cannot be based on facts, the curriculum would reflect the realist's concern for system, order, definiteness, planning, and organization. Such details as prerequisites, students' records, catalogue statements, and the like would be carefully worded, established, and processed. The major student would be expected to gain all requisite knowledges, skills, and so on— together with their connections with nature and with science (including mathematics).

The realist, like the idealist, uses lectures, textbooks, outside readings, recitation, and other traditional methods of teaching without apology. More attention is likely to be paid, however, to newer teaching methods and to preciseness of course content. In fact, the realist's penchant for analysis will probably be expressed in carefully organized course outlines, including relationships with other disciplines, especially the sciences.

Directed, cadet, or student teaching and internship, under the supervision of a realist, as can be expected, probably will be a combination of such admonitions as "follow these proved ways," "find out for yourself," and "learn to adjust." There would be considerable emphasis on applying "the nature of the child," "the nature of learning," and the other key factual and near-factual knowledges garnered during the previous years of study.

Should a realist be in charge of graduate study in physical education, the fifth year is apt to consist of a continuation of the scientific approach, culminating in a respectable thesis rather than some more casual hurdle. Certainly in advanced graduate study one would expect rich offerings in scientific-type courses and experimental types of research, with motivation toward the development of independence in thought and work.

The Administrator and Administration

As an administrator, the realist is a detailed organizer, a stickler who demands systematic work from the students and faculty. He is business-like, open-minded, fair, and objective. Although he may ask faculty members for proposals and opinions, he maintains the ultimate responsibility for decisions. He stands ready to modify procedures as more efficient methods are established. His decisions are dictated by impersonal factors. He favors objective experimentation. As Henry Suzzalo, former president of the University of Washington once said as he discussed the realist, "He is like the honest butcher who keeps his hands off the scales as he weighs the meat."

Promotion of faculty members is based on achievement as evidenced by facts regarding technical competence. Merit pay is acceptable if valid, reliable means for determining merit are available.

Curriculum changes under the realistic administrator incorporate and are based on research findings. He also would expect students to be or become interested in the scientific reasons for physical education.

Comments and Criticisms

Because of the diversity within the philosophic position known as realism, it is more difficult to find a precise and universally accepted definition for it than it is for idealism. By now it should have become evident that realism does *not* represent a single, near-unanimous position, for within philosophic realism at least the following variations have been identified: Aristotelian realism, classical realism, Scholasticism or Thomism, naturalism, neorealism (the new realism), critical realism, and direct realism. (Pragmatism, progressivism, and perennialism, as well as important aspects of analytic philosophy, borrow from the realist position.) This diversity notwithstanding, there is one extremely important point upon which realists find agreement. It is the view that the physical world is real in its own right and exists independent of the sense experiences and the human mind. Thus, realism is opposed to idealism, which holds that things only exist as they are perceived by the human mind and denies the commonsense realist view that material things exist independently of their being apprehended by the human consciousness.

The strength of realism may be said to lie in its commonsense approach to the world. At a time when what seems to be needed to solve man's natural and social problems is concrete action, realism does not resort to conjecture and speculation which critics say characterizes idealism. Many people find it comforting to believe that one exists as a real entity in a world composed of real objects and events. Knowing that trees, beautiful sunsets, other human beings exist independent of our awareness of them provides a certain sense of stability. For some individuals such a belief eliminates—or at least reduces—the transient and ephemeral malaise which some have come to regard as a hallmark of the twentieth century. Man's own actions matter here and now; within his potential grasp are the means to modify and control nature for the betterment of humankind. Such an awareness can provide an enormous sense of human value and importance. It is the empirical method of science and the inductive method of reasoning which have enabled man to test his growing abilities and, in general, he has achieved remarkable success.

Realism, of course, is not without its critics. Titus describes how both idealists and pragmatists criticize the realist position by maintaining that in the last analysis it is impossible to prove that there is an object independent of the knower.[110] Some idealists contend that by making everything scientific and objective the realist has minimized the importance of human life. The empirical explanation of man, they claim, can never present us with the whole of man. To use an example from sport and physical education, the value of empirical investigation in the quest for and the attainment of improved performance records can scarcely be doubted. Some individuals, however, would question whether what seems to be a headlong rush to better quantitative records may be worth the losses in human values, human dignity, and human potential—or to use George Leonard's term "human intentionality."[74a]

TO SPEAK, THEREFORE, OF THE UNIVERSAL VALIDITY OF A LAW OF NATURE HAS ONLY MEANING IN SO FAR AS WE REFER TO A CERTAIN TYPE OF PERCEPTIVE FACULTY, NAMELY, THAT OF A NORMAL HUMAN BEING.

—Karl Pearson

11

Pragmatism

PRAGMATISM RESTS ON NO CERTAIN ASSUMPTIONS. IT IS
NOT DEDICATED TO PURSUE ANY PARTICULAR DESTINATIONS.
IT VALUATES IDEAS IN TERMS OF THEIR SIGNIFICANCE. IT
EXAMINES THOUGHT IN TERMS OF OPERATIONS AND CON-
TROLS.

—William James

Pragmatism is regarded as a contribution of America to the history of philosophic thought, although it is related to the British empiricists' movement and has progenitors in early philosophic thought. For example, hints of pragmatism may be found in the relativism or "inevitability of change" propounded by Heraclitus, in Protagoras' declaration "Man is the measure of all things," in Bacon's advocacy of inductive logic, and in Kant's principle of the "primacy of practical reason."

Charles Sanders Peirce, William James, and John Dewey are generally recognized as the three greatest contributors to American pragmatism. They were, for a period, contemporaries.

Although Kant coined the term "pragmatisch," the publication of Peirce's essays, "The Fixation of Belief" (November, 1877) and "How To Make Our Ideas Clear" (January, 1878) in the *Popular Science Monthly,* are said to mark the birth of pragmatism as a philosophy.

Pragmatism has been known by a variety of names: pragmaticism (Peirce), instrumentalism, functionalism, and experimentalism (Dewey). The term "pragmatism" is derived from a Greek word meaning action, deed, or affair from which the words "practice" and "practical" come.

The philosophy of pragmatism is basically a *method* for determining the meaning of ideas. The experimental method is carried into all realms of human experience in providing a basis for beliefs about both facts and values including those of ethics and religion. Emphasis is placed on the biologic and social sciences in the attempt to extend the scientific spirit and knowledge to deal with the changing world and its problems. In the following paragraphs, the concepts of pragmatism are elaborated under philosophic categories, followed by a discussion of the ideas of Dewey, James, and Peirce, and then a discussion of the meaning of pragmatism for various aspects of physical education.

Metaphysics

Pragmatists are wary of committing themselves to self-contained metaphysical notions and theories of reality in general. The pragmatic viewpoint does not accept rationalism which finds truth and reality in the realms of generalized ideas, in the absolutes of divine revelation, and in the symbolic intuitions of the mind. Naturalism, which finds truth and reality in the material things of the universe, in nature, in empirical data, and in the findings of science, also is repudiated by the pragmatist. Such ultimate realities are unprovable, beyond the ability of man to demonstrate.

The *pragmatic* theory of truth then is that truths emerge from verification, from being experimentally tested. Ideas are not apart from experience or independent of knowledge. What is real is what experience shows it to be. Experience, then, is the only ultimate reality.

As stated by Burke:

> Philosophers of extreme Empiricism (especially the Sensationalists) believed that ideas and knowledge originate in human experience and sensations, or even that human sensations were identical with knowledge. They seem to expect truth to emerge automatically or spontaneously from observation of the material world. To pragmatist John Dewey, however, sensations were not 'bits' on a memory drum, awaiting a somewhat mechanical selection and combination into ideas by an acquiescent computer-mind. Only when empirical findings are employed in the formulation of new theories and hypotheses, and only when these are used as instruments for experimentation (that is, reconstruction of experience) is human experience efficient and effective. Dewey regarded sensations not as knowledge but as stimuli tending to disrupt a previously established adjustment. The organism is thus incited to action. The action alters the environment, which in turn reacts upon the organism.[24]

In Dewey's view, "the living creature undergoes, suffers the consequences of its own behavior. This close connection between doing and suffering or undergoing forms what we call experience."[34]

Epistemology

Pragmatism, being primarily a method of knowing, is epistemologically rather than metaphysically oriented. The term "truth" is used synonymously with knowledge. The pragmatic method begins with the question "How do we know what is true?" and conceives of knowing as an active process. That is, the pragmatist rejects the "spectator view of knowledge," looks to experience, to possibilities of action, rather than beginning with any eternal or universal truths. The mind, then, is active and exploratory, not passive and receptive. This mind helps form knowledge or truth by transactions between man and his environment.

Before knowledge is attainable, objective criteria for validating assertions must be established. The pragmatist's method of intelligence is to acquire knowledge by locating and solving problems. Pragmatism, therefore, embraces scientific methods of the inductive process of inquiry. It rejects such views as those of Kant, who placed emphasis on reason as an arbiter of experience. What Dewey called a "warranted assertion" results from a hypothesis that explains the facts and solves the problem most successfully and leads to the testing of further hypotheses.

Thought does not serve as an instrument for problem-solving unless it is a real problem. There is no separate "mind" which thinks. Mind denotes meanings that arise in the process of human adjustment. Thinking is biologic in nature, being concerned with the adjustment between an organism and its environment. Reflective thought arises when there is a problem. Because man's environment is outstandingly and inescapably social, the truth of a hypothesis is established not only by the criterion of individual experiment, but also by the criterion of *social experiment*. Social experiment leads inevitably toward *democracy*. Under a plastic, relative criterion, truth for an individual may be different from truth for society. In such a situation the pragmatist always gives precedence to social truth, because social needs must invariably reflect individual needs. What Dewey called a "critical engagement" describes what he envisioned as the blending of individual thought and group sanction.

Logic

Logic to the pragmatist is not a formalized or abstract system of thought, but a part of all reflective thought. It is an instrument for the solution of problems. Thus, logic is not absolute or unchanging, not isolated from meaning, consequences, usefulness. Rather, thinking occurs in a concrete biosocial context. It must be a real problem rooted in the situation in which the individual finds himself that provides something to think about.

The means of effective inquiry into problems is the scientific method. Thus, pragmatists speak more frequently of problem-solving, mediation, and analysis than of logic as such. Abstract thinking is an active experience which includes intellectualizing, conceptualizing, imagining, or whatever helps to sense the meaning of that which is going on.[70]

Axiology

For the pragmatist, judgments of values can be critically appraised on the basis of intelligent reflection on facts. Science, then, conceived in terms of its distinctive method is applicable to the realm of ethics and values. Because judging values (as with judging anything else) depends on facts, which are always specific to a particular circumstance, values are relative to the pragmatist. Values must be related to where and how the individual is living. Thus, values are not fixed or permanent; they arise from experience. They are subject to continuing criticism and reformulation, for, as Dewey pointed out, the best is the worst enemy of the better.

Pragmatism's theory of values, particularly that of Dewey, is applied most characteristically to social and political questions. The pragmatist's faith in democracy lies in his insistence on the individual as the focal point of social reconstruction. In Dewey's words, "Ultimate moral motives and forces are nothing more or less than social intelligence—the power of observing and comprehending social situations—and social power . . . at work in the service of social interest and aims."[28]

Religion, too, is considered to be examining experiences that give life true meaning rather than worship of the supernatural. Ethical values are arrived at by the individual's using critical examination of choices offered by each new situation, progressing by means of problem-solving from an indeterminate situation to a planned, purposeful course of action.

In order to understand aesthetics, one must begin with it in the raw, in the events of man. Interests are aroused and enjoyment is afforded as one hears or observes or tastes or smells or feels. Aesthetic enjoyment depends on whether the individual resolves indeterminate situations to his satisfaction. In short, aesthetic appreciation is related to the nature of one's experience. Art, for example, should carry the observer forward, not merely or chiefly by the mechanical impulse of curiosity, not by restless desire to arrive at the final solution, but by the pleasurable activity of the process itself.

Educational Theories

Pragmatism is popularly identified with the educational movement known as progressivism, although, according to Frederich Neff, a great many more of progressivism's tenets sprang from a romantic naturalism largely identifiable with Rousseau and his idealistic views of child nature.[17]

It is significant to note that physical education had been moving toward a progressive philosophy long before what came to be known in the 1920s as the "progressive education movement" occurred. Before the first decade of the twentieth century had ended, individual physical educators had spoken out for a more liberal approach to physical education—an approach that gave prominence to the educational potential of play and physical activity (an approach which would be expressed so eloquently in Dewey's *Democracy and Education,* 1916, and taken up and popularized by William H. Kilpatrick and others during the progressive education movement of the 1920s). Leaders in this early concept of a "natural program of physical education" were Thomas D. Wood of Teachers College, Columbia University and Clark W. Hetherington, who had studied with Wood at Stanford University. The philosophy of John Dewey and the learning theories of G. Stanley Hall and Edward Thorndike provided valuable background and support for the theories of physical education that Wood and Hetherington were developing. In 1910, Wood provided a lengthy report for the *Ninth Yearbook of the National Society for the Study of Education,* in which he emphasized the need to move away from formalized artificial gymnastics, which characterized physical education at the turn of the century (e.g., Swedish gymnastics, German gymnastics, free gymnastics with hand apparatus), toward a program of natural play activities and exercises which were in keeping with the actual abilities and needs of individual human beings. The subject matter of physical education, Wood declared, was to be found in "play, games, dancing, swimming, outdoor sports, athletics, and gymnastics (reconstructed to satisfy educational needs)."[126a] He also stressed the vital role of play in the life and education of the child, stating: "The fundamental impulse or motive to be considered in physical education is play."[126a] In 1910, Hetherington published "Fundamental Education," in which he declared the need for a "new physical education" that would place an emphasis on *education* rather than on training.[48b] He, too, viewed play and natural physical activities as superior to formal gymnastics, and he upheld the vital role of play as a socializing and character-building force. The "new physical education," Hetherington maintained, would be "*physical* only in the sense that the activity of the whole organism is the educational agent and not the mind alone."[48b] The educational process must be concerned with organic, psychomotor, social, and intellectual education.

The essence of pragmatism is the application of the master question "Does it work?" A pragmatist does not hesitate to change his methods or his values whenever they fail to satisfy needs. A pragmatist is not an unyielding systematist. He is appalled by biased educational reformers who merely replace archaic traditional authoritarianism with a new and revolutionary variety of authoritarianism. He does not replace a teacher-dominated system with a pupil-dominated system. Instead, he sees pupil needs and group and societal needs in a complex, fluctuating, interacting relationship. The complexity of these relationships does not confuse him. In the complexity he sees an orderliness, and finds an understanding that could never evolve from some arbitrary authoritarianism.

Reconstructionism, a contribution of Theodore Brameld, is in essence an extension of the educational theory of progressivism, stressing more heavily than does progressivism the reconstruction of culture. It is concerned with using the possibilities of group experience (social consensus) in remaking the culture according to design when the ideals of democracy become factual realities on a global scale. Reconstructionism is considered to be "the cutting edge of left-wing educational theory in the United States."[17]

Among other notable interpreters of pragmatism in education have been George Axtelle, Ernest Bayles, Kenneth Benne, Boyd H. Bode, John L. Childs, George S. Counts, Sidney Hook, William H. Kilpatrick, R. Bruce Raiys, Harold Rugg, William O. Stanley, and Lawrence G. Thomas. The philosophies of Peirce, James, and Dewey are presented as representative of pragmatism. An attempt also is made to describe the educational views of some of these proponents of pragmatism and the tenets of progressive education insofar as this movement stems from the philosophy of pragmatism.

Prominent Pragmatists

Charles S. Peirce (1839–1914)

Peirce (pronounced "purse") was an American logician and psychologist who wrote numerous articles and memoirs on logic, psychology, mathematics, metaphysics, astronomy, optics, chemistry, engineering, and other scientific subjects. In his essays, "The Fixation of Belief" and "How to Make Our Ideas Clear," the principles of pragmatism were first set forth.

Because he was a logician interested in the methods of the laboratory sciences, Peirce believed the meaning of ideas is best discovered by putting them to an experimental test and observing results. He believed Kant raised all relevant philosophic problems, although Peirce's intent was to correct what he regarded as an error in Kant's thinking—the lack of continuity between an inner world of ideas and the outer world of realities. All philosophy takes its start in logic, or the relation of signs to their objects, and phenomenology, or the brute experience of the objective world.

Peirce's pragmatic test for meaning, which is considered a test for the meaning of words or ideas and for the meaning of assertions, has been widely adopted by the language analysts as a tool of criticism to translate the words of philosophy into intelligible language. The criterion of meaningfulness advocated by Peirce amounted to putting an idea to work, and the practical consequences which appeared would thus determine the meaning of the idea.

Peirce held that pragmatism was not a doctrine of metaphysics, not an attempt to determine any truth of things, and that one cannot claim to be true what he does not know. Therefore, Peirce, as were later pragmatists, was not concerned with seeking some sort of ultimate reality. Peirce coined the word "tychism" by which he meant that sheer chance exists and is evident in the nature of the "pluraverse" (James's word for universe). There is logical continuity to chance events which through indefinite repetition beget order. This is illustrated in the tendency of all things to acquire habits. Peirce's view of ethics was that this desire of all things to come together in this certain order makes love a kind of evolutionary force.

In "The Fixation of Belief," Peirce considered four alternative methods of settling beliefs: *the method of tenacity; the method of authority; a priori method; the scientific method.* Peirce fully embraced the scientific method or the process of inquiry.

William James (1842–1910)

The rapid development of pragmatism in America was considered to be largely due to the brilliance and clarity of the writings of William James. He was said to have written psychology like a novel.

Receiving a degree in medicine but unable to practice it for health reasons, James began as an instructor of physiology, anatomy, and hygiene at Harvard. Later, as a professor of physiology, he helped to establish the first laboratory for psychologic research in the United States. Still later he became a professor of philosophy and began writing on pragmatism in 1897, 20 years after Peirce introduced the principle of pragmatism. Among his chief philosophic works are *The Will to Believe* (1897), *Varieties of Religious Experience* (1902), *Pragmatism: A New Name for an Old Way of Thinking* (1907), and *Essays in Radical Empiricism* (1912).

A major point in James's philosophy was his use of the criteria of utility, result, or usage in evaluating ideas and theories. Before considering whether or not an idea was true, its relative value should be ascertained. The question was asked, "What difference would it make if a particular idea were true?" If it would make no difference, then its truth or falsity was quite irrelevant.[23]

James made special application of pragmatism to morality and religion. His interpretation of religion was centered in "the will to believe." He followed the doctrines of pluralism (suggesting the word "pluraverse" as more accurate than universe) and meliorism (the world is neither completely good nor evil but capable of improvement). Since both possibilities of good and evil exist, no all-powerful good God could have created the universe. God, therefore, was to James an ideal of human experience, the many contacts man has with the "more" which brings comfort, happiness, peace. Man, then, was the measure of the universe.

In protesting the intellectualism of rationalists and objective idealists, James argued that their view of absolute truths was not practical or useful and did not correspond to the way people verify their beliefs.

Theories, ideas, and doctrines, according to James, were instruments to be utilized by man in order to solve life's problems. Effective workability also can become the criterion for determining what is good and bad, right and wrong. Morality and truth, then, for James were relative not fixed, truth being the expedient way of thinking and right being the expedient way of behaving.

James considered philosophy to be a set of convictions by which to live, not a matter of detached inquiry: "the philosophy which is so important in each of us is not a technical matter; it is our more or less dumb sense of what life honestly and deeply means. It is only partly got from books; it is our individual way of just seeing and feeling the total push and pressure of the cosmos."[57] The traditional concept of philosophy, which held that there was a supposedly objective and independent thing called truth, turns out, on examination, to be the continuing process of men throughout history trying to bring order and unity to their own human experience. Because the continuing attempts of human beings to bring order out of their experience will always lead to new inquiries, there will always be new theories put forward to be tested.

In his book, *Pragmatism,* James argued that pragmatism could satisfy both the rationalists and the empiricists, allowing man to live by a philosophy that fits him best and works most satisfactorily for him. Pragmatism could remain religious like the optimistic "tender-minded" rationalists, and preserve intimacy with the facts like the "tough-minded," often materialistic, empiricists. Both science and human values could be rationalized compatibly under the same philosophic system. Thus, James's "corridor" theory became the basis for much of neorealism.

Butler points out how through his own self-doubt James came to the conviction that the essence of well-being was to be found in putting into practice the idea of one's own free will.[18] In this sense, free will meant health, the ability to find one's place in things and to do one's work effectively and well; moreover, it meant the ability to enjoy all this. James was asked to address the female graduating class of the Boston Normal School of Gymnastics, and his remarks, entitled "The Gospel of Relaxation," appeared in *Talks to Teachers.*[58] James informed his audience of the importance of good mental hygiene and a sound moral character saying: "I cannot but think that the tennis and tramping and skating habits and the bicycle-craze which are so rapidly extending among our dear sisters and daughters in this country are going also to lead to a sounder and heartier moral tone . . . I hope that here in America more and more the ideal of the well-trained and vigorous body will be maintained neck by neck with that of the well-trained and vigorous mind as the two coequal halves of the higher education for men and women alike."[58] Women, too, must have the opportunity to develop and exercise free will. Even if muscular strength and vigor should become unnecessary for the kind of work which a person must perform, physical activity was still very much needed to contribute to a kind of "internal peace" which James believed to be of the utmost importance.

John Dewey (1859–1952)

Dewey was a personal friend and contemporary of William James although he survived James by many years. Dewey was born in the year Darwin's *Origin of the Species* was published, and some writers suggest that this circumstance led Dewey to create a philosophy for the age of evolution with its emphasis on relativity. It also has been suggested that his typical Vermont background may have been partly responsible for his practicality. Whatever the reasons, Dewey's prolific writings in logic, epistemology, ethics, aesthetics, and political, economic, and educational philosophy were instrumental in the growth and strength of pragmatism.

Dewey's instrumentalism emphasized that knowledge reshapes and changes the world; men must look toward the future, which will be novel, not to the past; the world, which is neither good nor bad, can be made better by man's efforts (meliorism). *Experience* is one of the key words in his instrumental theory of knowledge. In such books as *Logic*, *The Theory of Inquiry*, *The Quest For Certainty*, *Experience and Nature*, and *Art and Experience*, Dewey elaborated his theory of the nature of experience. Experience, to Dewey, included all processes of interaction between man and his social and physical environment. It is primarily practical. Knowing and acting are continuous. That is, the central concern of philosophy, for Dewey, was the *use* of knowledge. The principle he called "instrumentalism" was concerned with a conception of ideas that would function significantly. Associating knowledge with democracy, he believed that men could use their intelligence to attack social problems, to make the human conditions more human.

Dewey was critical of the traditional institutional church because he believed it stressed fixed ritual and authoritarian dogma. The religious aspects of Dewey's experimentalism, as defined in his book *A Common Faith*, in essence, deal with the method of discovering a religious attitude in everyday living. In the "something to live for," the God-idea, a religion is embodied in such concepts as brotherly love, compassion, cooperation, and sharing.

It has been suggested that the use of aesthetic terms would serve to designate what Dewey meant by religious experience. Morality is conceived of as a philosophic quest for the good life, not as timeless truths, divine inspiration, or a catalogue description of positive beliefs about what is right and wrong. For Dewey, the experimentalist's faith is built on human authorship, human thought and feelings.

To Dewey, values are capable of verification by the methods through which other facts are established, by the discipline most practical in method, namely, science. Scientific inquiry, therefore, is the means of testing phenomena in ethics and values as well as in any other sphere. As he stated in *Logic, The Theory of Inquiry*, "Experimentation enters into the determination of every warranted proposition."[33] In *The Quest For Certainty*, Dewey put forth the view of life as risk, adventure, experiment. Men are the heirs of a great scientific revolution and the search should not be for some haven of security.

Dewey was the first to recognize the educational mission of pragmatism. It was in education, Dewey believed, that all other problems—metaphysical, epistemological, ethical, logical—come together. So important did he believe education to be that in his autobiographical statement "From Absolutism to Experimentalism" (1930) he declared: "Although a book called *Democracy and Education* was for many years that in which my philosophy . . . was most fully expounded, I do not know that philosophic critics, as distinct from teachers, have ever had recourse to it. I have wondered whether such facts signified that philosophers in general, although they are themselves usually teachers, have not taken education with sufficient seriousness. . . ."[30] The interaction between philosophy and education described in *Democracy and Education* conceives of philosophy itself as the "general theory of education."

Dewey's educational theories are ultimately rooted in his concept of democracy. Education, for Dewey, being broader than schooling, involves all people and institutions that form or modify attitudes. The school should be concerned with the issues of society, he held, not something apart from its social context. The value of something studied is to be found in the process of living itself, not in some set of arbitrary hierarchical values. Value is found in how a study improves the quality of life. Those who plan the curriculum should be certain that what they include will provide "both direct increments to the enriching of lives of the pupils and also materials which they can put to use in other concerns of direct interest."[28] Dewey's pragmatic theory of knowledge assumes the continuity of meaningful knowledge (as opposed to divisions, separations, dualisms), the free exchange of ideas, the reorganization of experience, experimentation. He held that the experimental method of obtaining knowledge was the "remaining great force in bringing about a transformation in the theory of knowledge"; the function of knowledge is to make one experience freely available to other experiences. Such a theory of knowledge is vital to a society which stresses free interchange and social continuity—that is, to a democracy.[28]

Dewey believed that the education needed in a democracy was one that would prepare the individual for both useful labor and a life of leisure. The traditional dualisms present in assigning to some subjects liberal or cultural value (those in which it is assumed there is knowledge to be valued for its own sake) and to some subjects practical or utilitarian value (those assumed to be without intellectual or aesthetic merit) were based on historical and social distinctions. Such separations, Dewey contended, were neither intrinsic nor absolute. In a democracy such dualisms as theory and practice, knowledge and activity, intellectual and practical studies, labor and leisure must be eliminated.[28]

Dewey emphasized the importance of education for leisure in *Democracy and Education*. The word "recreation" is equated with *recuperation of energy:* "No demand of human nature is more urgent or less to be escaped. . . . Education has no more serious responsibility than making adequate provision for enjoyment of recreative leisure; not only for the sake of immediate health, but still more if possible for the sake of its lasting effect upon habits of mind."[28] Dewey also emphasized that work and play are not as antithetical as has often been assumed, the difference being "largely one of time-span, influencing the directness of the connection of means and ends." When people play they are not just doing something which is momentary or solely its own end; this would have no meaning. Play has educational value, Dewey declared, when it is infused with a "directing idea which gives point to successive acts."[28] It is the responsibility of the school to provide an environment in which play and work can be used to facilitate mental and moral growth. However, Dewey warned, it is not enough to just introduce play, games, and manual exercises in the curriculum. Everything depends on how they are used to foster growth. He also cautioned that the psychologic distinction between play and work must not be confused with the economic distinction.

References to the importance of play, games, and physical activities appear in a number of Dewey's writings. In *Lectures in the Philosophy of Education—1899*, he commented on the importance of play developing into games as the child becomes older and his need for order increases.[32] In *Schools of Tomorrow* he stated: "All peoples at all times have depended upon plays and games for the larger part of their education of children. Play is so spontaneous and inevitable that few educational writers have accorded to it in theory the place it held in practice, or have tried to find out whether the natural play activities of children afforded suggestions that could be adopted within school walls."[35]

Educational cliches and slogans have often been used as shortcuts in attempting to describe Dewey's epistemological position as applied to educational theory. They often have resulted in misconceptions of Dewey's philosophic thought. He is sometimes erroneously identified with all progressive educational theory and practice. In an attempt to correct some of the misinterpretations attached to his philosophy of education, Dewey wrote *Experience and Education* in 1938.

Neff pointed out that the distinction that can be made between these theories is that pragmatic education is based on a theory of knowledge-getting, whereas progressive education is based on a theory of "child nature." Neff argued that unqualified cliches such as "learning by doing," "child-centered," and "meeting the needs of pupils" scarcely represent an accurate reading of Dewey's educational ideas.[17] What is done, not the mere doing of it, determined the significance of learning for Dewey. According to Neff, "subject matter has a rightful place in the educational program, not in a position of isolated autonomy, but in a meaningful functional capacity; and that the basis on which pupil needs are to be decided is fully as important as meeting them."

Synthesis of Views on Pragmatism*

Although pragmatism is, in a manner of saying, on the other side of the fence from idealism, it developed in part as a reaction or alternative to extremes of materialism. Both idealists and materialists believed a real world exists independent of man. For idealists, this independent reality lay in the realm of ideas and the absolute. For materialists it lay in the material stuff of the universe. For both, truth existed whether or not man became aware of it. Pragmatists do not necessarily deny an independent, unknown, or unknowable reality, but advocate such a reality to be irrelevant, because it lies essentially in an area beyond man's comprehension. Pragmatists find reality in what man experiences. Whether the things he experiences have an independent existence is a moot point, but in any event a strictly academic one.

In short, pragmatism considers the classic debates concerning whether ideas or things are real as being arbitrary and artificial arguments. Experience is the master criterion, the source of truth, the only reality. All else is unknown and unknowable. *Experience*, then, is a first tenet of pragmatism.

Experience is not mere sensation, however, nor is it simply an adaptation to the environment by the organism. Adaptive adjustment is not a passive phenomenon or a reaction alone. The very fact of living implies reactivity which feeds back in such a fashion that the environment is modified and reconstructed. Experience, therefore, is a matter of dynamic and reciprocal changes within and outside the organism. As John Dewey stated, "There is no such thing in a living creature as mere conformity to conditions. . . . The higher the form of life, the more important is the active reconstruction of the medium."[34] Thus, the higher concept of *interactive adjustment* is a second tenet of pragmatism.

---

* We are indebted to Burke for his analysis of pragmatism and for his many ideas regarding the philosophic position. His writings in *The Philosophic Process in Physical Education*[23] and *Philosophies Fashion Physical Education*[24] are drawn on extensively in this and the following sections.

The organism in environment develops needs, which call for a reorganization of the environment through activity. In this process of resolving needs, man's thoughts, ideas, and theories become useful, or instrumental, in problem-solving. This principle of *instrumentalism* is the third tenet of pragmatism.

The instrument—this idea—is it true or false? Is an action based on this idea good or bad? To the pragmatist, the proof is in the pudding. If the action is successful in resolving the problem, it is good, and its theory is true. If the action is unsuccessful, it is bad and its theory is false. Idealists believe that if theories are true they work, whereas pragmatists believe that if theories work, they are true.[118] This if-it-works theory was more characteristic of James than of Peirce and Dewey. James maintained that an idea is true only if it has favorable consequences when scientifically tested.[70] This pragmatic test is called *experimentalism,* and it is a fourth tenet of pragmatism.

The ethics that evolve from such a pragmatic, experimental criterion are highly relativistic. "Good" and "bad" depend on the particular person, time, place, situation. Not only the ethics, but the entire world view, and indeed the whole philosophy of pragmatism is relativistic, involving constant fluctuation of relationship and changes of valence. The pragmatist does not explain change; he pre-assumes it and then deals with it. The whole system is diametrically opposed to the fixed, eternal, and absolute world view of the idealist. Therefore, the principle of *relativity* may be identified as a fifth tenet of pragmatism.

Man's environment is outstandingly and inescapably social. The truth of a hypothesis is therefore established, not only according to the criterion of individual experiment, but also by the criterion of social experiment. *Social experiment* is a sixth tenet of pragmatism, and it leads inevitably toward a seventh tenet, *democracy.*

In review, these are the seven tenets of pragmatism: (1) experience as the only ultimate reality; (2) interactive adjustment; (3) ideas and theories as instruments for problem-solving; (4) the experimental criterion for truth; (5) inevitable relativity and change; (6) social experiment as a preferred method; and (7) the principle of democracy.

Implications of Pragmatism for Physical Education

As Neff pointed out, there are inaccuracies in associating the philosophy of pragmatism with so-called progressive education.[17] Professor Dewey himself was one of the first critics, saying that the defects of progressive education "illustrate . . . a theory and practice of education which proceeds negatively or by a reaction against what has been current in education rather than by a positive and constructive development of purposes, methods and subject matter on the foundation of a theory of experience. . . ."[29]

Clearly, all contemporary progressive education practices do not mirror what education and physical education would be like under a philosophy of pragmatism. Such a practice would be distasteful to a pragmatist, anyway. A pragmatist prefers to examine human needs rather than contemporary practices.

A key concern in Dewey's philosophy is that of the social nature of man. The human organism is necessarily a part of the social whole, and all problems are to a greater or lesser extent social problems. The emphasis on the social nature of man and his problems, and the emphasis on the relative nature of the universe, led to the concept of biologic and psychologic adjustment as the critical task toward which all of man's behavior is oriented. Dewey believed that democratic social action is required.

The educational principles proposed by Dewey required a child-centered rather than a subject matter-centered curriculum, a democratic rather than an autocratic method, a natural motivation of felt needs rather than an imposed discipline, and a process of problem-solving rather than of information-absorbing alone. Education was to take place in a social setting. Needs, interests, abilities, and adjustment are to be emphasized.

With the several tenets of pragmatism, speculations are made in the following paragraphs about their application to the various broad categories of the language and concerns of physical education.

Objectives of Physical Education

According to the pragmatist, the aims or objectives of physical education should emerge from an examination of the nature of man, the requirements of his environment, and the subtleties of the interaction between the two. The objectives should be based on the needs, interests, and potentialities of the learners, and not on desires for prestige, profits, publicity, and public performance. The latter are invalidated by weight of evidence from biology, psychology, sociology, and the theory of democracy. (They are invalidated, but not yet eliminated!)

The pragmatist has little patience with the verbal debate about education of the physical versus education through the physical. Instead, he seizes avidly on Jesse Feiring Williams's phrase "to live most and serve best" not as a definition of health, but as an aim of education. The total of man's problems in his attempt to live most and serve best becomes the source of objectives of general education. Subject-matter fields, such as physical education, health education, history, and the rest, will be differentiated into separate entities only as required by the practical problems of organization and administration. Some people are capable of finding truth in literature; some can find truth in calculus; others find truth (and beauty and morality) in the experience of gross bodily movement. A broadly educated person will explore all of these avenues, seeking a breadth and variety of experiences which will enable him to live most and serve best.

A pragmatic physical educator must always aim to produce certain essential experiences that cannot be achieved consistently by any other subject-matter field. What other division of the curriculum can give every child the opportunity to feel, in the same way, the glorious experience described by R. Tait McKenzie in his sculpture The Joy of Effort? Physical education must not only pursue its unique aims, but also join the general educational endeavor to develop interpersonal communication and social relationships. Music and mind, habit and decision, skill and knowledge, individual and society are all elements in an interactive system: they need never eliminate one another, in the pragmatic view.

Curriculum or Program Building

Under a philosophy of pragmatism, what should a program of activities in physical education include? *First,* the pragmatist wants a variety of activities. *Second,* he wants socializing activities, and those best exemplifying the quality of experience elucidated previously. *Third,* he desires activities requiring individual adaptability, choices, self-evaluating consequences, self-expression, and creativity. *Fourth,* he favors activities that are broadly integrative with the total subject matter of the school and of life (in contrast with activities that are narrowly and artificially specialized into divergent spectra of interest).

The development of programs of physical education in the twentieth century reflects the acceptance of these pragmatic principles.

Turning to the area of program content in physical education, the pragmatist makes a catholic selection of activities. Variety is valued because variety itself represents an expansion of experience. The pragmatist is skeptical of a Day's Order of Exercise, and of any modern version of that plan. He dislikes static systems. He has little respect for tradition per se, but he recognizes historical inertia and cultural inheritance as dynamic elements in contemporary environment, and therefore examines them as sources of program content.

About the pragmatic desire for a variety of activities, recent history is most illustrative. Whereas the complete system of Swedish Educational Gymnastics was once published in a single thin volume, major publishing houses now compete with rival sports libraries and physical education series. Whereas, formerly, exercise could be classified under such quaint subdivisions as free exercise, light apparatus exercise, and heavy apparatus exercise, physical education now uses such inclusive and diverse headings as aquatics, team sports, individual sports, dual sports, gymnastics, dance, combatives, and so forth. Each subdivision can be further refined. Thus, aquatics is meant to include competitive speed swimming, lifesaving (water safety), springboard and platform diving, water ballet (synchronized swimming), water polo, skin diving, water skiing, board and body surfing, and numerous kinds of boating. The curriculum of sports is indeed diverse, and the diversity itself contributes to pragmatic educational ideas.

The pragmatist always prefers socializing activities. This does not mean, however, that all activities must be social. Even highly individual and solitary activities, like marathon running and weight training, can be instrumental as socializing agents, but they must be promoted in a particular way if they are to serve effectively as educational activities.

Team sports and group recreational activities have been found to satisfy pragmatic criteria especially well. The pragmatist is reluctant to promote essentially individual and solitary activities. Calisthenic drills and exercises on the stall bars largely have been discarded. To a pragmatist, a thousand people performing a mass drill in close-order formation in a stadium may not constitute a real social group activity. If individual performances, as exemplified in the track and field events, are conducted as a team effort, however, they could qualify as pragmatic educational experiences! Narcissistic self-developmental activities are frowned on, except when they appear to be prerequisite to participation in a more favored social activity.

Contemporary programs also illustrate a pragmatic bias toward certain qualities of experience. The program of the pragmatist cannot consist of positions to be held, bodily symmetry to be molded, repetitions to be counted, arbitrary routines to be learned, or scientifically programmed tables of maneuvers to be run through. Instead, there must be intriguing problems to be solved, challenges to be faced, adjustments to be made by creative and independent responses, cooperations to be worked out, competition to be undertaken, defects to be endured, initiative to be mustered, and social communications to be arranged.

From Dewey's definition of experience, it is obvious that physical education activities are much superior to many, if not most, classroom experiences as subject matter for general education. Where better can one "undergo and suffer the consequences of his own behavior" than in most physical education experiences? Failure to keep one's legs together while swinging between the parallel bars, failure to cooperate with the plans of the group in a team sport, or failure to take appropriate initiative when one receives the ball is inevitably followed by poignant consequences which are bound to result in the reconstruction of experience, for better or for worse. Successful responses in the same situations can go far beyond the acquisition of neuromuscular skills and specialized knowledges. They can involve expression, creativity, social adaptation, aesthetic appreciations, and contributions to personality and character development. For these reasons, physical education as a fundamental subject-matter discipline has prospered under pragmatic educational philosophy.

Pragmatic influences are obvious in the historical development of many specific activities during the past century. Dance has evolved from stylized ballet to aesthetic dance, to natural dance, to modern dance. Square and folk dances have been utilized in education for the purpose of gaining insights into social patterns of ethnic groups and of achieving correlation with social studies. Camping, in some instances, has followed a trend away from the traditional "gymnasium in the woods" toward emphasis on backpacking, wilderness living, conservation of natural resources, and survival techniques. School camping has achieved a definite integration of outdoor life with science, art, social studies, home economics, and general education in manners, morals, and democratic living.

With regard to the problem of specialization and fragmentation in the program of activities, pragmatists have some definite viewpoints and many implications for current practices. In general, the principle of integration of subject matter fits best into a philosophy emphasizing experience. Although the pragmatist favors the inclusion of practical and vocational subject matter in the curriculum (and even would erase many of the distinctions between those activities traditionally labeled "curricular" and "extracurricular"), integration is strongly preferred to specialization.

A pragmatist is not likely to favor such fragmentation. He would prefer those activities whose scope is richer and more inclusive, which lend themselves to curricular integration. Experiences in outdoor education and school camping can blend many separate activities into a meaningful pattern of lifelike experience. Dance, with its integrated aspect of conditioning, skill, expression, creativity, aesthetic appreciation, and deep symbolic meaning, is more valuable than a course in bowling. Intensive experiences in the competitive team sports are more pregnant with educational potential than courses in juggling and stilt walking.

Values

Physical education activities provide an almost ideal sort of experience under pragmatic criteria. Except in their most artificial form, they create microcosms of aspects of real life. Sports and games, especially, meet pragmatic criteria for lifelike educational situations, providing intensely meaningful emotional involvement, requirements of social and democratic interaction, competition with natural restrictions, and imposed adversities and responses to the challenges of the sociophysical environment. Although the subject matter of physical education never has suffered at the practical hands of the pragmatist, it is strange that it has not been even more vigorously advocated and promoted in the writings of the pragmatic educators.

The pragmatist sees education as life, as a natural life activity. He sees physical education as an undifferentiated phase of general education and as an invaluable subject-matter area of general education. He sees physical education as:

—an experience for achieving development and adjustment according to social standards
—an experience promoting social efficiency
—an opportunity for the development of social effectiveness and personal well-being
—a medium for developing the individual's potentialities in all phases of life, and
—a way of total education of being—intellectually, emotionally, and developmentally.

The foregoing phrases are adapted from the works of Hetherington, Wood and Cassidy, Wayman, Davis and Wallis, Nixon and Cozens and Oberteuffer. Within their stated definitions and aims of physical education, these writers were careful to include and repeat more traditional phrases such as health, big-muscle activities, vigor, endurance, physiologic and hygienic values, movement, physical activities, and muscular responses. It is hardly fair to blame the philosophers and theorists if *some* of their readers and followers lost the idea of physical fitness while absorbing the concept of total fitness. The really new emphases supplied by the pragmatists (most notably Dewey) were those of sociality and democracy as critical elements in the educative process. Traditional values were not all rescinded, although it became necessary to interpret them in a new context.

The Learner and the Learning Process

Because learning is more than the stimulus–response description of behavior, motivation must be present to elicit student effort. Under the pragmatic banner, true learning blooms when the student is actively involved. The learn-by-doing approach recognizes man's biologic nature. Because questions arise out of this biosocial human organism interacting with his environment, the problem-solving method offers the best psychologic method for learning.

The pragmatist builds his philosophy on the fundamental postulation of the existence of a living organism in an environment, accompanied by a basic process of interactive adjustment between the organism and the environment. For human beings, the most obvious and pertinent aspect of the environment is its social element. This social element is absolutely inescapable. Even the possibility of being a hermit describes an organismic reaction to a social condition. Personality, individuality, and growth are social outcomes.

If individual needs and adjustments are primary, one person's needs and adjustments inevitably will come into conflict with another's, or at the very least, will alter the environment of another person. Thus, new needs and adjustments are created which will in turn feed back into the environment and the first person. The social situation is envisioned as a dynamic field of fluctuating and interacting supraorganismic valences. The social needs for communication, cooperation, and resolution of conflict are as real as the personal physiologic needs, and generally, more stimulating, challenging, or threatening to the adaptive capabilities of the individual. Individual experiment becomes social experiment.

The Teacher and Teaching

Pragmatic educational method arises out of several prerequisite assumptions: (1) educational activity originates in a recognized problem of the learner or of the social group of which he is a member; (2) educational activity should require creativity, choice, decisions, and initiative by the participants—something more than routine, automatic, mechanical response to signals or specific directions; (3) pupils should participate in the determination of subject matter, activity, and method; (4) pupils should evaluate their own individual and group performance; (5) pupils should participate in the reorientation of the educational activity, to the greatest extent of their capabilities; and (6) educational activity should be in a democratic and social process.

Authoritarian or arbitrarily restrictive *methods* violate a fundamental pragmatic assumption, namely, that the individual's ability to change, adapt, or adjust requires freedom. It also requires responsible acceptance of an active part in the shaping of the group adjustment, and this in turn is an aspect of individual growth. Individual existence and survival depend on social existence and survival; individual growth requires social organization and growth; and as individual needs become social needs, the social good transcends the individual good. "Democracy . . . is but a name for the fact that human nature is developed only when its elements take part in directing things which are common, things for the sake of which men and women form groups."[34]

An ideal educational method, from the pragmatic viewpoint, might take place during a basketball game, for example. To play to win the game is a recognized desire of the participant. This need originated through a combination of natural, learned, and artificially created motivations. The situation is complex and lifelike, involving dedicated activity, social interaction, independence and interdependence, decisions, choices, and responsibility. There are arbitrary restrictions (natural laws of the physical environment, rules of the game, styles of play), but there is an abundant opportunity and a necessity for freedom, initiative, self-control, self-evaluation, creative expression, character and personality development, and democratic cooperation and competition. Although there are authorities whose control must be recognized (coaches, officials, captains), it is possible to appeal to them or utilize them as resources for assisting individual actions and choices in the effort to achieve the immediate objectives. A team huddle in a hastily called time-out after an adverse tendency in the course of the game is a situation filled with true educational potential. This potential might, of course, be subverted partly or markedly if the time-out is an occasion for the coach to assume all initiative and responsibility for maneuvers to solve the problem.

To the pragmatist, the role of the teacher is that of leader, not of director; that of resource-person and counselor, not of commander; that of motivator and stimulator, not of dictator. The teacher should guide and aid the individual and the group to make appropriate choices and responses. The response-to-command method of teaching should be avoided. To the extent that commands, signals, and cues calling for conditioned responses are unavoidable, the pragmatic teacher attempts to make these a functional adjunct to the learner's pursuit of his own goals. Where strict formations and alignment patterns are an essential part of the activity (as in a relay race or in offensive and defensive systems in team sports), the functional and cooperative aspects are emphasized; furthermore, the participants have a part in the selection, evaluation, and modifications of the formal pattern. Those alignments and formal movement patterns that contain options and that encourage intelligent choice, creative and expressive responses, and versatility of participation receive definite preference.

In the determination of teaching methods, broad educational effectiveness is the criterion. Methods designed or employed exclusively for the purpose of class control and discipline, in a restrictive or punitive sense, are not used. Class control and discipline are approached positively, and are accomplished through appeal to spontaneous or intrinsic motivations, and through the teaching of self-discipline, self-control, and cooperative effort. The pragmatist abhors the response-to-command method because it produces regimentation when he wants self-discipline, obedience when he wants initiative, and conformity when he wants creativity.

Evaluation

When the matter of evaluation is approached, some distinct philosophic differences appear. The scientific measurement movement in education is basically a product of the philosophy of realism. The emphasis on objectivity and standardization in educational measurement is abhorrent to both pragmatists and idealists. Pragmatists object most to the element of standardization, which also tends to standardize and stabilize the whole educational process. Idealists object most to the application of scientific criteria to subject disciplines other than science, for they tend to depend on historical, comparative, and philosophic criteria more than on scientific measurement. Idealists would measure, but they would measure different things and in a different way. The pragmatist parts company with both the idealist and the realist because he does not accept their assumption of the independent existence of real or ideal things. He rejects, on philosophic grounds, the very premise of absolute or direct measurement; namely, that anything that exists, exists in some amount and therefore can be measured. Wahlquist cited Dewey's point that the teacher is concerned primarily with things that do not in any definite sense exist—the process of growth, the transformation of capacity into achievement, the solving of life problems.[118]

Testing has progressed from anthropometry (dimensions) to dynamometry (mechanical function) to cardiorespirometry (physiologic function) to sociometry (social efficiency). Likewise, the measurement of physical and physiologic attributes has been supplemented by the measurement of knowledge, attitudes, appreciations, adjustments, and personality. In general, measuring has been supplanted by evaluation. In the former, tests were administered by a teacher or proctor; in the latter, the process is conducted primarily by and according to the standards of the participants, and the results are expected to lead to immediate changes in self-direction. Pragmatists are not oriented toward the measurement of muscular strength by a dynamometer, but toward the ability to respond successfully to an unpredictably changing life situation.

Evaluation, rather than measurement, is the alternative proposed by the pragmatist. Objective evidence may be taken into account, but evaluation is essentially subjective judgment used by a competent participant in order to determine whether his purposes have been achieved in practice. Evaluation involves participation and is internal, essentially a function of the individuals or groups involved in the activity being evaluated. Evaluation encompasses the identified needs, the chosen activities, the resultant outcomes, and the relationships of these to each other. It is not a matter of applying external or absolute criteria. For example, it would not be enough for the pragmatist to know the overall percentage of children who could pass a minimum fitness test. (There is no doubt that he would find more meaning in the concept of total fitness than in the concept of physical fitness.)

To the pragmatist, evaluation is continuous. It is not a separate topic, but an integral part of the pragmatic method. As a matter of fact, the emphasis on evaluation is perhaps the crowning virtue of a pragmatic educational philosophy, from the functional point of view.

The Administrator and Administration

Health, physical education, and recreation, according to the pragmatist, would be unified within the school system because they are basically related, and when they are coordinated they serve the needs of children more effectively. Any effort to fragment the curriculum into separate areas of physical education, health, recreation, intramurals, and so forth would need to be carefully and thoroughly evaluated, and possible effects on the learner considered, before any division of studies would be effected. The pragmatist would also hold that students, faculty, and administrators should take a share, according to the unique contributions each can make, in planning, carrying out, and evaluating the whole educational enterprise.

For the pragmatist, democratic living is fostered best when all who are affected share in the planning and execution of policies. Departmental policies, therefore, are determined through democratic group process.

The administrator views administration as a social science. He acts as a servant of his colleagues to provide the best learning conditions and an atmosphere conducive to everyone's making fullest contributions to the department. All members of a department are treated as co-workers and all participate in committee projects designed to improve departmental functions.

In-service training programs are teacher-centered and -conducted. Faculty promotions are effected by group-determined standards. Merit raises, if given, are based on individual growth in democratic group behavior.

Teacher Preparation

The appearance of differentiated collegiate majors in physical education, health education, recreation, dance, and athletic coaching would be questioned. Are the professional abilities required in these areas mutually exclusive? Are there discrete employment possibilities in these professions? Will not the narrow specialization of teachers increase the difficulty of providing an integrated educational experience in elementary and secondary schools?

Because the pragmatist would be concerned with unity and integration, the various aspects of physical education, health, safety education, driver education, and recreation education, for the pragmatist, are all included under one teacher preparation curriculum rather than in separate major programs.

The pragmatist would have the social sciences form important parts of the content of the professional curriculum. This curriculum would be directed toward helping the student solve his professional problems. Problems teachers encounter on the job (job analysis based on graduates' experiences) are examples of content that would provide a framework for major student learning experiences. The curriculum is flexible, rather than standardized or systematically arranged, and the student is given the opportunity to make choices in changing and planning the program.

Guidance of major students is personal, but nondirective. Teacher placement is primarily the concern of the student rather than the institution because it is a learning experience for him.

Standards for accreditation of college and universities offering teacher preparation programs are not strictly applied by the pragmatic physical educator. Rather, greater acceptance is given to concepts of self-evaluation.

Comments and Criticisms

Pragmatism, also referred to as instrumentalism and experimentalism, with its emphasis on getting things done, dealing with problems that are of immediate interest to man and a truth that works, has been called a typically American philosophy. It became the most influential philosophy in the United States in the first several decades of the twentieth century, and seems to retain that role. The pragmatic movement represented a rejection of the traditional absolutism in philosophy, and its emphasis on the nature of human affairs was compatible with the needs and aspirations of a democratic society. In stressing the social role of education, the unified nature of the individual child, and the responsibility of the school to provide for all phases of the child's life (social, emotional, intellectual, physical), the educational philosophy of Dewey provided an especially supportive rationale for including physical education in the curriculum.

Its critics, Titus points out, contend that pragmatism is based on unsound foundations and an inadequate metaphysics.[110] Although they may grant that its methods for solving problems do have usefulness in certain circumstances, many critics hold that pragmatism places too much emphasis on activity and not enough on goals. Man has interests and needs in the realm of aesthetics and ideals, as well as in practical affairs. Pragmatism is also criticized for its view that truth is man-made. We do not create truth by living right, it is suggested, we live right when we grasp and follow the truth.

Perhaps pragmatism has been most severely criticized for its contention that truth is to be verified on the basis of what works. It is not really possible to tell what works, critics assert, because the consequences may continue indefinitely. Moreover, to evaluate whether or not something works actually implies that there already exist some criteria to which to appeal; if criteria already exist, pragmatism's basic tenet is contradicted. Critics also point out that the contention that what works has no clear point of reference: is it what works for the individual, for society, under certain conditions, or for what? Pragmatism has also been criticized on the basis that personal preference is no reliable guide for judging truth. Some individuals have questioned pragmatism's tendency to rapidly change its character to meet new needs. As Smith notes, the pragmatic belief that philosophy should concentrate on immediate and specific problems to the exclusion of general, speculative problems led, in some instances, to a general skepticism of philosophy itself.[105] Because pragmatism emphasized problems of a social nature (politics and education), some critics found it relatively easy to conclude that these were matters for the social sciences not philosophy to deal with.

Translated into educational matters by Kilpatrick and others, and most notably in the progressive education movement, the pragmatic attitude, through Dewey's instrumentalism, encouraged educators to free the learner from the constraints of the traditional formal curriculum and authoritative teaching methods. Although progressivism may have helped free the schools from excessive formalism, it was also severely criticized as being anti-intellectual and overly concerned with concepts like life-adjustment.

> THE ANCIENTS DID THINGS BY DOING THE BUSINESS OF THEIR OWN DAY, NOT GAPING AT THEIR GRANDFATHER'S TOMBS—THE NORMAL MAN TODAY WILL DO LIKEWISE.
>
> —*William James*

> WE CAN RECOGNIZE THAT ALL CONDUCT IS *interaction* BETWEEN ELEMENTS OF HUMAN NATURE AND THE ENVIRONMENT, NATURAL AND SOCIAL. THEN WE SHALL SEE THAT PROGRESS PROCEEDS IN TWO WAYS, AND THAT FREEDOM IS FOUND IN THAT KIND OF INTERACTION WHICH MAINTAINS AN ENVIRONMENT IN WHICH HUMAN DESIRE AND CHOICE COUNT FOR SOMETHING. THERE ARE IN TRUTH FORCES IN MAN AS WELL AS WITHOUT HIM.
>
> —*John Dewey*

12

Other Ways of Thinking

BUILD NOT AN EMPIRE WHERE EVERYTHING IS PERFECT IF
YOU SCORN BAD TASTE, YOU WILL HAVE NEITHER PAINTING
NOR DANCING, NEITHER PALACES NOR GARDENS.
                                        —*Antoine de Saint-Exupéry*

This chapter discusses the principal themes to be found in a number of other philosophic ways of thinking: personalism, analytic philosophy, and existentialism, and the educational positions referred to as perennialism, aritomism, and essentialism. In contrast to the more traditional and long-standing philosophies like idealism and realism, these ways of thinking are restricted in their scope. They usually are limited to only one aspect of the larger whole of philosophy. Analytic philosophy, for example, hovers around science, mathematics, logic, and language. Its adherents have relatively little technical interest in metaphysical questions. Existentialism, on the other hand, reflects a preoccupation with metaphysical speculation and description, especially concerning the nature of being.

Each of these other ways of thinking may be said to be traceable to an attitude which opposes certain tendencies of the modern world. The growth of analytic philosophy, for example, occurred during the twentieth century largely as a reaction against the dominant beliefs of traditional Western philosophy, especially the idealism of the nineteenth century. Existentialism has been described as a revolt against the increasing modern tendencies to treat human beings as things, or objects, instead of *individual persons* (subjects). Personalism opposes such tendencies which many have found to be on the rise in contemporary society, such as materialism and moral breakdown. In the educational sphere, perennialism, aritomism, and in some respects, essentialism represent reactions against a number of the tendencies to be found in progressivism and seek a return to various aspects of the more traditional philosophies.

Some individuals are critical of what they feel is a too limited scope within these "other ways," a seeming lack of some of the variants to focus clearly on fixed definitions and an embarrassingly divergent point of view or interest which is sometimes to be found in the expressions of the adherents of these ways of thinking. Nonetheless, these modes are tendencies with which any thinker must be familiar in order to understand the more recent trends of formal philosophy.

PERSONALISM

Although fragments of philosophies from Heraclitus (c. 562–470 B.C.), Anaxagoras (c. 500–430 B.C.) and René Descartes' (1596–1650) maxim "I think, therefore I am" may support personalistic idealism, it is considered to be a rather modern development. The word "personalism" first appeared at the close of the eighteenth century, serving as a general term descriptive of theism as distinct from pantheism.[71] The name "personalism" appeared for the first time in 1908 as the title of a book by Borden Parker Bowne. There are also various forms of personalism including personalistic realism. However, personalistic idealism is regarded as typical personalism because it has most consistently held to the personal structure of reality. The most significant exponents of personalistic idealism are Rudolph Herman Lotze, Borden Parker Bowne, Edgar S. Brightman, Albert C. Knudson, Ralph Tyler Flewelling, and Mary Whiton Calkins.

Borden P. Bowne (1847–1910) taught a theistic idealism at Boston University to which he gave the name "personalism." His book attacked the view that all knowledge must be interpreted from the standpoint of the human personality.[11] Calkins (1863–1930) combined absolutism with personalism. Both a psychologist and philosopher, she contributed to developing the concept of personalistic psychology with the conclusion that "every idea is the experience of a self who is conscious." Her study of Gestalt theory suggested psychologic support for her doctrine.

Personalists, protesting mechanistic naturalism, argue that belief in matter or nonmental being is not reasonable. Nature is a reality to the personalist, but persons transcend nature in interpreting it.

The basic difference between personalism and other forms of idealism is that personalism holds a pluralistic rather than a monistic or dualistic view of reality. Unlike other idealistic theories such as Hegel's (which portrays universal reality as one mind which is absolute, eternal, final), the phenomenon of personhood involves many individual, personal minds which are ultimately parts of an integrated whole. Personalism, according to Flewelling, seeks in personal experience not only the meaning of reality, but the ground of universal cooperation in government, in society, and in religion.[41]

Personalistic idealists have shown considerable interest in ethics. Because personality is the prime value, they stress the realization of the full powers of the person through freedom and self-control. The person's acts determine him, and he determines his acts. Society must be organized so as to provide each person opportunity for fullness of life.

According to Flewelling, the will, then, is the particular and unique act of personality.[41] Even the movements of the body depend largely on the will and become the means of expression of desire. The inner consciousness finds objective expression through physical movement. By means of play the child prepares for the activities and situations that will become a part of his later workaday world, prepares mind and body to meet the crisis when it occurs. In play activities, therefore, there must be provision for imaginative self-development.

Because will is exercised often by performing laborious tasks, it is necessary to master the mechanical side of a skill, for example, until it becomes habit. The learner must master the material and himself.

In personalism as in idealism, the place and power of teacher suggestion, teacher character, and sympathetic contact with students are important in arousing student imagination and helping the student find his highest expression.

ANALYTIC PHILOSOPHY

The enormous impact which the scientific method had on the twentieth century also influenced philosophy. It soon became evident that although philosophy had traditionally claimed that it provided knowledge about the world, the philosopher did not carry out experiments, make empirical observations, quantify data, or perform any of the other acts usually associated with scientific undertakings. This prompted such questions as: What kind of knowledge is it that philosophy does provide? How does this knowledge differ from that which can be discovered (perhaps better) through science? Some suspicion was raised that philosophic activity had actually been nothing more than hopeful, but futile, musings. Bertrand Russell, one of the leading figures in the development of the new philosophic attitude, contended that a great deal of the confusion in thinking throughout the history of philosophy had stemmed from the failure to distinguish clearly between "a theory as to the nature of the world" and "an ethical or political doctrine as to the best way of living."[97] It was in reaction to nineteenth century idealism and the speculative metaphysical views of traditional philosophy that the movement which has come to be known as analytic philosophy arose.

Because it was Russell's view, Jones contends, that much of what had passed for philosophy was based on what the new thinkers believed to be logical confusions, the primary task of the new philosophy was to be critical.[61] Philosophy must now base its work on the only methods that, to date, have provided mankind with any real knowledge—that is, the methodology of science. In *On Scientific Method in Philosophy* Russell states that there are two ways in which philosophy may base itself on science: (1) on the general *results* of science and (2) on the *methods* of science. Philosophy may endeavor to give greater generality and unity to the results of science, or it may apply the methods proved useful in science to its own particular province.[98]

Although it has roots reaching back to the materialism of Anaximander and the ancient atomists, the philosophy of science being as old as Greek philosophy itself, analytic philosophy is usually considered to be of quite recent origin. It has been predominant in departments of philosophy in British and American universities since the 1920s. Analytic philosophy reflects the British philosopher G. E. Moore's assertion that most difficulties have been caused by attempting to answer a question before discovering precisely what the question is one is trying to answer. It includes such specialized forms of investigation as logical atomism, language philosophy, logical empiricism, scientific empiricism, logical positivism. These are all concerned, in varying ways, with the use and function of language and with how to clarify statements of ordinary language. The central task of philosophy, according to the philosophic analysts, is the *analysis of statements,* not the determination of whether or not these statements are true. Philosophy is now intended to serve science by clarifying those questions with which science can deal empirically.

In the *Principia Mathematica* (1910–1913), written with Alfred North Whitehead, Russell developed a new logic based on mathematical calculus. The main difference between this new logic and Aristotelian logic, which had influenced philosophy for over 2,000 years, is described by Popkin and Stroll.[87] Whereas Aristotelian logic was essentially a logic of *classes* (all men are mortal), Russell's was a logic of how *propositions* in ordinary language relate to each other.

Three important expressions of analytic philosophy (logical atomism, the later views of Wittgenstein, and logical positivism) are presented in the next sections. These are followed by a statement regarding the general application of analytic philosophy to education, and by selected examples of how analytic philosophy may have relevance to physical education.

Logical Atomism

Russell and Ludwig Wittgenstein, his student at Cambridge, in the years preceding World War I, developed a theory of language analysis known as "logical atomism." Logical atomism holds that the world is composed of a number of simple facts, each independent of all other facts, yet capable of being related to them. A distinction is made between what are called "atomic propositions" and "molecular propositions."

An atomic proposition is a single statement giving a particular fact. A molecular proposition is made up of more than one atomic proposition and involves the relationship between propositions. Molecular propositions must be logically analyzed into their constituent atomic propositions because only atomic propositions can describe actual facts of nature.[87]

One of the most severe criticisms to be lodged against logical atomism is that, even if its doctrines should be true, they could not be stated without being in violation of its basic tenets. This, Warnock points out, was the conclusion of Wittgenstein's *Tractatus Logico-Philosophicus* (1921). Wittgenstein concluded that most of the propositions of logical atomism did not state facts—they purported to say something *about* facts, especially about the relationships between facts and propositions. According to the logical atomist's own assertions, he noted, such propositions cannot be meaningful because they purport to say what actually cannot be said. Wittgenstein then concluded that most of the statements of philosophy, including those he had made himself, were actually without sense.[119] His famous dictum states: "Whereof one cannot speak, therefore one must be silent."

Later Views of Wittgenstein

Wittgenstein left university life and spent several years in his native Austria where he taught elementary school and associated with members of the Vienna Circle (which developed the philosophy called "logical positivism"). He returned to Cambridge in 1929, and over the years his views on language changed considerably. He contended that language was actually not as he and his contemporaries had pictured it to be. There is no *one* pattern—language is not essentially used for one purpose. Language is, in fact, much like games and, as with games, the ways of using language are diverse.

In his posthumously published *Philosophical Investigations*, Wittgenstein asks what is it that is common to all those proceedings which we call "games" (board games, card games, ball games, Olympic games). You must *look* and *see*, Wittgenstein insists, not just think about the problem. When you look at those activities called "games," you do not find something common to all but a whole series of similarities, sometimes general, sometimes in detail. (These may be referred to as "family resemblances.") Compare, he suggests, skill in chess and skill in tennis; compare skill and luck; compare activities in which there is competition between players and those of a child throwing a ball at a wall. "How can we explain what a game is?" he asks. We can start by describing it! "This *and similar things* are called games." But this, too, Wittgenstein holds, can cause problems because any general definition can also be misunderstood, and he provides the following example. "Someone says to me: 'Show the children a game.' I teach them gaming with dice, and

the other says, 'I didn't mean that sort of game.' Must the exclusion of
the game with dice have come before his mind when he gave me the
order?" As a step toward clearing up difficulties in understanding the
meaning of a word (in this case "games"), we should ask ourselves "how
did we learn the meaning of this word . . . from what sort of example?"
Wittgenstein declares.[126]

Wittgenstein, like Russell, was trained in higher mathematics and his
philosophy is often difficult to comprehend. Drawing again from Warnock,[119] Wittgenstein's message might be summed up as what a philosophic problem actually states is: "I don't know my way about." Philosophy should help us to see more clearly what was there all the time—to
see connections or relations. It is not the job of philosophy to add to
our information or to alter our language. To be able to see things more
clearly is, of course, extremely important.

Logical Positivism

In the late 1920s a group of Austrian mathematicians, scientists, and
philosophers became attracted to Russell's and Wittgenstein's ideas concerning the use of words. This "Vienna Circle" included Moritz Schlick,
Rudolf Carnap, Otto Neurath, Ernst Mach, Hans Reichenbach, and A. J.
Ayer. The philosophy which the Vienna Circle originated is called "logical
positivism." Its aim was to show that all knowledge is dependent on
logic, mathematics, and the natural sciences. Warnock describes the
essential features of the Vienna Circle as (1) an extreme distaste for
metaphysics and (2) an extreme respect for science and mathematics.[119]
Knowledge of anything not given in ordinary experience is not possible;
therefore, it is not a concern of philosophy. Most logical positivists contend that metaphysical statements are nonsense. Statements that are
neither empirical nor analytic are meaningless or, at best, they are expressions of personal feelings.

The "verifiability principle," the method by which logical positivists
hope to eliminate metaphysics, is explained by Matson.[79] It stipulates that
the meaning of a proposition is to be found in its method of verification.
If we know how to verify a proposition, we know its meaning; if we
know the meaning of a proposition, we know how to verify it. Because
it is not possible to specify those conditions under which we could verify
a statement like "the absolute is perfect," the statement can have no
meaning. It cannot be claimed to be true, nor can it be claimed to be
false. It simply is not the kind of statement with which either philosophy
or science can deal.

Although they contend that science and sense-observation are the
only true sources of knowledge (ethics, morality, aesthetics, and the like
cannot be examined by means of sense-observation), the logical positivists do not suggest that other concerns are unimportant to human

beings. Of course they are! What the logical positivists are saying is that statements about such things express an attitude or feeling on the part of the individual and should not be considered universal or unassailable truths. These things may be of interest to psychology, sociology, art, and other disciplines, but not to philosophy.

Implications of Analytic Philosophy for Education and Physical Education

The significance of analytic philosophy for physical education as for other aspects of education may be summarized in the main themes put forth by George F. Kneller.[70]

The discipline of education should be independent of traditional philosophies, which are allegedly biased, unreliable, unprovable, and have no implications necessarily for education. The problems of education should be solved by methods that are relevant to education. These methods are to make education more logical and scientific. Educators, therefore, must observe the rules of formal logic, reason consistently, avoid ambiguity, clarify the terms and rules of all discourse and debate, and apply principles of inductive probability to the verification of hypotheses, generalizations, and theories. The knowledge that educators claim must be objective, reliable, free from personal and cultural bias, and judgment must be withheld until the evidence is adequate for deciding the question. Knowledge also must be publicly testable by specialists. Most especially, analytic philosophy requires educators to redefine their basic terms, untangling the network of mixed definitions, slogans, and metaphors, which may hide an uncritical adherence to a particular educational ideology.

Although it rejects system building and has no formal theory of education, the methods of analytic philosophy can be applied to reevaluate the special language of education and physical education—to help clarify the meaning of such terms as "adjustment," "motivation," "interest," "need," and "human movement," and such statements as "sports build character" and "dance is an experience in living."

One example of how philosophic analysis might be valuable to physical education involves the matter of stating precisely what physical education *is*. During the 1960s the American Academy of Physical Education and the Big-Ten Body-of-Knowledge Project in Physical Education undertook investigations dealing with knowledge–discipline–profession relationships in physical education. The December 1967 *Quest*, devoted to the theme "The Nature of A Discipline," raised questions regarding syntax, relationship, and clarification of statements in physical education.[108] In an article in the June 1973 *Quest*, Renshaw raised the question "Is Human Movement an autonomous discipline or is it more logical to view it as a field of knowledge drawing on several distinct forms of thought?"[92] Reflecting the attitude of analytic philosophy, Renshaw concluded that, although philosophy by itself cannot solve the problems raised in his article, it could help to refine, restate, and clarify the questions which should be asked.

Another example of how the methods of analytic philosophy might be used to benefit physical education is suggested by Best, who points out that different kinds of statements need to be tested in different ways.[10] Not all questions of human behavior are empirical, therefore, not all questions can be treated in the same way. We must be careful to recognize what it really is we are asking, Best cautions: "if our interest in dance is exclusively *aesthetic*, then the notion of empirical examination is inappropriate. Aesthetic interpretation is a matter of reasons, not causes."[10] A similar warning is given by A. J. Ayer, an Oxford philosopher whose views have had a considerable currency in British physical education. Ayer contends that "the only information which we can legitimately derive from the study of our aesthetic and moral experiences is information about our own mental and physical make-up." On closer inspection, most questions of aesthetics turn out to be questions for psychology or for sociology.[4]

Comments and Criticisms

For the analytic philosopher, concepts such as being, God, and normative ethical standards are meaningless issues. Questions about good, evil, and value are outside the objective, empirical area of knowledge, and therefore have no meaning. A. J. Ayer stated: "In saying that a certain type of action is right or wrong, I am not making any factual statement, . . . I am merely expressing moral sentiments . . . it is impossible to find a criterion for determining the validity of ethical judgments."[4]

Critics of analytic philosophy, who also admit the value of formal logic and scientific method, argue that human beings have certain values, not all of which are subjective and arbitrary. Such critics say the analytic philosophers are too exclusive in their attention to the tools of philosophy, and they do not give attention to areas of human experience other than symbols and language. As John Wild pointed out: "Analytic philosophy which surrenders objective insight to focus on the logical and linguistic tools of knowledge is like a man who becomes so interested in the crack and spots of dust upon his glasses that he loses all interest in what he may actually see through them."[110]

Kaplan, however, pointed out that analytic philosophers do not undermine the basis for values and that such philosophers are concerned about the great moral issues of our time. His criticism is that what the analytic philosopher identifies as philosophy is not something he lives by, but is purely an intellectual pursuit.[63]

EXISTENTIALISM

Existentialism has been called a "movement," a "mood," an "attitude," a "philosophic outlook," a "point of view," and a "way of life." The continuing development of science and the "technological culture" based in part on it seem to be paralleled in the lives of many individuals by what they regard as the depressing insolubility of man's alienation in a machine-dominated impersonal world. The label "existentialist" gradually has been attached to those who have expressed deep concern about this human predicament. They have attempted to resolve the unfortunate human condition by motivating the individual to feel that he alone should be responsible for himself.

Existentialists protest the traditional emphasis in philosophy which deals with speculative questions and formulation of systems. They reject being labeled existentialists because doing so suggests they can be identified with a fixed body of propositions. Philosophy is not the doctrine of a philosophic school, they contend; it is life, and there are no answers to the problems of life in the back of a book. Although there are religious as well as atheistic existentialists, all existentialists "are irreligious in the sense that they consider traditional religious philosophies inadequate in defining the human condition in its most critical aspects."[63]

Existential efforts have had impacts in such areas as psychology, psychoanalysis, and charactology. Ralph Allport, Rollo May, Abraham Maslow, Victor Frankl, and others have written interesting applications to psychotherapy and motivation of ideas related to some existential premises. The existentialist himself admits "he is really a kind of literary psychologist;" he understands the human psyche, which he contends gives his philosophy human content. Some persons find existentialists more worth reading precisely when they turn their talents to psychologic questions, than when they plunge into the depths of ontology and logic.[63]

Whether or not existential psychology brings its insights into human nature within the purview of philosophy, existentialistic thought over the past few decades has been spun into poems, plays, novels, essays, criticisms, "creative" philosophy, and art. Tolstoi's short story *The Death of Ivan Ilych,* in which a modern man must face an agonizing death with no resources save the artificial conventions of a polite society, became a rich source for existentialists in their indictment of modern society. European writers such as Duerrenmatt (*The Visit*), Natalie Sarraute (*The Golden Fruits*), and Samuel Beckett (*Waiting for Godot*) grappled with what they regarded as the absurdity and the anguish of man isolated from himself and mankind. The plays of Jean-Paul Sartre (English translations: *The Flies, No Exit, Red Gloves*) and the works of his lifelong woman companion Simone de Beauvoir (*The Secret Sex, The Mandarins*) were platforms for the existential theme of the anguished, lonely individual condemned to the freedom of making his own choices.

Early and Contemporary Existential Thought

The intensity of insistence on individual responsibility is believed by some existentialists to be unique to philosophic thought. However, questions about human destiny and the individual, and concerns for the human situation have been philosophy's original problem. There are excellent illustrations in sports, for example, of man's long history (pre-Homer) of the human expectation that the individual performer is responsible for what he does. Both Simonodis and, before him, Hesiod in their poems point out this same theme. That is, before man expressed the individual's responsibility, he practiced it. Most systematic philosophies and philosophers have addressed themselves to the *individual*. Socrates, in his chief concerns for the inner man, asked 2500 years ago the same question being asked today ("What is the essence of man?") in his dictum "Know thyself." Bits of existentialism have been said to permeate many philosophies throughout the centuries. For instance, Heraclitus (c. 500 B.C.) insisted that all was flux. Rabelais' ideal Abbey of Thelma, whose motto was "fay ce que vouldras" (do what you like), and Rousseau's echo of Rabelais in his "man is born free but everywhere in chains," raised the issue of irreconcilable conflict in choice. Intellectual antecedents of Sartre's position may be found in René Descartes' "I think therefore I am," and in Blaise Pascal's "Man is a terrified thinking reed."

Although it seems that bits of existential thought may have been on the human scene for millennia, the orthodox precursor of modern Christian existentialism is said to be Soren Kierkegaard (1813–1955), a Danish theologian. His philosophy was based in part on the idea of permanent cleavage between faith and reason. For Kierkegaard, the remedy for man's ills was to cultivate the inner life, his own immortal soul, and to realize the reality of God. Rather than depersonalizing religion and attempting to make Christianity reasonable through intellectual arguments, man must embrace the absurd and paradoxical in taking the agonized "leap of faith."[65]

Kierkegaard denounced much in the Christianity of his day, the conventional unreflective church-goer or "unorthodox" Christians with their beliefs in reason, human progress, goodness of man. Removed from God by this naive humanism and pursuit of techniques, modern man, to Kierkegaard, was a "displaced person."

Friedrich Nietzsche (1844–1900) also occupies an important place in existential thought. This nineteenth century philosopher-theologian, who drove himself mad over his contempt for the world of his day, possessed an admiration for the Greek ideals of balance and moderation and the hardened life. Men such as John Stuart Mill and Herbert Spencer, according to Nietzsche, vulgarized the scientific spirit by using the techniques of science to make life easier. This was not the way to produce the "Super-Man," the man who had the "Will to Power." He opposed Christianity, also, because salvation was to be found in the creation of "Lords of the Earth," not in Christianity, democracy, or socialism. His classic proclamation in *Thus Spake Zarathustra*[85] that "God is dead" may be interpreted as emphasizing the belief that man was thrown into a world not fashioned beforehand by some benevolent Deity, and the death of God is proclaimed to make room for man to be *himself*.

Although Kierkegaard and Nietzsche had many points of disagreement, the lessons exerted by both on existentialistic thought may be summarized as follows: There is much that is wrong with human nature. Man is an existential being whose life is more than logic and who must discover the meaning of existence. There are no answers to the human predicament to be found in the back of a book; philosophy is to be lived, something to be proved in action, not something to be studied and put away.

Thus, the stage was set for the spirit of revolt, the emphasis on the inner life, and the passionate encounter with the human predicament, which was the adopted task of existentialists to describe, evaluate, and live in successfully. After World War I, two German philosophers, Martin Heidegger (1889–1976) and Karl Jaspers (1883–1969), exerted influence on existentialistic thought. They were influenced by both Kierkegaard and Nietzsche as well as by Kant. For Heidegger, man can know by insight into his own existence something of the nature of existence everywhere, the totality of being in its fullness.[49] For Jaspers also, there is the intimate human experience of love and hate, joy and tragedy, and the transcendent or authentic self which the sciences, like psychology, cannot discover.[59] For Heidegger and Jaspers it is this authentic self that gives life its meaning, and makes choice and freedom possible and the human predicament bearable.

Since its emergence as a cause célèbre after World War II, existentialism's most publicized spokesman has become the French novelist and playwright Jean-Paul Sartre (1905–   ). Sartre borrows from the men previously described. In Sartre, three contemporary streams of thought flow together: Marxism, existentialism, and phenomenology. His main philosophic works are *Being and Nothingness*[102] and *Existentialism*,[103] although he is perhaps best known for his novels, plays, and essays.

To the list of existential writers may be added Gabriel Marcel, Jacques Maritain, the novelists Fedor Dostoevski, Franz Kafka, Albert Camus, the Russian philosopher Nikolai Berdyaev, and such contemporary theologians as Karl Barth, Martin Buber, Paul Tillich, and Reinhold Niebuhr.

Some Meanings of Existentialism

Obstacles to understanding existentialism may be posed by differences of opinion among existentialists, the stylistic writings of existential proponents, the fact that existentialism lends itself better to literary than to philosophic treatment, and the use of terms which are not adequately translated or whose meaning is not agreed on. For example, the sparsity of English translations of the philosophic writings of Karl Jaspers and his involved reasoning, intricate writing style, and uniquely "Jaspersian" terms have thrown up roadblocks to some pursuers of many of his concepts.

Despite the confusion about the nature of existentialism, and despite the existentialist's objection to placing existential meanings within any set categories of philosophy, an attempt is made to describe some characteristics of existentialism.

1. The starting point for contemporary existentialist thought is with the individual's awareness of the human predicament in his *encounter* with the turmoil of life. The human being is, in Martin Heidegger's words, "forlorn" and "abandoned." On the peaks, Nietzsche proclaims, one is always alone. The existentialist is forever gazing into the void. Man is conceived as suffering from what Kierkegaard called a "sickness unto death." Facing the facts of life to which he gives his attention, so often in despair over the fact of death, the existentialist uses words such as "angst," "dread," "anguish," "care," "enduring life," "being able to stand it." The despair of which the existentialist speaks culminates in something like: the universe is without meaning or purpose; there is nothing in the world we can count on except our own wills. The starting point for some contemporary existentialistic thought lies in the metaphysical idea that "life is a tale told by an idiot, full of sound and fury, signifying nothing." The conviction of absurdity cuts all ties to history and nature.[63]

2. The name "existentialism" derives from the special sense that is given to the metaphysical category *existence*. Perhaps, then, the crux of the whole doctrine of existentialism, at least for some existentialists, lies in the metaphysical contention propounded by Sartre that "existence precedes essence." Sartre's celebrated aphorism presents a conception of man's existence. In its simplest terms that conception is: First man is, and what he is is not predetermined but is determined in the course of his existence. The world is, objects exist, man interprets them. The fact that things exist is prior to any essence or definition man gives them. Everything but man is subject to the law of identity (A is identical with A; A is A, was A, will be A). However, man exists only insofar as he shapes his own existence and thus confers an essence on it. "Because man's existence precedes his essence no definition of man is possible."[63] Sartre, in making the point that existence precedes essence, stated: "man

exists, turns up, appears on the scene, and, only afterwards defines himself . . . at first he is nothing. Only afterwards will he be something and he himself will have made what he will be . . . he is also what he wills himself to be . . . nothing other than what he makes himself."[103]

3. If man is the existent that determines his own essence, his most fundamental attribute is absolute freedom in his capacity for *choice*. These acts of choice express the conception that existence precedes essence. Because man is free, he makes himself. This is the significance of Sartre's "man is continually becoming what he was not," and Kierkegaard's "either/or."[63]

The supreme virtue is integrity or *authenticity*, honesty with oneself and others. For Jaspers, life is a drive toward honesty, toward really being what we are. Only the authentic man is what he is. Correspondingly, phoniness in whatever form, self-deception is the greatest vice.[63]

To be authentic, to the existentialist, means freely choosing one's own behavior, attitude, and mode of living regardless of what others expect one to be. Man's distinctive existence lies only in making a choice—to choose freely and to assume responsibility for the choice. Existence, then, in the existential lexicon implies something active, an emergence from passiveness ("Do something! Exist!"). Everyone can choose to lead an authentic existence or choose to be lost in the crowd: "to be different, as a matter of principle, is also a kind of conformity and negates freedom, responsibility, authenticity." He is truly *engaged* in discovering the meaning of existence through commitment of thought and action rather than middle-class drift.[63]

When he makes a choice, the existentialist is choosing not merely for himself but for all men. The awareness of the burden of this crushing responsibility for the fate of mankind in every choice the existentialist calls "anguish." Freedom of choice is a dreadful thing. Kierkegaard spoke of the "dizziness of freedom," while Sartre echoed, "man is condemned to be free."[63]

4. There must be alternative possibilities of action, or choice would be meaningless, and there must be alternative possibilities of existence, or existence would be predetermined by essence. These possibilities give rise to the final basic existential category *ambiguity*. Jaspers called it the "endless ambiguity of all existence and action." He said, "We live in a seething cauldron of possibilities."[63]

Educational Implications of Existential Thought

Although no existentialist has as yet addressed himself strictly to the application of his philosophy to the problems of education, a few writers have described approaches to education as viewed from the existentialistic platform. One difficulty existentialism has in educational application seems to be just how and when the teacher practices being an existentialist and when and how the student does.

Kneller attempted to establish points of contact by using such pertinent themes of education as (1) anguish and death; (2) the individual and the others; (3) knowledge and the knower; (4) values and the individual; (5) the teacher and the student; and (6) the educational process. Paraphrases of Kneller's viewpoints on each of these pertinent themes follow.[70]

Anguish and Death. Students should be shown that it is only the thought of death which makes us aware of the values of life. To die for an ideal may be finer than preserving one's life. The teacher should describe such examples (Christ, Socrates) and lead the student to examine the quality of his own life, letting him ask himself "Would it have mattered whether I lived at all?"

The Individual and Others. If the primary concern of an educational system is with the average rather than the exceptional student, mediocrity will be substituted for the possibility of brilliance and the individual will be compelled to conform to the average.

The educational system must permit much greater variety in its methods and organization. All children should not be educated at the same rate in the same way or in groups. Rather they should be educated as individuals. Group instruction is not rejected, but it is used for individual fulfillment. The school cannot be expected to do the educative job of the parents who should have the responsibility for the fullest development.

Knowledge and the Knower. There is no such thing as disinterested knowledge. Man is not an intellect alone but a creature of feeling as well. In order to know something he must be able to relate to himself personally. Knowledge brings freedom, because it delivers man from ignorance and prejudice.

Subject matter, therefore, is a means for the cultivation of the self rather than being an end in itself or an instrument to prepare the student for his career. Because the meaning of existence lies in man himself, the curriculum must shift from an emphasis on the world of objects to the world of the person.

Values and the Individual. Individualism is not essentially social individualism and values are not automatically those adopted by the group. Because the basis of morality is freedom of human choice, values must be freely chosen. The individual cannot be expected to conform to values that have been laid down independently of him. The teacher should not expect to condition the student into accepting timeless moral principles, but should bring home to the student the idea that he must accept the consequences of his own free choice.

Frustration and conflict are not to be avoided because they are part of the human condition. The school should acquaint the student with the darker side of life—with its pain, terror, brutality—as well as with its beauty, ecstasy, joy. The student must become personally concerned with what Tillich called "the courage to be."

The Teacher and the Student. Teaching is an intimate relation of two beings. Children are by nature curious to discover, pioneer, and invent and the teacher must enter into the kind of relationship with his pupil that releases creativity. The teacher's function, therefore, is to assist the student toward self-realization. He stimulates latent originality by urging the student to challenge and criticize his views, advising him not to be daunted by the fear of error, exhorting him not to take the opinion of others for granted or to merely imitate.

The teacher does not seek to ridicule the rebellious child or to berate the backward pupil. Each student is encouraged to commit himself to his work, handling what he learns in order to enhance his freedom and originality rather than merely to produce a lot of information on demand.

The Educational Process. Although the existentialist is less concerned with what is taught than the purpose for which it is learned, he subscribes to a considerable body of traditional subject matter. The student must discipline himself to learn thoroughly about the reality in which he lives and the "giveness" of the world in which his freedom is exercised. Great importance is attached to the humanities (history, literature, art, philosophy) because they reveal the nature of man and his conflicts with the world.

Subject matter should not be taught with so-called objectivity (for example, history taught merely as a catalogue of facts), but in such a way as to fire the student's thoughts and feelings and become part of him.

The existentialist opposes overspecialization, because it stunts the growth of the total inner life, and emphasizes vocationalism which trains him to be a particular kind of person.

The Socratic method of learning is the ideal, because by it the student learns what he personally asserts to be true. The teacher questions beliefs, and forces the student to probe the workings of his own mind.

The problem-centered approach to learning is rejected on the grounds that problems chosen concern the student chiefly in his role as a social being. Solutions insulated from the individual's feelings are valueless to the authentic individual.

Implications of Existentialism for Physical Education

As was noted in the previous section, existentialism has been largely concerned with various philosophic issues and has not applied those concerns to any great extent to the educative process. Certain inferences may be drawn from the existentialist's position, however, which relate to the educational enterprise or to the larger concern of pertinence here, that of man in physical activity. These inferences derive almost completely from what has already been described in existential theorizing.

In general, it may be concluded that various forms of physical activity are seen by the existentialist as a means of living humanly. Self is the primary frame of reference. There are no public standards, fictional heroes, or deliberate moral instructions to be used as ultimate reference points for determining what the individual should do, be, have, or get from physical activities. He is alone in the value enterprise, released from the expectations of other people and what is approved or disapproved. What is considered beautiful is the composing of his own personal work of art, the private expression of his own inner feeling. What is considered good is the awakening of self to responsibility.

In sports, dance, games, exercise, only the individual would be considered as having authentic knowledge of beauty, grace, skill, form. Whatever activities in a program of physical education would permit the individual his own private judgments and afford him a means to achieve on his own accord would be considered desirable. Among the most promising candidates within the school curriculum for stressing the existential ideal of personal liberation would be creative dance, movement exploration, and play activities.

Movement exploration, for example, may be regarded as basically existential in its approach. The song title "Every Little Movement Has a Meaning All Its Own" might be said to express the existential point of view, in the sense that the individual is free to explore space, shape, size, time, tempo, and relationships, and to find in this experience expressions of private feelings and what he wants to say about the world. Dance educators perhaps have been among the first to approach the existential theme of "to dance is to live." Laban defined dance as "an experience of living," and advanced the conviction that "man moving is a total human in 'being'"—man knows himself through his movement.[26]

The importance of the play element in sports and games is emphasized by some existentialists. The game is in the playing rather than in the result. Presumably the more impromptu the game, the freer the players are to achieve release in play, giving rein to creativity.

Team games are regarded as having little value by some existentialists when individual self-expression is subordinated to team effort directed toward winning. Moreover, from the existentialist point of view, the contestant in an athletic contest cannot achieve moral stature just by doing as he is told. He must come to decisions for himself. If he is coached on the answers, he demonstrates that he does not know himself. Perhaps this idea has application to such questions as: Should the athlete cut his hair or in other ways conform to decisions regarding behavior made by someone else? Should the coach call the plays? Kneller, discussing Sartre's analysis of play and sport, wrote:

> In sport, man abandons himself to his freedom, personally choosing the values and rules of his own physical activity, and the desire to play corresponds with the desire to *be* a certain type of person. . . . most varsity sports, parading such ideals as 'fighting for dear old Alma Mater,' have little place in the existential scheme of things because the hero of the day, who has scored the winning touchdown or knocked the winning run, may well be a completely unauthentic person. His athletic values may have been prefabricated for him.[70]

For the existentialist, the world of superstars and super bowls, wherein performance is measured only by the highest standard, would negate the meaning of sport as personal experiencing. Felshin contends that increasing concerns for the "products" of sport performance—victory, medals—has led more and more to devices that dichotomize the human from his own body and its effort.[40] The use of drugs and other efforts to improve or control the conditions of performance, such as training, team selection, and strategy choices, alter the mode of experiencing the essence of the struggle toward perfection and victory. This structure of sport has a nonpersonal, dehumanized essence.

The existentialist, as Vanderzwaag pointed out, would have a skeptical view of what he considers the addiction to sensationalism and superficial attraction of professional football "wherein millions of adult males are completely absorbed by the TV spectacles and boys throughout the nation are involved in the pass, punt and kick contests."[117] As Vanderzwaag put it, "Self-image has been sacrificed on the altar of group demand and tradition."

Sport situations such as those described, as well as jogging or any other activity done only because it is the "in thing" to do, might lead some existentialists to feel that participants may lose their social freedom through social pressures. Some existentialists would accept the goal of total fitness with a balance between competitive and cooperative activities, provided the individual was free to choose the values he wishes to derive and his accomplishments are based on self-evaluation.

The equality revolution in recent years has provided some illustrations of existential themes. The existentialist would resist what has been called the socialization constructs and constraints of "femininity" and "female-type-sports" in athletic programs for women. There are no suitable role-expectations for women in the sports world. Defined existentially, the essence of sport and sources of meaning in sport for women are not different from or less than those for the male athlete.

Comments and Criticisms

Some nonexistentialists commend existentialists who call attention to what they regard as the critical problems of modern civilization, the dehumanization of man and the destruction of moral values. The typical existentialist feels that most philosophies overlook such vital crucialities and become enmeshed in pseudoproblems of their own making. Some nonexistentialists find parts of existentialist thought most rewarding as it deals with psychologic questions and if it also succeeds in producing deeper insights into human nature. Some nonexistentialists also believe that existentialism emphasizes not only the constraints to which man is subjected, but also the importance of man's freedom and his vast possibilities for giving meaning to life.

Some criticisms of existentialistic thought center around its presumptuousness in putting man in the place of God.

> Of all the theories which attempt to account for man's aspirations, sense of purpose and of right and wrong in a world which does not clearly correspond at all times to all of them, the existential theory seems to me the most improbable and indeed to be a logical monstrosity . . . to say that the transcendental does not exist, that man is nothing but a part of a meaningless universe, but that, nevertheless, he can create meaning and purpose seems to me to involve a self-contradiction.[73]

Wells and Shaw, the two most influential utopians of the twentieth century, ended with the same conclusion as did Krutch: "Man," each said, "is not good enough to create Utopia—quite possibly not good enough to survive much longer."[73]

The reaction of some existentialists is that religion has not resolved the human predicament any better than science or philosophy. The view that sees a world with a God in it to care for us may be a comforting nostrum for our spiritual ache, says one existentialist, but the difficult problem of man encountering his own essence is not acted on.[81]

Some critics are concerned with the implications of existential *freedom*. They contend that man being free to do as he pleases proposes an irresponsible moral doctrine. They refer to many works in contemporary literature and the arts, suggesting that the writers and artists of these works have become so preoccupied with Sartre's type of freedom that they have distorted the existential concern over freedom into a puerile infatuation with license.

> Man must make the best of freedom, his singular and most cherished gift. But one gets the impression from reading the literature that its use, its unstinted and enthusiastic use is also its complete justification. One finds neither a deep concern for the restraint of freedom nor a search for an explanation of this unusual phenomenon in a world that largely lacks it. Existentialism takes freedom as a fact, not as a paradox.[77]

Works such as Duerrenmatt's *The Visit* (the world made me a pros-
titute so I've turned the world into a brothel) suggest to some critics
that the nihilistic, degenerate, and brutal repudiation of any moral code
by many leaders in the arts, literature, and music is at the core of the
increasing violence within our domestic life. What cannot be doubted,
according to Krutch, is that this is indeed an age of violence, both public and private.[73] "Publicly, it is an age of revolutions, small wars, and
riots; privately, an age of vandalism and brutal assaults that suggest the
'unmotivated act' of the existential novel, though the perpetrator usually
can give no such rationalized explanation."[73]

However, the existentialist contends he is not saying "freedom to
do anything"; he adds the phrase "with responsibility," which means
that when we choose we are choosing for mankind. Choosing honestly
that which one believes to be the meaning of man is magnificently moral,
according to many existentialists. Morris points out, "Here is the final
guard against rascality in Existential doctrine."[81]

Some critics of existential freedom describe it as being hyperpersonal,
as negating community values, and that this is not a realistic attainment
(excepting in nihilism). The viewpoints of Kierkegaard, for example,
who wanted his epitaph to read, "Here lies the individual," and of Sartre,
who said, "Other people are Hell," seem to illustrate a lack of concern
for others.

One existentialist's thesis, however, is that Dewey's experimentalistic
notion of shared experience represents an underlying reason for the
"supersocialized life." Most existentialists contend that the *social experience* does not represent the sum total of human reality, and that man
still feels lost in this age of social man. In becoming enmeshed in sharing, togetherness, or group dynamics, the individual has forgotten his
own private self as a choice-maker.

Perhaps the most prolific and compelling criticisms of existentialism
are directed at its emphasis on one set of feelings, as though this were
a clue to understanding life, for existentialism's preoccupation is largely
with the psychopathologic aspects of living. Although the existentialist
may say that much in contemporary literature and the arts is, as Buber
implores, teaching people to see reality around them, critics of this "tell-
it-like-it-is" position, call it *sick* because of its pessimism and morbidity.
Joseph Wood Krutch suggested that the difference between interludes
in some contemporary plays and those of burlesque is the difference between self-pity and laughter.[73] The existential hero cannot trip a police-
man or throw a custard pie in the face of his tormentors. It is always
he who gets slapped, never he who slaps. The clown makes us think,
"There but for the grace of God, go I." The existentialist's hero asks us
to conclude instead, "Since there is no God to grant the grace, there
in fact am I."

If man's existence is a "vexation of spirit," there is nothing in the world to count on except our will. "Why should this state of affairs drive us to despair?" Kaplan asks.

> The Stoics started from the same premise and drew from it quite the contrary conclusion, that it provides an unshakable basis for the cheerfulness and equanimity of a rational self. Spinoza made that premise the starting point of a logical progression to the blessedness of the intellectual love of God. Gautama Buddha, repudiating the metaphysics of both Self and God, found repose in the will to master the will, and from his deathbed charged his disciples, 'Be ye lamps unto yourselves!' If cheerfulness, blessedness, and repose seem so foreign to existentialism, it is because they are not as native to the human spirit as are anguish, nausea, and despair. . . .[63]

To this line of argument, the existentialist would agree that he dwells on the depressing aspects of the human predicament, but he does so only in order to cancel the pseudo-optimistic view that this predicament has been solved. This negative response to the human condition, the existentialist contends, is a positive, optimistic, affirmative approach because it frees man to redesign himself. This idea leads to a consideration that the physical educator may wish to make of some of the contemporary literature in the world of sports, particularly professional athletics. Emerging simultaneously with the cult of the candid in the arts, music, and drama is a literature spawned by the professional athlete and committed to illuminating "the real thing." As Reising points out, the image of the so-called anti-hero dominates much of contemporary sport literature.[91] Although a large segment of the public believes writers like Beckett and Albee are "speaking to their condition," others contend that their characters do not describe life in meaningful terms that are not dispirited, confused, and ugly.

If sports figures worthy of admiration are among those conspicuously absent in modern America, can the sport world really be used to provide examples of the ethics and morality of competition? On the other hand, does contemporary literature adequately describe life? If so, is this all that literature should do? Krutch referred to the comment "If it were not for poetry, few men would fall in love" as a way of saying that *great* literature describes life in terms which confer meaning on it. If honor, duty, and the like are to be salvaged, Krutch contends, then someone must write about them with conviction. If we should get along without them, then someone must describe a world where they are absent in a fashion which makes that kind of world seem worth living. Critics of existentialistic sports literature may concur with Krutch that they can know the good and beautiful not only through a portrayal of their opposites. Moreover, these critics may believe that one can hardly feel that a character is ennobled by adherence to such practices as rough language and lust, which are merely tawdry demonstrations of man's essence.

Whatever their philosophic position may be, members of the profession of physical education, as they read current literature about this discipline and its affiliate, organized athletics, should find it advisable to decide for themselves whether some book or article has been written as a serious concern for the sociomoral future of athletics. The person whose name is listed as author or ghostwriter may or may not be motivated to write out of an honest desire to get at solutions. Perhaps he may be motivated out of awareness for the marketability of his name, as well as for the current proclivity for finding something wrong with athletics or other kindred "fair game" for the cynical and the skeptical.

PERENNIALISM

Robert M. Hutchins and Mortimer J. Adler, who joined forces at the University of Chicago in 1929, formulated many of the basic principles of the educational philosophy known as perennialism. Other leading exponents of perennialism have been Nicholas M. Butler, Mark Van Doren, Stringfellow Barr, and Scott Buchannan. Hutchins and Adler criticized what they believed to be the extreme anti-intellectualism of public education in the United States, and developed the Great Books project which proclaimed that the great works of literature, philosophy, history, and science contain enduring ideas and truths that never lose their value for mankind. The fundamental belief of perennialism was articulated by Hutchins when he stated: "the function of a man as a man is the same in every age and in every society, since it results from his nature as a man. The aim of an educational system is the same in every age and in every society where such a system can exist: it is to improve man as man."[56]

Perennialism is critical of several of the theories advanced by progressive education, especially the progressivist's emphasis on relativism and change. The primary responsibility of the school, the perennialist holds, is to provide an intellectual education. Such things as life-adjustment and social reform which appeal to the transient interests of the child are minimized, if not totally rejected, by the perennialist.

According to Kneller, "Perennialism stipulates that the basic principles of education are changeless, or perennial. Its philosophical foundations are those of classical realism, although it is supported also by many idealists. The philosophers it quotes most often are Aristotle and Aquinas."[69] The six basic principles of perennialism cited by Kneller are: (1) because human nature is constant, the nature of education remains constant, too; (2) because man's most distinctive characteristic is his ability to reason, education should concentrate on developing the rational faculty; (3) the only type of adjustment to which education should lead is adjustment to the truth, which is universal and unchanging; (4) education is not a replica of life but preparation for it; (5) children should be taught certain basic subjects that will acquaint them with the world's permanencies, both spiritual and physical; and (6) these permanencies are best studied in what perennialists call the "Great Books."

Several of Hutchin's and Adler's general views regarding education and physical education are presented in the section entitled Aritomism which follows.

ARITOMISM

Although some important differences and distinctions may be found among perennialism and two other educational philosophies labeled intellectualism and formalism, adherents of the views of these three modes of thought would all find considerable agreement with characteristics identified in the philosophy which Brubacher has called aritomism.*

If the *theological* tenets of Scholasticism or Thomism (see Chapter 10, Realism) are avoided and the remainder synthesized with Aristotelianism, aritomism is the result. Like the realist, the aritomistic aim is human happiness. Whereas the realist proposes to reach it by adjustment to life and the world, the aritomist plans to reach it through reason, or through following supernatural laws. Aritomism requires a top role for man's intellect. Rational man, ever seeking truth, comes to see that one way of reaching toward it is through finding unchanging truths and then synthesizing them. The aritomistic emphasis given to such concepts as self-discipline, the development of the will, and formalism is also somewhat like that found in realism. The aritomist also agrees with the realist in believing that the senses bring in important information from the world, although the *degree* of importance he gives to the role played by science and to his senses is not to be compared with that of the realist. The aritomist sees these media bringing into man's consciousness only some truths; however, he regards any truths arrived at intuitively superior to the truths coming from science and his senses.

Because all men are born with tendencies toward immaturities and toward seeking the eternal verities (truth, good, beauty), the goals of a basic education are the same for all men in all places, circumstances, and times. This belief leads the aritomists to accept two words familiar to the idealist, *universal* and *absolute*. Such matters as *basic* educational curricula become universal and stable.

To some extent the aritomist recognizes a place for man's emotions and feelings. This is illustrated in an interest in beauty. However, some aritomists believe beauty becomes a reality to man only through his in-

*Aritomism is a word coined by Brubacher and used by Donn Baer in his doctoral study, in which he classifies philosophic positions into two broad categories (spiritualism and naturalism).

tellect. It is his mental abilities that bring him to the place where he can appreciate (feel) beauty in something. These same aritomists believe it is man's mind that guides him, pulling him here, pushing him there, in the direction of producing a thing of beauty. Then there is the view that man comes to distinguish that which is beautiful from that which is ugly through his mind, whereas other aritomists believe this is an intuitive experience. One *knows* that this sunset, this panorama, this rose, this movement is beautiful, and that certain others lack beauty.

One source of interest to the physical educator is a dualism inherent in aritomism. This dualism springs from those aritomists who emphasize their philosophy's God-centeredness and from others who emphasize man's rational nature. Both groups place a consideration of man's physical nature as of secondary, if any, importance.

Many physical educators in thinking of their profession wonder if the influence of aritomism can be anything but negative. Not only is it significant to them that Robert Maynard Hutchins is an aritomist, but also that, although aritomists refer to man as a rational animal, they seem to neglect him as a whole human being.

Championing the liberal arts tradition, Hutchins and Adler would make a somewhat truncated version of that tradition the subject matter on which college students would "cut their teeth" (the figure of speech is Adler's). Philosophy, literature, history, and the arts would be the instruments whereby the intelligence and sensibility would be trained. Hutchins, who declared that the university is not a custodial establishment nor a body-building institution, protested against extracurricular activities such as big-time intercollegiate athletics. He implied that athletes may be compelled to demonstrate the four cardinal virtues (courage, justice, prudence, and tolerance), but their contribution, important as it may be, does not justify the time, money, and effort that go into them, and such activities hardly help answer the question of what is the special role of an institution of higher learning.[55]

By way of contrast, John Henry Cardinal Newman's *The Idea of a University*, as reported by John Williams, sets forth the idea that physical education is suited for inclusion in a liberal education which aims at achieving a "habit of mind . . . which lasts through life, of which the attributes are freedom, equitableness, calmness, moderation, and wisdom."[125] In contrast with a narrow view of *liberal*, Newman presented the idea that "there are bodily exercises which are liberal, and mental exercises which are not so." Newman explained, "That alone is liberal knowledge, which stands on its own pretensions, which is independent of sequel, expects no complement, refuses to *be informed* (as it is called) by any end, or absorbed into any art, in order to duly present itself to our contemplation."

One might ferret out further positive implications of aritomism:

1. One aritomistic influence is its emphasis on the great importance of teaching moral-spiritual standards, conduct, and values. Although the orthodox aritomist may not admit that some of the most fundamental standards of human conduct are taught in and by means of physical education, the aritomistic physical educator *knows* they are taught here.

2. The emphasis given man's intellect should find ready response from the modern physical educator who uses searching, brief questions in his teachings, motivating the student to use his rational skills.

3. Neither the orthodox aritomist nor the aritomistic physical educator apologizes for the old-fashioned emphasis he makes on students performing difficult, demanding and even disagreeable tasks toward the end of developing the will. They are not embarrassed in advocating the need to exercise a good deal of self-discipline if the student is to improve.

4. Some aritomists see physical education in the role of an antidote to the rigors of prolonged periods of mental activity.

5. Closely related to 4 is the aritomistic belief that physical education is accepted as a catharsis, providing a channel for relieving pent-up energies of youth.

6. Persons interested in dance find the aritomistic physical educator interested in the aesthetic aspect on the basis of "art-for-art's-sake." Again, it is man's mind that feels drawn to that which is beautiful.

7. The aritomist, somewhat like the idealist, believes that some of man's potentialities should be developed to their capacity. These, of course, are restricted to man's mental, moral, and spiritual abilities. An associated influence of aritomism is belief in encouraging the topnotch performer. This belief is not apt to apply to the development of highly skilled athletes, but the principle applies to them if they are intellectually gifted.

8. Some aritomists prefer calisthenics to games and sports not only because of the supposed greater demand for greater self-discipline, but also because they believe calisthenics demands a greater use of the memory and the will. Other aritomists prefer an emphasis on games and sports because they lead more directly to happiness, the avowed aim of aritomism.

9. The aritomistic teacher does not apologize for his belief in old-fashioned drill, regardless of student attitude. In fact, believing in faculty psychology, he may feel that the student develops more self-discipline and willpower if he objects to doing drills.

10. The aritomist is a businesslike teacher, and like the realist, places importance on a well-organized, systematic program and its execu-

tion. Somewhat related is the similarity between the realist and aritomist who exercise more social distance and impersonality than does the idealist. The idealist's great emphasis on development of the student's personality is of no more particular concern to the aritomist than to the realist.

11. The aritomistic administrator of a physical education department would be expected to maintain quite impersonal relations with staff members and students. He would maintain high standards of efficiency and effectiveness for himself and those under him. At the college level, he would expect his staff to demonstrate scholarly attainment.

12. The aritomist tends to go to great pains to build the best programs possible (based on the best of the past, plus the indicated additions suggested by science), and then persistently adheres to this "best" program. He is of short patience with those who advocate constant changes in the physical education program. He does not see why every physical educator everywhere at each educational level cannot agree to a permanent core of activities and then stick with this core, adding others according to climate, topography, and facilities.

ESSENTIALISM

Essentialism was founded in the early 1930s primarily as an educational movement. Brameld said the word "essentialism" was coined by M. J. Demiashkevich, an educational philosopher. In 1938, William C. Bagley described "An Essentialist's Platform for the Advancement of American Education."[6]

Essentialism is compatible with various philosophies. Theodore Brameld, noting the common grounds of the educational aspects of the philosophies of idealism and realism, suggests that both groups are represented within the school of educational thought designated essentialism.[12] John Brubacher described four primary philosophic positions under essentialism:[15] namely, idealism, naturalistic realism, rational humanism, and Catholic super-naturalism, although he sees idealism as being on the border line in relation to the other essentialistic positions. Zeigler illustrated a "refined educational philosophy spectrum" charting two broad positions: progressivism (including romantic naturalism, experimentalism, reconstructionism) and essentialism (including naturalistic realism, rational humanism, scholastic realism), with idealism being between the two and somewhat nearer essentialism.[129]

Essentialism also has been described in relation to an antithetical position—that of educational progressivism. Vanderzwaag pointed out the relationship of essentialism to political and social conservatism, and the relationship of progressivism to political and social liberalism.[116] Similarly, Brameld, describing essentialism as "cultural conservation," stated that essentialism is not opposed to progressivism as a whole, only to some specific progressive doctrines.[70]

Contemporary essentialism has been identified with such educational figures as Arthur Bestor, Bernard Bell, James Conant, Paul Woodring, and Mortimer Smith, and with the political position of the "new conservatives." It also has the support of Herman H. Horne.

The educational position of essentialism is that there is a fundamental or essential core of knowledge, skill, and values that should be transmitted to all students. That which is considered essential is based on the tried and the true, the accumulated wisdom of the race. For most essentialists, moral values do not change although man's concepts about them may vary. Because the history of the race has disclosed essential realities, the essentialist takes the view that it is important to transmit the established values of the past. Man has proclivities to strive toward truth, to seek the good, and to create and recognize beauty. Left to express his own nature he seeks to attain these eternal verities.

Essentialism differs from perennialism in that it is not so much concerned with certain eternal truths as with adjustment of the individual to his environment. Great achievements of the past are sources of knowledge to the essentialist for dealing with general problems of the present. Many essentialists believe that physical science rather than behavioral science has contributed more to educational practice.

In sharp contrast with the progressive educators, the essentialist is critical of specialization, or vocational training, and calls for a broad discipline in the liberal arts. Differing from progressivism, essentialism reestablishes the teacher as the authority in the classroom. The essentialist tends to resist the school as an institute of social reconstruction; rather, he characterizes the school as the educational arm of society and as such it has a unique function.

Essentialist doctrine emphasizes industriousness (the effort that leads to interest rather than the interest that leads to effort), discipline, thoroughness, logical organization of subject matter, cultivation of the intellect, and moral stamina.

NEW THINGS ARE SELDOM ESTABLISHED EXCEPT BY INSINU-
ATING THEMSELVES INTO THE OLD—A LESSON WHICH YOUTH
LEARNS WHEN YOUTH IS GONE.

—Will Durant

References—Part II

1. Agard, W. R.: *The Greek Mind.* New York: D. Van Nostrand Company, Inc., 1957.

2. Avey, A. E.: *Handbook in the History of Philosophy.* New York: Barnes & Noble, Inc. 1961, p. 181.
3. Axtell, J. L.: *The Educational Writings of John Locke.* Cambridge: University Press, 1968, pp. 344–346.
4. Ayer, A. J.: *Language, Truth and Logic.* Harmondsworth, England: Penguin Books, 1946, pp. 149–151.
5. Ayer, A. J., et al.: *Revolution in Philosophy.* New York: St. Martin's Press, Inc., 1956, pp. 108–109.
6. Bagley, W. C.: An essentialist's platform for the advancement of American education. *Educational Administration and Supervision,* XXIV, 241–256, 1938.
7. Baker, A. E.: *How to Understand Philosophy.* New York: George H. Doran Company, 1926.
8. Ballou, R. B., Jr.: *An Analysis of the Writings of Selected Church Fathers to* A.D. 394 to Reveal Attitudes Regarding Physical Activity. Unpublished Doctoral Dissertation, University of Oregon, December, 1965.
9. Barrett, W.: *Irrational Man: A Study in Existential Philosophy.* New York: Doubleday & Company, Inc., 1958, pp. 6–7.
10. Best, D. N.: Empirical examination of dance—a reply. *Br. J. Phys. Educ., IV,* xii–xiii, 1973.
11. Bowne, B. P.: *Personalism.* New York: Houghton, Mifflin and Company, 1908, p. 2.
12. Brameld, T.: *Philosophies of Education in Cultural Perspective.* New York: Holt, Rinehart & Winston, 1955.
13. Breasted, J. H.: *The Dawn of Conscience.* New York: Charles Scribner's Sons, 1947.
14. Broudy, H. S.: *Building a Philosophy of Education.* Englewood Cliffs, N.J.: Prentice-Hall, Inc., 1954, pp. 322–326.
15. Brubacher, J. S.: *Modern Philosophies of Education,* 3rd ed. New York: McGraw-Hill Book Company, Inc., 1962, p. 311.
16. Bryn-Jones, D.: *The Dilemma of the Idealist.* New York: The Macmillan Co., 1950.
17. Burns, H. W., and Brauner, C. J.: *Philosophy of Education.* New York: The Ronald Press Company, 1962, pp. 16, 26–33, 42, 172, 240, 273, 284, 318–319.
18. Butler, J. D.: *Four Philosophies,* rev. ed. New York: Harper & Brothers, 1957, pp. 155, 162–163, 165, 169–170, 208, 435–438.
19. Cairns, G. E.: *Philosophies of History.* New York: Philosophic Library, 1962.
20. Ceram, C. W.: *The Secret of Hittites.* New York: Alfred A. Knopf, 1956.
21. Cornford, F. MacD.: *Before and After Socrates.* Cambridge: University Press, 1964.
22. Cottrell, L.: *The Anvil of Civilization.* New York: The New American Library, Inc., 1957.
22a. Czula, R.: Pierre de Coubertin and modern olympism. *Quest, XXIV,* 10–18, 1975.
23. Davis, E. C.: *The Philosophic Process in Physical Education.* Philadelphia: Lea & Febiger. 1961, pp. 12, 17, 26, 51–52, 74–77.
24. Davis, E. C. (Ed.): *Philosophies Fashion Physical Education.* Dubuque, Iowa: Wm. C. Brown Company. 1963, pp. 6–15, 21, 28–31, 43–57, 86.
25. Davis, J.: Physical Education in Christian Colleges. 59th Annual Proceedings, Physical Education Association, 1956, p. 264.
26. de Laban, J.: Modus operandi. *Quest, II,* 15–18, 1964.
26a. Demarest, G.: Hero worship harnessed. *JOHPER, 21,* 30–31, 1960.
27. Dewey, J.: *Art As Experience.* New York: G. P. Putnam's Sons, 1934.
28. Dewey, J.: *Democracy and Education.* New York: The Macmillan Co., 1916, pp. 42–43, 194–203, 205, 228, 239–244, 338–344, Chapter 19.
29. Dewey, J.: *Experience and Education.* New York: The Macmillan Co., 1938, p. 10.
30. Dewey, J.: From absolutism to experimentalism. *The Golden Age of American Philosophy* (C. Frankel, Ed.). New York: George Braziller, 1960, p. 392.

31. Dewey, J.: *Human Nature and Conduct*. New York: Henry Holt and Company, 1922.
32. Dewey, J.: *Lectures in the Philosophy of Education—1899*. New York: Random House Publishers, 1967, p. 103.
33. Dewey, J.: *Logic, the Theory of Inquiry*. New York: Holt, Rinehart and Winston, Inc., 1938, p. 461.
34. Dewey, J.: *Reconstruction in Philosophy*. New York: The New American Library of World Literature, 1950, pp. 82–83, 162.
35. Dewey, J., and Dewey, E.: *Schools of Tomorrow*. New York: E. P. Dutton and Company, 1915, p. 103.
36. Dray, W. H.: *Philosophy of History*. Englewood Cliffs, N.J.: Prentice-Hall, Inc., 1964.
36a. Durrant, S. M.: And who may compete? *Quest*, XXII, 104–110, 1974.
37. Durant, W.: *The Story of Philosophy* rev. ed. New York: Garden City Books, 1938, xxii, xiii, xxviii, 45, 46–47, 253–255, 256, 261, 278, 288, 289, 349–350.
38. Edwards, I. E. S.: *The Pyramids of Egypt*. Baltimore, Md.: Penguin Books, Inc., 1954.
39. Emery, W. B.: *Archaic Egypt*. Baltimore, Md.: Penguin Books, Inc., 1963.
40. Felshin, J.: The Socialization of Sport. In *Sport and the Body: A Philosophical Symposium*. E. W. Gerber (Ed.). Philadelphia: Lea & Febiger, 1972, pp. 222–229.
41. Flewelling, R. T.: *The Person; or the Significance of Man*. Los Angeles: Ward Ritchie Press, 1952, pp. 90–97.
42. Frankfort, H., et al.: *Before Philosophy*. Baltimore, Md.: Penguin Books, Inc., 1951.
43. Fuller, B. A. G., and McMurrin, S. M.: *A History of Philosophy*, 3rd ed. New York: Holt, Rinehart and Winston, Inc., 1960.
44. Gardiner, E. N.: *Athletics of the Ancient World*. Oxford: Clarendon Press, 1955.
45. Gerber, E. W.: *Innovators and Institutions in Physical Education*. Philadelphia: Lea & Febiger, 1971, pp. 90–92.
45a. Gerber, E. W. (Ed.): *Sport and the Body: A Philosophical Symposium*. Philadelphia, Lea & Febiger, 1972.
46. Greene, T. M.: A Liberal Christian Idealist Philosophy of Education. *Fifty-Fourth Yearbook of the National Society for the Study of Education*, Part I. Chicago: University of Chicago Press, 1955, pp. 50, 116–117, 119–120.
47. Hamilton, E.: *The Greek Way*. New York: The New American Library, Inc., 1963, pp. 56–57.
47a. Hanford, G. H.: An Inquiry into the Need for and Feasibility of a National Study of Intercollegiate Athletics. *A Report to the American Council on Education*, March 22, 1974.
48. Hansen, K. H.: *Philosophy for American Education*. Englewood Cliffs, N.J.: Prentice-Hall, Inc., 1960, p. 45.
48a. Hazlitt, W. H. (Ed.): *Essays of Montaigne*, Vol. I. C. Cotton (Trans.). London: The Navarre Society Ltd. 1923, pp. 196, 216.
48b. Hetherington, C. W.: Fundamental education. *Am. Phys. Educ. Rev.*, XV, 629–635, 1910.
49. Heidegger, M.: *Existence and Being*. Chicago: Henry Regnery Company, 1949.
50. Hocking, W. E.: *Human Nature and Its Remaking*. New Haven: Yale University Press, 1963.
51. Hocking, W. E.: *Types of Philosophy*, rev. ed. New York: Charles Scribner's Sons, 1939, p. 383.
52. Horne, H. H.: An Idealistic Philosophy of Education. *Forty-First Yearbook of the National Society for the Study of Education*, Part I. Chicago: University of Chicago Press, 1942, pp. 154, 186.
53. Horne, H. H.: *The New Education*. Nashville, Tenn.: Abingdon Press, 1931, pp. 125–236.
54. Horne, H. H.: *The Philosophy of Education*, rev. ed. New York: The Macmillan Co., 1930, pp. 75, 95, 310.

55. Hutchins, R. M.: *Freedom, Education and the Fund.* New York: Meridian Books, 1956.
56. Hutchins, R. M.: *The Conflict in Education in a Democratic Society.* New York: Harper and Brothers, 1953, p. 68.
57. James, W.: *Pragmatism: A New Name for Some Old Ways of Thinking.* New York: Longmans, Green and Company, 1908, pp. 4–20.
58. James, W.: *Talks to Teachers on Psychology and to Students on Some of Life's Ideals.* New York: Dover Publications Inc., 1962, pp. 99–112.
59. Jaspers, K.: *Man in the Modern Age.* New York: Doubleday & Company, 1957.
60. Johnson, W.: *People in Quandaries.* New York: Harper and Brothers, 1946, p. 7.
61. Jones, W. T.: *A History of Western Philosophy.* New York: Harcourt, Brace and World, Inc., 1952, p. 983.
62. Jorgensen, J.: *The Development of Logical Empiricism.* International Encyclopedia of Unified Science, Vol. II, No. 9. Chicago: University of Chicago Press, 1951.
63. Kaplan, A.: *The New World of Philosophy.* New York: Random House, Inc., 1963, pp. 50, 56, 63, 88, 101–105, 108, 110–111, 113, 114–115, 117.
64. Kemeny, J. G.: *A Philosopher Looks at Science.* New York: D. Van Nostrand Company, Inc., 1961.
65. Kierkegaard, S.: *The Sickness Unto Death.* New York: Doubleday Anchor Books, 1954, p. 217–218.
66. Kingdon-Ward, F.: *Footsteps in Civilization.* Boston: Beacon Press, 1951.
67. Kirk, G. S., and Raven, J. E.: *The Presocratic Philosophers.* Cambridge: University Press, 1963.
68. Kitto, H. D. F.: *The Greeks.* Baltimore, Md.: Penguin Books, Inc., 1958.
69. Kneller, G. F. (Ed.): *Foundations of Education.* New York: John Wiley & Sons, Inc., 1963, pp. 94–99.
70. Kneller, G. F.: *Introduction to the Philosophy of Education.* New York: John Wiley & Sons, Inc., 1964, pp. 48, 50, 58–70, 90, 113.
71. Knudson, A. C.: *The Philosophy of Personalism.* Boston: Boston University Press, 1949, p. 17.
72. Kramer, S. N.: *History Begins at Sumer.* New York: Doubleday & Company, Inc., 1959.
73. Krutch, J. W.: *If You Don't Mind My Saying So.* New York: William Sloan Associates, 1964, pp. 19, 59, 93, 194–196.
74. Lawson, J., and Silver, H.: *A Social History of Education in England.* London: Methuen and Company, Ltd., 1973, pp. 154, 162.
74a. Leonard, G.: *The Ultimate Athlete: Re-Visioning Sports, Physical Education and the Body.* New York: Viking Press, 1974, p. 254.
75. Locke, J.: *Some Thoughts Concerning Education.* (Introduction and Notes by R. H. Quick) Cambridge: University Press, 1913, pp. 1, 20 87–88.
76. Mandelbaum, M.: *Philosophy, Science and Sense Perception.* Baltimore, Md.: The Johns Hopkins Press, 1964.
77. Margenau, H.: Science As A Humanistic Adventure, Address given for Phi Beta Kappa Day at Occidental College, March 22, 1956.
78. Margolis, J.: *Philosophy Looks at the Arts.* New York: Charles Scribner's Sons, 1962.
79. Matson, W. L.: *A History of Philosophy.* New York: American Book Company, 1968, pp. 469–472, 479–482.
80. McDermott, W. C., and Caldwell, W. E.: *Readings in the History of the Ancient World.* New York: Holt, Rinehart & Winston, Inc., 1964.
81. Morris, V. C.: *Philosophy and the American School.* Boston: Houghton Mifflin Co., 1961, pp. 389–391.
82. Muller, H. J.: *The Uses of the Past.* New York: The New American Library, Inc., 1956.
83. Nahm, M. C.: *Selections From Early Greek Philosophy.* New York: Appleton-Century-Crofts, 1964.

84. Neef, J.: *Sketch of a Plan and Method of Education.* Philadelphia: printed for the author, 1808, Chapter 11.
85. Nietzsche, F.: *Thus Spake Zarathustra.* New York: The Macmillan Co., 1923.
86. Park, J. (Ed.): *The Philosophy of Education.* New York: The Macmillan Co., 1958, p. 3.
87. Popkin, R. H., and Stroll, A.: *Philosophy Made Simple.* London: W. H. Allen, 1973, pp. 274–276, 285–287.
88. Price, L.: *Dialogues of Alfred North Whitehead.* New York: The New American Library, Inc., 1956.
89. Ralph, P. L.: *The Story of Our Civilization.* New York: E. P. Dutton and Company, Inc., 1959.
90. Reinhold, M.: *Greek and Roman Classics.* New York: Barron's Educational Series, 1960, p. 197.
91. Reising, R. W.: "Where have all our heroes gone?" Some insights into sports figures in modern American literature. *Quest,* XVI, 1–12, 1971.
92. Renshaw, P.: The nature of human movement studies and its relationship with physical education. *Quest,* XX, 79–86, 1973.
93. Robinson, C. A., Jr.: *The Spring of Civilization—Periclean Athens.* New York: E. P. Dutton & Company, Inc., 1959.
94. Robinson, J. H.: *The Mind in the Making.* New York: Harper and Brothers, 1921.
95. Rousseau, J. J.: *Emile: Or Treatise on Education.* William H. Payne (Trans.) New York: D. Appleton and Company, 1893, p. 54, 161, 259–266.
96. Royce, J.: *Lectures on Modern Idealism.* New Haven: Yale University Press, 1964, pp. viii, 239, 247.
97. Russell, B.: *A History of Western Philosophy.* New York: Simon and Schuster, 1963, p. 834.
98. Russell, B.: On scientific method in philosophy. In *Mysticism and Logic and Other Essays.* London: Longmans, Green and Company, 1921, p. 98.
99. Ryle, G.: *The Concept of Mind.* New York: Barnes and Noble, Inc., 1949, pp. 11–24, 48.
100. Santayana, G.: *The Life of Reason: Or the Phases in Human Progress,* rev. by D. Cory. New York: Charles Scribner's Sons, 1954, pp. vi, 4–9.
101. Santayana, G.: *The Sense of Beauty.* New York: Random House, 1955, pp. 7–8, 17–19, 34–36.
102. Sartre, J.-P.: *Being and Nothingness.* New York: Philosophical Library, Inc., 1956.
103. Sartre, J.-P.: *Existentialism.* New York: Philosophical Library, Inc., 1947, p. 75.
104. Slusher, H. S.: Existentialism and physical education. *The Physical Educator,* 153–156, Dec. 1963.
105. Smith, J. E.: *The Spirit of American Philosophy.* New York: Oxford University Press, 1963, pp. 198–200.
106. Smith, T. V.: *From Thales to Plato.* Chicago: The University of Chicago Press, 1956.
107. Schweitzer, A.: *The Philosophy of Civilization.* New York: The Macmillan Co., 1960.
108. The nature of a discipline. *Quest,* IX, December, 1967.
109. Thomas, H.: *Understanding the Great Philosophers.* New York: Doubleday and Company, Inc., 1962.
110. Titus, H. H.: *Living Issues of Philosophy,* 3rd ed. New York: American Book Company, 1959, pp. 42, 43–45, 63–68, 69, 262–264, 285.
111. Titus, H. H.: *Living Issues in Philosophy,* 4th ed. New York: American Book Company, 1964, pp. 270–272.
112. Tomlin, E. W. F.: *The Western Philosophers.* New York: Harper Colophon Books, 1963, pp. 12, 36.
113. Toynbee, A. J.: *Greek Civilization and Character.* New York: The New American Library, Inc., 1953.

114. Toynbee, A. J.: *Greek Historical Thought.* New York: The New American Library Inc., 1953.
115. Van Dalen, D. B., Mitchell, E. D., and Bennett, B. L.: *A World History of Physical Education.* Englewood Cliffs, N.J.: Prentice-Hall, Inc., 1963, pp. 175–179, 184–185, 190.
116. VanderZwaag, H. J.: Essentialism and physical education. *The Physical Educator,* 147–149, Dec. 1963.
117. VanderZwaag, H.: Sport: Existential or essential? *Quest, XIII,* 47–56, 1969.
118. Wahlquist, J. T.: *The Philosophy of American Education.* New York: The Ronald Press Co., 1942, pp. 72, 246.
119. Warnock, G. J.: *English Philosophy Since 1900,* 2nd ed. London: Oxford University Press, 1969, pp. 32–35, 62–65, 72.
120. Wiener, P P., and Noland, A.: *Roots of Scientific Thought.* New York: Basic Books, Inc., 1958.
121. Whitehead, A. N.: *Adventures of Ideas.* New York: The Macmillan Co., 1933, p. 53.
122. Whitehead, A. N.: *The Aims of Education.* New York: The Macmillan Co., 1929, pp. 60, 67.
123. Whitehead, A. N.: *Process and Reality, An Essay in Cosmology.* New York: The Macmillan Co., 1930, p. 9.
124. Whitehead, A. N.: *Symbolism.* New York: The Macmillan Co., 1959.
125. Williams, J.: John Henry Newman's consideration of physical education as a "liberal pursuit." *Peabody J. Educ.* 42, 343–348, 1965.
126. Wittgenstein, L. : *Philosophical Investigations.* G. E. M. Anscombe (Trans.). New York: The Macmillan Co., 1953, pp. 31e–41e.
126a. Wood, T. D.: Physical education. In *Ninth Yearbook of the National Society for the Study of Education,* Part I. Chicago: University of Chicago Press, 1910, pp. 75–104.
127. Woolley, L.: *A Forgotten Kingdom.* Baltimore, Md.: Penguin Books, Inc., 1953.
128. Yu-lan, F.: *A Short History of Chinese Philosophy.* New York: The Macmillan Co., 1964, p. 2.
129. Zeigler, E. F.: *Philosophical Foundations for Physical, Health and Recreation Education.* Englewood Cliffs, N.J.: Prentice-Hall, Inc., 1964, pp. 252, 322.
130. Zeller, E.: *Socrates and the Socratic Schools.* O. J. Reichel (Trans.). London: Longmans, Green and Co., 1885.

III

PHILOSOPHY
AS QUEST

III

PHILOSOPHY
AS QUEST

YOU MUST BE WILLING TO COMMIT YOURSELF TO A COURSE,
PERHAPS A LONG AND HARD ONE, WITHOUT BEING ABLE TO
SEE EXACTLY WHERE YOU WILL COME OUT.

—*Oliver W. Holmes, Jr.*

The philosophic process may be characterized by its action or by its heritage. Another singular feature of philosophy is a sustained searching. The search moves from the prosaic known to the mystical unknown. It is for whatever has worth for man. Such questing is rarely satisfied with appearances. It pursues reality, the way things are. Part III, then, is concerned with the nature of such questing. Rather than *talking about* quest, however, the four essays in this part try to take up the quest itself. Brief examples though they may be, they deal with ethics in amateur sport, humanistic education, deceptions in the athletic–physical education relationship, and the idea of the questing method of phenomenology as used in physical education. Each essay is followed by a short critique, inviting the novice philosopher to actively take up the quest himself, to rethink what others have thought.

13

Needed: Ethical Guidelines for Amateur Sport

INTRODUCTION

Few persons today are so unaware that they believe that twentieth century Western civilization will go down in history as a time noted for its ethical concern, ethical behavior, or ethical promise. Ethics in education seems to be a topic that typically produces a sly smile or an abrupt change in conversation. Smart people, sophisticated people, the "in crowd" and even the self-styled intellectual are incredulous or at least painfully patient with one who attempts to motivate them *to think* about any aspect of ethical conduct in educational sport, as a case in point. If this expression of an observation is exaggerated, evidence to the contrary escapes serious searching.

As unpromising as it may appear to be, the purpose of the present discussion is to seek help from those who are not so fully indoctrinated, and who are not so accustomed to low-order ethical behavior in educational sport that they see nothing that challenges them to *go to work!*

ESSAY

THE AFFIRMATIVE ATTITUDE CAN PRODUCE OF ITSELF ONLY A PARTIAL AND IMPERFECT CIVILIZATION. ONLY IF IT BECOMES INWARD AND ETHICAL CAN THE WILL-TO-PROGRESS WHICH RESULTS FROM IT POSSESS THE REQUISITE INSIGHT TO DISTINGUISH THE VALUABLE FROM THE LESS VALUABLE, AND STRIVE AFTER A CIVILIZATION WHICH DOES NOT CONSIST ONLY IN ACHIEVEMENTS OF KNOWLEDGE AND POWER, BUT BEFORE ALL ELSE WILL MAKE MEN BOTH INDIVIDUALLY AND COLLECTIVELY, MORE SPIRITUAL AND MORE ETHICAL.

—Albert Schweitzer

The title of this chapter should be further delimited. The comments embrace amateur sport in American schools and colleges. Ethics are restricted to but one of its phases—ethical conduct. The guidelines refer to principles. Of the three major categories of the 19 definitions of principles, only the one referring to guides and rules of conduct is of present concern.

Principles are assumed to emerge from man's judgment. Some students of ethics would add intuition and conscience as other sources. Still others would insist that some guidelines to right conduct are givens or immediate knowledge.

The title proposes that sport today needs guidelines to ethical conduct; that is, it is *action* that needs emphasis. The value of today's theorizing about ethics in amateur sport is admitted and supported. It will not be discussed in these pages. This limitation points to another disadvantage of fragmenting the complex unity of ethics.

Nevertheless, the need for action guidelines in sport is urgent. That something more cogent than the current skirmish of words is necessary is obvious to those who are concerned for the future of both sport in educational institutions and those who participate. It is more than being dramatic to point to some of the West's threatened values which have moved from the marketplace to amateur sport.

The purpose of this treatise is limited to attempting to identify a few reasons underlying the difficulty of delivering the needed action before the consequences of current conditions become irreversible.

One obvious difficulty in trying to turn the trend around is the large variety of peoples who are indirectly or directly involved. Principles of ethical conduct held by the individual parallel this variety. Feelings about ethics in general, as well as those applied to sport, also lack similarity. The ideas of those who are concerned about the proposed ways to counter the trend also differ considerably. The list of representatives from various vocations, as well as the organizations and services such as the public communications media, who are interested in school and college sport is astonishingly long.

Another source of difficulty springs from one of democracy's rights. Americans avow a concern for individual rights and the dignity and uniqueness of the individual. Decisions regarding rights that affect the individual perforce must face the fact that there is usually more than one individual to be considered! James H. Breasted, eminent American Egyptologist, estimated that it took about 2000 years for man to learn that society and the individual had to coalesce their beliefs about ethical conduct.[2] This is a one-world lesson that some individuals eschew. Fortunately, most of them think it through, even if painfully and resistantly at first.

A third reason it is difficult to take positive action, in opposition to indifference and unconcern about the slipping away of sport's ethics, is tied to the second. It is the general frustration facing those who attempt to guide ethical conduct by formal group action, whether it be an athletic team, a professional organization, or a nation. In spite of the worthiness of the cause, this may be baffling endeavor. After years of work attempting to codify ethical beliefs for teachers or for coaches, often the project is abandoned. Sometimes a few persistent dissident members influence the entire group over those favoring such an effort, because of the latter's lack of courage, firm conviction, or indifference. The familiar claim that an ethical code is a threat to individual freedom often carries the day, and the need for standards of ethical conduct loses support for another generation.

If a code for ethical conduct is adopted, subsequent members of the group may covertly oppose it. Although rare, cases have occurred in medicine and law. Under pressure, members may break their pledges to follow and uphold the ethical standards. Their allegiance buckles under the weight of economic, social, or domestic forces and allurements. On the other hand, some professions continue to hold to selective criteria for entrance into their respective preparation curricula, as well as for licensure to serve the public. Some of these criteria attempt to prevent admission of persons who seem to be apt to flaunt or subvert the principles of ethical conduct of their profession.

Whether or not physical education currently is an authentic profession, or whether those admitted into this vocation are interested in ethical conduct of teachers and educational administrators (to the same degree as members of the three ancient and honored professions) may not be an appropriate question. The basic nature of sport in educational institutions, however, suggests that teachers and coaches should be extremely interested, even though the contemporary picture is discouraging. At the same time, few members of other professions undergo the pressures to which instructional personnel are subjected in sport in high schools and colleges. Yet, these pressures are seldom used as an excuse for violating the ethical conduct that even the man and woman in the street traditionally expect of educational sport. On the other hand, physical education teachers and coaches are expected to teach ethical conduct even in the heat of contests that rub through the thin veneer of adolescent self-control, and appear to obtain little support from academic-type teachers or even the administrator. This support, of course, is needed today. Is not this the day when teachers generally have experiences that lead them to conclude that larger proportions of children and youth come from families in which ethical conduct is not demonstrated or taught.

Nevertheless, any such attempt to see the difficulties facing this aspect of ethics as action in educational sport's instructional and administrative staffs is not an effort to overlook or whitewash unethical acts associated with this broad program. For instance, do you recall that coach (or was it only a rumor?) who violated an ethical principle in all facets of his work in order to be a "winner"? Do you recall the office clerk in the Admissions Office accused of changing the grades on entrance examinations of the All-State champion, the principal who _____, the state superintendent of public instruction who _____, or the rural high school English teacher who revised the final grades of the school's only pitcher?

Heaped on the familiar criticisms are the avowed dangers of sport competition: professionalism, loss of self-responsibility and individuality, and the noisy clatter about the ills of educational sport. What school or college program is a better target for the critic, whether motivated by feelings of inferiority, envy, or academic superiority? Is there, then, little substance in or foundation for these accusations and viewings with alarm? It could be said with considerable justification that educational sport per se is neither right nor wrong, neither good nor bad. And is it not those involved in sport who permit it to serve such claimed negative ends?

Even the previous statement misses the mark, if the attempt is to seek that which should be of most concern. How much of the failure of ethics in sport descends on and negatively influences the sport performer? What is this failure's impress on him, now and later? Is this not the forgotten question? Who, then, is left in the educational setting to turn the picture around, if those who teach, coach, and administrate in educational sport permit ethics for this vast human endeavor to continue to deteriorate? Who is left to prevent its floundering in a sea of easy virtue? These two questions trigger a third one directed at those who are preparing to become teachers and coaches of educational sport: Is ethical conduct in sport important enough to make you want to do something about it?

Who *will* turn around the defaulting of ethics in sport? From present evidence, it will be the *intending* young men and women now preparing for the profession who will soon be teaching and coaching. They are aware of the downward drift of ethics in sport and oppose it. Is there no one to help them? Can they expect help from those who are experienced and will regain their former concern for, belief in, and appreciation of the need for ethical standards in action, and who have the professional savvy, once they see the intent, will, and energy of their younger professional compatriots? Perhaps the newcomers prefer to go it alone!

Whether future teachers and coaches will have to instill ethics in sport alone or will have help, there are some triggers for action which may prove useful. They are but words on a page of a book. They represent, however, forces that drive humans into action. They are familiar to any student who recalls some of the elements of the psychology of motivation. The first one is a great purpose. Large-scale values leading to that purpose are second. Third are emotionalized, affirmative attitudes toward both the master purpose and the basic values. Fourth are major personal motives, such as the desire to excel and to cooperate, that compel the individual to initiate and sustain his best effort and thought.

Other triggers also may help. One respected philosopher has presented the idea that, if philosophy is to be philosophy (and not something else), it must conform to six conditions. One of these is that in answering an ethical question it "be conducted as a *public* (sic) enterprise."[1] The remaining pages of this chapter will continue to attempt to meet this one condition.

The selection of two triggers will enable examples to illustrate the practicality of starting action to upgrade ethical conduct in sport by means of these triggers. The first example is the master purpose. Consider the active, powerful role that a great master purpose plays in one's ordinary daily living (see pp. 21–23). Recall the ability of a magnet purpose to pull all of life into a meaningful whole. Albert Schweitzer's Reverence for Life is a master purpose that was formulated only after years of thought. We do not know what his previous magnet purposes were. They were, of course, whatever was of most importance to him at that time. The various master purposes in one's life reflect not only personal experiences and lessons learned therefrom, but also the level of maturity, the quality of thinking, and the particular wording used to identify each of the succeeding magnet purposes.[9]

A college student's master purpose at a given time may seem quite naive to the professor who does not understand him. For instance, there is the senior athlete with one year of eligibility left. He is not a star. He has never won a sport letter. Competition for his position this year promises to be as keen as last year. Playing enough to win a letter becomes, literally, the most important thing in his life. This has become his master purpose in life.

On the other hand, some coaches report that today a few players do not include their sport among their major values, even though they possess the requisite skills and seem to enjoy playing it. These observations are based on the fact that these young persons do not put out enough to earn the honor to be selected to play often, even though in their own opinion they do. Toward the season's end, they realize that they will not earn a letter. They confront the coach. They aggressively assert that he is prejudiced, unfair, unobserving, and even incapable of judging their ability. Obviously, neither the sport nor the letter nor their efforts constitute the elements of a master purpose.

The question may arise, "Do they have *any* master purpose whatsoever?" The coaches interrogated were unable to answer the question, although it was their judgment that some of the athletes seemed to have none. On the other hand, some of them *appeared* to have the major purpose of downplaying the purposes and values of the Establishment. There is, of course, nothing unusual in this phenomenon during the growing-up stage of development. It is of interest that among these malcontents were many who in a matter of a few years appeared to possess master purposes that triggered them to take worthwhile places in their communities. Perhaps the point needs explication. It appears that one may become involved in an activity—sport, art, music, and the like—without being challenged or attracted enough by it to bother to try to excel. It also seems reasonable to conjecture that human beings may experience "dry seasons" when no master purpose emerges.

If the prime purpose of educational sport does not include ethical conduct, no one would expect it to be practiced by or of concern to anyone. If it once was purported to be almost synonymous with the school or college program and no longer is, should not the public be informed? Continual failure in expectations of this kind may become a threat to a program's survival.

Let us now turn to the second example of a trigger. Four decades after Albert Schweitzer noted the absence of or confusion over values (as a cause of the deterioration of ethical behavior in the West),[9] Paul Roubiczek's *Ethical Values in the Age of Science* was published.[8] The ethical picture had not improved.

The major values of an individual, irrespective of his purpose, are forceful initiators of human action. When he works with his purpose, his values become more powerful as triggers. The fact that a few philosophers have been unwilling to define the word "value" does not mean that a working definition cannot be helpful in clarifying its general meaning. Most persons understand value to be something desirable, important, significant, and worthwhile; something leading to another thing of value; or something possessing admired or wanted qualities. Often happiness and satisfaction are backdrops to the word's meaning. Such values as justice, right, truth, and good often are regarded as ethical values, and usually are significant in decisions regarding sport.

The reader interested in more detailed and critical ideas about this controversial subject is referred to E. A. Burtt,[3] Shepard B. Clough,[4] William Lillie,[5] G. E. Moore,[6] Lewis Mumford,[7] Paul Roubiczek,[8] and Charles L. Stevenson.[10] The reader should not be perturbed over disagreements among these writers. The word "values" is a recent arrival in philosophy's lexicon.

It is not difficult to talk about ethical conduct in sport and the mild ripples it causes in today's civilization. Standards of ethical behavior applied to sport and their neglect in educational institutions no longer cause alarm even among educational administrators (who still talk the ethics-in-sport game). *Where else may they find an area of activity so teeming in possibilities?* The public needs to be informed of what is almost imperceptibly happening to the bases of their belief that educational sport, whatever else it is, is an experience for the community's youth which upholds and practices ethical behavior. They also ought to be informed of the *consequences* of unethical conduct in sport as the results spill over into the life styles of even young adults who unawarely assume that ethics in amateur sport in schools and colleges is an old-fashioned idea.

Should a skeptical reader wonder about the public's concern over the defaulting of sport's ethics let him communicate with responsible persons in civic organizations; public office; business and parent groups; certain foundations, corporations, and agencies interested in the welfare of youth; and even the policymakers of the public communications media. Through an exploration of how the public feels the investigator will find that over and above other considerations they will be *most* concerned about the influence of the defaulting on the individual performer. As hackneyed as the term "worthy citizen" has become, no thinking adult chooses to stand for any educational program that does not contribute to the development of *potentially* worthy citizens.

For decades some professional men and women in physical education and sport have persistently, effectively, and eminently though modestly given of their time, energy, thought, and even means to their students, regarding the students as *potentially* worthy of the best that they had to give. This seldom recognized giving has been done with but one thought in mind, the potentiality in human beings. This deep conviction has become their *summum bonum*. These individuals are a part of the *avant-garde*, without escutcheon, without appreciation, and without recognition or even a name. Hesiod spoke of them three millennia ago: "long is the road thereto and rough at first./But when the height is won, then there is ease,/Though grievously hard in the winning."

Precisely what the ethical values of sport should be is best determined by those most genuinely involved in, concerned with, and affected by the future's impact on those who participate. Who will be counted in this company? Could most of them be found in some college class today?

In spite of the discouraging state of affairs hanging over the heads of those who have given up the struggle for ethics in sport, it is hoped that this effort is at the trough of the wave, the dip in the cycle. The new breed faces, then, a contest that challenges their thinking, understanding, courage, and belief in man's potentiality. They will need patience and foresight, too. The task is almost overwhelming. The challenge is to their depth of dedication. When will they begin?

OF ALL THE WILL FOR THE IDEAL WHICH EXISTS IN MAN-
KIND ONLY A SMALL PART CAN BE MANIFESTED IN ACTION.
ALL THE REST IS DESTINED TO REALIZE ITSELF IN UNSEEN
EFFECTS, WHICH REPRESENT, HOWEVER, A VALUE EXCEEDING
A THOUSANDFOLD AND MORE THE ACTIVITY WHICH ATTRACTS
THE NOTICE OF THE WORLD.

—Albert Schweitzer

CRITIQUE

This essay is so limited in coverage and depth that one is puzzled as to a suitable place to begin. Even the narrow channel followed is too restricted to enable the reader to gain a foothold for rebuttal.

Apparently, the writer assumed that readers are familiar enough with the state of ethical behavior in educational sport to make the citing of examples unnecessary. It also appears to be an assumption that readers will agree with the view that this particular aspect of ethics represents a multiplicity of ills, without exception. Although the purpose of the treatise is not in these directions, it would have been preferable to lay out, first, a foundation on which a case might be established.

Two other quasi-assumptions might be mentioned. One of these is that contemporary teachers, coaches, and administrators of sport are either so disinterested or incapable that they cannot be counted on to reconstruct the ethical picture of sport in schools and colleges. The other quasi-assumption is that nothing much can be done to rectify this situation until those now preparing for professional service begin to work on this problem.

The treatise does point unwaveringly to a trend in ethics that plagues and threatens not only educational sport but education, the established professions, and most phases of the Western world.

References

1. Adler, M. J.: *The Conditions of Philosophy.* New York: Atheneum, 1965, p. 68.
2. Breasted, J. H.: *The Dawn of Conscience.* New York: Charles Scribner's Sons, 1947, pp. 29–42, 115–207.
3. Burtt, E. A.: *In Search of Philosophic Understanding.* New York: The New American Library, Inc., 1965.
4. Clough, S. B.: *Basic Values of Western Civilization.* New York: Columbia University Press, 1960.
5. Lillie, W.: *An Introduction to Ethics.* New York: Barnes and Noble, 1963.
6. Moore, G. E.: *Principia Ethica.* Cambridge, England: The University Press, 1965.
7. Mumford, L.: *The Conduct of Life.* New York: Harcourt Brace Jovanovich, Inc., 1970.
8. Roubiczek, P.: *Ethical Values in the Age of Science.* Cambridge, England: The University Press, 1969.
9. Schweitzer, A.: *Out of My Life and Thought.* New York: The New American Library, Inc., 1953, pp. 154–158, 170–188.
10. Stevenson, C. L.: *Facts and Values—Studies in Ethical Analysis.* New Haven: Yale University Press, 1964.

14

Humanistic Education: Another Bandwagon?

INTRODUCTION

In 1949, Gabriel Marcel gave the Gifford Lectures at the University of Aberdeen. Early in those lectures Marcel spoke of our world as a "broken world." Among some of its characteristics were the increasing efforts to social man, the extension of the powers of the State, and the general disinclination towards privacy, brotherhood, creativity, reflection, and imagination. In short, the world has lost its real unity.

One clear symptom of the degree to which our world is broken is the tendency to surrender more and more frequently to the power of words. For the most part, many of these words have been emptied of their original content:

> Such words as *liberty, person, democracy,* are being more and more lavishly used, and are becoming slogans, in a world in which they are tending more and more to lose their authentic significance.[8a]

To this list we might add the word "humanism." The essay that follows makes an effort to help one understand the uses and abuses of this fashionable term, particularly as it is used in the idea of humanistic education. In searching for a steadier meaning of humanism in education in general and physical education in particular, the question is asked: Is humanistic education another bandwagon?

ESSAY

Many contemporaries find humanistic education full of semantic confusion and paradoxes. Some no doubt will say that humanistic education theories and practices have made a difference in man's humanity to man or at least have had some impact on reducing antisocial behaviors. Others are curious as to why humanistic education apparently seems to have no possible application to lawlessness and violence, which are on the increase. In fact, the question is raised as to whether it is honorable to be perverse and sadistic, to kill for fun. Here and there, individuals wonder why praying in the school is forbidden, whereas the language of the gutter is so permissive as to have become commonplace in some halls of academia. It seems almost ridiculous to fret over humanistic education when a person, although decrying the evils of polluted air and the killings of wars, tears up the terrain and spews noise and dust from his motorbike, or races his car at dangerous speeds on crowded streets, after his momentarily reviving shot of heroin. Nor is it less ridiculous for those who cheat on examinations to become diligent advocates of enlightened humanistic social reforms.

In the world of sport the paradoxes abound. On the one hand, excitement seems to be increased by mass hysteria, violent action, materialism, greed, and even the use of drugs to enhance athletic performance. On the other hand, compelling arguments support the claim that sport teaches ethical behavior and provides avenues to challenge man's own performance potential.

Whether or not Carl Rogers's "revolution" in education really was intended to settle such concerns, obviously the accomplishments, methods, and goals claimed for humanistic education do not go entirely unchallenged. Such quaint inconsistencies cast doubts on attempts to deal with the problems of modern man by educational methods based on understanding the individual, as the assumption is made that our technological society is responsible for the entire, tragic mess.

What seems to be necessary, but lacking in order to clarify any general discussion of humanistic education, is a clear definition of humanism on the one hand, and on the other an identification of the subject matter that the humanist believes he deals with and the methods he uses. It also would help to clarify his position if he proposed some major purposes for whatever the subject matter is claimed to be.

As to the meaning of humanism, there seems to be a feast of assumptions and a famine of straight thinking. Although, according to Rune's *Dictionary of Philosophy,* there are *seven* different kinds of humanism, one searches far for an article or a talk by a self-claimed humanist which identifies exactly which one of the seven types of humanist he is.[10] Within the kaleidoscope of humanism, for example, one person can claim to be a humanist and believe that God is a necessary concept in religion, and his neighbor can claim to be a humanist and believe that a deity is not a necessary part of religion.

With reference to confusion over the terms "humanism" and "humanist," Fuller and McMurrin in their *History of Philosophy* give this current meaning of humanism: "indicates especially naturalistic or nontheistic philosophy with positive emphasis on human values."[5] Gerald

Heard's classic *The Five Ages of Man* uses *humanic* in an effort to avoid the morass of differing meanings of humanism and humanist.[6]

Is what is called humanism by humanists today actually humanitarianism, what Gerald Heard called humanics, or what others simply call humane? Rune gives the meaning of a word, which it becomes apparent many self-styled humanists actually are. The word is "humanitarianism," to which Rune gives three definitions. The first definition is any moral or social program seeking to lessen suffering and increase human welfare leading to social reform, which closely resembles "any view in which interest in human welfare is central," and is Rune's primary meaning for *humanism*.

As to the beginnings of what sometimes is called the "new humanism," one encounters still more confusion. Although several writers refer to the new humanism, there is no "new" humanism. Usually such movements, as the revival of "humanism" (note the quotes—since there are so many kinds, which humanism is being talked about is a question of import), are under way long before they are recognized by some nickname or an assumed name. The only one of the seven kinds of humanism with a beginning date is the Humanist Manifesto (May, 1933), in which left-wing ministers of the Unitarian Church and some college professors took the view that God was not necessary for religion.

Originally, of course, humanities referred to secular learning, knowledge about human affairs as contrasted to the divine—the kind of discourse found in writings of the Greeks and Romans before Christian revelation made knowledge of the divine possible. Later, science, which originally meant knowledge of any kind, came to mean a certain kind of technical knowledge, whatever is measurable and subject to experimental verification. Thus, humanities came to mean whatever could not be measured or experimentally verified. Humanism eventually came to represent a kind of counterrevolution to science and the technology it spawned. Sidney Hook, for example, wrote articles in the early 1900s which were labeled humanistic. Hook and Mumford are old standbys who early and continually sharpened their pens attacking technology, its satellites, and the ills which they associated with this phenomenon.

Many mature persons, of course, avoid taking the view that something, especially some one thing such as technology, is all bad. They argue that many "goods" are related to technology. When asked what there is about life today that is good for mankind, most persons will mention such things as improved medical and pharmaceutical services, transportation, distribution of food, and many more.

Humanistic psychology appeared on the American scene in the past 30 years. Psychologists, attached to this frame of reference, call themselves by such names as self-psychologists, transactionalists, existentialists, perceptualists, and the like.[3] The contemporary humanistic education movement, considered as having developed as an alternative to the Freudian and behavioristic psychologic models, is rooted in this "third force" psychologic movement.

Abraham Maslow is generally regarded as the most popular spokesman for the humanistic or third force psychology movement. Maslow, repudiating nineteenth century science and contemporary professional philosophy, which he calls essentially a technology, described the goal of humanistic education as the self-actualization of the individual.[9] Much of that which has followed in educational literature and practice has hinged on Maslow's concept of self-actualization. Words such as "self-identity," "self-acceptance," "selfhood," "unique potential," "students' concerns," and those characterizing affective learning (interests, appreciations, emotions, motives) have become prominent in the literature of education. Self-actualization, in fact, has become a fetish for some and a shibboleth for many.

In parallel with the general contempt for the so-called "bads" of our technological society, the explanation is given that such problems as school dropouts, for example, represent a rejection of nineteenth century technology as this is manifested in educational institutions. There is widespread skepticism in educational circles about the wisdom of trying to quantify the outcomes of education. The negative argument is that measurable outcomes represent only a portion of individual learning, while entailing much risk of warping students. The viewpoint of *The Humanistic Education Sourcebook* is that behavioral objectives provide too narrow a basis for proper assessment of educational outcomes, and that answers to problems of accountability need to be sought in such human qualities as positive self-concepts, feelings of identification, openness to experience, creativity, effective human relationships, and so forth.[3]

Although the variety of goals of humanistic education are not easily unraveled, Alschuler suggested that most courses in humanistic education have the common goals of development of a person's imagination by using one's fantasy, development of better communication skills by using nonverbal exercises, exploration of the individual's emotional responses to the world, and emphasis of the importance of living fully and intensely here and now.[1] Some of the many techniques and strategies developed under the sobriquet of humanistic education include free-learning or open classrooms, emotion in the classroom, creativity training, sensitivity training, encounter groups, role playing, psychodrama, aikido, yoga, zen, body awareness, strength training, simulation games, movement exploration and movement-oriented tasks, and many other experiences designed to develop self-awareness. However, even this panoramic array does not account for all seven kinds of humanism.

Open education, as one illustration of a humanistically oriented curriculum, is viewed by its proponents as a way to facilitate the ability to

live successfully with other human beings, to develop positive self-concepts, to develop skills at one's own individual pace. The materials for
learning consist of multimedia types of sources that are claimed to operate on varying levels to meet the many learning styles and achievement
levels. Few failures are experienced in open education. Its devotees
believe that those who experience this new type of success develop positive attitudes toward learning. The teacher, as the orchestrator of the
learning environment, is considered as approachable, receptive to students' needs, and a modeler of intellectual curiosity.

Some humanistic conceptions of physical education focus on human
movement experiences as a way to facilitate the development of self-
actualization and to experience human feelings ranging from agony to
ecstasy. A sampling of approaches to "body/movement/nonverbal experiences," assiduously extracted by Caldwell from growth center literature,
included an incredible array of titles, such as Gestalt awareness, sensory
awakening, nudity, Gestalt psychosynthesis, bodily masks, biofield, energy
body, massage, body awareness, chanting, meditation, bioenergetics,
structural integration, Hatha yoga, energy awareness, sensing, psychomotor therapy, primal encounter, tai chi chuan, aikido, breathing techniques, acupuncture, biofeedback, sensory relaxation, structural awareness, nonverbal communication, karate, arica sufism, sensory encounter,
body consciousness, Alexander technique, body language, body rhythms,
touch, mudra, neuromuscular reintegration, body therapies, sense height-
ening, sensory bombardment, polarity therapy, body flow, bodily identity,
body sounds, inner space, nonverbal encounter, psychodrama, dervish
dancing, body journey, Feldenkrais exercises, trance dances, kung fu,
body Gestalt, movement flow, and Reichian methods.[2] Still, not all seven
varieties of humanism are represented.

The panoramic interpretations of humanistic physical education strategies also include elimination of dress standards, mandatory uniforms and
showers, and such traditional directives to success as sacrifice, dedication,
and discipline. Under the humanistic banner, published articles appear
concerning sport and the business ethic, the changing image of the sport
hero to the anti-hero, factors in the ecology of sport, and the morality of
sport. Some writers address themselves to the concern that the humanistic spirit of play in sport has been repressed by the competitive spirit,
which others consider so essential in top performance, and which they
associate with desirable personality attributes judged to be essential for
human life in this universe.

Although the concept of self is of central concern to the humanistic
education movement, there is considerable mysticism about what is
meant by the term "self." It would not be the first movement founded on
and headed toward uncertainty. Basic questions such as "Is the child self-
educating or does he need a set of planned experiences in order to learn

to be self-educating?" are being raised by those concerned with creating a humanistic physical education.[11] Real and crucial concerns indicate the need for *clarity* in the goals and methods of humanistic education. Should humanistic methods be ends in themselves? What kinds of teaching and subject matter are in the best interest of students? What is a humanistic educator? In the selection and preparation of humanistic educators, should greater emphasis be placed on social and therapeutic skills than on educational skills (what they know and how they can teach) in the traditional sense? And, lest it is forgotten, which of the seven kinds of humanism does the adjective humanistic as used here reflect? This is but a beginning of the challenging queries.

Whenever the concept of humanistic education becomes a methodological debate or a defense of some philosophic school of thought over another, there seems to be considerable gerrymandering of definitions as to what constitutes good teaching. Much bandying of slogans and catchwords is characteristic. The fact that almost no one is happy with the current nature of the educational system appears to be obvious. Reverberations on a common theme coming from one culture include complaints about the pressure of large and impersonal classrooms, factorylike instruction geared to turning out quantity more than quality, irrelevant examinations and grading practices, lack of relevance to social problems, and so forth. Another subculture argues just as strongly from a countering view that contemporary education has been turned into unstructured free-floating "rap-sessions," and has failed to teach either fundamentals or aspiration. Critics contend that humanistic education is a current hurrah, another ism, for relativism or the unfettered rights of the individual, so typical of the open, self-freedom extremists' position.

Indictments facing education today are not necessarily peculiar to education. The roots of these accusations also appear to be sociopersonal maladies typical of current times. Such indictments have been analyzed and classified into numerous subject headings, scores of subheadings, and endless topics and instances. Even the insensitive reader cannot but note the frequent recurrence of the terms "ecology," "pollution," "energy crisis," "overpopulation," "genetic manipulation," "the urban crisis," "the ghetto," "government-industrial-military complex," "the impersonalized society" of "don't fold, staple or mutilate," and the like.

The problems of contemporary society, of course, are not new. Take from the library shelf Plato's *Republic*. Therein will be found such contemporary concerns as communism and socialism, feminism and birth control. If you find central government today in a chaotic state, so did Plato in his day. The student concerned with current ecological problems will savor Rousseau's idea that nature is good and civilization is bad.

Nonetheless, problems of society seem to demand new solutions or at least new terminology. On the other hand, the assumption that the resolving of man's human problems lies in the mere altering of terms or styles and methods of teaching seems shallow and narrow-visioned. It also seems to lead to shifts of teaching fashions no more gargantuan than the rise and fall of hemlines.

Thus, should not the issue of what is humanistic education be distinguished from debates about better or worse methods or styles of teaching? For one thing, every method of teaching can be shown to be functional or dysfunctional in terms of the results of the manipulations performed and deified. For another, teachers, students, and the teaching process, being what they are, are not discrete entities, but complexities of liquid amalgams. Teaching styles spill over retaining walls, and merge or coalesce. Effective teaching behavior and outcomes cannot be pigeonholed under categories such as formal versus relaxed, drill versus discovery, serious versus humorous, lectures versus free-learning, relevant versus traditional, and the like. To illustrate, many traditional-type classrooms may be fraught with dogmatism and unjustified generalizations, yet is it *not* specious to conclude that only methods of introspection, discussion, and group-oriented techniques belong under the humanic tent?

May not a thoroughgoing drillmaster who spends considerable time in skill practice and who suppresses all conversation be as humanic as one who acts only as a guide while children "freely explore"? Does the teacher who believes that it is important to feel as well as to think need to be apprehensive about what happens emotionally to the young person who is expected to obey adult authority? Is that teacher less than humanic if he believes that authority is a part of living? Moreover, should not what is to be taught and the variability of the students—gradations of interest, purpose, and talents—be taken into account? For example, if learning to swim is the terminal behavior sought, is there any reason to suppose that the fundamental facts of how to swim will be revealed in, say, a sensitivity session?

There is further confusion generated by the question of "What is relevant?" in *any* curriculum. A few years ago, Stanford University, often regarded as having a liberal curriculum, undertook an intense study of its entire curriculum. In 10 volumes (concise and readable), the final published report made deep-reaching recommendations on curriculum, dealing with both trivia and profundities (both essential to a candid, realistic study). The report freely acknowledged that students can learn quite as much from their involvement in outside activity as they do in the classroom, but that such activities do not necessarily belong in the curriculum. It is a mistake, the report pointed out, to expect the university to accept primary responsibility for satisfying the demand for both relevance and experience. "Rather, such activities should arise from the intellectual and social ambience which the university fosters." More recently, the President of that University, describing a fresh attack or series of attacks on the problem of relevance, declared: "*Education that does not cause you to change your ideas as to what is relevant can hardly be called education.*"[8]

If the premise that humanistic education is to be found more in existential experiencing than in disciplined drill, more in pragmatic problem-solving than in idealistic exhortations to perfection, more in dance improvisation than in ballet, or more in group enrichment sessions than in solo efforts at thinking is dismissed, *what then* is *humanistic education?* What does it mean to be *a humanistic teacher?* Socrates could have asked his students these questions over 2000 years ago. The answers obviously are far from being found. But philosophy lies in the quest, in the searching, and one may assume that there are certain unchangeables deep in the soul of Socrates' time which are still valid.

One might simply call humanistic education humanness or humaneness, and quest after not only more humaneness, but also a finer quality of being a human, and then bring these qualities more consistently to those taught—regardless of the likeableness or repulsiveness of the student and regardless of how the day has gone for the teacher. Students of this kind of teacher obviously learn more whether the curriculum is conventional or progressive.

To be a humanistic teacher, from most vantage points, may be to strive to be humane and to recognize human qualities in others. To be humane is to be capable of being agonized; to have feelings, not a heart of stone; to have a benevolent attitude toward others—caring, sensitive, empathic—as opposed to seeing one's more urgent problems in terms of the deficiencies and shortcomings of others.

To be human, it might be added, is in itself a continual act of self-assertion. However, if the major concern of the humanist is to be "the individual," at what point and how deeply does one have a concern for *other* individuals? Most great thinkers of the past have more lessons to give us in answering this question than most contemporaries. Also relevant are their views of human problems that still confront and perplex us today. The early Greeks remind us to practice moderation. Yes, and after Socrates, *moderation* applies to even concern about self, and even concern about others. The practice of individualism may focus on the good, but can it not be pushed too far? One objective pushed to the fore by John Dewey was to make students and teachers allies, not peers, in the quest for knowledge. Some of his third generation devotees confuse schooling with personal license to do whatever the individual wants.

Frankfort and co-workers in *Before Philosophy* strikingly report on what happened to Egypt during the millennium of individualism.[4] One can imagine somewhat similar situations in the Orient which led a Confucius to formulate the first Golden Rule (worded negatively), which later became a part of the New Testament. "Do unto others" is not an idea that just came out of the blue. Such truths are generalizations drawn from the observations and experiences of people. One becomes quite aware of this as Frankfort quotes from the Pyramid Texts, wherein the inner walls of pyramids tell of the devastation that individualism caused as it became every man for himself and an utter disregard for the welfare of others.

Perhaps the most humanistic teacher in rapidly changing times is not the zealot of change but the person of *unchanging* values. Shakespeare and many other spirits of former days still speak to us of timeless human values and about the potential *within* man. Louis Wright reminds us that men and women of Elizabethan times, whom Shakespeare dramatized, were possessors of courage and daring with a lusty zest for life, sometimes pious, sometimes bawdy. Unafraid and willing to enjoy an imperfect world, they were ready to face, without flinching, the worst of fates. Many of them, heirs to poverty and inequality, with problems that almost parallel ours, "wrote no long-winded descriptions of their nothingness, no tedious epics of ugliness, no hog-wallows of slimy words without meaning, no apologies of insecure ignorance." Perhaps we still like to read about them because we admire and envy the secret of their outlook. Perhaps that is why Shakespeare, who knew so much about human nature, may have more to say to us, as well as to our great grandchildren, about humanism than many contemporary humanistic educators.

An authentic humanistic education could mean self-discipline as much as self-expression. Obviously, it is important to educate the heart as well as the head, but as Edmund Burke cautioned, we must place a "controlling power upon will and appetite." Humanistic education which liberates us to do only what we like to do could never be called humanizing! Socrates declared that education teaches us to harness the worst elements within us in the interest of the better. Comparing man's soul to the tasks of the chariot racer, he pointed out that the driver had to learn to control two contrary horses—one was good and wise and beautiful, the other ugly, unruly, and ignorant. To cut the reins of the ugly would be disastrous; the chariot race would be lost.

Today, Joseph Wood Krutch, considered by some to be an inveterate humanist, and certainly the severest critic of the behaviorist B. F. Skinner, sounds the persuasive warning that it is more productive of personal happiness to be a candle throwing its beam into a naughty world than to cry revenge from the gutter.

Perhaps in the final analysis there is no better way to determine what is humanistic education than by a distinction which Krutch draws: "Whenever an attempt is made to convey knowledge or influence opinion in such a way that the person addressed becomes, as a result, less merely passive, more capable of criticism, and better prepared to make an effort to learn and think for himself, then what has been done to him comes under the heading of education. Whenever, on the other hand, the attempt to convey knowledge or influence opinion is such as to encourage his indolence and his passivity, whenever it aims to require the least possible effort on his part and confirms him in, rather than frees him from, the existing limitations of his powers of attention and analysis, then it is propaganda or indoctrination."[7]

CRITIQUE

One can hardly expect an essay dealing with something as fuzzy as humanism to escape being fuzzy itself. It is indeed difficult when reflecting on the uses of a term which seems to say something about everything to not be carried along to say something about everything. It might have been helpful to the reader if the writer had drawn a tighter circle around the topic, perhaps excluding the excursions into psychology, contemporary problems in society, and maybe even humanistic physical education itself.

A close reading of this essay may reveal its genuine theme to be the smaller theme of humanistic *teaching*, not the larger theme of humanistic education. Indeed, the message is clear—that whatsoever and howsoever one teaches, humanistic education appears when teachers are human: when they know their subject, are cheerful, kind, compassionate, patient—when they are guided as much by the heart as by the head.

In any case, the reader of this essay ought now to be wary of the term "humanism"—in and out of the educational context—and its various forms forevermore. No doubt the word has become nearly meaningless. The term is in serious need of having its content stripped of abstractions and filled with authentic meaning.

References

1. Alschuler, A. S.: Humanistic education. In *Humanistic Education Sourcebook*. D. A. Read and S. B. Simon (Eds.). Englewood Cliffs, N.J.: Prentice-Hall, Inc., 1975, pp. 63–64.
2. Caldwell, S. F.: The human potential movement: Body/movement/non-verbal experiencing. *The Physical Educator*, 35, March, 1975.
3. Combs, A. W.: Humanistic goals of education. In *Humanistic Education Sourcebook*. D. A. Read and S. B. Simon (Eds.). Englewood Cliffs, N.J.: Prentice-Hall, Inc., 1975, pp. 91–100.
4. Frankfort, H., et al.: *Before Philosophy*. Baltimore: Penguin Books, Inc. 1951.
5. Fuller, B. A. G., and McMurrin, S. M.: *A History of Philosophy*, 3rd ed. New York: Holt, Rinehart and Winston, Inc., 1960.
6. Heard, G.: *The Five Ages of Man*. New York: Julian Press Inc., 1964.
7. Krutch, J. W.: *And Even If You Do*. New York: William Morrow & Company, Inc., 1967, pp. 130–131.
8. Lyman, R.: What's ahead for Stanford? *The Stanford Observer*, 5, April, 1971.
8a. Marcel, G.: *Mystery of Being*, Vol. I. Chicago: Henry Regnery Co., 1960, p. 41.

9. Maslow, A. H.: Peak experiences in education and art. *The Humanist*, 29–31, September–October, 1970.
10. Runes, D. D.: *Dictionary of Philosophy*. Totowa, N.J.: Littlefield, Adams and Co., 1960.
11. Siedentop, D. L.: The humanistic education movement: Some questions. In *Issues in Physical Education and Sport*. G. H. McGlynn (Ed.). Palo Alto, Calif.: National Press Books, 1974, pp. 3–14.

15

Some Reflections on the Athletics-Physical Education Problem

INTRODUCTION

What is, or should be, the relationship of interscholastic or intercollegiate athletics and physical education? To the extent that this has been one of the most persistent and intricate questions to face the American physical educator, it might be called the profession's Gordian knot. Since the founding of the American Association for the Advancement of Physical Education, forerunner of the American Alliance for Health, Physical Education, and Recreation (A.A.H.P.E.R.), in 1885, this has been one of the more frequently recurring and stubbornly perplexing of the dilemmas confronting many physical educators. A broad range of opinion exists regarding the proper relationship of athletic programs and physical education programs. For example, interscholastic athletics have often been seen as an outgrowth and natural extension of physical education, yet they also have been viewed as being in conflict with physical education. At times intercollegiate athletics and physical education (often with intramurals and recreation) have been placed together in one departmental structure; at other times intercollegiate athletics and physical education have been organized into separate departments, each with its own administrative structure, sources of funding, and personnel.

The decades of the 1960s and 1970s would seem to be one of those periods in which what is here called the "athletics-physical education problem" has assumed a prominent position. The pervasiveness of sport in contemporary American society, the growing visibility and popularity of professional sports, the increasing criticisms of recruiting practices carried on by some institutions, the enormous athletic budgets yet financial difficulties of numerous colleges and universities, the enactment of federal guidelines for Title IX of the Education Amendments Act of 1972, and other important issues suggest that it may well be time to once again take a long, careful, and unemotional look at the question "what should be the relationship between interscholastic or intercollegiate athletics and physical education?"

ESSAY

Although the complexity of the issues associated with the athletics-physical education problem makes the attainment of a universally accepted solution extremely difficult, efforts to achieve a clearer understanding of the essential nature of the problem should not be discouraged. The history of human thought demonstrates that the dedicated search for better understanding may, indeed, lead to important discoveries and much needed changes. In a book aptly entitled *The History of Ideas,* George Boas emphasized the continuing need to reevaluate, reject, and revise what we have thought our ideas to be.[2]

From Wittgenstein's admonition that we should *look* and *see* what a problem consists of (Chapter 12), this short essay attempts to set forth and discuss briefly five "deceptions" which often seem to give rise to considerable confusion when dealing with the athletics-physical education problem. It should be clearly understood that these are not intentional deceits. They are called "deceptions" because our habitual ways of thinking, our misuse of terms, our reliance on slogans, and our disinclination to examine possible unspoken assumptions which may lie behind statements often obscure the real nature of the problem.

Deception of the Spurious Continuum

The literature of professional physical education frequently implies (and often directly states) that there is a natural developmental continuum from play to games to competitive sports to interscholastic (or intercollegiate) athletics. It is, moreover, usually implied that as one passes through this assumed continuum certain attributes of the preceding function are (or at least should be) carried over into the next. Most major students are familiar with the pyramid of a broad-based instructional physical education program with intramurals, competitive sports clubs, and athletics; even the words seem to suggest this transfer of attributes along a continuum: children are said to play games, youths play sports, and so on.

There is, however, no basis in fact for the belief that participation in an interscholastic basketball contest, for example, will *necessarily* be playful, although it certainly *may* be. On the other hand, there have been many instances when the behavior of participants in athletic contests appears to have been anything but playful. The British authors Philip Goodhart and Christopher Chataway contend that twentieth century sports have become, and will continue to become, increasingly like warfare without weapons.[9] It is germane to the present discussion to recognize that at many American colleges large numbers of young men and a growing number of young women are *recruited* directly into an intercollegiate athletic program with many of the attributes of a commercial enterprise, rather than being drawn from the instructional physical education program of the institution.

It may be worthwhile to reflect on whether or not an assumed continuum of a broad-based instructional physical education program leading to an intercollegiate or interscholastic program is any longer a viable concept. In this context one must surely ask "what is the relationship between athletics and physical education?"

Deception of the One Viable Model

There is a tendency on the part of many Americans to measure the success or failure of any given sports program by the gauge of a single model. The most prominent model for recent sports competition in the United States has surely become the professional sports athlete, although in earlier decades it was the model offered by intercollegiate athletics, especially football. The professional model is the one which represents the greatest degree of readily observable "success"—success that can be measured in terms of such things as the most games won, world championships (although opponents are rarely to be found outside of the United States), players whose skills enable them to command enormous salaries, franchises that amass incomes in the millions of dollars. Such successes all share one thing: in the final analysis they are all *quantitatively* determined. It is not denied that individual participants may have a substantial interest in the *qualitative* aspects of their involvement, but the *models* themselves are quantitatively defined. The professional sports model, it should be realized, exhibits a large number of the characteristics and attributes of the entertainment and business enterprises.

The model provided by professional sports increasingly seems to have become the pattern that today's intercollegiate athletic programs (especially at the larger institutions) seek to emulate. These intercollegiate programs, in turn, usually become the model for high school athletic programs. In 1957 a book with the intriguing title *The Astonished Muse* was published. Reflecting rather sadly on the decline of what he called the "lyric" attitude toward sport in America, Reuel Denney observed: "To the degree that they [big-time sports] build the entertainment system rather than individual participation, they may distort our ideals of human growth in a free society."[4] Denney believed that three standards for sports participation existed in the United States: (1) the business standard; (2) the social class standard, which included that of the gentleman (amateur) and that of the "non-gentleman" ("non-amateur");

and (3) the standard of the educational community. The educational community, he contended, was caught squarely between the first two standards (or models), and it had suffered as a consequence.[4]

It may be worth considering whether there is any logical reason to believe that the athletic model of the educational community should seek to emulate the model of professional sports, or whether sports and athletics in educational institutions should devise and foster their own unique models.

Deception that Attitudes Are Inherent in the Game

One often speaks as if such attitudes as sportsmanship, fair play, cooperation, teamwork, aggression, competition, dominance, tough-mindedness, and the like are inherent parts of games. It is clear that rules and those who enforce them (umpires, referees, judges) set limits which are not to be transgressed without penalty, but there is no logical reason to proceed as if the game itself had attitudes or dispositions. Various behaviors may enhance chances of winning or losing, but sportsmanship, cooperation, aggression, and such are attitudes and dispositions held by the *participants*. (It may be helpful to recall Ryle's example, presented in Chapter 10, of a spectator observing his first cricket game.)

Except for the legacy of our traditional ways of thinking, there is also no reason to believe that all sports contests must necessarily stress the same attitudes, an assumption frequently associated with the deception of the one model. Such difficulties as may arise from an exclusive emphasis on competitive behavior in sports have been discussed by Sadler, who asks whether we can continue to tolerate *so much* competition. "If organized sports are to have a beneficial role in a future, more humane society, those of us who are interested in both sports and human values will have to demonstrate meanings and values in sporting activity which transcend the level of competition. . . . [those which stress] personal growth, freedom, creativity, love, reason, happiness, beauty, and justice."[17]

It may be worthwhile to ask whether there may, indeed, be too great an emphasis on the competitive aspect at all levels of sport in contemporary American society; and also whether it may be time to reemphasize the development of such attitudes as fair play, sportsmanship, understanding, personal growth, and creativity through the medium of sports.

Deception of Definitions in Athletics and Physical Education

Despite attempts made in recent years to clarify their meanings and usage in the English language, the words "play," "games," "sport," and "athletics" (all of which are important in a discussion of the athletics-physical education problem) are still used with a considerable amount of imprecision in ordinary conversation. In some contemporary languages (French, for example), at least the words for "to play" (*jouer*) and "games" (*jeux*) are etymologically much closer than they are in English, where it is often necessary to resort to a number of lengthy explanations to try to achieve the desired connection.

"Play" seems to be the most vague of the four words. The contemporary Dutch historian Johan Huizinga, referring to the word "play," noted the persistent failure of civilizations throughout recorded history to solve the problem of vagueness: "Now it appears at once that a general play-category has not been distinguished with equal definiteness by all languages everywhere, nor expressed in one word; . . . it is arguable that one language has succeeded better than others in getting the various aspects of play into one word."[10] A few examples will illustrate the breadth of usage which the word "play" has in the English language. Sparshott points out that play is deemed nonserious, whereas work is considered serious;[20] Stone talks of the antithesis between work and play;[21] Dewey speaks of the relatedness of work and play;[5] Santayana and Huizinga refer to play as a creative force in culture;[10,18] Miller views play as being akin to a religious attitude;[14] Schiller declares that man is only wholly man when he is playing.[19] These are but a few of the connotations given to the word "play." Although play is usually regarded as nonproductive in a utilitarian sense, it is much less rarely referred to disparagingly. There often is, in fact, an underlying implication that somehow play has a positive, recreative, reaffirming quality. It might be worth noting that popular usage suggests that one plays games and, sometimes, that one plays sports, but it is rarely said that one plays athletics.

The situation is not much improved when the word "games" is considered. There are, as Caillois points out, all kinds of games: games of competition, games of chance, games of simulation, games of vertigo, and games involving various combinations of these elements.[3] There are games like dodge ball, which have only a few general rules, and games like baseball, which have highly structured, restrictive rules. To say that someone is game is to imply that he has a certain spirit or courage. The social psychologist George Herbert Mead viewed games symbolically as a phase in the socialization of the human being.[13]

With the word "sports" difficulties still remain. The term "sports" has an extremely broad meaning. Its regular use for athletic activities is of relatively recent origin. Elias reports that a German author in 1844 declared that since his language had no word for sport it was forced to introduce it.[7] There is talk of *recreational* sports and *competitive* sports, of *amateur* sports and *professional* sports. There are sports in which the identifiable central purpose is a contest between two teams or individuals for an eventual victory which can be designated in terms of some quantitative standard; there are sports like mountain-climbing in which the challenge is the encounter between an individual human being and a natural phenomenon. Maheu is one of several authors who contend that sport as a job cannot really be considered sport; sport, like play (and culture), contains its own intrinsic justification and reward.[12] This is a considerably different point of view than that offered by Noll, who maintains that "The professional sports industry provides a fascinating subject for students of the relationship between government and business. Virtually every major public policy toward business—anti-trust, labor relations, taxation, even the constitutional prohibition against slavery—has a potentially significant application to sports."[15]

There is, perhaps, slightly more unanimity regarding the meaning and usage of the word "athletics." In general, athletics seems to signify those competitive physical activities for which participants engage in long and arduous training programs in preparation for contests requiring significant physical strength, stamina, highly specialized neuromuscular skill, and an attitude which rejects the possibility of potential defeat. Considerable emphasis (sometimes, it would seem, the only emphasis) is placed on *winning*. When it is recalled that the word "athletics" is derived from the Greek word "athlein," meaning "to contend for a prize," this emphasis becomes more understandable. Although in many countries athletics refers only to track events, in the United States the term is habitually used interchangeably with sports. Whether or not there may be an inconsistency which accentuates the deception of the vagueness of words in the American proclivity for saying *professional sports* and *intercollegiate athletics* may be an important question.

These brief comments regarding the possibility of confusion arising from the vagueness of words dealing with the athletics-physical education problem have certainly not solved the problem. If, however, they have prompted further thought concerning potential difficulties and an attempt to clarify the expression of ideas, they will have served a useful purpose.

Deceptions from Disregarding Historical Origins

In an article entitled "Can Philosophers Learn from Historians?" Alan Donagan suggests that the bridge to better understanding must be constructed from both ends.[6] It is the intention of the following paragraphs to point out that knowledge of how athletics and physical education began in American institutions of higher learning might help to clarify a number of important (but often overlooked) aspects of the athletics-physical education problem. In an essay as brief as is this one only a limited account can be given. The interested reader should study the historical development of athletics and physical education in the United States more fully.

Before turning to the United States, however, it might be helpful to take a brief glance at the classical Greek world—the source of so much of Western tradition. In ancient Greece, Forbes declares, a clear distinction was made between the teacher of general physical education(*paidotribes*) and the coach (*gymnastes*) whose role was the care and instruction of those who were preparing for an agonistic career as professional athletes.[8] The impact of this early distinction between athletics and physical education has come down through history (sometimes acknowledged, sometimes obscured) with far greater force than is often recognized, and this recognition is vital to the achievement of a clearer understanding of the present situation.

During the last decades of the nineteenth century and first two decades of the twentieth century, America experienced an unprecedented rise and expansion of sporting activities. The American historian John Rickards Betts has documented the establishment of intercollegiate athletics as a thoroughly entrenched American phenomenon during the period 1890 to 1920.[1] In the 1880s and 1890s collegiate athletics developed largely outside the official structure of institutions of higher learning. Conducted by students, alumni, and individuals who had little or no preparation in education, and usually no responsibility to the college, these athletics often took on many of the characteristics of a haphazard business enterprise. Before long, such practices as the employment of professional players, recruiting, abuse of academic standards, gambling, and dangerous forms of play made it necessary for college administrations to take steps to attempt to control or regulate the conduct of intercollegiate athletics.

The same decades (1890 to 1920) also constitute the period of the rapid rise and expansion of American colleges and universities. Many college presidents and boards of trustees found that a winning team (especially a football team) was a most useful means to attract students, encourage donations, and provide publicity for the institution. College football teams often were, Frederick Rudolph claims, the best publicity agents a college or university could have.[16] In this respect, intercollegiate teams provided a vital *service* to the institution.

Although there was growing concern before the turn of the century that all was not right with intercollegiate athletics, it was the football crisis of 1905 that triggered the events leading to the formation of the National Collegiate Athletic Association (N.C.A.A.).[11] Directors of men's physical education departments, several of whom were physicians, were among the early members of important N.C.A.A. committees. Almost from the outset, however, concern was voiced that intercollegiate athletics were not being carried out in a manner in keeping with the aims of an educational institution. Chancellor James Day of Syracuse University provided an often heard criticism in the 1909 *N.C.A.A. Proceedings:* "If athletics are for the students they should be so diversified that an adaptation may be made to all classes of students." In 1915 William Foster, President of Reed College, declared: "first of all the question must be decisively settled, which aims are to dominate—those of business or those of education." President Foster went so far as to recommend that all intercollegiate athletics be suspended for an entire college generation in the effort to establish the "tradition of athletics for education." C. W. Savage, Director of Physical Education at Oberlin College, stated in the same year: "The facts of the case are that there is little or no justification of the present status of intercollegiate sport as a legitimate interest of an educational system." In 1922 Elmer Mitchell, the major force in the intramural sports movement, maintained that those individuals who argued that intercollegiate athletics were essential because they developed qualities like leadership, sportsmanship, courage, and a healthy demeanor actually weakened their own position because "the more argument you present that athletics develop these qualities, the more you prove likewise that athletics are needed by all, and that a few are monopolizing the benefits."

The American Association for the Advancement of Physical Education was founded in 1885. During the first years its membership evidenced only a mild interest in athletics. Before the early 1900s, physical education in the United States consisted largely of gymnastic systems imported from Europe, a variety of indigenous calisthenics and anthropometry. It soon became evident, however, that students would rather derive their exercise through games than through programs of disciplined formal exercise. As early as 1903 Lucille Hill stated that women should become "exponents of the New Athletics, whose platform is largely idea at present." Leaders in physical education like Thomas Wood, Luther Gulick, and Clark Hetherington spoke out in favor of "the new athletics," which were to be evolved from an educational base in physical education. At a meeting of the Athletic Research Society in 1910 Hetherington reported: "We distinguish sharply athletics organized primarily as spectacle for the amusement of people from athletics organized as play. . . . Professional spectacles should be distinguished from educational athletics."

The contrast between attitudes held by members of many departments of intercollegiate athletics and those who advocated the new athletics was made even more evident in the 1920s, when steps were taken at many institutions to combine athletics and physical education into one department. The newly created administrative units were frequently placed under the direction of an individual who had no professional preparation in physical education. The Carnegie Foundation for the Advancement of Teaching, in its report *American College Athletics* in 1929, criticized this practice on the grounds that men who possessed physical education backgrounds seemed to have broader interest in all forms of sport and were inclined to develop more comprehensive programs. The 1929 report also questioned whether an institution whose primary purpose was to foster intellectual life should at the same time serve as an agency to promote athletics on an extensive commercial basis. It may be worth noting that the 1974 American Council on Education inquiry into "The Need for and Feasibility of a National Study of Intercollegiate Athletics" raised as still-not-solved problems a large percentage of the issues which the 1929 Carnegie report had discussed.

CRITIQUE

Sometimes an essay bent on asking one question answers another. The essay has not failed. It has only deceived us somewhat.

The question "*What* is, or should be, the relationship of athletics and physical education?" has not been answered. It is not surprising. The question is a tough one. Instead, what is discussed though not stated is "*Why* is the relationship between athletics and physical education a problem?" The relationship is a problem because there are a number of myths which interfere with straight thinking about the matter. This essay introduces several of these myths or deceptions, or probably better, assumptions.

Frequently, more confusion is created when choosing to discuss a *number* of confusions. There is a sense of helplessness, a feeling of not having the vaguest notion of where to begin to set things straight. Consequently, some people never begin.

One wonders if more information would have been gained if the essay had concentrated on a single assumption. Any one of them would have done. The exploration of one common assumption to its root would quickly take us far beyond the question of why directly toward the more fundamental question of what.

References

1. Betts, J. R.: *America's Sporting Heritage: 1850–1950.* Reading, Mass.: Addison-Wesley Publishing Company, 1974.
2. Boas, G.: *The History of Ideas.* New York: Charles Scribner's Sons, 1969.
3. Caillois, R.: *Man, Play and Games.* M. Barash (Trans.). Glencoe, Ill.: The Glencoe Free Press, 1961.
4. Denney, R.: *The Astonished Muse.* Chicago: University of Chicago Press, 1957.
5. Dewey, J.: *Democracy and Education.* New York: The Macmillan Co., 1916.
6. Donagan, A.: Can philosophers learn from historians? In *Mind, Science and History.* H. E. Kiefer and M. K. Munitz (Eds.). Albany, New York: State University of New York Press, 1970, pp. 234–249.
7. Elias, N.: The genesis of sport as a sociological problem. In *Sport: Readings from a Sociological Perspective.* E. Dunning (Ed.). Toronto: University of Toronto Press, 1972, pp. 88–115.
8. Forbes, C. A.: *Greek Physical Education.* New York: Century, 1929.
9. Goodhart, P. and Chataway, C.: *War Without Weapons.* London: W. H. Allen, 1968.

10. Huizinga, J.: *Homo Ludens: A Study of the Play Element in Culture*. London: Routledge and Kegan Paul, 1949.
11. Lewis, G.: Theodore Roosevelt's role in the 1905 football controversy. *Res. Quart.*, XC, 717–724, 1969.
12. Maheu, R.: Sport and culture. In *International Research in Sport and Physical Education*. E. Jokl and E. Simon (Eds.). Springfield, Ill.: Charles C Thomas, 1964, pp. 9–22.
13. Mead, G. H.: *Mind, Self and Society from the Standpoint of a Social Behaviorist*. C. W. Morris (Ed.). Chicago: University of Chicago Press, 1934.
14. Miller, D. L.: *Gods and Games: Toward a Theology of Play*. New York: World Publishing Company, 1970.
15. Noll, R. G.: *Government and the Sports Business*. Washington, D.C.: The Brookings Institution, 1974.
16. Rudolph, F.: *The American College and University*. New York: Alfred A. Knopf, 1962.
17. Sadler, W. A.: Competition out of bounds: Sport in American Life. *Quest*, XIX, 124–132, 1973.
18. Santayana, G.: *The Sense of Beauty*. New York: Dover Publications, Inc., 1955.
19. Schiller, F.: Play and beauty. *In Essays and Lectures, VIII*. A. Lodge, E. B. Eastwick, and A. J. W. Morrison (Trans.). London: Anthropological Society, 1882.
20. Sparshott, F. E.: Play. In *Aesthetic Concepts and Education*. R. A. Smith (Ed.). Urbana: University of Illinois Press, 1970, pp. 107–134.
21. Stone, G. P.: American sports: Play and display. In *The Sociology of Sport*. E. Dunning (Ed.). London: Frank Cass and Company, Limited, 1971, pp. 46–65.

16

Phenomenology

INTRODUCTION

Useful in the understanding of philosophy as quest is to learn how some expert philosophers actually do quest after understanding, knowledge, wisdom. Among the various ways to know (some of which were discussed in Chapter 4), one in particular (not discussed in Chapter 4) is the subject of this essay. As a method of philosophizing, phenomenology could be of great significance to the exploring physical educator. Accordingly, this essay introduces *phenomenology,* especially the possibilities for phenomenological description in physical education.

ESSAY

SELF-EVIDENT DATA ARE PATIENT, THEY LET THEORIES CHATTER ABOUT THEM, BUT REMAIN WHAT THEY ARE.

—Edmund Husserl

Among various rally cries, "To the things themselves!" does not rank among the most noteworthy. Most certainly, "Damn the torpedos, full speed ahead!", "Remember the Alamo!", and "Give me liberty or give me death!" are much better known. Nonetheless, to some "To the things themselves!" is as compelling a slogan in the contemplative world as were those more popular cries in the world of action. Let us attempt to approach the meaning and significance of this allegedly compelling cry.

The Term

That from which the cry "To the things themselves!" issues is *phenomenology.* Knowing this fact is not particularly helpful, for it may appear that we have merely substituted an obscure term for an obscure phrase. Indeed, the term "phenomenology" does have its "ponderousness and tongue twisting ugliness" (Spiegelberg). It is sometimes confused with similar sounding words, such as phenology (influence of climate on recurring annual phenomena such as bird migration), phenomenalism (the only objects of knowledge are phenomena), phonology (study of speech sounds), philogyny (love of women), phylogeny (evolution of a genetically related group of organisms), penology (science of punishment of crime), philology (study of written records, linguistics), physiognomy (face as an index of character), and even phrenology (prediction of mental powers by the shape of the skull).

We should not be deterred from understanding a little of phenomenology simply because the term is ugly and is easily confused with other words. In fact, the term itself is something we should get beyond rather quickly. Its historically strange career, its misleading nature, and its almost undefinable meaning force us to take a more productive and useful approach.

What Phenomenology Is Not

Sometimes it is quite helpful in studying what a unique thing is to learn what it is not—or better what it is not like. Because the misunderstandings of phenomenology both in and out of philosophy are legion, it behooves us to cut it loose at the outset from what it is often misunderstood to be or to be like.

First, phenomenology is *not a branch of knowledge.* Among the many "ologies," a number of them claim to be but a branch of that great tree. Together these various branches compose the full tree; or rather, without the myriad of branches, the tree of knowledge would not be complete. Immediately one can think of both the hard and the soft sciences (the physical or natural sciences and the human sciences) as appropriate trunks. Their various subdivisions are branches. Eventually, the various technical specialties make up the twigs. As the number of trunks, branches, and twigs grow and develop, knowledge is said to have proportionately increased.

Second, phenomenology is *not a branch of philosophy.* As the reader now knows, the various branches of philosophy include epistemology, metaphysics, logic, axiology, and aesthetics. Phenomenology, although strictly speaking understandable under the rubric epistemology, is not a new addition to or recast version of these ancient divisions of philosophy.

Third, phenomenology is *not a philosophy.* Throughout the second section of this book, the reader was introduced to or reacquainted with various philosophies (or philosophic positions), such as realism, idealism, and pragmatism. Each of these positions views the world from a different perspective. Although the philosophies themselves are rather difficult to fully characterize, they do point to different world views. There is within each a set of beliefs or doctrines, or at least some assumptions, distinguishing each from the other. Phenomenology is not such a school of thought. It is simply not one of a number of diverse positions from which one chooses or from which one puts together an eclectic view of things. In short, phenomenology does not consist of an ordered collection of propositions or statements to which one subscribes.

Fourth, phenomenology is *not a system.* Throughout the history of philosophy there have been individual thinkers who have tried to put together complete systems of thought. Some philosophers have been known to try to account for all things known and knowable in a massive internally consistent program. Almost all of the unsettled problems of mankind (which number many) come before the judgment of the system in the making. The thinker then tries to fit the unknown into the organized system. (This is not unlike the child trying to fit puzzle pieces into pre-cut slots—they fit, or else!) Although it lies within the capability of phenomenology to say something about everything, phenomenology is not a system against which things are judged and then expected to conform.

Fifth, phenomenology is *not measuring.* The primary way for the sciences of mankind (often called the "empirical sciences") to discover things by is measurement. Whether we study human beings, rocks, plants, agricultural processes, animals, or chemical compounds, we determine the consistency, the density, the components, the weight, the color, the location, the length, the shape, and hundreds of other factors. The measuring procedures depend on techniques which vary according to the object under scrutiny. Phenomenology does not depend on sense experience (seeing, hearing) which is necessary for all kinds of measuring.

Thus, phenomenology is not a lot of things. We know that it is not a branch of knowledge, a branch of philosophy, a philosophy, a system, or a kind of measuring. If it is not any of these things, then what is it? What of our slogan "To the things themselves!"?

What Phenomenology Is

The basic thing to remember is that phenomenology is *method.* It is a way—for some, *the* way—to know. It is method that has evolved gradually from a variety of different influences. Its central force was the life work of the German philosopher Edmund Husserl. There is much confusion about phenomenology, especially in the United States. A large part of this confusion is because much of Husserl's work remains to be translated. Even his translated material stubbornly resists being understood. It produces not only different levels of understanding but even multiple meanings, depending on choices made by the particular translator.

It should be no surprise that in light of a variety of historical influences surrounding phenomenology, the incomplete version by Husserl himself, and the often contradictory tales told by his numerous interpreters, there is considerable uncertainty about the message of phenomenology. Not only are battles being fought in the popular literature about the meaning and significance of phenomenology, but all sorts of technical issues are being raised in lesser known journals and symposia. All in all, although phenomenology has never had its day in court, persons from widely differing persuasions are preparing for its defense or its prosecution.

Nevertheless, in the midst of all the academic punching and counterpunching, there is agreement as to some of the basic features of phenomenology. Among these various features, perhaps one in particular will be most helpful to the student trying to gain a better understanding of phenomenology. Necessary to the successful use of the method is a full awareness of *the region or terrain to which the phenomenologist is restricted.* In short, what are these *things* we are to look for and just exactly where are we to find them?

Not long ago there was a professional golfer trying to explain in an interview why he had been in a slump. After a two-year dry spell, he had finally won a major tournament. "It turned out to be a little thing," he said. "It was in my grip." He explained how he had tried every conceivable solution. Nothing had worked. "Finally," he said, "I went to this older retired pro who analyzed my swing from start to finish." After a short session, the older pro quickly saw the flaw in the grip. The older pro told the younger pro, "Change your grip this way, back to the fundamental position." The senior told the junior that he must have forgotten the very basics of the grip, that he should get back to the foundations, "the very first principles of the golf swing."

How often do we hear from coaches about the importance of getting back to the fundamentals? Even when the accomplished player falls into a period of poor performance, the cause is more often something quite elementary. The player says, "I have to work on the fundamentals." Even pros are not free from the need to build their skill on fundamentals and basic sequences or patterns.

Much like the helpful suggestion from the older golf pro, Husserl recommended to the world that it return to the foundations, to original sources, to fundamentals. In Husserl's view, both science and philosophy, in spite of their apparent successes, remain *uncritical,* weak in their foundations. They are, and have been for some time, in a slump. Although quite without meaning to, science and philosophy have accepted without question far too many unverified claims to truth. Among other things, science and philosophy not only have taken for granted the existence of the entire world (and all that such existence entails) but have been prejudiced from the outset as to how best to *know* the world. Furthermore, these claims are quite beyond verification by the existing techniques and procedures of *either* science or philosophy. To begin again requires the development of a "universal science," a "first philosophy."

Instead of continued building and building and building on a largely unexamined foundation, the phenomenologist practicing this universal science must carry out the necessary activity of digging and digging and digging. Indeed, Husserl even likened the method of phenomenology to the science of archeology.

The difference between the digging of the archeologist (the careful poking around a dig), and the digging Husserl had in mind is exactly *where* one does the digging. The dig site is not anywhere in the world, especially not spatially located, but rather is in one's consciousness of the world. In short, the site to expose is none other than "my (and your) experiencing of the world."

"My experiencing of the world?" "Well," the careful reader might object, "not only is that an individual matter, but it certainly could not pass for a universal science, if we are to use as a source the subjective (and thus personal and relative) element of *my* consciousness."

However, in phenomenology the ideas of subjective and objective take on a new meaning. Instead of the subjective being individual and relative, it becomes an absolute source for knowledge. Once we suspend our interest in extant particular things (such as this person, that chair, our school, this team) and suspend our personal individual judgments about such individual things, including *my* opinion or point of view, *the region where the phenomenologist digs is left over*. It is "consciousness of the world, our awareness of the world, our mental grasping of our experiences." By mentally standing back (anonymous viewing), any object may be brought before my (and your) gaze. All things, even to be recognized as things, depend on a pre-given region of consciousness of the essences of these things. Even the objection voiced previously concerning what is or is not subjective and objective (insofar as legitimate sources for objective results) issues from the subjective region. A familiarity with the meaning of subjective and objective is presupposed.

That people do not regularly do such standing back does not mean people cannot do it. Once the proper stance has been taken (bracketing the individual and relative natural world of actually existing particulars), the essence of things known can be reflectively described. The existing philosophic theories, which depend on the unquestioned reality of the external world as well as all other theories, are not used in one's questioning. Rather, subjective reflection on the invariants of these realities (the problems and phenomena themselves) is the basic root of indubitable knowledge. Reflection is turned toward that which makes a thing what it is (essence) not what theories tell us it is, because to theorize about it already supposes knowledge of what the thing is.

In short, the phenomenologist makes use of what Husserl called the "wonder of all wonders"—that human beings are not only objects in the world, but also subjectively aware of their being in the world. Instead of consciousness being dismissed as entirely useless (or as only of second-order importance), this same subjective awareness becomes *the* source, *the* region, *the* terrain of all of our questing.

"To the things themselves!" means that the investigator must restrict, whatever the inquiry, to the region of consciousness (our mental experiencing of the world) *and* what is given or intended in it. The things themselves appear to consciousness when the reflective gaze apprehends them. Because chairs differ from tables, people from trees, shame from fear, love from embarrassment, religion from politics, and so forth; and because consciousness of these things (universals) can be made a theme of inquiring, the phenomenologist simply *notes the differences* between things and describes what is "seen." The phenomenologist *goes to* conscious experience and finds universal content, the *objects* of that experience.

Phenomenology and Physical Education

Most people shy away almost instinctively from any suggestion that we ought to rely on our experiencing of the world for the struggle to understand ourselves and our world. It is important, however, to remember the altered meaning of this phrase. We are now speaking *not* of my personally living through (autobiographical), let us say, running from here to there and then noting what that was like. We are speaking of reflecting on *what it is to run from here to there* (to run as such), whether or not I personally have ever actually run or even can run at all (perhaps not having the use of my legs).

If we were interested in the experience of running, we would set out to describe the fundamentals of running that distinguish it from other experiences like it. We would describe the *necessary* characteristics of the running experience. We would no doubt note what kinds of things can run. We would imaginatively vary the experience of running, describing various possible ways to run, possible functions of running, reasons or causes for running, relationship between possible motive and the act, purposes of running, possible individual differences in running, maybe even distinguishing the differences in categories of running depending on whether one runs fearfully, joyfully, aggressively. Furthermore, we could even describe various possible meanings of the act of running and its relationship to different or similar acts. Sometimes such reflecting and noting, as we dig deeper into the experience, eventually force us to ask such questions as "What difference does the possibility of running make in the world?" and "Why in the world would anybody want to be good (or better than others) at running?"

Not only could one select running (or any locomotor movement) as a theme, but one could describe running as it appears in something such as tennis. Does it appear? in what ways? How much of the game of tennis depends on running? More important, how is it that persons can do more than one thing at a time, namely, run *and* hit (or miss) tennis balls? What differences in the experiences are there between running and running *in* the game of tennis? If the running act has been complicated by inserting it as part of a larger whole, then how do these experiences interrelate? In short, the phenomenologist describes what happens to humans when the experience becomes complex. What does one think about? Does one think at all? How is this description affected by various levels of ability? What does it mean to be skilled? What does a skilled player command that is not within the ability of the unskilled player? How are others (partners and opponents) a part of the game? How is space used? How is time involved? Is the temporal aspect of tennis different from ordinary time?

Questions like the aforementioned begin to lead us into the game of tennis itself. The phenomenologist tries to describe what tennis is, in fact. What are the essential characteristics of the game? People talk of strategy in tennis, but how is it possible for the *experience* of tennis to be complicated even more to include some kind of mental deceiving or feigning? What makes up this mental activity? Is it conscious? Does one think automatically while playing tennis? How does this happen? Is there really such a thing as a mind telling a body what to do? In what way? Is this distinction abstract? How does the strategy in tennis differ from that in other activities in which one wants the upper hand? If there is such a vast realm of tennis beng played as an inner (mental) game, what are its characteristics? What are the common ploys used in tennis to gain the advantage? Why does one want the advantage? to win? why? What are the essential characteristics of the game that distinguish it from other games? Is it a game at all? What is a game?

Digging further and further into our example, we soon begin to wonder whether tennis is a game. Description of its components still seems to leave out something fundamental. What, after all, is a game? How do games differ? What other examples of games are there? Why are they games? Could they be sports? Are games and sports different? if so, why? if not, why not? Many people seem to think that games are not too important. Others think they are far too important. What value is there in a game? in sport? Is sport valuable in itself, or only because we value it?

Before we progress much further we run into the claim that there is some kind of educational benefit from sport and game. The phenomenologist physical educator now turns the "anonymous seeing" directly into the characteristics of sport or game insofar as they may relate to education. What is it to be educated? What are the characteristics of education? Is it merely going to school? Is there more to it than that? To what degree can we relate the essential characteristics of sport or game to education? Does it make any sense at all to speak of these together? Are they really "oranges and apples?" Is there some possible connection between them? If so, what is the connection? Are there different kinds of education? If so, do sport and game belong to one kind of education and not another? If sport and game are of different possible kinds or layers of education, are some of these possibly more educational than others?

We shall not go on. We already have come quite a distance from the description of running to the description of education. It can be seen that once one begins the digging, there seems to be almost no end to the possible directions the inquiring might take.

Descriptive phenomenology in physical education would be the primary excavating tool to probe all those frustrating mysteries haunting physical education. At the moment, physical education crosses over many other disciplines. Its roots currently seem to be in all the various arts (liberal and fine) and sciences (natural and human). There is little question that physical education is included in Husserl's recommended massive art and science archeological dig. Perhaps even more than other disciplines, physical education is in need of sustained, rigorous, methodical, and communal root exploration.

Physical education and its alleged components really have never been carefully and thoroughly grounded. Its polymorphous structure far too often resembles whatever is in fashion. Over the years it has grown chiefly by adding on rooms, by building and building and building.

However, remember that phenomenology digs. It does not build (at least not until the ground has been fully excavated). What is necessary at the moment is for professional physical educators to make use of this fundamental method of original description of the problems and phenomena in physical education. It is sensible to begin where there is already some agreement.

It may be best to back up and take a look at the basics of that which seems to pull physical educators together. Some of us might choose to describe fundamental movement experiences, others sport experiences, yet others dance experiences, and possibly even some, play experiences. We might be able to describe exactly how these things are experienced, in short, what they are in themselves. We might find some basic categories of physical activity which could serve as ground. These basic categories would then reveal what kinds of foundations we actually do have, and whether or not there is enough uniqueness in the categories to allow the discipline to stand alone. The results of such careful and patient *objective* (subjective sources) inquiry will tell us rather clearly what, or even if, physical education *is,* and knowing this will surely be one guide to present and future professional action.

Such digging calls for large numbers of mental archeologists in order to complete and verify the various finds. Learning how to carry out phenomenological descriptions and analyses is a first step all of us ought to consider taking. We have been given the necessary tools, that is, the ability to reflect on experiences and their objects. All that remains is to put that ability into action and "go to the things themselves!"

> COMPLETE CLEARNESS IS THE MEASURE OF ALL TRUTH, AND THOSE STATEMENTS WHICH GIVE FAITHFUL EXPRESSION TO THEIR DATA NEED FEAR NOTHING FROM THE FINEST ARGU- MENTS.
>
> —*Edmund Husserl*

CRITIQUE

It was Adolf Reinach, in "Concerning Phenomenology" (*The Personalist*, Spring 1969), who wrote: "To talk about phenomenology is the most idle thing in the world. . . ." A major criticism of this essay may be in the choice of writing about phenomenology instead of doing it. It is much easier to spin off a short treatise on what needs to be done. It is more difficult to set to work doing it. The uninitiated reader might have benefited more from a good example of phenomenology. In such a way the reader would have something to hang onto, some results of phenomenological description by which to judge its effectiveness.

In regard to the content of the essay under scrutiny, there are points at which the reader may have become weighted down with technical jargon. Although there is a minimum of such loaded words, perhaps more synonyms could have been provided. Furthermore, for those students interested in following up the method of phenomenology, a few guidelines could have been included to demonstrate just *how* one does phenomenology.

On the whole, there is enough introductory material presented in this essay to whet the appetite of the scholar-physical educator. The invitation stands: "Go to the things themselves!"

Selected Reading

Primary Sources

Husserl, E.: *Ideas*. W. R. B. Gibson (Trans.). New York: The Macmillan Co., 1931/ 1962.

Husserl, E.: *Logical Investigations*. J. N. Findlay (Trans.). New York: Humanities Press, 1970.

Husserl, E.: Phenomenology. In *Encyclopedia Britannica*, 14th ed. Reprinted in *Realism and the Background of Phenomenology*. R. Chisholm (Ed.). Glencoe, Ill.: Free Press, 1960.

Husserl, E.: Phenomenology as a rigorous science. In *Phenomenology and the Crisis of Philosophy*. Q. Lauer (Trans.). New York: Harper & Row, 1965.

Husserl, E.: *The Crisis of European Sciences and Transcendental Phenomenology.* D. Carr (Trans.). Evanston, Ill.: Northwestern University Press, 1970.

Secondary Sources

Edie, J. M. (Ed.): *Phenomenology in America.* Chicago: Quadrangle, 1967.

Farber, M.: *The Aims of Phenomenology.* New York: Harper & Row, 1966.

Farber, M.: *The Foundations of Phenomenology.* Albany: State University of New York Press, 1969.

Gurwitsch, A.: *Studies in Phenomenology and Psychology.* Evanston, Ill.: Northwestern University Press, 1966.

Kockelmans, J. J.: *Edmund Husserl's Phenomenological Psychology.* Pittsburgh: Duquesne University Press, 1967.

Kockelmans, J. J.: *Phenomenology.* New York: Doubleday, 1967.

Lauer, Q.: *Phenomenology: Its Genesis and Prospect.* New York: Harper & Row, 1958.

Lawrence, N. and O'Connor, D. (Eds.): *Readings in Existential Phenomenology.* New York: Prentice-Hall, 1967.

Schmitt, R.: Phenomenology. In *The Encyclopedia of Philosophy.* P. Edwards (Ed.). New York: The Macmillan Co. and Free Press, 1967.

Sheets, M.: *The Phenomenology of Dance.* Madison, Wisc.: University of Wisconsin Press, 1966.

Solomon, R. C. (Ed.): *Phenomenology and Existentialism.* New York: Harper & Row, 1972.

Spiegelberg, H.: *The Phenomenological Movement (An Historical Introduction).* The Hague: M. Nijhoff, 1960/1971.

Thévenaz, P.: *What Is Phenomenology?* Chicago: Quadrangle, 1962.

Zaner, R. M.: *The Way of Phenomenology.* New York: Pegasus, 1970.

IV

PHILOSOPHY
AS DISCOVERY

IV

PHILOSOPHY
AS DISCOVERY

PHILOSOPHY WILL ALWAYS, TO MY WAY OF THINKING, BE AN
AID TO DISCOVERY RATHER THAN A MATTER OF STRICT DEM-
ONSTRATION.

—Gabriel Marcel

Questing presupposes something after which one quests. Whatever the object or subject pursued, it is the discovery or the hope of discovery that completes or perpetuates the quest. Be it the child discovering a lost toy, the natural explorer discovering uncharted regions, the person discovering himself, or the thinker discovering an idea, the discovery usually justifies the pain, uncertainty, and frustration of the questing.

The essays in this part attempt in a small way to point toward the delights of discovery. They include such subjects as one barrier to knowing thyself, the problems of being an administrator, philosophy in the Eastern world, and some reflections on leisure. In each case, as with the essays in Part III, a short critique immediately follows the essay to encourage the novice philosopher to challenge the discoveries of others preparatory to making discoveries for himself.

17

Presuppositions: A Barrier to "Know Thyself"

INTRODUCTION

Major hidden difficulties face those who make the effort to accept the challenge "know thyself." One of them, strangely, has escaped adequate acknowledgment and discussion. This usually hidden force is one of those umbrella concepts which covers not only science and philosophy but most of man's endeavors. Yet, it has operated, without a sobriquet, in the discipline of philosophy until relatively recently. In fact, its name does not appear in the glossaries of some rather recent textbooks purporting to discuss philosophy.

Presuppositions have been so little known that the individual is apt to be unaware of the ones that underlie his behavior and thought. Yet, they are among the powerful influencers of what he believes, says, writes, and is. Their hiddenness increases their strength as influencers.

The implication is that presuppositions may bar the individual not only from "know thyself" but also from straight thinking.

The reader is challenged to find his own presuppositions if he expects to "know thyself." He is reminded that it is easy to be trapped by one's assumptions, and that the searching-examining task is never completed.

ESSAY

AS MAN SUCCESSFULLY DIGS FOR AND FINDS HIDDEN PRE-SUPPOSITIONS TOGETHER WITH THEIR MOTIVATIONS, HE TAKES A STEP FORWARD AS A PHILOSOPHER.

—Adapted from E. A. Burtt

According to legend, Thales' answer to the Miletus youth's question "Master, what is most difficult?" was "To know thyself." Delphi's later invitation "know thyself" has become more widely accepted. It also was

10

carved in stone, if the visible inscription is authentic. Either thought serves our purpose here. It challenges moderns as well as ancients to perform this difficult, never completed task.

Many modern adult persons actually or figuratively are attempting to engage in this intriguing duel with themselves. So slippery is mind, so puzzling is self, and so uncertain is to know, that barriers to responding to Delphi's tempting call are many and formidable. Why, then, be concerned with one barrier?

The barricade selected on this occasion seems to be appropriate to men and women in and preparing for a profession embracing physical education and amateur sport. Historians, scientists, professional philosophers, sociopsychologists, and many persons outside any academic circle also are involved, although they may not be aware of it, as will be seen later.

This blockade, one may conjecture, made its initial appearance with early evidence that Homo sapiens was capable of reasoning. This rampart's strength to thwart the ability to generalize and hypothesize, however, is a relatively recent acknowledgment. We shall first recall some familiar examples of this barrier to straight thinking, sound reasoning, and wise judgment.

Among the more commonly practiced barriers are prejudice, dogmatism, intolerance, gullibility, and incuriosity. Even a brief list of others would be incomplete without this one: "There is a principle, proof against all argument, a bar against all progress, and which, if persisted in, cannot but keep the mind in everlasting ignorance, and that is contempt, prior to examination." (In spite of efforts to find full information of the source of this quotation, all that can be reported is its author, William Paley.)

The barricade selected for attention in these pages is *presupposition,* a comparative newcomer to academic philosophy. It is similar to examples given previously. For instance, all presuppositions gain their force from human emotions. All often work incognito. Frequently, the individual is unaware of them. He often sincerely believes that he is not prejudiced, dogmatic, and the like. He feels no need to doubt his strongest biases or to examine what to him is plain common sense or obvious fact.

The need to examine the obvious is of historical interest. Here is but one example. It took centuries for mankind to acknowledge that the axioms and postulates on which euclidean geometry was built should be examined, as Burtt points out. Only as several differing sets of postulates and presuppositions were formulated and verified did other kinds of geometry emerge. Today, scientists and mathematicians acknowledge not only that their disciplines rest on presuppositions, but also that progress depends substantially on the process of *examining* currently held presuppositions, *searching* for new ones, *verifying* them, and *using* them.[1]

Burtt has written extensively about the role and place of presuppositions in most areas of mankind's work and thought. To emphasize this point he presents two simple examples. (1) "I eat my peas with honey;/ I've done it all my life./It's true they do taste funny,/But they don't roll off my knife." (2) Mr. A: "Every evening I drink five cups of coffee." Mr. B: "Man, doesn't it keep you awake?" Mr. A: "It helps." Burtt then adds, "The reader will find it good practice to formulate them—and likewise (formulate) the presupposition that the two examples have in common."[1]

Burtt's discussion of presuppositions recalls Robinson's prior emphasis on the difficulty human beings experience when requested to give up firm beliefs, regardless of evidence to the contrary.[2] Burtt's report a half-century later pictures little improvement in this respect. However, this little improvement is found in the fact that several disciplines are increasingly subjecting their established presuppositions to doubt.[1] Researchists in physical education are a part of this improvement, as witnessed by a testing and measuring program in a department of physical education. Those in charge do not assume the accuracy of the measuring devices. At regular intervals the devices are checked for accuracy with still more accurate mechanisms. Necessary adjustments or replacements are made.[1] This example enables a statement to be made as to the meaning of presupposition. The researcher *antecedently* considered it logically necessary to examine the devices periodically. This examination was considered to be necessary if the resulting data were to be as accurate as possible throughout all testing periods. Runes states that a presupposition is that antecedent which is logically necessary if a desired result is to be obtained.[3]

Shall we follow Burtt's suggestion that we try to formulate a presupposition? Here is a tentative one for the movement movement in educational institutions: in terms of man's development, it is important that schools and colleges provide programs of human movement, as well as opportunities to study the field embracing this knowledge related to the phenomenon that man can and does move. Many physical educationalists would prefer that a clause be inserted to the effect that this program and study operate within the overall curriculum of physical education.

The profession covering amateur sport and physical education in educational institutions *has never formulated its basic presuppositions*. There appears to be little effort to take such a logically necessary step, in spite of a considerable interest evidenced in transforming this field into a discipline. The guess is hazarded that many members of this profession are unaware of the need for such a step. Once these basics have been carefully formulated and then verified by knowledgeable professional persons, the profession will have taken a long step toward recognition by other disciplines as a possible candidate for this honor. Nevertheless, never should it be considered that the resulting presuppositions are beyond doubt, nor should a continual examination of them cease until they have been proved beyond question, as relevant research continues. Physical educationalists, with their involvement in some of the sciences and scientific methods, should have little difficulty in appreciating the logical necessity of this basic step. This observation does not mean to suggest that this self-examination of their profession is limited to the methods of the natural sciences.

The spread of a willingness to doubt the obvious and the givens and to give up or revise long-assumed presuppositions which may be doubtful and/or questionable is encouraging. It speaks for open-mindedness toward new and even conflicting presuppositions. It also speaks for cooperative efforts to seek alternative presuppositions, many of which may not yet have been discovered. This statement should not be considered without appreciating the integrity and courage shown by women and men who have started to question presuppositions, particularly if they help to formulate or to assume the presuppositions undergirding the profession but which now may be discarded, replaced, or severely revised. Sometimes one wonders whether one of the barriers to the progress of physical education and sport in educational institutions has not been the strength of the persistence of its leaders, holding to a way and/or a goal of thinking in contrast to adapting to and even seeking change in such essentials as presuppositions.

Those who continually search for truth also demonstrate the quality of patience. One who begins to be such a searcher soon encounters well-meaning associates who cling to the tried and true of yesterday. (They may feel that the open mind sometimes becomes a bit drafty!) Yet, to fail to examine cherished presuppositions, to fail to consider alternative valid presuppositions, and to fail to try out the latter constitute a triad of possible reasons that help to explain why physical education has not yet tackled the inescapable, logical necessity of formulating at least its foundational presuppositions.

In fact, the several national-level professional organizations concerned with physical education and sport in educational institutions have seldom united their strength, thought, and resources toward any major goal except to aid the nation in time of war. As vital, admirable, worthy, and helpful as these efforts have been, one wonders about the results if such unity were directed to the attack on the neglect of the major presuppositions undergirding physical education and sport, which *now* are considered to be beyond doubt or question, are assumed to exist, or are beyond the need to be examined.

The unexamined basics form a veritable chain against "know thyself." The assumption that there are undergirding presuppositions and that they are beyond doubt becomes a habit of the mind. It also becomes a habit of the heart. As admirable as loyalty may be, it becomes a surreptitious part of the barrier to know thyself. Exactly what is one loyal to —a given movement, a favorite professor's ideas, a certain textbook, one's alma mater, the department, a cause, or the profession? Other forces join such habits of mind and heart. For example, a popular "in" theory, way of thinking, underlying assumption, deep personal interest, or long-delayed personal ambition, as vital as it may be in the lives of all of us, also may serve as an effective barricade against even being aware of the presuppositions which form the foundation stones of one's personal and professional life. Other activities captivate our thinking and feeling so easily and pleasantly that their force tends to be unrecognized. How then do we know that they crowd out such unrecognized things as presuppositions? That is, they *prevent* coming to know thyself. Once again Robinson's uncovering of how stubborn man is to continue to believe whatever he believed before is pushed to the fore of thinking. How easy it is to be *certain* that firm beliefs are beyond question, beyond concern. How logical it seems that we are reasoning when we assiduously dig up arguments to believe as we did before.[2]

There must be some reason for such strange mental activities among rather intelligent men and women. Do we perhaps lack confidence in our ability to formulate better beliefs? Do we doubt our ability to choose wisely between alternative beliefs? Do we think we lack the ability to reliably evaluate the beliefs of a life time, or is it that we are afraid of the result of such evaluation? Could some of the reason stem from mental laziness?

Such possible shortcomings help to explain the imitation of the beliefs of someone admired, some writer who makes sense, or someone whom "everyone" says is tops-in-his-field. The shortages explain the "bandwagon jumper" who thinks the way to become a leader is to leap from one fad to another as each new one arrives. One exhausted "jumper" confided, "I began by joining the progressive movement, then the group method, then group process, then group dynamics, then of course existentialism. I finally found final truth and became a phenomenologist."

From whence come such unrecognized presuppositions that personal convictions should always be firm, certainties unquestioned, and beliefs fixed? One source may be those outside influences which tend to operate without being recognized and at the same time indirectly suggest some of the presuppositions underlying both personal and professional belief and conduct. Familiar examples are home, state, church, and local culture. Less readily recognized sources are one's hierarchy of values and major purposes, which are regarded as self-selected but frequently spring from either outside sources or are unawarely the result of imitation.

The young individual eventually feels a need to determine what it is he believes. This vital, complex, and frustrating task is carried on into postadolescent years. As a set of beliefs that seem reasonably satisfactory or as feasible as possible is formed, the individual tends to become engaged in other activities of day-to-day living and his profession. Beliefs then are seldom examined or reasons for holding them questioned. Defense of them is the common response, if another person should point out the need to question or scrutinize them. Usually, this challenge is not made. Thus, personal beliefs lie fallow, except as they may be deepened and extended.

The individual's major beliefs, such as presuppositions, tend to become so much a part of him that it does not occur to him that alternative beliefs about a given thing might be held tentatively, so that they also might be tried out in his personal or professional life style. In addition, workaday activities claim his attention and time to such an extent that it does not occur to him that such major underlying beliefs are seldom beyond doubt until verified for all times and conditions. In addition, the mature, aware individual should be expected to want to know why he believes such important foundational concepts as presuppositions.

Presuppositions that spring from that which the world teaches and from the wisdom of the body are examples of large-scale beliefs which offer alternatives verified through the experiences of millions of individuals beginning at least in the third millennium B.C., according to American Egyptologist James H. Breasted. Certainly, every schoolboy knows of one or two that have the mark of Ancient Greece stamped on them: "The unexamined life is not worth living." "Moderation in all things." Presuppositions verified by means of scientific methods and tested in the cauldron of the living of the human race offer basic beliefs of another kind, which also may spawn alternative presuppositions to those which are never examined or questioned. Even the practice of becoming alert to the *possibility* that some of one's presuppositions may be modified, with benefit to him and to others, is a step forward. Even the conscious thought that one might possess presuppositions (which determine or influence his conduct), which lie hidden from consciousness, is a step forward. Even daring to *evaluate* a cherished major conviction is a step toward opening the mind. Actually, trying any such measures helps lead the individual to begin to think in terms of better understanding himself.

To try the new merely because it is new and the different merely because it is different, and to change merely to change are not the equivalent of taking a step that promises *improvement*. This pedestrian statement is packed with challenge. One's decision as to whether a given step's desirability outweighs its cost depends on the impact of temperament, personality, and some would add, digestion. What of the influence of those familiar catalysts of human conduct—personally selected values, purposes, attitudes, motives, and interests? How easy it is to mention and to read this familiar string of words. Too much wordy education without application is responsible for that! However, even that does not siphon off the power of these human triggers for action, which make undigested knowledge a pale weakling when it comes to changing oneself or anybody else. How could one have even a miniscule amount of knowledge about himself if such triggers are not released for use.

Some reader might well respond to much that has been discussed by countering with "Yes, but through the years I have *not* been aware of presuppositions, their nature, strength, role, or operation in my personal or professional life." Nevertheless, once this reality is faced, presuppositions no longer need to be hidden. Is there an exception to this view?

Recall for a moment some of the other sources of influence as one selects or formulates presuppositions and other vital, major beliefs. Examples are parents, siblings, professors, friends, readings, communications media, experiences, as well as personal imagination, feelings, and the like. In addition, there appears to be evidence that genetic heritage should be added to the list.

Pediatricians join many other specialists in emphasizing the importance of early habit formation in infants. Smiles and encouraging vocal noises of family members and others reinforce preferred behavior. Facial gestures and verbal encouragement are some of the springboards for the beginnings of value formation, attitudes, and so forth. The world of the infant is apparently assimilated, osmosislike, to varying degrees. A veritable plethora of experiences partially explain natural responses, which emerge later as shyness, outgoingness, and much later, the phenomenon of choking when the chips are down in a tight athletic contest. The beginnings of such a thing as racism or chauvinism and their opposites apparently are rooted in the infant's experiences and guided responses to them even *before* his awareness begins. Teachers in physical education who *understand* the behavior of small children and know of their home upbringing are forced to conclude that negative attitudes toward this discipline may begin long before their school years.

Habit formation is a reservoir of early body and other memories, together with later inputs and impacts, which remain *hidden* as sources of presuppositions, as do the presuppositions themselves. The responses seem to be so much a part of the individual that it is extremely difficult for him to ferret them out. If a friend should mention some presupposition, which the individual by word or act demonstrates, and which the friend believes is harmful, unseemly, or fallacious, the individual usually is astonished. He says "Why that's me! That's the way I am! I've always been that way!" Should the individual sincerely *desire* to jettison the offending presupposition or its expression, he has taken a step ahead. Accomplishment of this goal is difficult. To come to regard it as a something to be eliminated means actually finding and digging it out. One of the reasons for the difficulty of this operation is that many of our cherished convictions rest on these hidden beliefs. They have been nurtured, clung to, and are the source of satisfactions.

Some presuppositions of course are the foundations of commendable, desirable, pleasurable, worthy conduct, yet still are hidden from the individual. That is, he remains ignorant of the force which these presuppositions have, as well as being unaware of the presuppositions themselves. He cannot understand a professional discipline or himself if he is not knowledgeable of the appropriate presuppositions underlying the discipline or himself, respectively.

The focus of these incomplete remarks has been on but one small target. No attempt has been made to examine that presupposition which was formulated in Grecian antiquity. For most of the intervening years of Western civilization little heed has been given to "know thyself," in spite of Socrates' and Plato's influences. Only recently have we of the West belatedly picked up this forgotten torch. It might well be carried on somewhat in the manner of Schweitzer's examination of his prime presupposition, Reverence for Life.

Thus, we have been caught in the web of our own net! We have assumed that the presupposition "know thyself" is beyond doubt or question! Is it?

AN OBJECT IS PERCEIVED IN SUCH A WAY THAT IT FITS INTO THE STANDARD HABITS THAT PERCEIVERS IN GENERAL, OR PERCEIVERS IN OUR CULTURAL MILIEU, HAVE FORMED.

—E. A. Burtt

CRITIQUE

Among the limitations of this essay are the following:

1. Applications to physical education are limited.

2. Discussion of presuppositions initiated in infanthood is too brief.

3. The assumption that presuppositions and beliefs may be treated similarly in some instances needs verification.

4. More examples of the definition of presuppositions would have been helpful.

5. More reasons for one's ferreting out presuppositions would have strengthened the essay.

6. Explaining how one might locate presuppositions would make the essay more convincing.

7. Those who regard themselves as beyond the novice level would have preferred a more technical discussion.

8. At best, the essay does little more than open the way for further and deeper discussions of the place of presuppositions in physical education, as well as the role of "know thyself" in this profession's thought and work.

9. Appraisal of the essay would have been facilitated if the basic purpose of the discussion had been made explicit. However, had this been done, the crux of the treatise would have been tipped off prematurely.

References

1. Burtt, E. A.: *In Search of Philosophic Understanding*. New York: The New American Library, Inc., 1965, pp. 101–102, 131, 132, 140–145.
2. Robinson, J. H.: *The Mind in the Making*. New York: Harper and Brothers, 1921.
3. Runes, D. D.: *The Dictionary of Philosophy*. New York: Philosophical Library (n.d.), p. 249.

18

The Administrator and the Philosopher

INTRODUCTION

It is frequently the case that the manner in which various departments of physical education are administered (at whichever educational level) determines the effectiveness of the program. Although it is occasionally true that good faculty and students survive in spite of bad administration, and that good administration can sometimes exist in spite of miserable faculty or students, it is generally the case that good administration breeds effective programs. This essay is concerned with the characteristics of *effective administration*. It is no accident that these characteristics are essentially related to the *reflective posture* of the philosopher at work.

ESSAY

The problems of being an administrator of physical education and athletics are not greater than those of being an administrator anywhere else in the academic community. Nonetheless, there are particular, if not peculiar, problems. For example, one problem produced in a large measure by past events and persons in our profession is the separation of men and women physical educators and coaches. They have experienced a checkered relationship as partners and adversaries over the years. This trend has been paralleled by a general mistrust of the "other side."

Another problem connected with administration of physical education and athletics is that all sorts of people move into or are thrust into administrative positions. Some of them were formerly top-notch teachers. Others had been outstanding athletes or coaches who produced winning teams. Some may have been selected on the basis of their business management skills. The mandate of Title IX to equalize educational opportunity prompted many almost instant mergers of departments of physical education and athletics for men and women. Thus, new administrative titles and roles were created for some women. Women athletic directors, as well as heads of integrated departments of physical education, ceased to be an anomaly as the number of women administrators in such situations increased.

To the wide assortment of personalities must be added the panorama of types of programs (physical education, dance, recreation, health, safety and driver education, athletics) usually placed under the physical education umbrella. In addition to the multiplicity of programs are the disparate philosophic positions, not easily recognized as being interrelated.

A study of the history of great educational institutions and their subdivisions reveals that they have not died as a result of such problems. Rather, have they not died of rigidity, or a "failure of nerve," to use Gilbert Murray's phrase? In the mergers of formerly separated departments, if success is attained, perhaps the one thing that men or women cannot have a failure of nerve about is in changing their old polarized views of themselves. They can no longer risk alienation. Is it not the duty of men and women, most particularly administrators, to quietly build a new synthesis to take the place of people's former patterns of thought, judgment, attitude, and practice?

Men and women of goodwill, together, can work out an understanding of what administration is and can become. The results of such efforts should not be pious manifestations about everyone's good intentions. Genuine dialogues about togetherness become difficult if one cannot find at least shared basics from which to start. If, for example, the portents of the past suggest that physical education will flounder, then this phenomenon may indeed be a consequence of the nature of *administration.* That is, if mergers between men's and women's departments, and between physical education and athletics lead to administrative commitments being fashioned solely to protect the athletic dollar, then such a view cannot carry the merged departments toward the outcomes inherent in their programs and their personnel.

What then is effective administration in the diverse and complex field of physical education and athletics? Perhaps, as Epicurus warned, we should not avoid pleasures but select them. Proposing that we seek such pleasures as tranquility and equanimity, rather than those which disturb the soul, he held that there was nothing nobler than to apply one's self to philosophy. As one attempts to make such selections and to find experiences to be cherished along the administrative way, one is inescapably concerned with values, ethics, and purposes. They enter administrative policies and practices, over any opposition. Let us take a look at a few elements of administration through the philosophic perspective. We may discover a profitable clue or two to multiplying challenges and added maturation, rather than frustration, during the administrator's journey.

The problem is simplified somewhat if it is realized that the *human* reference point cannot be dismissed. The administrator's values, ethics, purposes, and other philosophic considerations are major bases of her or his assumptions and theories, in addition to the practical aspects of administration. As the mosaic of administrators' duties is studied, some major guides emerge. For example, the administrator should be an educator, a decision-maker, an interpersonal psychologist, and able to *understand* the philosophic position reflected in her or his own behavior and that of the others involved.

As an *educator*, the administrator's *primary* responsibility is attending to those conditions which "bring the young under the intellectual influence of a band of imaginative scholars," to use the words of A. N. Whitehead. As the administrator tackles this foundational responsibility, acute problems arise. There are decisions to be made regarding enrollments, diverse programs and services, a bureaucracy of personnel policies and procedures, all of which tend to demand of the administrator qualities and abilities somewhat akin to those of the big business executive.

How does the administrator immersed in a mass of such operational detail become a leader among scholars rather than lead what some administrative theorists describe as a "descent into trivia"? In one sense, being an *educator* means engaging in genuine study of the knowledge phases of one's discipline. The ability to perceive and anticipate problems and the ability to communicate are related, in part, to adequate knowledge of the area in which the problem resides. Faculty members tend to profess appreciation for the administrator who can "talk our language," even though an authentic vocabulary may be nonexistent.

As an educator, the administrator also works to infuse the department and its personnel with values beyond the technical requirements of the tasks at hand. The old axiom, "a whole is greater than a sum of its parts," expresses a basic about the climate of a department which has institutional character and group integrity. Identification with such a department creates resources of energy that help create day-to-day effort, motivating faculty members to say, "What we are proud of around here is_____."

Another central function of the administrator is to develop and regulate the *decision-making process*. Many people generally do not work as well in situations characterized by obvious authority, fiat, and command, as they do in situations reflecting persuasion, consent, and agreement. Thus, the making of decisions is not equivalent to the giving of orders. The administrator needs to be skilled in such areas as questions, challenges, and uses but not abuses of the committee device. He is, in the words of Enarsom, the "majority leader," the "devil's advocate." Apparently, however, the willingness to accept and act on decisions made by those higher in authority relates to a zone of acceptance which broadens as those affected by decisions have a voice in their determination.

Decision-making, particularly in matters of integrating formerly separated departments, seems to call for making imaginative decisions—those that call for new policy, change in thinking, change of activity of the members of the organization, or even change in the organization itself. Many of these decisions cannot be delegated, may be rarely shared, and may depend on proper timing and the administrator's ability to think fearlessly yet speak softly. Fearlessness in thought is often revealed in the willingness to take certain chances and a readiness to experiment. Without fearlessness in thought, an administrator may stay on dead center, a nonentrepreneur perhaps concentrating on sheer survival, unable to live with what Christopher Fry called "the patter of tiny criticisms."

Moreover, fearlessness in thought means accepting the loneliness of decision-making. After a faculty committee makes its report on some matter which it has been studying for a semester or a year, and after the faculty spends a few meetings discussing the recommendations and implications of the report, the top-notch administrator has to have the courage to do what his best judgment dictates. In the last analysis, it is the administrator who will be *held responsible* for the matter and its consequences. The old hat trick of saying, "I have a mandate from my faculty to _____" is responsibility-dodging, flim-flamming. The administrator is paid more money for several reasons, not the least of which is to judge rightly, in terms of what he or she knows and believes and thinks, and given the situation that is faced.

Above all, effective administration appears to be an art requiring acute perception and understanding of and empathy in human nature, as well as skills in *interpersonal psychology*. Knowing how to deal with people might be likened to what John Dewey called "knowing where to tap," when he wrote that for knowledge to function it must be internalized. Perhaps it is what Herbert Thelan called the "instinct for the jugular" developed through reflection on experiences that have importance for people. Perhaps it is what Gerald Kennedy meant when he said "I like men with hard heads and soft hearts."

Regardless of how one comes by the skill, the successful administrator is a person no less than the leader Gardner Murphy envisioned when he stated: "It is not knowledge of the task, but interpersonal skill—and toughness, shrewdness, persuasion, tact, knowing when to use the tweezers, when the sledge hammer—that produces results." Apparently, the administrator should be as unobtrusively obvious, simple, and human as the situation demands. He or she needs to be expert in quietly noting details, capturing the flavor of occasions, forming preferences, wording awkward truths acceptably. With this easy openness, on occasion, the administrator is a consummate actor, without being thought of as such. His or her extroversion, or covertness, may lead to being misunderstood. This, however, should not concern the administrator if he has done his best.

The search for an acceptable theory of administration may bring an unwanted degree of systematization to what is now guesswork, even in human relations. In the entire gamut of human operations and relationships, no theoretical proposition, hypothesis, or theory stands inviolate, regardless of persons and situations involved. The outcome of administration's multiple procedures depends on the *persons* involved. It is possible to have a catch-as-catch-can administrative pattern and operation which works beautifully *if* the faculty and students have confidence in and respect and admire the administrator, and if the administrator sincerely feels this way about them. They make it work without knowing it. They make up for gaps and errors without reflective thinking. And, if and when new students and faculty arrive, the "hopscotch" administrative pattern and operation may become utterly ineffective.

The possible major guide for the administrator, therefore, would seem to be *understanding the philosophic positions* reflected in his own behavior and in the behavior of others. Surely the administrator of top rank is one who knows *what are* his or her values and other philosophic ingredients. Only then does one know what is being given up if compromise and consensus are asked or requested. Only then does one know on what personal assumptions and hypotheses are based, and only then can judgments be made circumspectly. As judgments are made is not the administrator continually appraised by all who are involved (and by knowledgeable observers)? To what degree is a judgment fair, sound, and wise? Underlying the ability to make good administrative judgments are balance in outlook, balance in appraisal of people, and balance in value system. These kinds of balance are possessed by the synthesizer, the amalgamator, one who focuses on large-scale goals, who sees life whole and who has perspective. Wisdom and weakness are interlaced in all philosophic positions and neither stampedes this kind of novice philosopher.

Without a synthesized set of philosophic concepts, the administrator relinquishes his or her leadership role and swims without direction through a sea of management minutiae. Lacking a consistent, sensible modus operandi, one's only alternative may be to resort to expediency. The administrator then shifts willy-nilly in acquiescence to what administrative theorists call "opportunism" (the pursuit of immediate short-run advantages and excessive response to outside pressures), and utopianism (avoiding hard choices by a flight to abstraction and expediency).

The acid test of administration, then, seems to be what happens to all those within the administrator's jurisdiction, not only their capabilities and potentials, but also their reasonable hopes and aspirations.

As an educator, decision-maker, and interpersonal psychologist—and, throughout all, as a philosopher—an administrator's ultimate pleasure, the exhilaration in his or her work, is that of enjoying the flavorful experience of being one of the faculty as well as being concerned with the quality, direction, vitality, and worthiness of the department. The prevailing possibility of the *collective* performance and achievement of all members of a department enables an administrator to pick herself or himself up from many a "slip on a banana peel and serve the next ball." Unless he or she has "wit enough to keep it sweet," surely over the doorway, as over Dante's *Hades*, might be inscribed the words "Abandon hope all ye who enter here."

Finally, if one were to ask what will be the future of merged departments, perhaps the most eye-opening estimate is provided in the cornerstone of the Prudential Life Insurance Building in Minneapolis where were placed predictions by 20 leading citizens as to what life in the United States would be like at some future date. Among the forecasts for the future was this reminder: "men and women will struggle for happiness—which will continue to lie within themselves." So is it with departments.

CRITIQUE

The characteristics of effective administration, or rather the characteristics of persons who effectively administer physical education programs, also happen to be reasonable characteristics of effective teachers. It may be that in an age that prefers the community of administrators to the community of scholars, this essay might be a good argument for eliminating administrators, or for decentralizing the control of various departments.

At least one original meaning of the verb *to administrate* is "to serve." It is too much to ask for the return of the original idea of the administrator being the slave of the faculty, but there may be good reason for the faculty to be more master than slave. This essay describes postures and attitudes quite within the range of individual faculty members to master their own fate. Take away the assumption of this essay that there even ought to be administrators, and remaining is a good, if general, argument for the rebirth of the community of scholars managing their own affairs. In short, were administrators *and* faculties *to be* as described in this essay, there would most likely be little need for people called "administrators."

19

Philosophy in the Eastern World

INTRODUCTION

From time to time ways of thinking that arose and developed in the Eastern world have become attractive to a substantial number of individuals in the United States and in other Western countries. There have also been several Western philosophers who have displayed an interest in Eastern thought; Leibnitz, Hegel, Kierkegaard, and Jaspers are among those who have evidenced an interest in the thought and value systems of Eastern philosophy. The United States at mid-twentieth century has been witness to such an interest in the East—an interest ranging from thoughtful, sympathetic, scholarly study to superficial, thoughtless, even blind and fanatical fads. Noting that modern technology has facilitated communication among the different cultures of the world, a number of thoughtful writers have suggested that valuable consequences might ensue from a greater rapprochement between the thought systems of the East and those of the West. Many have suggested that an understanding of the more meditative aspects of the philosophies of the Eastern world might help the Westerner to minimize some of the psychologic problems which a rapid pace of life and a one-sided materialism seem to have created. In 1938 Sarvepalli Radhakrishnan, one of the twentieth century's leading figures in the introduction of Indian thought to the Western world, wrote: "The supreme task of our generation is to give a soul to the growing world-consciousness, . . . To this great work of creating a new pattern of living, some of the fundamental insights of Eastern religions, especially Hinduism and Buddhism, seem to be particularly relevant, . . . No culture, no country, lives or has a right to live for itself. If it has any contribution to make towards the enrichment of the human spirit, it owes that contribution to the widest circle it can reach."[9] More recently, P. T. Raju stated in his *Introduction to Comparative Philosophy:* "when educated men see that men in other parts of the globe have the same aspirations, are guided by identical or similar motives, and think and act like themselves, the strangeness of other cultures

and apathy toward them is bound to be lessened, and a sense of the oneness of humanity will be strengthened."[11]

In the United States during the last decade many college and high
school students have requested, and often initiated, a variety of courses
and study groups which have sought to explore a broad spectrum of
various Eastern cultures. Included in their interest have been such
physical activities as judo, akido, t'ai chi ch'uan, and yoga. Although
many students have enrolled in these and similar classes solely for the
physical activity which the courses may offer, other students have expressed an interest in learning something of the philosophic orientations
of the cultures in which these activities arose. It is because of this seeming interest in Eastern thought, especially as it may have a valuable
contribution to make to Western physical education, that this brief essay
is presented.

ESSAY

JUST AS A FLETCHER MAKES STRAIGHT HIS ARROW, THE WISE
MAN MAKES STRAIGHT HIS TREMBLING, UNSTEADY THOUGHT.
. . . THE CONTROL OF THOUGHT, WHICH IS DIFFICULT TO RE-
STRAIN, FICKLE, WHICH WANDERS AT WILL, IS GOOD; A
TAMED MIND IS THE BEARER OF HAPPINESS.
                    —*The Dhammapada (The Path of Virtue)*

It is necessary to understand that there is no single Eastern philosophy—no one way of thinking which is characteristic of the millions
of people who live in the countries of the Orient. Just as a variety of
philosophic orientations can be found within the Western philosophic
tradition (idealism, realism, pragmatism, and so forth), so may numerous orientations be found within Eastern philosophic tradition (Hinduism, Buddhism and its derivatives, Confucianism, Taoism, Jainism). As
Nakamura points out, "we must acknowledge the fact that there exists
no single 'Eastern' feature but rather that there exists diverse ways of
thinking in East Asia, characteristic of certain peoples but not of the
whole of East Asia."[7]

It is important to recognize that philosophy and religion in the East
are often intimately associated and that they are frequently difficult, if
not impossible, to separate. It is also important to realize that the historical development of many Eastern philosophies (especially Hinduism
and Buddhism) often covers a much longer time than those of the West.
Over the centuries variations within these philosophies may have developed, which render more complex and difficult an understanding of
their basic tenets. Moreover, the teachings of the Eastern philosophies

frequently do not easily lend themselves to verbalization, and are often presented in a form which the Westerner finds obscure and perplexing. The *Vedas* of Hinduism, for example, have been described as "half-formed myths" or "crude allegories."[10] The *Analects* of Confucius and the *Koans* of Zen Buddhism present their teachings more as parables than as declarative statements. Last, but certainly not least, it is extremely important to realize that many of the more exaggerated and flamboyant movements and fads which have recently appeared in the West usually provide an erroneous and extremely distorted (sometimes even dangerous) picture of what Eastern philosophy really endeavors to teach.

Although the immense complexity of Eastern philosophic thought renders generalizations dangerous, a few cautious observations may provide a perspective by which the reader can begin to grasp how an understanding of Eastern thought might be of some value to the person born and reared in the West. Hinduism and Buddhism (and sometimes Confucianism) are usually considered to be the major philosophies of the Eastern world. The total number of adherents of one or more of these philosophic systems constitutes, by far, the greatest percentage of peoples of the Asian continent and subcontinent. Each has a large body of recorded literature which has developed a great complexity. Huston Smith has suggested that the world's three broad cultural traditions actually express the three main aspects of man's basic nature (natural, social, psychologic): "Generally speaking, the West has accented the natural problem, China the social, and India the psychological."[16]

D. T. Suzuki, one of the leading contemporary authorities on Eastern thought (especially Zen Buddhism), has provided a statement which seems to sum up about as well as it can be expressed in words the basic difference between much of the philosophy associated with the West and much associated with the East. In the West, Suzuki says:

> We generally think that philosophy is a matter of pure intellect, and, therefore, that the best philosophy comes out of a mind most richly endowed with intellectual acumen and dialectical subtleties. But this is not the case. It is true that those who are poorly equipped with intellectual powers cannot be good philosophers. Intellect, however, is not the whole thing. There must be a deep power of imagination, there must be a strong, inflexible will-power, there must be a keen insight into the nature of man, and finally there must be an actual seeing of the truth as synthesized in the whole being of the man himself.[17]

Knowledge must be accompanied by a personal experience or it is only superficial—someone else's knowledge—Suzuki contends. Buddha's whole philosophy comes from experiencing or seeing (the term "seeing" here implies an intuitive grasp of things, not the physical act of using the eyes). It is the seeing of what is called "prajna"—intuition. To have any chance of understanding what is meant by this way of experiencing the world, Suzuki cautions, we must try to give up the typical Western method of dividing things into subject and object, into self and other, into either/or.[17] This is, of course, not an easy thing for anyone raised in the Western tradition to accomplish. Nevertheless, if we are to begin to understand the Eastern orientation, Suzuki insists, we must begin to replace discursive knowledge (vijnana), which analyzes knowledge into subject and object, with intuitive knowledge (prajna), which enables one to grasp the oneness or wholeness of reality.[18]

Brief Overview of the Basic Teachings of Hinduism and Buddhism

Hinduism

Hinduism can be regarded as a religion, a vast and complex philosophy, and a social institution. One must be *born* a Hindu, it is held, it is not something that can be acquired. However, persons who are not born Hindu may come to discover, by diligent effort, many of Hinduism's philosophic insights. The earliest literature of Hinduism is a vast collection of religious texts known as the *Vedas,* the oldest (*Rg Veda*) having been committed to writing about 1000 B.C. Not so much a book in the customary sense, *Veda* is the name given to the extremely diverse system of beliefs gathered by a priestly class over 1000 years. For the orthodox Hindu, the *Vedas* constitute eternal truth and are the acknowledged source of authority. Although Hinduism has experienced numerous modifications since the creation of the *Rg Veda,* its *basic* beliefs have remained constant: the belief that on mortal death the soul is reborn into another body (reincarnation); the belief that the world is eternal (it had no beginning and will have no end); the belief in the "law of the deed" by which man is compensated in kind in his next incarnation (*karma*); the belief that when one has continuously good karma over an extremely long series of successive incarnations a state of perfection or release (*nirvana*) will be reached. It is the ultimate goal of every follower of Hinduism to reach this perfection of nonbeing or nirvana. Hinduism has no formalized creeds or standardized forms of worship, and it is extremely tolerant of other views. Popular Hindu theology is polytheistic; in its more sophisticated form it may be monotheistic or even monistic.

Radhakrishna and Moore have identified seven characteristic attitudes of the Indian philosophic mind: (1) a concentration on the spiritual; (2) a belief in the intimate relationship of philosophy and life; (3) an introspective approach to reality; (4) a tendency to idealism (and in Hinduism, to a monistic idealism); (5) an openness to reason, but a conviction that intuition is the only method by which the ultimate can be known; (6) an acceptance of authority; and (7) an overall synthetic tradition, which is essential to the spirit and method of Indian philosophy. Indian philosophy holds that reality is *ultimately* one and *ultimately* spiritual. Metaphysics, epistemology, ethics, religion, psychology, facts and values are not cut off from one another but are seen as the natural unity of a single comprehensive reality.[10] Indian philosophy tends to be otherworldly. Its central emphasis has been on the one unchanging reality which transcends time, space, and the particular. The individual self, which we see as characterized by change, is illusionary; the true self or soul (*atman*) can never be destroyed. The true destiny of the self is to identify with Brahman. It is this nondualism which holds that ultimate truth is the oneness of existence, Nikhilanada contends, which is "the highest achievement of India's mystical insight and philosophical speculation, and her real contribution to world culture."[8] The Hindu view of the individual and his relation to society is summarized by Radhakrishnan as consisting of three disciplines: (1) the fourfold object of life (desire and enjoyment, interest, ethical living, and spiritual freedom); (2) the fourfold nature of society (the man of learning, the man of power, the man of skilled productivity, and the man of service); (3) the fourfold succession of the stages of life— *asramas* (student, householder, forest recluse, and free supersocial man). It is by means of these three disciplines that the Hindu is to strive to change body into soul and to discover the world's potentiality for virtue.[9]

Unquestionably, in Indian philosophy soul or spirit is deemed superior to body. "The Upanishad tells us," Radhakrishnan states, that "the natural half-animal being with which [man] confuses himself is not his whole or real being. It is but an instrument for the use of spirit which is the truth of his being. Nevertheless, soul and body, however different, are yet closely bound together. The things of spirit are in part dependent on the satisfaction of the body."[9] This theme has been emphasized by the contemporary Indian philosopher Sri Aurobindo. The body, according to Hindu philosophy, cannot be the self because it is changeable and transitory, yet the uninformed identify the person with the body. It is through the body, however, that one may practice spiritual discipline. This is one of the teachings of Hatha Yoga, which uses discipline of the body and concentration as a means to higher consciousness. The Yoga system (of which Hatha Yoga is only one of eight) seeks the attainment of perfection through control of the physical and psychical elements of human nature.[10]

Buddhism

Through Buddhism, the philosophy of India has influenced the culture of many other Asian countries. Millions of human beings adhere to one or the other forms of Buddhist faith. It is generally accepted that Siddhartha Gautama, the historic Buddha, was born in northeastern India in 563 B.C. At the age of 29 years, Gautama renounced wife, family, and worldly possessions and set out to discover the cause of human suffering and its cure. After years of self-mortification (which he decided was ineffectual), then of self-discipline and meditation, Gautama finally achieved enlightenment while seated under the Bo tree. The term "Buddha" means "the Enlightened or Awakened One," and Gautama never believed that he, or any other great teacher, could do more than help others who sought salvation to find enlightenment. One of the famous sayings ascribed to the Buddha is "Look within, thou art the Buddha"; that is, each of us, through our own efforts and compassion, must find the path to knowledge and peace. Buddhism's teachings are practical and down-to-earth, rather than otherworldly (as Hinduism tends to be). In contrast with the Indian Brahmanic view that only a special class could attain *dharma* (merit, virtue, moral law), Gautama maintained that dharma was available to everyone. The method by which this might be achieved constitutes the essence of Buddha's teaching. Buddhism rejects the concept of a universal, unchanging, permanent self (which is essential in Hindu philosophy). For Buddhism, everything is subject to change; everything is "becoming."

From its early beginnings in India, Buddhism spread throughout Asia and ultimately settled (having assumed a variety of forms) in what is now China, Korea, Japan, Southeast Asia, Sri Lanka, Burma, and Tibet, where it coexists amicably with other religious views. About A.D. 1200 Buddhism largely died out in India. The two major branches of Buddhism recognized today are *Mahayana* (the greater vehicle), located mainly in China, Japan and Korea, and *Hinayana* (the lesser vehicle). Mahayana Buddhism tends more toward social compassion. The basic tenets of Buddhism are contained in the *Four Noble Truths* and the *Noble Eightfold Path,* which can aid man's attainment of nirvana. The Four Noble Truths teach that the essence of existence is bound up with suffering (birth, illness, death, desire, and the like); the origin of suffering is found in desire, craving, and grasping (we can never possess that which is external to ourselves); the cessation of suffering is to be found in the elimination of desire, craving, and grasping; and the way to the cessation of suffering is to be found by following the Noble Eightfold Path. The eight stages of this path, which constitute the essence of Buddhist teaching, are right views, right aspirations, right speech, right conduct, right means of livelihood, right effort, right mindfulness, and right contemplation or meditation. The Eightfold Path leads to the cessation of craving, to truth, and to ultimate insight. Buddhism seeks to put an end to the endless cycle of cause and effect (*samsara*) and to reach ultimate insight, or salvation (nirvana), by release from the continual cycle of rebirth. Closely associated with the cycle of rebirth and its escape is the concept of karma (the law of the act or deed). A good deed, provided it is motivated by good intentions, creates good consequences; a bad deed (or bad intentions) creates bad consequences. Mental discipline is also of extreme importance in Buddhism. By controlling the mind, Buddha taught, we can discover things as they actually are, not as they *appear* to be.[2] Both body and mind, which in traditional Western thought are usually taken to comprise the individual life, do not constitute the real self, Buddhism holds. Body and mind will wear away but the nature of Buddhahood cannot be destroyed. Buddhism teaches that a "wise man . . . should break away from any attachment to body or mind, if he is ever to attain Enlightenment." The way to enlightenment is the "life of the Golden Mean," or the avoidance of extremes: the avoidance of ascetic discipline and the degradation of mind and body (the inclination of those who renounce the notion of life); and the avoidance of desires of the body and whims of the mind (the inclination of those who believe that this life is an end in itself).[19]

Zen Buddhism, a form of Mahayana Buddhism found chiefly in Japan, has gained a considerable popularity in Western countries in recent years. The term "zen" means meditation, and disciplined meditation is the basis of Zen Buddhism's teachings. Zen is the Japanese pronunciation of the Chinese term "Ch'an," which is, in turn, a translation of the Sanskrit term "dhyama." Having slowly traveled for centuries through China, Zen acquired certain aspects of Chinese philosophy. Ross suggests that Zen involves a subtle blend of Indian metaphysical abstraction, Taoistic paradox, and Confucian pragmatism. Zen Buddhism emphasizes the search for the Buddha nature in oneself. Its aim is the attainment of ultimate knowledge or enlightenment(*satori*), which lies beyond the world of apparent change. It rests on Buddha's insight "Look within, thou are the Buddha." Satori, the state that defies verbal description, has been likened to the state which Gautama, the Buddha, reached while seated under the Bo tree.[13]

According to Zen Buddhism, the search for enlightenment cannot be carried out intellectually by rational thinking; it must be done intuitively. The guidance of a master is necessary, however; one cannot learn Zen by oneself. The Zen *Koans* constitute a kind of allegorical tale, meanings of which must be grasped intuitively, not by discursive thought. The most important practice of Zen Buddhism is usually taken to be *za-zen* or "sitting meditation," although the term should not be taken too literally for there are a number of zen practices which are active. Rinzai Zen, for example, uses such secular arts as the tea ceremony, kendo, and archery as means of spiritual training.

Eastern Thought and Physical Activity: Selected Contemporary Views

Charles Moore has described Aurobindo Ghose (generally referred to as Sri Aurobindo) as one of India's leading contemporary philosophers.

Aurobindo, who was educated mainly in England, sought to provide a reinterpretation of traditional Indian philosophy in light of his Western training. His philosophy, which reflects the traditional Eastern attitude of nondualism, seeks a "reconciliation between matter and spirit, God and man, the finite world and absolute reality, and the one and the many."[10] For Aurobindo, the attainment of "the life divine" is tantamount to achieving identity with the absolute of traditional Indian philosophy. It is, however, the achievement of the divine life *on earth* (not solely in some superconscient "other life") which Aurobindo seeks. If man is to attain this goal, he must prepare himself by means of what Aurobindo has called "integral yoga," described as a philosophy and practice which integrates, in ever higher evolutions, man's physical, mental, cultural, and spiritual dimensions. Haridas Chaudhuri states that its essence "lies in free, active, and effective co-operation with the superconscient force of evolution, . . ." and that its two essential aspects are a "balanced unity of meditation and action" and an "intelligent correlation of the ascending and descending movements of consciousness. . . ." The ascending movement is described as a gradual broadening of spiritual outlook and a rising level of consciousness; the descending movement is described as the opening of the insights of the higher consciousness to all aspects of our material existence.[3]

If mankind is to progress then, it is by means of a divine life lived through a divine body. At his ashram in Pondicherry, Aurobindo placed considerable emphasis on physical and practical education. He writes:

> A divine life in a material world implies necessarily a union of the two ends of existence, the spiritual summit and the material base. The soul with the basis of its life established in Matter ascends to the heights of the Spirit but does not cast away its base. . . . The Spirit descends into Matter and the material world . . . and transforms life in the material world so that it becomes more and more divine.[1]

According to Aurobindo's view, neither mind nor spirit can fully evolve without also achieving perfection of the body. He declares:

> If our seeking is for a total perfection of the being, the physical part of it cannot be left aside; for the body is the material basis, the body is the instrument which we have to use.[1]

A large portion of Aurobindo's small volume *The Mind of Light* is devoted to matters of the education of the body. In the chapter entitled Perfection of the Body, he advocates sports and physical exercises for children and youth as means to strengthen the mind, the will, and the character.[1] Rishabhchand, who has elaborated on Aurobindo's views concerning physical education, maintains that the Western world has erred by placing too much emphasis on the mental in education while neglecting the natural wisdom of the body. He asserts that "the body has its own consciousness and its own instinct, which must be carefully evolved and given free play. . . . In a sound physical education, the student should be taught to study his own body and its subtle mechanism and foster the growth of its natural instincts till, with the development of its consciousness, they turn into infallible intuitions."[12] In accord with his view of the fourfold nature of man, Aurobindo's concept of the proper educational program would provide for the psychic, the mental, the vital, and the physical dimensions of man.

Although Za-zen (sitting meditation), with its emphasis on correctness of posture and method of breathing, is basic to Zen Buddhism, there are several forms of Zen practice which utilize ordinary work and physical activity as means of meditation. This is exemplified in such things as the tea ceremony, brush painting, garden care, archery, kendo, judo. Nancy Wilson Ross points out that although judo is increasingly taught in the West as a form of self-defense, its roots actually "lie deep in Zen philosophy for it teaches the instinctive—or intuitive—wisdom of the body. . . ." In judo the emphasis is not on physical strength, competitive spirit, or calculated moves, but on nonresistance or "awareness without tension."[13] The story usually associated with the historical development of judo (which means "gentle art") points up the Buddhist principle of nonresistance. An observer, it is said, noted one day that the weight of heavy snow caused the branches of the fir tree to break while the more supple and yielding reeds relaxed and were only bent by the weight of the snow. Western man, it is suggested, is much like the fir tree; he lacks the physical and mental suppleness to adjust to many circumstances in life without breaking. In kendo (the art of swordplay), Takano Shigeyoshi asserts, as soon as displaying one's skill or winning becomes important, all is lost. It is when such desires are done away with that the state of oneness is most likely and unexpectedly to occur. It is then that "I seem to transform myself into the opponent, and every movement he makes as well as every thought he conceives are felt as if they were all my own. . . ."[15] Robert Linssen considers the importance of judo, Hatha Yoga, Zen masters, and the like to be that they can provide a means to reinform the West of the instinctive wisdom of the body by focusing an attention which is entirely nonmental and completely physical.[6]

Caution must be exercised, however, when dealing with thought systems of the Eastern world. Christmas Humphreys, one of Britain's best-known interpreters of Buddhist thought in the West, has noted the extreme folly which can ensue when the Western world attempts to import the spiritual techniques of the East by means of traditional Western intellectual processes. Eastern teachers suggest, Humphreys contends, that Eugen Herrigel[4] may be one of the few Westerners to have captured the spirit of Zen.[5] Herrigel dedicated himself to a long and arduous course of instruction under a Zen master. After years of discipline Herrigel asked his master: "Is it 'I' who draw the bow, or is it the bow that draws me into a state of highest tension? Do 'I' hit the goal, or does the goal hit me? . . . Bow, arrow, goal and ego, all melt into one another, so that I can no longer separate them. For as soon as I take the bow and shoot, everything becomes so clear and straightforward and so ridiculously simple. . . ." To Herrigel's inquiries, the master retorted: "Now at last . . . the bowstring has cut right through you." When Herrigel took his final leave after many years, the master declared: "You have become a different person in the course of these years. For this is what the art of archery means—a profound and far-reaching contest of the archer with himself."[4] Such responses, which may to the Western thinker seem unsatisfactorily vague and incomplete, are typical of Zen Buddhism.

> THE GREAT TAO FLOWS EVERYWHERE, TO THE LEFT AND TO THE RIGHT. ALL THINGS DEPEND UPON IT TO EXIST, AND IT DOES NOT ABANDON THEM. TO ITS ACCOMPLISHMENTS IT LAYS NO CLAIM. IT LOVES AND NOURISHES ALL THINGS, BUT DOES NOT LORD IT OVER THEM.
>
> —*Lao-tzu*

CRITIQUE

Could this essay have stopped on the brink of possible discoveries? There is little doubt that physical educators could learn much from study of the Eastern way. Indeed, this brief sketch of some of the major Eastern orientations may speed some along in that long overdue study.

However, of even more benefit to the reader would be a description of just exactly what benefits there may be for physical educators to study Eastern philosophies. The background information on them is an important beginning—however brief it is. If there are some possible discoveries available through this orientation, then they ought, by all means, to be searched for. One has the feeling that this essay was but a mere introduction to what might most interest the professional physical educator: the "intuitive wisdom of the body." If there is a future in this wisdom, whether it is a peculiarly Eastern notion or not, then it needs to be brought out.

References

1. Aurobindo, S.: *The Mind of Light.* New York: E. P. Dutton and Co., Inc., 1953, pp. 7–29.
2. Chan, W.-T.: *A Sourcebook in Chinese Philosophy.* Princeton: Princeton University Press, 1963.
3. Chaudhuri, H., and Spiegelberg, F.: *The Integral Philosophy of Sri Aurobindo.* London: George Allen and Unwin, 1960, pp. 32–34.

4. Herrigel, E.: *Zen in the Art of Archery*. New York: Pantheon Books, 1953, pp. 88–92.
5. Humphreys, C.: *The Buddhist Way of Life*. New York: Schocken Books, 1969, pp. 194–196.
6. Linssen, R.: *Living Zen*. Abrahams-Curiel (Trans.). London: George Allen and Unwin, 1958, pp. 267–270.
7. Nakamura, H.: *Ways of Thinking of Eastern Peoples: India, China, Tibet, Japan*. Honolulu: East-West Center Press, 1964, p. 21.
8. Nikhilanada, S.: *Hinduism: Its Meaning for the Liberation of the Spirit*. New York: Harper and Brothers, 1953, p. xix.
9. Radhakrishnan, S.: *Eastern Religions and Western Thought*. New York: Oxford University Press, 1959, pp. viii, 351–352, 379.
10. Radhakrishnan, S., and Moore, C. A. (Eds.): *A Sourcebook in Indian Philosophy*. Princeton: Princeton University Press, 1957, pp. xxii–xxix, 3, 453–485, 575–576.
11. Raju, P. T.: *Introduction to Comparative Philosophy*. Carbondale and Edwardsville, Ill.: Southern Illinois University Press, 1962, pp. 3–4.
12. Rishabhchand, S.: "The Philosophy of Education. *Sri Aurobindo Mandir Annual, 11*, 93–96, 1952.
13. Ross, N. W.: *Three Ways of Asian Wisdom*. New York: Clarion Book, 1968, pp. 139–144.
14. Reference omitted.
15. Shigeyoshi, T.: The Psychology of Swordplay. In *The World of Zen: An East-West Anthology*. N. W. Ross (Ed.). New York: Vintage Books, 1960, pp. 292–293.
16. Smith, H.: Accents on the World's Philosophies. *Philosophy East and West, VII*, 7–19, April–July, 1957.
17. Suzuki, D. T.: *Mysticism: Christian and Buddhist*. New York: Harper and Brothers, 1957, pp. 36–51.
18. Suzuki, D. T.: *Studies in Zen*. New York: Delta Books, 1955, pp. 85–128.
19. *The Teaching of Buddha*. Tokyo: Kenkyusha Printing Company, Limited, 1968, pp. 35–60.

Selected Reading

Aurobindo, S.: *The Life Divine*. New York: The Greystone Press, 1949.
Benoit, H.: *The Supreme Doctrine: Psychological Studies in Zen Thought*. New York: Pantheon Books, 1955.
Cairns, G. E.: *Philosophies of History: Meeting of East and West in Cycle-Pattern Theories of History*. New York: The Citadel Press, 1962.
Hopkins, T. J.: *The Hindu Religious Tradition*. Belmont, Calif.: Dickenson Publishing Co., Inc., 1970.
Lin Yutang (Ed. & Trans.): *The Wisdom of Confucius*. New York: The Modern Library, 1938.
Noss, J. B.: *Man's Religions*, rev. ed. New York: The Macmillan Co., 1956.
Robinson, R. H.: *The Buddhist Religion: An Historical Introduction*. Belmont, Calif.: Dickenson Publishing Co., Inc., 1970.
Suzuki, D. T.: *The Field of Zen*. C. Humphreys (Ed.). New York: Harper & Row, 1970.
Watts, A. W.: *The Way of Zen*. New York: Pantheon Books, Inc., 1957.
Wright, A. F.: *Buddhism in Chinese History*. Stanford, Calif.: Stanford University Press, 1970.

20

Leisure Lost—and Found?

INTRODUCTION

There is an Aesop fable that relates the story of a dog and his shadow. The dog had stolen a piece of meat from a butcher shop. On his way to a safe place to eat his take, he crossed over a bridge. Glancing down, he saw his reflection in the water. Thinking that the reflection was another dog with a piece of meat in his mouth, he snarled and made a grab for the other dog's meat. As he greedily opened his mouth, out dropped the piece of meat into the stream. The application is *grasp at the shadow and lose the substance.*

It may be that the Western world is to the subject of leisure as the dog was to his reflection in the water. There is no want today of the use of the term "leisure," whether it is found in magazine articles, Sunday newspaper supplements, clothing styles, book titles, convention themes, communities for the aged, housing developments, and even education. But with the proliferating use of the term "leisure," the basic *idea* of leisure may be becoming obscured. In short, this essay suggests that we are so busy grasping at the shadow of leisure, that we are on the verge of losing its substance altogether.

ESSAY

LEISURE, IT MUST BE REMEMBERED, IS NOT A SUNDAY AFTERNOON IDYLL, BUT THE PRESERVE OF FREEDOM, OF EDUCATION AND CULTURE, AND OF THAT UNDIMINISHED HUMANITY WHICH VIEWS THE WORLD AS A WHOLE.

—Josef Pieper

Somehow or other, physical educators have gotten it in their collective heads that at least one proper contribution of physical education to modern American society is what has come to be called "leisure education." Let us examine the origin of, the plausibility in, and an alternative to such a belief.

I

It is generally believed that the essential component of twentieth century America is what has come to be called the "work ethic." Guiding most of the arguments defending the system of capitalism is a firm belief in the necessity, desirability, and innate goodness of work. In the words of a recent former president of the United States:

> The "work ethic" holds that labor is good in itself; that a man or woman becomes a better person by virtue of the act of working. America's competitive spirit, the "work ethic" of this people, is alive and well on this Labor Day. . . .[8]

In operation, the work ethic not only justifies the act of working in itself, but with everyone working it makes possible a sharing in the antithesis of that work: leisure. During these past 100 years or so, the right of leisure has moved from the sole possession of the jobless rich to the masses. As the country tooled up (Industrial Revolution) so to speak, more and more leisure was available to the everyday person. The work week was gradually reduced from 75 hours to somewhere around 40 to 45 hours. A land of labor became a land of leisure.

Indeed, leisure has seemingly increased, if by leisure we mean *time*. In fact, there is no strain on our ears when we speak today of *leisure-time*. If we are collectively working less, it is only natural that more time is available for nonworking activities. Leisure then becomes our uncommitted, discretionary, or unobligated *time*.

Leisure-time is not only a popular phrase in newspapers, magazines, and on radio/television. Even well-known leisure scholars seem to agree that leisure is to be conceived *in terms of time*. Joffre Dumazedier, the French sociologist, believes leisure to be "activity—apart from the obligations of work, family and society—to which the individual turns at will. . . ."[4] Miller and Robinson tell us that leisure-time is a portion of free time "devoted to activities undertaken in pursuit of leisure values."[7] Brightbill suggests that "Leisure is a block of unoccupied time, spare time, or free time when we are free to rest or do what we choose. . . ."[2] Leisure then, in what some have called the "age of leisure," is not necessarily all our nonworking time, but is definitely at least a portion of time within our nonworking time. Typically this time, Dumazedier states, is for relaxation, diversion, or broadening one's knowledge.

Where there is thought to be leisure-time for such pursuits, it is not surprising that there is interest in the wise use of leisure-time. An apparent need is created for educating the citizen to use this discretionary time. Physical education, broadly viewed, has contributed its share of wisdom to the category of what has come to be called the "worthy use of leisure." With all these hours available and in need of being filled, there are implications for various physical education activities, sports, games, and other pastimes. The last 15 years of physical education leisure literature has shown a general agreement that a valuable contribution can be made by physical educators to this obvious national problem. Physical education becomes valuable insofar as it can help people do something in their nonworking time.

In review then, it is work that makes leisure possible. Leisure is our unobligated time off the job. Physical education can assist in momentarily diverting the worker from his job in order to restore, repair, or recreate him for his work.

II

That physical education can train for leisure is a tidy view, but it may not be good for the country in general or physical education in particular. Not only is the view based on some rarely questioned assumptions about work and leisure, but it settles for a diminished picture of the capacities of man. Presumptuous though it may be to call into question our entire present-day world view, we confidently push forward, remembering Hesse's aphorism: "Time and time again we cling to the things we have learned to love; we call this fidelity, but it is only inertia."[6]

There is some question as to whether or not the work ethic is alive and well. Perhaps in the days when almost all work was necessary, work was desirable and definitely contributed to making better persons. When persons had trades, crafts, family businesses, or were workers of the land—that is, when one's work was unquestionably meaningful and quite likely valuable—work may have had a great degree of intrinsic good. People felt good at the end of their very long day. They liked what they did. There was pleasure in fatigue; knowledge of a thing well done.

Over 20 years ago, Paul Goodman noticed that our youth were *Growing Up Absurd*. American society, he wrote,

> has tried so hard and ably to defend the practice and theory of production for profit and not primarily for use that it now has succeeded in making its jobs and products profitable and useless.[5]

What we have apparently lost, according to Goodman, is the entire idea of doing valuable work, work that is "useful and necessary, requiring human energy and capacity, and that can be done with honor and dignity."[5]

The youth Goodman was talking about 20 years ago grew up and took their places in today's work world. One gets the feeling that some of these people were among those interviewed by Studs Terkel in his study called *Working*.[8] One cannot read Terkel's popular book without seriously wondering about the veracity of statements like those of our quoted former president. Terkel simply recorded people talking about their jobs, be they piano tuners, mechanics, teachers, assembly line workers, salesmen, waitresses, or office workers. Although an occasional enthusiast slips in among the interviewed work force, most sadly report their daily doings as forced work. They dislike what they do. They meet their jobs with indifference, boredom, bitterness, sometimes even hatred. Typical is Nora Watson (magazine editor) who is among those searching for a calling:

> Jobs are not big enough for people. It's not just the assembly line worker whose job is too small for his spirit, you know? . . . It's so demeaning to be there and not be challenged. It's humiliation, because I feel I'm being forced into doing something I would never do of my own free will—which is simply waste itself.[8]

In absence of what Goodman calls "real work" and what Nora Watson calls "big enough jobs for one's spirit," it seems hardly possible to speak seriously of that kind of worship of work necessary to keep the work ethic alive and well.

We are living a paradox: work is not worshipped by the worker, yet it is still glorified by society. Strange indeed is a world in which what we have learned to do is done out of the tradition of having loved to do it, not out of the actual love of doing it. To some extent we are playing in a game for which the final whistle blew years ago.

Like it or not, Hanna Arendt may be on the mark when she states that such glorification of labor has resulted in a factual transformation of our entire society into a laboring society. Indeed,

> What we are confronted with is the prospect of a society of laborers without labor, that is, without the only activity left to them. Surely, nothing could be worse.[1]

It is not necessary for everyone to work. It may not even be desirable that everyone work, and it is increasingly difficult to find any "real work" anyway. Yet only work carries any societal meaning. The originally meaningful and virtuous work ethic has cast a foreboding shadow over this age.

So glorified is work that even our idea of leisure is conceived in terms of the much celebrated workaday world. Leisure is time free from work (and other necessary duties). So impoverished is our view of leisure that we justify leisure only insofar as it supports the hollow work ethic. Things are so upside down that we now have *leisure for the sake of work*, not the other way round.

To have leisure for the sake of work, strictly speaking, is not to have leisure at all. In fact, some scholars are so bold as to announce that there is no leisure today. Free-time has been so commonly allowed to substitute for the idea of leisure that even the time we may have won gets filled with empty pastimes. In the pursuit of time the original idea of leisure has been sacrificed. We have exchanged a qualitative view of leisure for a quantitative one. Sebastian deGrazia, in the readable study of leisure in the industrial world, freely admits that Americans have approached a new level of life:

> Whether it is a good life is another matter. This much is clear: it is a life without leisure. . . . Indeed, the contemporary phrase "leisure time" is a contradiction in terms. Leisure has no adjectival relation to time. Leisure is a state of being free of everyday necessity, and the activities of leisure are those we would engage in for their own sake. As a fact or ideal it is rarely approached in the industrial world.[3]

An accurate view of leisure is one that has no bearing at all on the notion of time, free or otherwise. Leisure is not fragmented like our concept of free-time is. Leisure is not worklike as the activities pursued in our free time so often are. Leisure action is not done for the sake of something else like our free-time engagements (for diversion, for relaxation, for recreation, for money). Leisure is not dependent on other people. Leisure is not tied to any sort of materialism (having or buying things with which one then can have leisure). Rather, leisure in the classic sense is not a moment (or series of moments however connected in time) but a way of life. It is not time, but living the good life.

Whether we read the ancients, such as Aristotle or Seneca, or the moderns, such as deGrazia or Pieper, leisure is always the same. Leisure is intrinsic activity (ars liberalis) bearing the mark of the celebration of life. Chiefly residing in the activity of the mind, it is capable of liberating persons. The components that seem to belong to the life of leisure include freedom from necessity, tranquility, peace, dignity, calm, silence, serenity, festivity, timelessness, and a sense of mystery.

If the aforementioned description of the leisure life is unfamiliar, it is because our tradition in leisure is not a strong one. Were things otherwise we would not today speak so regularly of the *problem* of leisure. In truth, that leisure has become problematical to our age is the real problem. We have lost or forgotten the basic nature of that for the sake of which work was originally necessary. As deGrazia reminds us:

> Work, we know, may make a man stoop-shouldered or rich. It may even ennoble him. Leisure perfects him.[3]

III

The thinking professional physical educator no long can afford to mistake what appears to be the problem of leisure-time for the real problem of the nature of leisure itself. The real problem, manifested as the possibility that ours is a society without leisure (in the classic sense), is in desperate need of serious attention. What may apparently serve the immediate needs of the state—namely, leisure-time pursuits—may not serve the proper ends of physical education, or for that matter even the long-range survival of the state itself. We must learn what leisure properly is before it can ever be cultivated.

Are we so taken with our apparently valuable contribution to society that we are deaf to any other calls? Could man the worker be a bankrupt view of the capacities of man? Are there any other views by which physical educators could assist in transforming the matrix of society from labor to leisure?

One way to assist the world to exchange work for leisure as the basis of culture is to confront the possibilities of *play*. After all, if leisure is not the mother of play, play is at very least a taste of genuine leisure. Were physical educators to listen to the unmistakable secrets available in the world of play, a gradual transformation to a leisure-based society could conceivably take place.

For any legitimate start to be made toward a leisure-based society, physical educators must study play. Having either implicitly or explicitly bought the present-day ideal of man the worker, physical educators have been largely unreceptive to the inherent play possibilities. Consistently foisted on play have been characteristics quite foreign to it. Trying so hard to make play what it is not, to make it conform to or reinforce various economic, political, and educational priorities (often conflicting in themselves), has resulted in play becoming but a vestige of a better world. Even play has taken the form of being a means to other ends, such as fitness, health, therapy, winning in life, social skills, and the like. Consequently, having been shaped into a purely instrumental form, play has been both used and abused.

Amid all the clamor for physical education (both inside and outside the profession) to contribute to the wise use of leisure-time, the actual leisure-wisdom available in play itself has been ignored. Fortunately for us, and consequently for the world, things are what they are. Although unnoticed beneath the various appearances it takes on, play is and always will be what it is. As a basic "in itself," play not only *is*, but *is* insofar that it serves no other ends beyond itself. We do not play for the sake of something other than play. The sharing of this absolutely necessary characteristic with the basic essence of leisure makes play and leisure an amalgam. They are mutually reinforcing. It is inconceivable to have the one without the other. It is no surprise, therefore, that a society that has managed to become un-leisurely has also become un-playful.

Alert physical educators courageously using the philosophic process can help turn the world toward real leisure. Play may be our way. Perhaps someday in the future, if the winds of change are toward a more playful world, a president of the United States just may be quoted as saying:

> The "play ethic" holds that play is good in itself; that a man or woman becomes a better person by virtue of the act of playing. America's co-operative spirit, the "play ethic" of this people, is alive and well on this Play Day. . . .

CRITIQUE

If this essay distinguished, generally speaking, between the shadow and the substance of leisure, there was a preference shown for exposing the shadow to the neglect of the substance. Although some good clues were presented about the proper direction of thinking on leisure, further investigation would have more clearly revealed the connection between the idea of leisure and the idea of play.

It is especially important for physical educators not to be misled into believing in another mere fashion. There may be some significance in play for physical education. Indeed, the elements of play available in physical education have been largely ignored—mostly because physical educators have historically been accused of being idlers, of dabbling in mere play. "Mere play" does not have any place in educational institutions, so it is commonly thought.

Had this essay devoted equal time to the implications of play for physical education, a discovery or two might have been made. It is important that we do not give up what may be one shadow (the twentieth century idea of leisure) for another (play). It is in substance that such discoveries are made.

References

1. Arendt, H.: *The Human Condition.* Chicago: University of Chicago Press, 1950, p. 5.
2. Brightbill, C. K.: *The Challenge of Leisure.* Englewood Cliffs, N.J.: Prentice-Hall, Inc., 1960, p. 4.
3. deGrazia, S.: *Of Time, Work and Leisure.* New York: The Twentieth Century Fund, 1962, pp. 327, 437.
4. Dumazedier, J.: *Toward A Society of Leisure.* New York: The Free Press, 1967, pp. 16–17.
5. Goodman, P.: *Growing Up Absurd.* New York: Vintage Books, 1956, p. 19.
6. Hesse, H.: *Reflections.* R. Manheim (Trans.). New York: Farrar, Straus and Giroux, 1974, p. 51.
7. Miller, N. P., and Robinson, D.: *The Leisure Age.* Belmont, Calif.: Wadsworth Publishing Co., 1963, p. 6.
8. Terkel, S.: *Working.* New York: Arm Books, 1972, p. 675.

11
L

APPENDIXES

A

Practice in Philosophizing

Some recommended activities for the student who wants to further improve his or her philosophizing ability are listed below. These activities appear in two categories: activities for philosophic individuals and activities for students in philosophic classes. If these suggestions can assist in the improvement of individual and collective philosophic skills, or in the devising of further philosophic projects not included, then this list will have served a most hopeful purpose.

ACTIVITIES FOR PHILOSOPHIC INDIVIDUALS

1. Try to answer the question "Why should anyone bother to improve philosophizing ability?" Pretend a friend or relative has challenged your interest in improving your skill. Explain your interest in improved philosophic activity in clear, nontechnical language. (A rereading of Chapter 1 *may* assist in this undertaking.)

2. Try the same activity as suggested in 1, but narrow the scope of your response to physical education. That is, "Why bother to improve one's skill at philosophizing in or on physical education?"

3. Review Chapter 2, Getting Under Way. Try the exercises listed in this chapter again. Remember you were asked to write short statements or "telegrams" in each of three categories: life, education, and physical education. Pick a few representative examples in each category. Are there any differences in your choices, values, or approach *now* as compared with your earlier effort?

4. During any single week, chart the frequency with which the word "philosophy" appears, whether in conversations with friends or relatives, in the various forms of mass media, or perhaps in various classrooms. Ascertain the different *meanings* that various persons or groups attach to the word "philosophy." What does that tell you about the everyday understanding of philosophy?

5. Pick an article or short essay of interest which has appeared in a professional physical education journal. Study the piece carefully. (1) State all the presuppositions on which the article or essay depends. (2) Try to find the types or sources of evidence included in the piece. (3) Find and analyze the major and minor arguments contained therein. (4) Discover any of the known dangers into which the author has stumbled. (5) Synthesize the entire piece, indicating the probable consequences of what the article or essay communicates, if you can.

6. What is the philosophic process? Try to explain what you know of the philosophic process to someone unfamiliar with its details. A review of Chapters 2 through 6 *may* be of some help in undertaking this activity.

7. Tentatively try to indicate where you might stand with regard to the philosophic positions (slants, schools) discussed in this book, such as idealism, realism, pragmatism, and the like.

8. Pick one of the philosophic positions which may be of particular interest. Beyond the information presented in the appropriate chapter of this book (Chapters 9 to 12), conduct further inquiry into the particular philosophic slant. Draw out your own implications for physical education from your further study.

9. Pick at least one major philosopher who is of interest to you. In detail, study the person, his views, and what others have said about his views. In short, read a bit of his biography (or autobiography), study some of his original works, and look over some secondary sources about the philosopher.

10. After having met more thoroughly at least one major philosopher, such as through activities suggested in 9, look for possible implications of his views for physical education. Also, see whether you can learn anything from this philosopher which might be useful in your own particular life, personal and professional.

11. Pick at least one essay from Part III *and* from Part IV of this book. Study the essay, much in the same way as was recommended in 5. Look over the brief critique following the essay. Think the entire effort through on your own. Write your own critique. You might even want to criticize the existing critique.

12. Write a short essay on a theme of your choice in physical education. Select a subject you know something about, or are willing to learn something about. Apply what you have learned about the philosophic process to this essay. Pretend that you are trying to get your article published, either in a physical education professional journal or in a popular magazine.

13. After having written an essay on a subject of your choice (activity 12), criticize your own essay. Objectively distance yourself from your own work. Read it as a disinterested professional student of physical education. Look for the major and minor faults, ambiguity, and loose thinking or writing.

14. Remember one of the possible outcomes of philosophizing, knowing thyself? Write on the theme (or perhaps, some other mode of communication would be more appropriate than writing, such as graphics, poetry and so forth): "Knowing Thyself." You might want to tell your story.

15. Pretend you have been asked to *review this book* for a professional journal. Read a few book reviews in order to see the various ways a review is handled. Then set out to review this book just as though you were expected to publish your efforts. Include judgments on the intended purpose of the book, whether or not the purpose was fulfilled, the content of the book, its format, and something of the significance of the book. To become better acquainted with the background of your activity, you might even wish to study other comparable textbooks to see what differences exist between books written for the same general audience.

16. You have been asked to design a school course in Philosophy of Physical Education. Outline in detail what you would include in your course, especially the general format or style, types of readings (if any), and some representative assignments. You may find helpful some of the ideas suggested in Activities for Students in Philosophic Classes.

ACTIVITIES FOR STUDENTS IN PHILOSOPHIC CLASSES

1. Each class member selects one side of an approved controversy, becomes well prepared, and stands the rest of the class. He may use his notes. One side of each controversy is limited to one person.

2. Each class member selects one great physical education thinker of the past and becomes well informed about him and his beliefs about physical education. Views are epitomized at a simulated meeting such as an "Academy meeting."

3. Detailed reports about great persons in 2 are duplicated and made available to all class members.

4. Each class member reads several books by writers of philosophic-type books. Areas of agreement and disagreement are identified and reasons given therefor. (These are *not* book reviews.)

5. A number of stimulating questions are selected for discussion during the term. The class prepares for each discussion. Topics may include "Why is man here?" "What is the most powerful master magnet purpose a person can select for living?" "What is the significance of the naturalistic direction of physical education?" "How valid are the reasons for required physical education at the college level?"

6. Each class member conducts a poll of 50 typical American adults and asks "What's wrong with physical education?" Results are synthesized and speculations made about the overall answers which are philosophic in nature.

7. Interpreting one's philosophy: each class member gives a simulated talk with a school principal or college dean regarding the meaning of physical education; each member gives a capsule address to a lay group about the values or purposes of physical education.

8. Have the class read famous authors and decide which of the philosophic aspects of their writings are idealistic, realistic, and the like, and supply supporting evidence.

9. Each class member makes a study of a play, a movie, a speech, or an article that was presented for propaganda purposes, analyzing the techniques and tricks of thinking as well as the underlying assumptions.

10. Each class member selects his own number one value of physical education and presents it in some new form or pattern of expression.

11. Each class member talks off-the-cuff for five minutes about an assigned or self-chosen topic or point of view to which he is opposed. He attempts to make use of appropriately qualified statements rather than sweeping generalizations.

12. The class conducts a "heckle session" in which one student speaks while others heckle, trying to get him to change the subject and lose confidence under fire.

*13. Each class member throughout the term is responsible for writing two or more articles appropriate for publication in a professional periodical such as *Quest, The Physical Educator, JOHPER* or possibly *The Research Quarterly*. The point of the article is not only that it focus on some philosophic aspect of the discipline, but also that it typify the basic viewpoints of one given philosophic slant, such as idealism or aritomism.

14. This same kind of project may be undertaken for the writing of a proposed speech, radio or television talk, or discussion.

---

* Because courses in the philosophy of physical education are now being offered at both the master's and doctoral levels, some of the sample projects are inappropriate for some classes.

15. Groups of three to five class members prepare a simulated television program in which a vital issue facing physical education is discussed with each class member's part representing a different philosophic slant.

16. At the outset of a class, each student writes out a response to the question "What is physical education?" During the weeks of study in the class, the students are introduced to the myriad of answers to this question in the literature of physical education. Each approach is discussed and criticized. At the conclusion of the course, the student tries to respond a second time to the question. Will there be a difference in the before and after answers? If so, is this difference significant?

*17. Simulate a convention or symposium where a series of papers on appropriate philosophic themes are given. Include reaction papers and discussion.

18. Orient a class toward studying one or more aspects of physical education, such as sport, dance, play, and games. Combine reading with first-hand observation of these experiences, either as spectator or as participant. Collectively try to know more about these activities after than before immersion in them.

B

Chronological Perspective of Some Philosophers

A summary of some Western philosophers from Thales to Sartre is listed below. Where exact dates of birth and death are unknown, approximate dates (c.) or dates when they flourished (fl.) are provided. A few dates of related matters are provided.

Thales—fl. c. 585 B.C.
Anaximander—fl. c. 560 B.C.
Xenophanes—fl. c. 530 B.C.
Pythagoras—fl. c. 530 B.C.
Heraclitus—fl. c. 500 B.C.
Parmenides—fl. c. 475 B.C.
Zeno—fl. c. 475 B.C.
Anaxagoras—fl. c. 460 B.C.
Empedocles—fl. c. 450 B.C.
Protagoras—481–411 B.C.
Socrates—469–399 B.C.
Democritus—fl. c. 420 B.C.
Plato—427–347 B.C.
Aristotle—384–322 B.C.
Pyrrho (founder of the skeptical movement)—c. 360–270 B.C.
Zeno (founder of Stoicism)—c. 350–258 B.C.
Epicurus (founder of Epicureanism)—342–270 B.C.
Lucretius (Epicurean)—95–52 B.C.
Philo (Jewish Platonist)—c. 20 B.C.–A.D. 54
Seneca (Stoic)—4 B.C.–A.D. 65
Plutarch (Neo-Pythagorean)—c. 46–120
Epictetus (Stoic)—c. 60–120
Fourth Gospel (beginning of Christian philosophy; Platonic influences)—written c. 100
Marcus Aurelius (Stoic)—121–180

Clement of Alexandria (Christian)—c. 150–220
Tertullian (Christian)—c. 155–222
Origen (Christian)—c. 185–254
Plotinus (Neo-Platonist)—204–269
Council of Nicaea (Doctrine of the Trinity formulated)—325
Augustine (Christian)—354–430
Boethius (Christian?)—480–524
Closing of the Schools of Athens. End of ancient philosophy
Mohammed (founder of Islam)—c. 569–632
John Scotus Erigena (Christian)—c. 800–877
Avicenna (Moslem)—979–1037
Anselm (Christian Platonist)—1033–1109
Abelard (Christian)—1079–1142
Roger Bacon (Christian)—c. 1214–1294
Thomas Aquinas (Christian Aristotelian)—c. 1225–1247
William of Occam (Christian) died c. 1349
Leonardo da Vinci (Italian)—1452–1519
Machiavelli (Italian)—1469–1527
Copernicus (Polish astronomer)—1473–1543

Luther (German reformer)—1483–1546

Montaigne (French)—1533–1592

Francis Bacon (English)—1561–1626

Galileo (Italian astronomer and physicist)—1564–1642

Hobbes (English)—1588–1679

Comenius (Czech)—1592–1670

Descartes (French)—1596–1650

John Milton (English)—1608–1674

Pascal (French)—1623–1662

Spinoza (Dutch-Jewish)—1632–1677

Locke (English)—1632–1704

Newton (English astronomer and physicist)—1642–1727

Leibnitz (German)—1646–1716

Berkeley (Irish)—1685–1753

Voltaire (French)—1694–1778

Jonathan Edwards (American)—1703–1788

Hume (Scot)—1711–1776

Rousseau (French)—1712–1778

Kant (German)—1724–1804

Pestalozzi (Swiss)—1746–1827

Bentham (English)—1748–1832

Fichte (German)—1762–1814

Hegel (German)—1770–1831

Herbart (German)—1776–1841

Froebel (German)—1782–1852

Schopenhauer (German)—1788–1860

Comte (French)—1798–1857

John Stuart Mill (Scot)—1806–1873

Kierkegaard (Danish)—1813–1855

Lotze (German)—1817–1881

Karl Marx (German)—1818–1883

Spencer (English)—1820–1903

Peirce (American)—1839–1914

James (American)—1842–1910

Nietzsche (German)—1844–1900

Bradley (English)—1846–1924

Bowne (American)—1847–1910

Royce (American)—1855–1916

Bergson (French)—1859–1941

Dewey (American)—1859–1952

Husserl (German)—1859–1938

Whitehead (English)—1861–1947

Santayana (Spanish, educated in America)—1863–1952

Unamuno (Spanish)—1864–1936

Schiller (English)—1864–1937

Croce (Italian)—1866–1952

Flewelling (American)—1871–1960

Russell (British)—1872–1970

Moore (English)—1873–1958

Montague (American)—1873–1953

Cassirer (German)—1874–1945

Gentile (Italian)—1875–1944

Maritain (French)—1882–1973

Jaspers (German)—1883–1969

Ortega y Gasset (Spanish)—1883–1955

Tillich (German-American)—1886–1965

Heidegger (German)—1889–1976

Wittgenstein (Austrian)—1889–1951

Marcel (French)—1889–1973

Sartre (French)—1905–

Glossary

The technical vocabulary of philosophy is comprised largely of common-place terms often used with uncommon and highly specialized meanings. In most instances these definitions are not exhaustive. The student should rely neither on glossaries nor dictionaries, *but determine the meanings of terms within the context of their specific usage.*

Absolute. Unconditioned, unqualified, unrelated. In metaphysics, reality considered as a single entity, having no environment or relation to anything external to it. In Indian philosophy, *absolute* refers to the one changeless, eternal soul or consciousness.

Absolute idealism. Theory that reality is a single unconditioned and unrelated entity, spiritual, ideational, rational, or personal in character.

Absolutism. Opposed to relativism; indicates independence of relation. In metaphysics, theory that reality is an absolute. In ethics and aesthetics, theory that values are objectively real.

Activism. Any philosophic position that describes reality in terms of activity or otherwise emphasizes action. Opposed to intellectualism.

Aesthetics. Theory of beauty and ugliness. Study of art values and principles of art criticism.

Analysis. As a method, the resolution of a compound into its elements, or a complex situation into its constituents. In contemporary empiricism, logical analysis indicates the application of logical principles in the determination of meanings.

Analytic philosophy. Philosophic position holding that the central task (for some adherents the *only* task) of philosophy should be the analysis of the use and function of language. The purpose of philosophy is thought to be the clarification of statements of ordinary language, not the determination of whether these statements are true.

Anxiety. In contemporary existentialism, a rough synonym for anguish and dread. Usually an awareness by a being of nonbeing. A consciousness of the threat of nonbeing, death, or nothingness. A psychologic state induced by awareness of contingency, finiteness, guilt, or meaninglessness. Differs from fear in that it has no object.

A posteriori. Descriptive of knowledge and principles regarded as derived from or dependent on experience.

Appearance. That which is presented to the mind, especially in sensation or perception. In some philosophic systems distinguished from reality or from the thing in itself.

A priori. Descriptive of knowledge and principles of thinking that are not derived from experience and cannot be explained by experience, even if their only application is to experience. Such knowledge and principles being logically, though not temporally and psychologically, prior to experience are considered a priori.

Atomism. Any theory that describes reality as a pluralistic system composed of separate, discrete, and irreducible entities.

Attribute. In logic, that which is affirmed or denied of a subject.

Axiology. Theory of the nature of value.

Axiom. Proposition assumed to be true without proof and taken as a basis for proof of other propositions.

Being. As descriptive of metaphysical systems, often used to indicate opposition to change, or becoming. Whatever is, in and of itself. In current existentialism, opposed to existence.

Buddhism. Religious and philosophic thought system which is believed to have been originated in northeastern India in 563 B.C. by Siddhartha Gautama, the Buddha (or Enlightened One). Over the centuries Buddhism has spread to China, Japan, Southeast Asia, and other parts of the world, especially the Eastern world. The basic tenets of Buddhism are contained in the *Four Noble Truths* and *Noble Eightfold Path*. Buddhism, which rejects the concept of a universal, unchanging self, holds that everything is becoming.

Categorical. Unconditional, nonhypothetical. Proposition that asserts unconditionally.

Category. A wide and universal concept in which the mind habitually formulates its thought and judgments. A basic way of viewing or experiencing the world.

Causal law. Law asserting invariable and universal behavior or strict conformity.

Cause. Various meanings. Usually, whatever is the ground, occasion, or agency for an event.

Certainty. In technical usage, a quality of a proposition established by logical demonstration or otherwise requiring no evidence. An objective state of affairs rather than a subjective state of mind.

Certitude. Commonly indicates the mental state of being sure or certain. A subjective state of mind. Unquestioned assurance.

Coherence theory of truth. The truth of a proposition is a property of its logical coherence or consistency with a body of already accepted propositions.

Concept. An idea that is had by a mind. Distinguished from percept or sensation and from idea in the Platonic sense.

Conceptualism. Any one of several theories describing the status of universals in terms of mental concepts, and avoiding the extreme forms of both realism and nominalism.

Confirmation. Process of establishing, by evidence, a degree of probability for a proposition. Partial or incomplete verification.

Contingent. Whatever can be conceived equally well as existing or nonexisting. Propositions whose truth does not rest on logic or the necessities of rational thinking, but which must be verified in and by experience.

Contradiction. A proposition the falsity of which can be established by an examination of the proposition itself, that is, by an examination of the meanings of the symbols and the logic of the language. A proposition that is logically false.

Contradiction, law of. Traditional logical principle that "nothing can be both A and not A" and, when applied to propositions, that "no proposition can be both false and true."

Correspondence theory of truth. The truth of a proposition consists in its correspondence to the fact or facts that it asserts, and that falsity consists in noncorrespondence.

Cosmogeny. Theory of the origin or creation of the world.

Cosmological argument. Inference of the existence of God from the existence of the world. Founded on the assumption that whatever exists must have a cause or reason.

Cosmology. Study of the constitution of the sensible universe as an ordered whole and of the totality of the general laws that sum up its behavior.

Datum. That which is given, for example, in sensation.

Deduction. Inference from one or more propositions, taken as premises without denying or affirming their truth, to the conclusion logically implied in and necessitated by them.

Deism. In theology, has the technical meaning of indicating the view that God transcends and is totally other than the world, His creation, and has no intimate relation to it. Contrasts with a theology of immanence.

Determinism. Theory that every thing or event is totally conditioned by antecedent cause. Theory of governance of the universe by causal law.

Dialectic. Various meanings relating to the process of rational thought. In Plato, the science of first principles. In Hegel, the process of reason indicating the structure of the real.

Discursive. A term applied to processes of thinking that reach their conclusion step by step through a series of intermediary operations.

Dualism. Any theory that in any field of investigation reduces the variety of its subject matter to two irreducible principles; as, for example, the natural and the supernatural, good and evil, will and intellect.

Eclecticism. In philosophy, the combining of elements derived from different philosophic schools or doctrines.

Egotism. In ethics, the theory that the highest good is one's own pleasure or well-being.

Empiricism. In its rigorous form, the doctrine that all knowledge of fact must be validated in sense experience, and that whatever is knowable is knowable directly by sense data or is capable of being inferred from propositions based on sense data. Opposed to rationalism and to knowledge by intuition.

Entelechy. In metaphysics, the realization of the essence of a thing. Actuality.

Epistemology. Study of the nature of knowledge, its origin, limitation, and possibilities, and of the relation of the knowing subject to the known object. Concerns the problem of the validation of knowledge and the various ways of knowing, that is, by reason, experience, or intuition, and is closely related to the theory of the nature of truth.

Essence. In metaphysics, designates that which makes a thing what it is and nothing else, in contrast with the qualities which attach superficially and for the time being to the thing and may be detached from it. Contrasted also with the existence, or factual being and "thereness" of a thing in and for itself, or its presence as an experienced fact.

Eternal. Timeless, in the sense of having no duration, being outside of and independent of time.

Ethics. Theory of the nature of the good and of how it can be achieved.

Existence. Indicates the factual being and "thereness" of a thing, either independently of all actual and possible awareness and knowledge of it, or as an experienced fact. Modern existentialism, founded on the doctrine that existence is prior to essence, commonly ascribes existence only to human beings, on the ground that a conscious awareness of existence is necessary to authentic existence.

Existentialism. Philosophic position based especially on the idea that existence is prior to essence. In application this means that a man has no fixed nature, but is what he does or chooses.

Explanation. Traditionally, the attempt to account for events by finding ultimate causes, reasons, or purposes for them.

External relations. Theory that relations are not dependent on their terms, that the relations of a thing are external to it and not constitutive of its nature.

Extrinsic. In value theory, reference to the value of a thing in relation to something else. Opposed to intrinsic.

Fact. A state of affairs. That which objectively is. Not to be confused with a statement of fact or a factual proposition. Factual propositions are true or false. Facts simply are.

Hedonism. Reference to pleasure or happiness. Ethical hedonism is the moral doctrine that pleasure is the highest or only intrinsic good.

Hinduism. The vast and complex religious, philosophic, and social thought of the Indian subcontinent, which takes its basic tenets largely from the ancient *Vedas* (religious views collected over numerous centuries and committed to writing about 1000 B.C.), and the *Upanishads* (speculative treatises concerned with the nature of man and the universe which form a late part of the Vedic literature). Most Hindus believe in causality (karma), and look forward to ultimate salvation (nirvana).

Humanism. Traditionally referred to the humanities or humane learning. In current philosophy, an extension of individual traits which guide human conduct in impersonal groups; sometimes confused with humanitarianism, humane, and F. C. S. Schiller's pragmatism. Human welfare is a central focus.

Hylozoism. Theory that matter is alive or that life is a property of matter.

Hypothesis. A statement or idea whose truth is conditional, that is, dependent on the truth of another statement or idea.

Idealism. In metaphysics, the theory that reality is of the nature of mind or of idea. May be monistic (absolutistic) or pluralistic, impersonalistic, or personalistic. In epistemology, the theory that the known object is a product of its being known.

Induction. Usually, inference of a general proposition from observed particular instances or cases when the general proposition refers to all instances of the type indicated, whereas the observation is of only some of those instances. The laws of physics are induced from the observation of physical phenomena. In typical induction, the observations yield premises that support the probability of the conclusion without necessarily entailing it.

Innate ideas. Ideas or principles possessed by the mind independent of any experience, and incapable of being found in experience, though awareness of them may be occasioned by experience.

Instrumentalism. Dewey's pragmatism based primarily on the theory that the mind is an instrument in the service of the life of the organism.

Internal relations. Theory that relations depend on their terms; especially in metaphysical absolutism, theory that all relations are internal to the absolute. Theory that the relations of a thing are constitutive of its nature.

Intrinsic. In value theory, reference to value of a thing in and of itself. Opposed to extrinsic, or instrumental.

Intuition. Immediate apprehension of the object. Direct, nondiscursive, nonmediated knowledge.

Karma. In Eastern philosophy, the metaphysical law of cause and effect. The implication is that good deeds create good consequences and bad deeds create bad consequences.

Logic. Theory of inference. Often identified with deduction. In absolute idealism, logic is involved with or identical with metaphysics. In pragmatism, logic is the theory of inquiry.

Logical atomism. Form of contemporary analytic philosophy developed by Russell and his student Wittgenstein in the early twentieth century. Logical atomism holds that the world is composed of a number of simple facts, each independent of all other facts, yet capable of being related to them.

Logical positivism. The philosophic position developed by the Vienna Circle in the late 1920s. (See **Positivism.**)

Logistic. Especially the theory that mathematics is reducible to logic. Sometimes synonymous with symbolic logic.

Materialism. Theory that the total universe, including all life and mind, can be reduced to and explained in terms of matter in motion. Applied also to systems that, although they regard consciousness as irreducible to terms of physical energy, still consider it dependent on matter for its existence and find its processes explicable only when correlated with physiologic processes and thus subject to the laws governing physical motion and energy.

Meaning. Cognitive or knowledge meaning is of two types: formal and factual. Statements having cognitive meaning, being assertions, are true or false. Noncognitive meanings, for example, emotive, affective, volitional, are sometimes identified.

Mechanism. Any theory that explains phenomena by reference exclusively to causation in terms of antecedent conditions, eliminating the notions of design, purpose, final causation, determination of the part by the whole, and of causation by occult powers.

Meliorism. Theory that the world is neither totally evil nor totally good and that there is a possibility of increasing the good. View that things can be made better. Opposed to optimism and pessimism.

Metaphysics. In its popular and general sense, investigation of the essential and absolute nature of reality as a whole or of the nature of being as such. *Ontology.* The search for first principles. Originally meant what comes after physics.

Methodology. Analysis of the principles of inquiry, usually involving the problems of logic, evidence, verification, primary assumptions, and the like.

Monad. Usually, following Leibnitz, a simple living or sentient individual or atom, conceived as an elementary and irreducible unit of reality.

Monism. In metaphysics, the theory that all reality (1) is of the same kind, for example, material or spiritual, and/or (2) is quantitatively one single entity rather than a collection of things independently real.

Mysticism. The doctrine that the fundamental nature of reality is ineffable; that is, inaccessible through either the senses or the intellect, indescribable in any of the terms and categories at the command of ordinary human consciousness, and approachable only in and through a special state of ecstasy which transcends every form and activity—sensible, emotional, intuitive, volitional, and rational—of normal human experience.

Naturalism. Theory that the universe has no supernatural origin or ground and needs no supernatural explanation; that it is self-existent and should be explained solely by reference to itself; that its behavior is not teleologically explicable by final causes and purposes; that human life and behavior are in no way exceptional and outside the course of natural events, and are to be explained by the same principles as obtain throughout the rest of nature; and that human values, moral ideals, and conduct are determined entirely by the organic structure and needs characteristic of the human species.

Nihilism. Usually used loosely to describe theories that deny reality, values, knowledge, or, especially, moral distinctions.

Nirvana. In Hinduism and Buddhism, the attainment of final enlightenment which leads to freedom from the endless cycle of rebirth.

Nominalism. Theory that universals are not real but are only names or words, and that reality is limited to particulars.

Normative. Relating to norms or standards, especially in ethics, aesthetics, or politics. Valuational in contrast to factual.

Noumenon. In Kantian philosophy, opposed to phenomenon, or appearance. Reality not known in perceptual knowledge.

Ontological argument (proof). Argument for existence of God based on the idea of God, that is, the logical analysis and definition of His nature. The idea of a perfect being, it is argued, is necessarily the idea of an existent being, since a being that lacked existence would not be perfect.

Ontology. The science or knowledge of beings as such. Usually synonymous with metaphysics or with the central core of metaphysics as a theory of reality.

Operationism. Position in contemporary empiricism that the meaning of a term or concept is the set of operations performed on the occasion of its employment.

Pantheism. The teaching that God and the universe are one and the same thing.

Parsimony, law of. Principle of economy in ideas, that explanation should employ as few ideas as possible.

Particular. An individual thing or event. Opposed to class, of which it is a member, or opposed to universal.

Peripatetic. Pertaining to the philosophy of Aristotle.

Personalism. Pluralistic form of idealism that regards personality as the key to the explanation of reality as well as the locus of value.

Phenomenalism. Theory that knowledge and/or reality are limited to phenomena, that is, to appearances.

Phenomenology. Especially the philosophy identified with E. Husserl and his followers and described as a science of the subjective and its intended objects. Phenomenological method is an a priori method that seeks exact knowledge by describing objects given in the experiencing of the world.

Phenomenon. What appears to consciousness, appearance. What is perceived.

Physicalism.   Theory in contemporary positivism that holds that only those statements are cognitively meaningful that can be expressed as physicalistic propositions, that is, propositions designating observable properties.

Pluralism.   In metaphysics, any system according to which reality is composed of many individual, independent, ultimate constituents, which cannot be reduced to terms of one another, or to aspects of some single common principle underlying them.

Positivism.   Theory that equates all knowledge with scientific knowledge and regards metaphysics as impossible. Logical positivism regards metaphysical sentences as meaningless because they are, in principle, incapable of empirical verification.

Pragmatics.   Study of the use and effects of signs. Distinguished from semantics and syntactics.

Pragmatism.   Philosophic position identified especially with Peirce, James, Schiller, Mead, and Dewey, and based on a theory of the mind as an instrument for problem-solving, and on theories of meaning and truth that emphasize the results or consequences of ideas.

Presupposition.   A logically necessary antecedent to a statement, an argument, or a theory.

Primary quality.   Originally intended to indicate qualities regarded as belonging to objects taken independently of their being known.

Probability.   In knowledge, a value less than certainty but more than ignorance.

Proposition.   What is either true or false, sometimes synonymous with statement. Not identical with sentence. A proposition is what has meaning, either factual or logical.

Psychophysical parallelism.   The doctrine that every physical event is accompanied by and corresponds to a psychical event and vice versa. Used more particularly of the teaching that every psychical event accompanies and corresponds to a physiologic event, but not that every physical event necessarily has a psychical concomitant.

Rationalism.   As a way of knowing, the method of establishing propositions by reason or deduction, usually involving premises stating general ideas or principles. A priori method. Opposed to intuition and empiricism. Pure mathematics is the prime example of rationalism.

Realism.   In metaphysics, usually any system that denies the possibility of reducing the universe to mind and thought, and that maintains that something would still exist if all consciousness whatsoever were extinguished. In epistemology, the theory that the objects of knowledge and experience are real independent of their being known and experienced. Realism and idealism are opposites when used in an epistemological context, but used metaphysically they are not necessarily opposed.

Relativism.   Usually indicates the view that truth or moral and aesthetic values vary in relation to the knowing or experiencing subject or to other circumstances. Opposed to absolutism.

Scholasticism.   As a method, usually the subordination of science and philosophy to theology and the use of deductive techniques in proving theses by reliance on authorities. As a philosophy, especially the general type represented by Anselm, Abelard, Aquinas, and Duns Scotus, culminating historically in the neoscholasticism currently popular and approved in the Roman Catholic Church.

Secondary quality. Usually indicates qualities believed to belong not simply to objects as such, but rather to result from their being perceived by the senses.

Semantics. Study of the signification of signs. Analysis of language meanings. Relation of signs or symbols to that for which they stand. Distinguished from syntactics and pragmatics.

Semiotic. The theory of signs, including semantics, syntactics, and pragmatics.

Sense data language. In recent empiricism, language that describes, or purports to describe, sense data only, without referring to the properties of material objects.

Sense datum. Used variously, but usually refers technically to the sensory content of the mind in sense perception, that is, the sensation itself rather than the object sensed.

Sign. Something that stands for or means another thing.

Skepticism. Theory that reliable knowledge is impossible.

Solipsism. In metaphysics, a form of subjective idealism in which an individual affirms that he alone exists and all other reality, the external world and other selves, is a product of his own mental operations, without independent existence. The interpretation of the world as our private sense data. In language, the view that significant propositions cannot be communicated because the significance of language is limited to possible experience.

Subject. That which experiences and thinks and unifies the multiple and varied content of consciousness into an objective world of things.

Subsistence. Used by some modern philosophers to indicate the kind of being possessed by abstract entities, universals, logical propositions, formulas, types, laws, and the like, as distinguished from the existence of concrete, particular objects.

Substance. What exists in and by itself and not as a modification or relation of anything else. That which constitutes the essential nature of a thing, that makes a thing what it is.

Substratum. A synonym for substance in the sense of a permanent, self-identical support for modes and accidents and changes.

Symbol. Often synonymous with sign. Sometimes sign that substitutes for other signs.

Synoptic. Used to designate an act or thought or point of view in which a whole and all its constituents are grasped and seen together simultaneously in their entirety and in their necessary connection with and implication of one another.

Syntax. Formal arrangement of symbols in a symbolic system. Logical syntax indicates the formal rules of a symbolic system.

Synthesis. The operation and result of piecing together comparatively simple elements into larger and more complicated wholes, the fusion of opposed ideas, thesis, and antithesis, in a new, higher idea or proposition in which their contradiction is overcome and their essential identity is revealed.

Teleological. Explanation of events not by their antecedents but by their results and purposes, that is, not by efficient but by final causation.

Teleological argument (proof). Inference of the existence of God from the teleology discoverable in the world, that is, the operation of final cause, purposes, or adaptation to ends.

Tertiary quality. Sometimes indicates value qualities that belong not to an object but that result from the subject's relation to the object.

Theism. Religious philosophy asserting existence of God as a living being.

Theory. Usually an idea expressed by a hypothetical proposition or set of propositions. Sometimes erroneously used to indicate an idea that is probably false. Also frequently used *erroneously* in contrast with fact. Opposed to practice.

Transcendental. Transcending ordinary experience.

Universal. In metaphysics, usually an entity that is apprehended by the intellect rather than by the senses, and whose reality is independent of any exemplification in space and time.

Universal proposition. A proposition that asserts or denies a property of all the members of a specified class.

Utilitarianism. Empirical and altruistic hedonistic moral philosophy emphasizing the greatest happiness of the greatest number.

Validity. In logic, a proposition is valid if it follows necessarily from the accepted premises. When this is the case, the argument or reasoning is valid. *Validity is not to be confused with truth.* A valid proposition may or may not be true.

Verifiability. The possibility in principle of a proposition being verified, that is, established as true or false. By some empiricists, verifiability refers technically to confirmability. In current empiricism, for example, logical empiricism, the verifiability in principle of a factual proposition is the criterion of its cognitive meaningfulness.

Verification. Process of determining the truth or falsity of a proposition.

Vitalism. Theory that living things are identified by a property of life or a life force that is not reducible to physical or chemical processes.

Yoga. Indian (Sanskrit) term meaning yoke or union. The chief Yogas include devotional, intellectual, work, health (Hatha Yoga). The object of Yoga is to gain peace of mind, greater insight into the nature of reality, and union with the universal spirit (Brahma).

Zen. Japanese term for the Chinese Ch'an, which is, in turn, a translation of the Sanskrit term "dhyana" (religious meditation). Zen Buddhism is a form of Mahayana Buddhism found chiefly in Japan, but with adherents in all parts of the world. The aim of Zen Buddhism is the attainment of enlightenment (satori), or the discovery of the Buddha–nature within oneself.

Index